ESTABLISHING DEMOCRACIES

ESTABLISHING DEMOCRACIES

edited by

Mary Ellen Fischer
Skidmore College

WestviewPress
A Division of HarperCollinsPublishers

Copyright © 1996 by Westview Press, A Division of HarperCollins Publishers, Inc.

Published in 1996 in the United States of America by Westview Press, 5500 Central Avenue, Boulder, Colorado 80301-2877, and in the United Kingdom by Westview Press, 12 Hid's Copse Road, Cumnor Hill, Oxford OX2 9JJ

A CIP catalog record for this book is available from the Library of Congress.
ISBN 0-8133-2552-8 (hc.) — ISBN 0-8133-2553-6 (pbk.)

The paper used in this publication meets the requirements of the American National Standard for Permanence of Paper for Printed Library Materials Z39.48-1984.

10   9   8   7   6   5   4   3   2   1

CONTENTS

PREFACE

The idea for this book originated several years ago in discussions among colleagues at Skidmore and the Russian Research Center at Harvard as we all were trying to make sense of the momentous events in Eastern Europe. I myself was reading the comparative literature on democratization in other areas of the world to see how it could be applied to postcommunist systems, and I felt the need for more information on past attempts to establish democratic systems. I also wanted my students to see contemporary developments in a broad historical and theoretical context. These chapters try to provide that context and at the same time to present a number of case studies in sufficient detail for comparative analysis.

We hope the chapters that follow will be of use to scholars exploring new areas of research or to their students who may be approaching the study of democratic systems and democratization for the first time. In the few pages at our disposal, we could provide only brief surveys of these exciting but complicated periods in the founding of democratic systems. Each chapter ends with a chronology to simplify its complexities, and the general index should facilitate comparisons across cases. Our hope is that this material can stimulate further research by students and scholars, and so we have included extensive notes and suggestions for further reading after each chapter.

I should like to express my thanks to my colleagues at Skidmore and the Russian Research Center for their cooperation in this effort and their patience with my many demands and deadlines. My own tasks were made much more enjoyable by the help of Chris DeLucia, whose skills were crucial in the project's early stages. Deep appreciation goes also to my husband, Erwin L. Levine, for his significant contributions to this work, both academic and personal. We are all grateful to Phyllis A. Roth, Dean of the Faculty at Skidmore, for helping to support the fall 1994 conference in Saratoga that began the project, and to the many participants in those discussions, especially Erik P. Hoffmann, for comments and advice. Special thanks must also go to the Skidmore students in Government 365 during spring 1995 who read these chapters in an earlier form and whose insights and suggestions contributed significantly to the outcome. It is to those students that we dedicate the volume.

Mary Ellen Fischer

INTRODUCTION

MARY ELLEN FISCHER

The global balance of power between the Soviet Union and the United States that dominated the international system for almost a half-century during the cold war has ended, leaving in its wake a residue of instability, political violence, and war—both civil and international. Nevertheless, one of the most notable features of the 1990s has been the widespread attempt to replace authoritarian regimes with democratic institutions. Those recent efforts to create democratic political systems did not, however, begin in 1989 with the fall of East European communist governments. Indeed, in the fifteen years from 1974 to 1989, a "wave" of new democracies, to use Samuel Huntington's term,[1] spread across the world, mostly concentrated in Southern Europe and Latin America. Such countries as Portugal, Greece, Spain, Ecuador, Argentina, Brazil, the Philippines, and South Korea introduced new political systems based on constitutions, elections, and civilian rule.

Then, in 1989, there came another surge of potential new democracies as communist regimes of Eastern Europe collapsed one by one, followed by the disintegration of the Soviet Union itself in 1991. What factors caused these recent waves of new democracies? What are the basic features of these new systems? Will they be successful in establishing permanent democracies? These questions and others are addressed in the chapters that analyze contemporary attempts to establish democracies in Argentina, Romania, Poland, and Russia. Before studying these recent cases, however, we should ask similar questions with respect to earlier attempts to establish democratic political systems—in England, the United States, Germany, and Japan—to see whether they can help us understand the contemporary processes of regime change and democratization. Do the earlier attempts have any features in common? Can we discover any lessons for the new and fragile democracies in examining successful efforts to create democracies in the past?

Our first four case studies, therefore, focus on crucial founding periods in democracies that have faced the test of time: the Cromwellian period in seventeenth-century England; the framing of the U.S. Constitution near the end of the eighteenth century; the creation of the German Federal Republic after the defeat of Nazi Germany in World War II; and the origins of the Japanese Constitution under U.S. occupation after the same war. There are, of course, significant differences among these cases with respect to timing, geography, culture, political and economic structures, and international conditions. Even surface similarities reveal deeper disparities. War, for example, played a major role in each of these transitions, but on closer examination the circumstances turn out to be varied: England experienced a civil war and the execution of a monarch, the American colonies fought a colonial war of independence, and Japan and Germany suffered total military defeat and occupation by one or more foreign powers.

The differences are just as great when we focus on outcomes: the institutions and procedures of the democratic systems that emerged from these four founding periods. The United States, for example, is a presidential system, whereas the others are parliamentary. Germany and the United States are federal structures, whereas Britain and Japan are unitary. Britain and Japan retain hereditary monarchs; Germany and the United States are republics. Britain and the United States have two major parties, Germany has a multiparty system with coalition governments, and Japan has been called a "one-and-a-half" party system because the Liberal Democrats (until 1993) always formed the government. Britain and the United States elect their representatives in single-member districts, whereas Japan and Germany combine different versions of proportional representation with single-member districts. Britain does not even have a written constitution. Nevertheless, we consider these four countries to be successful democracies,[2] and the crucial early years of their formation may reveal features or patterns that will help us to understand their success—and provide lessons for current attempts to create democratic systems.

Our second set of cases involves four recent attempts to establish democracies: Argentina during the 1980s, with its background of both populist and military authoritarianism; and three cases from Eastern Europe, all postcommunist but otherwise quite different: Romania, Poland, and Russia. Whether any of these states will consolidate fully democratic political processes remains an open question. What factors will determine whether these recent cases become stable democracies? What factors might cause them to fail?

Most theories of successful democratization before 1974 were derived from studies of Western Europe and the United States. However, these pre-1974 theories provide little basis for optimism in regard to our recent cases, for the early literature often describes as prerequisites for democracy certain features that we find missing from the contemporary attempts: for example, specific historical sequences of political, social, or economic development (such as the decline of a landed aristocracy or the appearance of national consciousness and unity); society-wide economic, social, or cultural conditions such as economic prosperity or potential for growth; a diversified social structure with a propertied middle class and/or an organized working class; a national culture that tolerates diversity and prefers compromise.[3] Such factors may be useful in explaining the growth of democratic systems in England or the United States, but if indeed they are prerequisites for democracy, why the post-1974 wave of democratic systems in countries that had not met some or all of them? Again, we need to take a fresh look at the earlier cases to explain the recent explosion of new democracies and seek behavioral and institutional guidelines for those involved in establishing them.

DEFINITIONS OF DEMOCRACY

Before moving any farther we must clarify what we mean by democracy. What type of system, after all, do those who are establishing democracies wish to create? The concept of democracy has often been defined in terms of its origin (a system that derives from the will of the people) or its goals (a system that seeks and comes close to achieving the common good or social justice), but such definitions are often very hard to prove or disprove in practice. Demagogues and dictators can, after all, claim to rule by the will of the people and claim to seek the common good and social justice. Yet defining "democracy" in terms of specific structures or institutions—like constitutions, parliaments, or courts—also presents problems. Communist systems, for example, had constitutions, parliaments, and courts—the institutions of democracy—but all were dominated by the communist party and rendered meaningless. Thus, the inherent ambiguities of such definitions led to widespread acceptance of another definition, a procedural conception of democracy, which holds that democracy is a set of "procedures" for "constituting government."[4] In other words, democracy involves a set of rules by which representatives are elected, policies are chosen, and laws are made and enforced.

In a democracy, therefore, the outcomes of elections or policy formulation are uncertain, but the rules cannot be uncertain. Indeed, most citizens accept the rules and agree to abide by their results. Rules can be changed only by established processes such as enacting legislation or amending constitutions. We might consider this a shift in the concept of regime legitimacy: from traditional or charismatic authority to rational/legal authority, to use Weberian categories.[5] In such a system, the uncertainty of the electoral or legislative results becomes a strength: If no one always wins or loses, the current losers will accept defeat because they can try again another day.[6] They accept the rule of law because they have had or hope to have a role in shaping and administering that law. In addition, actors in a democratic system must have sufficiently long time horizons to conceive of future victory and must be prudent enough to realize that there are advantages to playing the game according to the rules. As Adam Przeworski states, "The decisive step toward democracy is the devolution of power from a group of people to a set of rules."[7] This is the crucial task of those who are attempting to establish democracies.

Of course, rules alone are not enough. There must also be some substantive criteria to democratic systems, but, because the rules and structures vary so greatly from one system to another, there can be different ways of fulfilling such criteria. Robert Dahl argues that two critical requirements are political competition for office and widespread participation of the population to ensure "the continuing responsiveness of the government to the preferences of its citizens."[8] In other words, a democratic government must be accountable to the citizens who elect it, and the process of selection should rest on the broad inclusion of all individuals and groups in the society—universal suffrage. As Huntington puts it, "elections, open, free, and fair, are the essence of democracy, the inescapable *sine qua non*."[9]

Most analysts also agree that simple majority rule is not sufficient; indeed, successful democracies "tend to qualify the central principle of majority rule"[10] in order to protect minority or individual rights through local autonomy or federalism, concurrent majorities, or constitutional guarantees such as a bill of rights and an independent judiciary to enforce those rights.[11] A democratic system therefore requires (1) *government accountability* achieved through elections (and other political processes) open to the participation of virtually all adults, and (2) *respect for individual and group rights* guaranteed through legal processes and constitutional structures. These and other substantive criteria associated with democracy are achieved, however, by means of clear and established rules and procedures.

In the modern state, "democracy" also implies representative government, which, according to Robert Dahl's typology, is actually a combination of two types of democracy: *referendum democracy*, or elections, in which all voters use ballots to choose the representatives; and *primary democracy*, the process by which elected representatives formulate laws and policies in a legislature through discussion and voting.[12] This two-tiered system of *representative democracy* means that citizen electors "end up choosing decision-makers rather than [making] decisions."[13] Such a system in turn requires the formation of political parties as organizations to win votes—first in the elections and later in the legislature.

Moreover, there should develop among the elected officials many of the behavioral norms and expectations often associated with democracy: a sense of responsibility to constituents and colleagues; a long-term view of needs, priorities, and interests; a pragmatic attitude toward legislation; and an acceptance of compromise as both necessary and positive. These behavioral norms are, of course, only goals, and are not always reflected in reality. As a result, accountability and respect for individual and group rights are requirements, whereas the ideal behavioral norms are merely preferred outcomes. Their absence may make democracy less effective and more difficult to maintain but does not necessarily destroy the system, at least at first. As Giuseppe Di Palma observes, "Genuine democrats need not precede democracy. . . . Democracy's rules, being a means for coexistence, need not be more than a second best for the parties that negotiate their adoption."[14] As long as the alternatives seem worse or any attempt to end democracy (by administrative or military coup, for example) seems fraught with danger, democracy may well be supported by many skeptical nondemocrats. In sum, "democracy"—under the definition that we have outlined here—supplies the rules for the game called politics, and, as long as the players and groups foresee a chance of winning, they will continue to participate in that game.

Semidemocracies and Protodemocracies

One question to keep in mind is whether to treat democracies and nondemocracies as separate categories or, instead, as points along a continuum ranging from full democracies, on the one hand, to nondemocracies on the other, with space in the middle for semidemocracies (those governments fulfilling some democratic criteria but not all)[15] and protodemocracies (those that seem to be in the early stages of developing into full democracies).[16] For some studies it might be best to use completely separate categories[17]—a country is either democratic or not democratic—but in this volume the continuum approach supplies some needed flexibility; hence, we shall place our contemporary cases—Argentina, Romania, Poland, and Russia—near the center of the continuum, because they have yet to prove over time that they are "real" democracies.[18]

REGIME TRANSITIONS

Scholars have searched for theories to justify the apparent success of the post-1974 democracies in Southern Europe, Latin America, and Asia, and the result has been a number of case studies and considerable theoretical literature examining the characteristics, causes, and methods of "transitions" away from authoritarianism.[19] Most transition literature suggests that societal factors—such as high levels of socioeconomic development or political traditions of participation and tolerance—are not prerequisites but outcomes of democracy. This view implies that contemporary postauthoritarian and postcommunist cases that lack these features can still establish stable democratic regimes. Indeed, the transition literature contends that we should abandon any search for identical preconditions to democracy and focus instead on the choices made by individuals and groups during the transition process.

Regime transitions, the argument goes, are times of great uncertainty, when political structures cease to function effectively, when almost anything is possible.[20] Indeed, a change from one type of *regime* to another implies just that: change not just in the individuals holding positions of political power but change in the assumptions and methods of the political system, in how the system legislates, formulates, and implements policies, and in the ways individuals gain access to power. Unless there is a revolution, formal *state* (institutional) structures—parliament, president, prime minister, bureaucrats—may remain in place, but the way the system works changes profoundly under a new type of regime.[21]

The Old Regime

Among the variables identified by Guillermo O'Donnell and Philippe Schmitter as crucial in shaping transitions toward democracy, at least in Latin America and Southern Europe, are the duration and methods of authoritarian rule, that is, the previous regime.[22] All authoritarian regimes are alike in that they are not account-able to the population and do not permit citizen participation in most decisions, but there are also differences among them. Authoritarian regimes may be governed by one person—a monarch, autocrat, or dictator—or by a group of individuals—an oligarchy. A traditional authoritarian system is based on custom and habit, and property rights and social status, along with political power, are inherited rather than acquired—a typical example being a monarchy with an aristocracy. Seventeenth-century England was just such a society but colonial America was not (despite its close ties to England), and the differences between the two would affect their transitions to democracy.

Modern authoritarian regimes usually exercise authority on the basis of individual charisma (the extraordinary qualities of one person who assumes the right to rule) or some vague idea such as national interest (often the justification used by military rulers). Argentina, for example, experienced both types of regimes, a populist, Juan Perón, and a series of military rulers. Although not democratic, authoritarian regimes have limited power: This type of regime usually dominates only the public arena and allows individuals considerable flexibility to pursue private lives as they wish as long as they do not challenge the regime's right to rule. Regime policies will, of course, affect citizens—their physical security, jobs, and right to travel—but the authoritarian regime does not try to dominate every aspect of citizens' lives.

Another type of nondemocratic rule, the totalitarian regime, is much more invasive. A totalitarian regime is distinguished from an authoritarian regime by (1) a goal-oriented ideology that demands significant change in the behavior of citizens (communism, Nazism, or certain religious belief-systems), and (2) its determination to use its monopoly of political power to impose its ideology on all individuals, in both their public and private lives. The totalitarian regime also uses police terror to enforce ideological goals, directs the economy, and controls all social organizations and sources of information including the educational system and the mass media, thereby simultaneously mobilizing citizens and invading their private lives. Indeed, the ideology justifies the regime in creating a "monistic" center of power from which all groups derive their right to exist, and the new political relationships represent a break from the past, "a political creation rather than an outgrowth of the dynamics of the preexisting society."[23] Nazi Germany, Stalinist Russia, and Nicolae Ceauşescu's Romania were all examples of totalitarian systems.

Not all states ruled by communist parties remained totalitarian after Stalin's death, however; most turned authoritarian as the ideology lost its mobilizing force, the power of the police declined relative to other groups, and political influence moved outward to state bureaucrats and specialists.[24] Poland and Russia already had experienced significant liberalization before 1989, the result of dissent from below in Poland and change at the top in Russia. Romania, in contrast, had seen a renewed period of totalitarianism in the 1980s under Ceauşescu, and the features of these old regimes would produce differences in the patterns of transition.

Individuals and Groups

During the uncertainty of regime transition, background circumstances—the nature of the old regime, or economic, social, and cultural conditions, or international conditions—may limit available choices, but crucial roles often will be played by uniquely talented individuals; chance and mischance are also likely to affect the outcome. In other words, although certain preexisting conditions might make political democracy highly improbable, transition theorists argue that "outcomes depend less on objective conditions . . . than on subjective evaluations surrounding unique strategic choices."[25] There is hope, they contend, that many of these new regimes may overcome their disadvantages and create lasting democracies.

Transition theorists also focus attention on the sequencing of choices and political coalitions during the transition, as members of the previous regime and its opponents shape the breakdown of the old system and negotiate the creation of new structures. On the one hand, if members of the old regime initiate and lead a regime change, it will probably occur peacefully through compromise—what Huntington calls "transformation" and Juan Linz terms *reforma*. If, on the other hand, regime opponents dominate the process, some violence is likely; Huntington calls this "replacement," Linz *ruptura*. If both government and opposition groups join together to establish a democratic regime, the process would be "transplacement" (Huntington) or a "pacted" transition.[26]

The situation, however, is sometimes more complicated than that. Indeed, four major divisions among elites often appear during a regime crisis and transition: two groups within the old regime, *hardliners*[27] and *reformers*, and two among the regime's opponents, *moderates* and *radicals*. The balance among them can prove significant. If, for example, hardliners dominate the old regime and radicals dominate the opposition, then the dominant groups on both sides will be too far apart to allow for negotiation or compromise. The result will be repression, revolution, or, in the case of extended discord among the factions, civil war. The eventual victory of the hardliners will preserve the old system, whereas a victory for the radicals will likely produce a new dictatorship. If, however, regime reformers and opposition moderates have sufficient skill or strength to overcome the resistance of hardliners and radicals and persuade or compel them to negotiate, the result might then be an agreement based on compromise: a "pact" to begin a democratic transition.

In such cases, the relative strength and political skills of individuals among the regime reformers and the moderate opposition (as they negotiate with each other or mobilize mass support) can also produce more complex results. For example, if the reformers within the regime prove stronger than their moderate opponents, then any agreement or pact initiating the transition will be dominated by many features and structures of the old regime, and full democracy may never be achieved. If, however, the moderate opposition proves stronger (perhaps by threatening to join the radicals), the consolidation of a democratic system may proceed more quickly—or too quickly so that it provokes an authoritarian response from a coalition of hardliners and reformers. Thus, the political sensitivity and shrewdness of individuals—as well as a bit of luck on their part—may determine the success or failure of a transition.

The political stripes among the factions in a given transition might be even more complex. For example, regime reformers may be divided into *liberalizers*, who wish to reduce the repressive features of the old system in order to enhance its performance, and *democratizers*, who wish to bring real change. *Liberalization* thus involves loosened restrictions and expanded rights for groups and individuals within an authoritarian regime; "Liberalization is an unclenched fist, but the hand is the same and at any moment it could be clenched again into a fist."[28] If the fist remains unclenched too long, however, it may lose its strength—as in the Soviet Union under Mikhail Gorbachev. Thus, the critical struggle shaping the transition might evolve not between supporters of the regime and its opponents but among the regime supporters, between liberalizers and democratizers like Gorbachev and Boris Yeltsin (see Chapter 8).

Most observers agree that elites have always been crucial actors in democratic transitions. Individual leaders, however, may try to mobilize mass participation to support themselves and their goals, and thus the role of the masses during transitions remains controversial. Are mass mobilization and violence during regime change more or less likely to produce a democratic outcome? Such popular mobilization might simply increase the pace rather than the direction of change and convince the elite groups to reach a quick and definitive outcome through repression or revolution or even a negotiated agreement. Transition theorists who focus on Southern Europe or Latin America emphasize that although mass mobilization can play an important role in democratization, during the twentieth century widespread violence and mass revolution have been more likely to produce an authoritarian result rather than a democratic result, either preserving the old regime or establishing a new dictatorial system based on revolutionary goals.[29] More recent analyses of the postcommunist cases take issue with this, arguing that some violence can indeed play a positive role in bringing down the old regime.[30] The role of popular mobilization and mass violence in democratic transitions is therefore an issue for continuing study.

The findings of the transition theorists regarding the sequencing and nature of choices in the process of regime change reveal the crucial roles of individuals who establish new political systems, the options they choose, and the procedures they create. The importance of personality, choice, and strategy also helps justify our focus here on eight individual cases, each of which, despite differences, involves periods of crisis and regime change and strategies and choices of significant individuals. The roles played by Charles I and Oliver Cromwell in seventeenth-century England, Thomas Jefferson, James Madison, and Alexander Hamilton in the early United States, Konrad Adenauer and Kurt Schumacher in Germany, Emperor Hirohito, Shigeru Yoshida, and Douglas MacArthur in Japan, Raúl Alfonsín and Carlos Menem in Argentina, Ion Iliescu in Romania, Lech Wałęsa in Poland, or Gorbachev and Yeltsin in Russia were decisive in the success or failure of their attempts at preserving or reshaping political regimes, and the outcome for democracy in some cases remains unclear. Are there any attributes shared by these individuals that help to explain the results of their actions?

SOCIETAL CONSTRAINTS
AND INSTITUTIONAL CHOICES

The founding of any democracy is, in some ways, a unique process, based as it must be on the assumptions, desires, and skills of its leaders and population under specific historical circumstances, and so the wide variation in the constitutional structures produced by our cases should not surprise us. Indeed, as we examine the specific features of these different political systems, we see that variations in the institutional choices made during the transition period are often critical to the success of the democratic process.

For democracy to last, the new structures must not only be internally coherent, but they must also be constructed on the ruins of previous institutions that have left physical, organizational, and cultural imprints on the society. The new institutions must fit into what Douglass North calls the "informal constraints" of the society, in other words, "social attitudes," or "culturally derived norms of behavior," such as assumptions about property rights or the law. The new political system must be crafted so that it allows for these attitudes and is flexible enough to adapt to them; if there is tension, North argues, between these societal constraints and the new rules of the game, the result will be long-term instability.[31] Therefore, choices made during the transition, including those shaping the basic political structures and processes—parliamentary or presidential government? unitary or federal structure? elections based on proportional representation or single-member districts?—must create new institutions that are inherently viable and, equally important, also appropriate for that country.

There are deep disagreements within the political science literature regarding the inherent advantages and disadvantages of various constitutional systems—for example, the Westminster (British) system with a parliamentary government and single-member, winner-take-all electoral districts, the continental system of parliamentary government with proportional representation, or a mixed presidential/parliamentary system with or without proportional representation. All of these arrangements can be found among the world's successful democracies, and therefore such varied solutions have been wise choices for certain societies.[32] Even seemingly minor choices regarding one aspect of a particular process like elections—the formula for determining proportionality, for example, or the threshold requirement for a party's representation in parliament or even the design of the electoral ballot—will have major implications for the stability of the new system. Moreover, some systems have been carefully designed to avoid unexpected pitfalls experienced by others in the past. After World War II, for example, the German Constitution was consciously crafted to avoid the weaknesses of the Weimar Republic, and the Japanese Constitution was shaped to prevent a repetition of interwar militarism.

To what extent, then, do we find that successful systems are crafted to take advantage of societal norms? In those cases, were strategic choices by uniquely talented individuals crucial to the outcome? Do these factors help to account for the institutional differences among the earlier cases? And how have the choices been made in the contemporary cases and with what initial results?

THE INTERNATIONAL SETTING

External circumstances are also important in the founding of democratic institutions and their survival. The international state system experienced tremendous change during the period covered by our cases. Initially European-centered, the system became global due to imperial expansion during the nineteenth century and two world wars in the first half of the twentieth century. Divided into two military camps during the cold war, the world during the second half of the twentieth century saw the gradual rebirth of Europe and Asia, regions which joined the United States and the USSR as powerful global players. Then the collapse of the Soviet Union dramatically changed the distribution of power and left chaos and confusion across the center of the Eurasian land mass. Continuing throughout, however, has been the growing influence of the international system on its member states as modern methods of production and distribution have increased interdependence.

All of our cases illustrate the importance of external factors—positive or negative—when establishing democracies. In order to raise an army against the Scots, for example, Charles I was forced to call a parliament in 1640; but his quarrels with parliament brought about his own demise. The American colonies, in contrast, derived military and economic benefits from European rivalries (mainly among England, France, and Spain) during the American Revolution, and afterwards the comparative isolation of the North American continent enabled the United States to consolidate its new political system and expand its territory without foreign interference. Indeed, both England and the United States gained from positions that were peripheral to the international antagonisms of the European state system (England being an island and the United States being an ocean away).

For Germany and Japan, in contrast, humiliating military defeats and postwar occupations in the aftermath of World War II precipitated their transitions to democracy; the cold war simultaneously brought them crucial external support as the United States, Britain, and France responded to the Soviet threat with economic aid and military protection for their former enemies. Argentina also received backing for its transition during the 1980s, especially from trade partners and world financial institutions. By the 1990s, however, the international system was in disarray, with the cold war over and replacement structures not yet in place. No threat comparable to Soviet expansionism justified the commitment of U.S. funds or troops to help the postcommunist states establish stable democracies. Moreover, international financial organizations like the International Monetary Fund were demanding quick economic transformations, which produced inflation and unemployment and tended to destabilize the new states. In some ways, therefore, the international system in the 1990s placed the postcommunist democracies in Eastern Europe at a disadvantage.

At the same time, however, specific features of the post–cold war international setting benefited and encouraged transitions to democracy. The postcommunist states had models to follow, and certain features of democratic political processes could be copied from other systems. Just as the English experience had helped the founders of the American republic, so too the constitutions of the United States, France, and other European states served as models for Germany and Japan after World War II, and all of these examples then became available for the postcommunist transitions. In addition, a demonstration effect, sometimes called "snowballing," "diffusion," or "emulation"—as democratization in one or more states is followed by "waves" of new democracies elsewhere—has encouraged democratization efforts since 1974.[33]

For democracy to take root, of course, any features that are copied or imposed from afar must be adapted to their new environment, and this interaction between foreign examples and indigenous institutions affects the chances of democratization, as do the regional and global structures of the international setting. Powerful neighbors or distant great powers may facilitate or prevent transitions to democracy by support, by intimidation, or by taking sides in an internal struggle. Moreover, international organizations can play crucial roles, encouraging accountable government and respect for human rights, as the Council of Europe, the European Union, and the North Atlantic Treaty Organization have done in the transitions of postcommunist Europe.

ECONOMIC CHANGE AND DEMOCRATIC SYSTEMS

What is the purpose in establishing a democratic system? More specifically, can we expect that democracy will bring economic prosperity?[34] In fact, clearly democratic systems often do not produce higher living standards for many citizens, and this is one of democracy's shortcomings. Any democratic system requires a balancing act among major interests, and the need to preserve an equilibrium can prevent solutions to the enormous problems of poverty and inequality that often confront the democracy's founders. As Terry Karl argues, democracies might "guarantee a greater respect for law and human dignity ... [but] be unable to carry out substantive reforms that address the lot of their poorest citizens."[35]

Indeed, none of our eight case studies has yet produced a system that makes economic equality and economic security a priority of the political process. On such issues the nature of the old regime, the timing of the founding, and the structuring of the transition process are crucial. For example, powerful elements of former regimes survived intact due to the historical compromises worked out in England, Germany, and Japan, as in the negotiated compromises or pacts between regime supporters and opponents so characteristic of the post-1974 democracies. Whenever initial agreements establishing new systems depend on the cooperation of conservative forces, economic and social change occurs much more slowly than legal and political change. In fact, the transition literature on Latin America and Southern Europe has found that "virtually none of the surviving transitions to democracy ... combined a significant redistribution of political *and* economic resources. ... In every enduring case, dramatic redistributions of property were postponed, circumscribed, or rolled back."[36] Aldo Vacs reaches similar conclusions in regard to the Argentine experience (see Chapter 5), and such pessimistic findings may also have negative implications for the postcommunist cases.

Postcommunist Systems

Not only are postcommunist states attempting to establish democratic systems on the foundations of a Leninist-Stalinist political and cultural legacy antithetical to democracy,[37] but they are also trying to implement simultaneous transitions to political democracies and market economies.[38] Lenin's system was dominated by a highly centralized political party that monopolized all productive resources (except agricultural land) in the name of the working class and suppressed any opposition by force. Lenin died in 1924, and Stalin then collectivized agriculture and introduced mass terror against both friends and foes of the party, thereby atomizing society, preempting any opposition, and destroying any independent social groups. He organized the entire economy on the basis of central planning rather than market mechanisms and gave priority to rapid industrial growth financed by depressed living standards. Initially he justified his actions on the basis of Marx's ideology and Lenin's legacy, to which he added Russian nationalism and a perceived external threat.

After World War II, Stalin's totalitarian regime was emulated in Soviet-occupied Eastern Europe. Although much of the terror ceased after Stalin's death in 1953 and the Soviet Union and most of its allies then became authoritarian rather than totalitarian, the East European states retained the basic structural features of Stalinism: a political monopoly by the hierarchical communist party and direct state ownership of industry, agriculture, housing, commerce, transportation, communications, and other economic and social facilities. Citizens depended on the state for jobs, food, clothing, housing, medical care, and all the other necessities of life. Even elite status required access to political power rather than possession of property. Individuals and families did develop techniques to avoid the demands of the state, and a second (black market) economy emerged in most areas to supplement the formal structures. Nevertheless, these societies remained heavily dependent on the state while mistrustful of those in power.

Economic decline precipitated the collapse of the communist regimes, but the efforts of postcommunist governments to change their economies ran into immediate difficulties because no models existed for shifting from a planned economy to a market economy or from a state-owned system to private enterprise. Initial reforms produced rapid inflation, widespread unemployment, and a severe drop in production as prices were raised to reflect costs and government subsidies were reduced for inefficient industries. This drastic economic dislocation led to popular protests and such instability that economic reform for a time seemed incompatible with democratic governance in formerly communist Eastern Europe, and most parties or coalitions associated with these policies were voted out of office. Economic prosperity might not be a *prerequisite* for democracy in these states, but Przeworski might be right to assert that "the eventual survival of the new democracies will depend to a large extent on their economic performance."[39] Yet the dilemma for these governments remains: how to be accountable to the people and still carry on with the pain of economic transition.

An extended economic crisis in any new democracy might provoke revolt or repression. Yet compromises can emerge with previously dominant elites—political or social, civilian or military—that allow those critical groups to benefit from the new system and stave off efforts to overturn the new democracy. If such compromises include them in the political process, however, then those former elites can use their power to obstruct the redistribution of wealth. In postcommunist cases they can do so by slowing the processes of privatization and marketization or by directing these to their own advantage. Such actions can prolong and deepen the economic crisis and promote political instability, or a viable compromise may emerge to moderate the dislocation and help to preserve stability and democracy. Neither alternative will do much to promote economic equity in the short run, but long-term economic growth can remain feasible. In any case, understanding the dynamics of other political transitions should help us analyze the special problems of postcommunist political and social change and evaluate the potential results of choices made in these cases.

THE CASES

Each of our case studies is quite different, yet each reviews a period of societal crisis and analyzes the ways in which background factors and individual choices shaped the outcome. As Patricia-Ann Lee demonstrates in Chapter 1, England between 1640 and 1660 did not become a democracy, but the country and its politics changed in fundamental ways, the result of economic and military pressures, conflicting political and religious ideas, and choices made by individuals such as Charles I and Oliver Cromwell. After framing for us the background of the crisis—economic, religious, and international pressures, the English constitutional system, and Charles I's personality—Lee discusses the evolution of events that led to the king's execution, Cromwell's rule as Protector, and the eventual restoration of the monarchy. On a number of occasions during those years it appeared that a compromise might be worked out either to keep Charles in power (prior to his execution in 1649, of course) or to preserve a republic (before the monarchy was restored in 1660); such hopes did not prove feasible. Even so, the English political process and the ideas and institutions upon which it rested changed fundamentally in those two decades; the restored Stuart monarchy did not last, and the events of the period started England down the path of democracy.

Economic pressures also precipitated the American Revolution, but Chapter 2 reveals that the societal factors that shaped the outcome were indeed different than in the English case. Nevertheless, the new system could trace many attributes to its English heritage, including concepts of representation and religious toleration, local autonomy and participation, and legal and legislative structures. The ideas and choices of individuals were also crucial to the founding of the United States, starting especially with the truly revolutionary notion of basing the new system upon natural law and human reason rather than tradition. The transition from the original Articles of Confederation to the U.S. Constitution turned separate colonies into a unified country and supplied the procedures and rules for the future development of the political system; yet, as Tadahisa Kuroda and Erwin Levine conclude, the American founders in the 1780s did not immediately produce democracy in America but rather established the foundations for its later emergence.

The cases of democratization in Germany and Japan differ sharply from the examples set by England and the United States. Not only did the German and Japanese transitions occur in the mid-twentieth century, when the concept of democracy had been fully articulated, but each also took place in the wake of dictatorships (fascist in the case of Germany, military in the case of Japan), after both countries had experienced total military defeat, foreign occupation, and the destruction and discrediting of their political systems. However, as Roy Ginsberg and Steven Hoffmann emphasize in Chapter 3 and Chapter 4, individuals again played crucial roles, and their choices created and shaped each new system in a variety of ways. Both countries based their new institutions on indigenous traditions such as federal structures (Germany) or the emperor (Japan), and yet both changed these institutions in significant ways. And whereas the founders of the German Federal Republic were consciously trying to make the new state *strong* enough to resist a revival of fascism, those who shaped the Japanese Constitution wanted to make the new state *weak* enough to prevent a revival of militarism.

A combination of international and economic pressures also precipitated a democratic transition in Argentina, but this first of our contemporary cases presents a distinct contrast to the other studies. Its background of populist and military authoritarianism, for example, and the suddenness of regime change separate Argentina from the first two cases, and the internal impetus for its transition distinguishes it from both Germany and Japan. During the late 1970s, there seemed little reason to hope for democratization in Argentina, especially in light of the serious problems that were facing its economy. Peripheral to the international economic system, Argentina in preceding decades had tried both export-import and import-substitution models of economic development,[40] but— despite initial successes with each model—it had failed to sustain economic growth. Then, in the early 1980s, economic decline and military humiliation in the Falklands/Malvinas War combined to discredit the military regime, and major groups and crucial individuals saw the legitimacy of democracy as a means of implementing significant but painful economic changes. In Chapter 5, Aldo Vacs, a political economist, focuses on the political-economic causes of the transition from military rule to a democratic regime and the structural results for Argentine society. He also shows how the strategies and choices of specific individuals, notably Presidents Raúl Alfonsín and Carlos Menem, were major factors in the creation and survival of the democratic system and in the widespread disappointment engendered by Argentina's continuing economic inequities.

The remaining three cases—Romania, Poland, and Russia—share features common to postcommunist systems, such as simultaneous political and economic transitions to democracy and to a privatized, market economy; weakness of independent social groups; absence of a propertied class independent of the state; lack of governing experience on the part of many officials; the crucial roles of certain individuals (such as the presidents, Iliescu, Wałęsa, Gorbachev, and Yeltsin); and a deep mistrust of the state and distaste for politics that are combined, paradoxically, with excessive reliance on the state for many necessities. At the same time, significant differences also appear among these states in their attempts to establish democracy.

Ironically, Romania, the last to begin the transition from communism (December 1989), became the very first to establish new institutions and to approve a new constitution. Indeed, Romania's constitutional precedents go back to the 1880s and the 1920s, and Chapter 6 briefly addresses these efforts as background to the 1991 constitution. The chapter then surveys the communist period, including the devastating effects of the totalitarian regime of Nicolae Ceauşescu and his violent overthrow. Most of the chapter, however, focuses on events since 1989 including two sets of national elections, two parliaments, and crucial choices in the shaping of a constitution. Negotiations have largely replaced street violence as a method of resolving disputes and political learning has occurred—most notably on the part of President Iliescu—but the country remains politically polarized and economically devastated.

In Poland, regime transition began as early as 1980 under the dissident trade union movement known as Solidarity, a moving chapter in Polish history led by Lech Wałęsa. Change was blocked by the Polish military, however, until a pact between the communist government and opponents in the spring of 1989 led to elections and a noncommunist government. This in turn stimulated the downfall of communist rule throughout Eastern Europe, ending nearly a half-century of Soviet domination. Thus, we learn that the Polish transition was initiated from below by regime opponents and that Poland was the first East European state to end communist rule. Nevertheless, by 1995, after three elections and a series of unstable coalition governments, Poland had yet to ratify a new constitution. In Chapter 7, Sarah Terry examines the last years of the communist period and the pact negotiations in some detail, because they shaped the dramatic transition that followed. She next discusses the postreform elections and the various coalition governments, focusing on the impact of choices made by individuals such as Wałęsa on the political structures and economic policies of postcommunist Poland.

In contrast to the up-from-below change that Poland experienced, change in Russia was initiated from the top, by Mikhail Gorbachev. In Chapter 8, Carol Saivetz examines both the liberalization under Gorbachev and the democratization under Yeltsin, pointing out that Russia was slowed in its postcommunist transformation under Yeltsin by the very institutions Gorbachev created to speed political and economic change. Russia faced much greater problems than the East European states, not only because of the longer duration of communist rule, but also because of the difficulty of defining its external boundaries and dealing with an internal federal structure. The war in Chechnya intensified the difficulties Yeltsin faced in his efforts to create a stable constitutional system in Moscow, dividing his supporters and strengthening his critics. In all three of these postcommunist states, by mid-1995 steps had been taken toward establishing democratic systems, but nowhere was the outcome certain or even predictable.

Each case that we will soon examine—the early experiments in England and the United States, the post–World War II governments installed in war-torn Germany and Japan, Argentina's emergence from military rule, and the painful postcommunist reforms in Romania, Poland, and Russia—will help us evaluate the relative roles of human choices, societal constraints, and plain luck in the crafting of each new system. The chapters focus on critical periods in the founding of democracies, when the uncertainty of transitions and the collapse of institutions enhance the abilities of individuals to shape events. Thus, the authors look closely at the crucial individuals who played leading roles during the transition and evaluate their goals, their skills, and their choices. They also consider the major groups supporting and opposing the old regime and, in the recent cases, those taking part in the new system, to assess their objectives, their relative influence, and the nature of their interactions.

Crucial to the longevity of all democratic regimes, however, are the new institutions created during these formative periods. The authors consider the foundations upon which such new institutions must rest—preexisting economic and social conditions, the nature of the old regime and reasons for its demise—and the international setting and foreign models, because these factors influenced the choices of the human actors and the shape of the new institutions and their potential to survive in the long term. The authors also examine the institutions themselves, the democratic structures and processes created during the transition period, their inherent viability, and the ways they fit into their environment. What is the balance among these factors? Do the findings of the earlier cases support transition theorists in their assertion that traditional prerequisites for democracy should be considered outcomes? How have human choices crafted institutions to fit into societal constraints? Finally, how can the survival of democracy be explained in the earlier cases, and what are its chances for success in the contemporary transitions? Keep these questions in mind as you read each chapter; we shall return to them in the Conclusion.

NOTES

1. Samuel P. Huntington, *The Third Wave: Democratization in the Late Twentieth Century,* from the Julian J. Rothbaum Distinguished Lecture Series, vol. 4 (Norman: University of Oklahoma Press, 1991). The first two waves occurred in 1828–1926 and 1943–1962, each followed by a briefer wave of reversion to nondemocratic rule, in 1922–1942 and 1958–1975. The "third wave" began in 1974.

2. Japan does not meet Huntington's "two-turnover test" of democratic consolidation, which suggests that a democratic system can be viewed as consolidated only after the party or group that wins the first set of elections has been defeated in elections and turns over its power to another group, which in turn is defeated and yields its power. Nevertheless, Huntington agrees that Japan has been "universally and properly viewed as a democratic nation after World War II." Huntington, *The Third Wave,* pp. 266–267.

3. For a survey and critique of this literature on historical prerequisites, see Terry Lynn Karl, "Dilemmas of Democratization in Latin America," in Dankwart A. Rustow and Kenneth Paul Erickson, eds., *Comparative Political Dynamics: Global Research Perspectives* (New York: HarperCollins, 1991), pp. 165–167; for a detailed discussion of such "prerequisites," see Robert A. Dahl, *Democracy and Its Critics* (New Haven: Yale University Press, 1989), ch. 18, or Dahl, *Polyarchy: Participation and Opposition* (New Haven: Yale University Press, 1971), esp. p. 203; see also Adam Przeworski, *Democracy and the Market: Political and Economic Reforms in Eastern Europe and Latin America* (Cambridge: Cambridge University Press, 1991), p. 96; Barrington Moore, *Social Origins of Dictatorship and Democracy* (Boston: Beacon Press, 1966); and Dietrich Rueschemeyer, Evelyne Huber Stephens, and John D. Stephens, *Capitalist Development and Democracy* (Cambridge: Polity Press, 1992).

4. This is Joseph Schumpeter's definition; see the discussion in Huntington, *The Third Wave*, pp. 5–7. See also Richard Bellamy, "Schumpeter and the Transformation of Capitalism, Liberalism, and Democracy," *Government and Opposition* 26 (Autumn 1991): 500–519; and Dol Chull Shin, "On the Third Wave of Democratization: A Synthesis and Evaluation of Recent Theory and Research," *World Politics* 47 (October 1994): 142, and the sources cited.

5. Max Weber, *Economy and Society* (New York: Bedminster Press, 1968). Legitimacy involves popular acceptance of a government's *right* to rule. Weber asserted that it could be rooted in tradition, charisma (the special qualities of an individual), or rationality/legality.

6. See Giuseppe Di Palma, *To Craft Democracies: An Essay on Democratic Transitions* (Berkeley: University of California Press, 1990), pp. 40–44, or Przeworski, *Democracy and the Market*, ch 1.

7. Przeworski, *Democracy and the Market*, p. 14.

8. Dahl, *Polyarchy*, pp. 1, 6–7.

9. Huntington, *The Third Wave*, p. 9.

10. Philippe C. Schmitter and Terry Lynn Karl, "What Democracy Is and Is Not," in Larry Diamond and Marc F. Plattner, eds., *The Global Resurgence of Democracy* (Baltimore: Johns Hopkins University Press, 1993), p. 43. See also Lincoln Allison, "On the Gap Between Theories of Democracy and Theories of Democratization," *Democratization* 1 (Spring 1994): 8–26.

11. Leszek Kolakowski, "Uncertainties of a Democratic Age," in Diamond and Plattner, *The Global Resurgence of Democracy*, pp. 321–323.

12. Robert A. Dahl, *After the Revolution? Authority in a Good Society*, rev. ed. (New Haven: Yale University Press, 1990), pp. 56–57.

13. Bellamy, "Schumpeter and the Transformation of Capitalism," p. 509.

14. Di Palma, *To Craft Democracies*, p. 30.

15. Such as O'Donnell's "delegative democracy"; Guillermo O'Donnell, "Delegative Democracy," *Journal of Democracy* 5 (January 1994): 55–69.

16. Daniel N. Nelson likes this term to describe some of the states in Eastern Europe; see Nelson, "The Comparative Politics of Eastern Europe," in Stephen White, Judy Batt, and Paul G. Lewis, eds., *Developments in East European Politics* (Durham, NC: Duke University Press, 1993), p. 255.

17. As Huntington does when he poses the question "whether to treat democracy and nondemocracy as a dichotomous or continuous variable" and chooses the former option. Huntington, *The Third Wave*, p. 6. Yet even he prefers the continuum approach when discussing the East Asian dominant-party systems; Huntington, "Democracy's Third Wave," in Diamond and Plattner, *The Global Resurgence of Democracy*, p. 18.

18. Japan, without a second electoral turnover, would be closer to the center than the other three historical cases.

19. See, for examples, Guillermo O'Donnell, Philippe C. Schmitter, and Laurence Whitehead, eds., *Transitions from Authoritarian Rule: Comparative Perspectives* (Baltimore: Johns Hopkins University Press, 1986); Di Palma, *To Craft Democracies*; Huntington, *The Third Wave*; Karl, "Dilemmas of Democratization"; and Diamond and Plattner, *The Global Resurgence of Democracy*. The authors of such studies initially did not wish to prejudge the outcome by analyzing transitions "to democracy" and instead adopted the more cautious "from authoritarianism."

20. Guillermo O'Donnell and Philippe C. Schmitter, *Transitions from Authoritarian Rule: Tentative Conclusions About Uncertain Democracies* (Baltimore: Johns Hopkins

University Press, 1986), pp. 4–5. See also the review article on this literature by Nancy Bermeo, "Rethinking Regime Change," *Comparative Politics* 22 (April 1990): 359–377.

21. O'Donnell and Schmitter define a regime as "the ensemble of patterns, explicit or not, that determines the forms and channels of access to principal government positions, the characteristics of the actors who are admitted and excluded from such access, and the resources and strategies that they can use to gain access." *Transitions from Authoritarian Rule: Tentative Conclusions*, p. 73. See also Przeworski, *Democracy and the Market*, pp. 88ff.

22. In their *Transitions from Authoritarian Rule: Tentative Conclusions*, Introduction, p. x. For distinctions among authoritarian regimes, see Juan J. Linz, "Totalitarian and Authoritarian Regimes," in Nelson Polsby and Fred Greenstein, eds., *Handbook of Political Science*, vol. 3 (Reading, MA: Addison-Wesley, 1975), pp. 175–411.

23. Linz, "Totalitarian and Authoritarian Regimes," pp. 191–192. For a recent study of the term, see Abbott Gleason, *Totalitarianism: The Inner History of the Cold War* (New York: Oxford University Press, 1995).

24. Linz, "Totalitarian and Authoritarian Regimes," pp. 336–350.

25. Terry Lynn Karl and Philippe C. Schmitter, "Modes of Transition in Latin America, Southern and Eastern Europe," *International Social Science Journal* 128 (May 1991): 271.

26. Huntington, *The Third Wave*, p. 114; Juan J. Linz, "Crisis, Breakdown, and Reequilibration," in Linz and Alfred Stepan, *The Breakdown of Democratic Regimes* (Baltimore: Johns Hopkins University Press, 1978), p. 35. On pacts, see O'Donnell and Schmitter, *Transitions from Authoritarian Rule: Tentative Conclusions*, ch. 4.

27. Huntington calls them "standpatters." Huntington, *The Third Wave*, pp. 121ff.

28. Shin, "On the Third Wave of Democratization," p. 142. The quote is from Alexander Gelman, a supporter of Gorbachev, quoted by Shin from Zbigniew Brzezinski, *The Grand Failure: The Birth and Death of Communism in the Twentieth Century* (New York: Charles Scribner's Sons, 1989), pp. 45–46.

29. Karl, "Dilemmas of Democratization," p. 173; Huntington, *The Third Wave*, ch. 3.

30. See, for example, Valerie Bunce, "Should Transitologists Be Grounded?" *Slavic Review* 54 (Spring 1995): 126.

31. Douglass C. North, *Institutions, Institutional Change, and Economic Performance* (New York: Cambridge University Press, 1990), p. 140.

32. For debates over presidentialism and parliamentarism, or the advantages and problems of proportional representation, see part 2 of Diamond and Plattner, *The Global Resurgence of Democracy*, and Alfred Stepan and Cindy Skach, "Constitutional Frameworks and Democratic Consolidation," *World Politics* 46 (October 1993): 1–22. See also the debates in the *East European Constitutional Review*, e.g., vol. 2, no. 1 (Winter 1993), and Juan J. Linz, ed., *The Failure of Presidential Democracy* (Baltimore: Johns Hopkins University Press, 1994).

33. For examples of international influence in the contemporary context, see Huntington, *The Third Wave*, pp. 85–106, or Di Palma, *To Craft Democracies*, ch. 9. For a brief survey of earlier examples and theories including dependency theory, see Karl, "Dilemmas of Democratization," pp. 166–167.

34. On the connection between democracy and alternative economic systems, see Larry Diamond and Marc F. Plattner, eds., *Capitalism, Socialism, and Democracy Revisited* (Baltimore: Johns Hopkins University Press, 1993). See also note 12 in Chapter 5 of this book.

35. Karl, "Dilemmas of Democratization," p. 178. See also Przeworski, *Democracy and the Market*, ch. 4, esp. p. 161.

36. Bermeo, "Rethinking Regime Change," p. 365. Some of Karen Remmer's recent work on Latin America does find a positive relationship between democratic regimes and economic growth; see Karen L. Remmer, "The Political Impact of Economic Crisis in Latin America in the 1980s," *American Political Science Review* 85 (September 1991): 777–800. See also Shin, "On the Third Wave," p. 155, and the sources cited.

37. For details, see Ken Jowitt, *New World Disorder: The Leninist Extinction* (Berkeley: University of California Press, 1992), ch. 8.

38. See Sarah M. Terry, "Thinking About Post-Communist Transitions: How Different Are They?" *Slavic Review* 52 (Summer 1993): 333–337; Valerie Bunce, "Should Transitologists Be Grounded?"; and Bunce, "Comparing East and South," *Journal of Democracy* 6 (July 1995): 87–100.

39. Przeworski, *Democracy and the Market*, p. 95.

40. Free trade as opposed to economic protectionism: export-import strategies open the country to the international market, in Argentina's case to export raw materials and import manufactured goods; import substitution strategies protect domestic production despite higher costs.

SUGGESTIONS FOR FURTHER RESEARCH

The most important works to consult on recent processes of democratization include: Samuel P. Huntington, *The Third Wave: Democratization in the Late Twentieth Century* (Norman: University of Oklahoma Press, 1991), a broad assessment of changes throughout the world; Giuseppe Di Palma, *To Craft Democracies: An Essay on Democratic Transitions* (Berkeley: University of California Press, 1990), an optimistic view emphasizing the role of individuals and their choices; and Adam Przeworski, *Democracy and the Market: Political and Economic Reforms in Eastern Europe and Latin America* (Cambridge: Cambridge University Press, 1991), a more pessimistic appraisal with special stress on the problems of postcommunist states.

The basic tenets of transition theorists were set forth in Guillermo O'Donnell, Philippe C. Schmitter, and Laurence Whitehead, *Transitions from Authoritarian Rule: Prospects for Democracy* (Baltimore: Johns Hopkins University Press, 1986), available in four separate volumes subtitled, respectively, *Southern Europe, Latin America, Comparative Perspectives*, and *Tentative Conclusions About Uncertain Democracies*. For a succinct discussion of this new approach, see Terry Lynn Karl, "Dilemmas of Democratization in Latin America," in Dankwart A. Rustow and Kenneth Paul Erickson, eds., *Comparative Political Dynamics: Global Research Perspectives* (New York: HarperCollins, 1991), pp. 163–191. See also the review article by Nancy Bermeo, "Rethinking Regime Change," *Comparative Politics* 22 (April 1990): 359–377. Terry Lynn Karl and Philippe C. Schmitter extended these theories to postcommunist states in their "Modes of Transition in Latin America, Southern and Eastern Europe," *International Social Science Journal* 128 (May 1991): 269–284. More skeptical appraisals for postcommunist systems are cited in note 38 of this chapter.

The single most important journal on these issues is *Journal of Democracy*, and an excellent collection of articles from its pages may be found in Larry Diamond and Marc F. Plattner, eds., *The Global Resurgence of Democracy* (Baltimore: Johns Hopkins University

Press, 1993). Other relevant journals include *Democratization* and *East European Constitutional Review*. On the difficulties of shaping institutions to fit societal needs, see Douglass C. North, *Institutions, Institutional Change, and Economic Performance* (New York: Cambridge University Press, 1990); Alfred Stepan and Cindy Skach, "Constitutional Frameworks and Democratic Consolidation," *World Politics* 46 (October 1993): 1–22; and the pages of the journals mentioned above.

1

ENGLAND:
AN UNFINISHED REVOLUTION

PATRICIA-ANN LEE

On January 30, 1649, in the backwash of a civil war and after a trial stage-managed by the victorious parliament, Charles I of England was executed. This was not the first time an English king had been removed from power, but it was the first time a king had been charged with crimes against his people, tried by a court composed of his subjects, and publicly executed. These deliberate and considered acts of policy were part of a process that dismantled and reconstituted what had until that time been universally accepted as the Ancient Constitution. In the weeks and months that followed Charles's execution, the House of Lords was abolished and monarchy itself was formally ended. Kingship having been found "unnecessary, burdensome and dangerous to the liberty, safety and public interest of the people," England temporarily became a republic.[1] But a true settlement of the nation, a permanent political solution that would attach to a new government the legitimacy, loyalties, and staying power of the old system, was to prove more elusive. Indeed, it was never to be achieved during this period, because the Stuart monarchy was restored in 1660 under Charles II.

When viewed in this way, the seventeenth-century revolution would seem to have been a failure. However, despite the fact that a Stuart king was restored and the formal acts and ordinances of the Interregnum were swept away, the institution of monarchy would never be the same. Limitations on the king's power, limitations that had been formally accepted by Charles I and were designed to prevent the continuance or resumption of arbitrary royal government, remained in place. Even more significant were the changes that had taken place in the substratum of ideas, assumptions, and understandings that supported the institutional framework. Experience and historical memory after 1660 included not only the martyrdom of Charles I but also the army debates at Putney, not only the rule of the army leaders but also calls by Levellers and other visionaries for a democratization of government. Above all, by 1660, it had become clear that monarchy was neither natural nor essential; the nation could choose some other system if it wished to do so. Never would it be possible thereafter to reconstitute an authoritarian monarchy on the old customary and theological basis. The English had been freed to question the nature of their political process, to speculate about what made power legitimate, and to examine other modes of political activity. Finally, there was the matter of religion, which had played so large a part in igniting the troubles of midcentury and in shaping events of the Interregnum. In that area there was also restoration, with the Anglican church officially reestablished. However, that restoration too was incomplete since it was no longer possible for Anglicanism to compel universal belief or even to include within itself all English Protestants.

These changes formed the foundation for the future development of British political life and thought. They also had an impact upon colonies overseas, because settlers carried with them a view of their traditional rights and liberties that was based on their understanding of what had happened during the century just past.

Classes, Politics, and the Ancient Constitution

The England in which these events took place was a small country, its population numbering perhaps 4.5 million persons, most of them engaged in agriculture. Woolen cloth was still the most important national export, although war and changes in European markets had caused some difficulty for the trade in the first three decades or so of the seventeenth century. There were several important ports, many agricultural villages, a number of smallish market towns, and one large city, London, which was the center of economic as well as national political affairs. However, except for the king, his court, and a group of professional administrators, lawyers, and judges, some merchants, and members of parliament when parliament was in session, life centered in the counties. Ordinary people thought in terms of their neighborhoods, and the gentry focused on their county (or "country"), where local government was carried out in the name of the king by local landowners who served without pay. In the counties the most important officials were the Lord Lieutenants, who were drawn from the highest nobility, the peerage. The real workhorses, however, were omnicompetent local agents of royal government called justices of the peace, who were usually members of the gentry. Through intermarriage, and by working together at the local level, established gentry families formed the county community and were a major force in national as well as local politics.

As Peter Laslett has pointed out, seventeenth-century England was a one-class society.[2] That class encompassed all socially, politically, and economically privileged persons, from the peers at the top to the greater and lesser gentry beneath. In terms of actual numbers, the nobility was a small group. By 1633, there were 122 lay peers and twenty-six bishops, who together made up the House of Lords. In contrast, untitled gentry numbered between 18,500 and 24,800, some of them great and wealthy landholders but many others "mere gentlemen."[3] All were men. Women took their social status from their fathers and husbands and did not normally participate in the political process. This was a society in which hierarchy and patriarchy were accepted as natural and provided discipline and control. Authority flowed downward from the top, where status, land, and wealth were concentrated. Deference was expected by those above and accorded by those below as a matter of course. Nevertheless, despite limits set by such a pattern of organization, English society was remarkably permeable when compared to societies of other European states. In England, gentle birth certainly gave high status, but there were other ways of gaining entry to the privileged class. For example, important royal officeholders could claim gentility and so could graduates of the two universities. Successful lawyers who bought land moved upward quite easily, and wealthy merchants married their children into well-born families.

Members of this privileged group belonged by definition to the political nation, that is, to that body of persons who traditionally participated in political life and dominated decisionmaking at the national and county levels. For such men, parliament was the most obvious and important arena of political activity. Within parliament, peers and bishops were summoned individually to the House of Lords, but members of the House of Commons (burgesses from the towns and knights of the shire from the counties) had to be elected. Voter qualifications differed from town to town, although in the counties there was a fairly broad and uniform franchise. Under the county franchise all property owners worth forty shillings per year could vote. Yet, whether they came from town or county, those elected under this system were always prosperous and well connected and almost always drawn from among the greater gentry. Their wealth and influence, in addition to the elective nature of the body, tended to give the House of Commons greater and greater importance, so that by the reign of Charles I the lower house was as significant as the once-dominant House of Lords.[4]

Although most seventeenth-century Englishmen could not vote, the number qualified to do so was increasing. Simple population growth played a part in this as did inflation, which reduced the exclusionary effect of the forty-shilling freeholder franchise. In addition, constitutional and religious controversies drew more people to the polls.[5] In the 1640s, one recent estimate suggests that between 27 percent and 40 percent of adult males could have voted. The numbers are small by modern standards, but the English electorate was a large one for its day.[6] Numbers of voters alone, however, do not tell the whole story of political participation. Outside the traditionally privileged group were other ordinary English subjects who attended county courts, served on juries, and acted as petty constables or filled other minor offices. By so doing they learned how to represent and be represented and acquired experience in leadership and participation that could be translated into political activity if the occasion arose. Such a group was to be of particular importance in a period in which issues were increasingly national and engaged English men and women at all social levels.

The constitution was the framework for political thought within which national political activity took place. This so-called Ancient Constitution was not a single written document but rather a body of law, custom, and traditional practice that had developed over a long period. It was an understanding about the proper relationships thought to exist among the king, his councillors (including parliament), and his people. The English believed this supposedly ancient and immutable arrangement was based on fundamental laws and embodied their rights and liberties. In practice, however, the constitution was in a constant state of renegotiation, and its laws and liberties could be modified or even abolished by new parliamentary legislation. The English state was described at the time as a mixed monarchy in which both king and parliament had a recognized place. To be sure, the precise nature of their relationship had never been defined, but there was no need to do so as long as crown and parliament were in substantial agreement or the state was under so much pressure from foreign events that disagreements could not be too harshly pressed.

Within this mixed monarchy the king still possessed considerable power. Although parliaments were an accepted part of the system, they met only occasionally, whereas he was continuously present. The king selected his own ministers, judges, and other officials, controlled the money—even that granted by parliament—and made foreign policy. He alone had authority to call a parliament into being, and he could dismiss it whenever he wished. In addition, parliamentary legislation required his assent to become law (giving him an effective veto power), and his officials guided deliberations in both houses. On its side, parliament was a court and the maker of statute (the most important kind of law), and when the king needed more money than he could raise from his rents and other customary sources, he had to obtain its assent to any legislation that imposed taxation. Control of the purse strings gave great potential power to parliament and particularly to the House of Commons (where tax legislation had to originate), but it was a power the members were not at first eager to exploit. Ideally, parliament was thought of as an occasion upon which all elements of the constitution were to be brought into a natural relationship of harmony and unity rather than as an opportunity for working out conflicts. Nevertheless, in spite of such confusions and difficulties, parliament was recognized as a national institution through which the voice of the community of the realm (a broader concept than the political nation) could make itself heard. In parliamentary deliberations, all Englishmen were considered to be represented, whether or not they could actually vote (an idea that would later be called virtual representation).

Within this system, the king was preeminent but not absolute. When, in the course of divorcing Katherine of Aragon, Henry VIII (1509–1547) split with Rome and took over the Catholic Church and its jurisdictions in England, he added greatly to his power and was able to claim the exclusive and undivided loyalty of all his subjects. Yet, without a standing army, a police force, or a paid bureaucracy to collect taxes, and with local government in the hands of the gentry, practical absolutism was harder to achieve. The English, even Henry's sixteenth-century subjects, did not think of their monarchs as absolute. Seventeenth-century parliamentary critics of the Stuart kings liked to quote Henry de Bracton, a medieval royal judge who had said that the king ruled not under men but under God and the law.[7] There was also great veneration for the Magna Carta, which had been wrested by the barons from King John in 1215. Although in reality a rather limited feudal document, the Great Charter was believed to embody the basic rights of the English subject. It also showed the community of the realm imposing the rule of law on a lawless king.

In time, differing views of the constitution would pit king and parliament against each other, but not because either was consciously seeking a new kind of power. Quite the contrary. The early Stuart monarchs, James I (1603–1625) and Charles I (1625–1649), were determined to preserve their rights by turning back parliamentary encroachments upon royal authority, and parliament was equally intent upon preserving its place within the system. Each could and did claim to be defending the proper balance of the constitution. However, these kings, who were Scottish in origin, had a view of kingship different from that held by most of their English subjects. Having obtained the throne by default when Elizabeth I (1558–1603) died without heirs, their claim depended upon birth and blood. This was determined by God, who, they believed, had thus ordained their rule and justified their power as his vice-regents on Earth. But such divine right was historically alien to English constitutional thinking and could be used to justify a kind of monarchy in which the king was not just preeminent within the law and the Ancient Constitution but superior to both. Thus, when the first Stuart monarch (James I) began to theorize about his rights as an absolute ruler, his parliaments were forced to define their own position on the issue. Even so, the members never claimed parliament's rights were superior to those of the king. What they did do was to claim a coordinate place in the constitution and to maintain that "the liberties, franchises, privileges, and jurisdictions of parliament are the ancient and undoubted birthright and inheritance of the subjects of England."[8] Indeed, Sir Edward Coke, the noted lawyer and judge, argued that the privileges of parliament were more ancient than monarchy, because they rested upon immemorial law and custom that predated the Norman Conquest. In this view, matters pertaining to parliament could only be changed by parliament itself. In the end, although both king and parliament could agree that parliament had a role within the constitution, they differed on what it was supposed to be.

FINANCIAL PRESSURE, STALEMATE, AND CRISIS

The Stuart monarchs, like other European rulers of the early seventeenth century, faced a crisis of government and, more particularly, of government finance. This was based in part on rapid inflation caused by the infusion of large amounts of bullion from the Americas into the European economy. Studies also emphasize the inflationary results of debasing the coinage, the sharp rise in unproductive military expenditures, and an increase in population (which doubled between 1500 and 1650).[9] The particular problems of England in the 1640s went back to the preceding century, a period during which prices increased more than 600 percent and royal income (between 1510 and 1602) doubled. Such inflation put great pressure on the crown, which, like other landlords, had to live on a relatively fixed income of declining value. Elizabeth I, who was notoriously careful about money, had ended her reign £400,000 in debt, which makes it less surprising that her Stuart successors regularly outspent their incomes. The monarchy was in fact running out of money. Not only were the Stuarts prodigal in expenditure, but their income from the taxes parliament authorized was also declining. For example, a parliamentary grant (subsidy) that had yielded £130,000 in the early sixteenth century was bringing in only £55,000 by 1628.[10] Although this owed something to the eroding force of inflation, the privileged class refused either to assess itself realistically for tax purposes or to act through parliament to authorize enough taxes to make up for the depreciated values of its grants and cover the rising cost of government.

Times were difficult in other ways as well. The 1630s were marked by a series of bad harvests that pushed up grain prices and caused much discontent. Trade, which suffered from changes in traditional markets and from the disruptions of war, was also in disarray and brought the monarch less money through customs duties. Attempts to solve the crown's financial problems, either by obtaining a fixed income from parliament or by reducing expenditures, also failed. Thus, by the reign of Charles I, when critics demanded that the king live on his ordinary (nonparliamentary) income, they were asking for what was already impossible. Perhaps in a climate of trust and good will these difficulties could have been dealt with. Suspicion and mistrust, however, increasingly marked Charles's relations with his parliaments.

Charles was in fact singularly ill-suited for kingship. Small in stature and handicapped by a lifelong stutter, he had great dignity and a high sense of his position as king but no practical political ability. Charles believed parliament had a place in the constitution, but one theoretically and practically inferior to his own as hereditary monarch. In practice, he felt no obligation to defer to its wishes, resented anything he saw as a demand, and was unwilling to adhere to concessions he believed had been forced upon him. These attitudes made real political interaction impossible and encouraged him to act in ways that appeared untrustworthy and treacherous. A poor judge of others, the king was also a weak leader. He sometimes failed to protect able but unpopular ministers such as the earl of Strafford, who was tried by parliament and executed in 1641. At the same time, he depended too much on personal favorites such as the duke of Buckingham (assassinated in 1628) and Henrietta Maria (Charles's French Catholic Queen). Worst of all, the king was committed to an outmoded and unrealistic view of the constitution. Doomed not only by the events of his reign but by his own defects of personality and leadership, Charles was a man "who knew not how to be or to be made great."[11]

A major cause of trouble for the king was his religious policy, in particular his efforts to impose a High Church system of liturgy and discipline, Arminianism, upon the Anglican church. Although Arminians were not Roman Catholic, many English men and women believed that they were, or at least that they were leading the church in that direction. This was a great disadvantage for Charles because hatred of "popery" (Roman Catholicism) was deeply embedded in English minds. To the English there was a natural connection between Catholicism, tyranny, and attempts by foreign powers to subvert and destroy their national independence. These attitudes dated back to the long Elizabethan struggle with Catholic Spain and were reinforced by events of the Thirty Years' War (1618–1648), which pitted Catholic against Protestant in Europe. Even in terms of domestic policy, Arminianism was bound to be unpopular. Its ceremonials offended religious Puritans, and its political implications alarmed many of Charles's other subjects. Because clerical advisers such as Archbishop William Laud also supported the king's absolutist political views, there was some logic in these fears.

Throughout the reign, politics and religion were matters of continuing concern, although concerns over finance actually precipitated the first major conflict and established a lasting pattern of tension and mistrust between the king and the House of Commons. The issue was customs duties, of which the most important was Tonnage and Poundage. Unlike other taxes, which were for a fixed sum and were reenacted as needed, Tonnage and Poundage was awarded to the king for life at the beginning of the reign. Thus, this revenue source was not subject to continuing control, and it could not be used to ensure that the king would call frequent parliaments or compel him to cooperate once a parliament had been summoned. This worried the House of Commons, whose power and influence depended upon its control of the governmental purse strings. Accordingly, at the beginning of Charles's reign in 1625, the Commons decided to examine all such grants and, while doing so, to authorize Tonnage and Poundage for only a single year. The House of Lords (which was more conservative than the Commons) refused to agree, and no authorization was given. In theory these duties could not be collected.

In fact, Charles had little choice. As customs duties constituted a significant part of his regular income, and because he was desperately short of money, he continued to collect Tonnage and Poundage on the basis of his own royal authority. Such a violation of parliamentary privileges was deeply resented by this and all succeeding parliaments. A specific financial problem was turning into a more general issue of arbitrary taxation and arbitrary government. So serious did the controversy become that in 1628 the leaders of Charles's third parliament decided to seek a formal confirmation of the rights of the subject in this area. The resulting Petition of Right reaffirmed the principle that taxation required common consent (that is, in parliament). It also went on to request an end to coercive practices such as arbitrary imprisonment, the billeting of troops in private homes, and imposition of martial law, by which the king had enforced his demands. To petition in this way was an ancient right, and supporters claimed they were breaking no new ground, but in fact they were attempting to limit Charles's power to authorize and enforce taxation.

Charles accepted the Petition of Right very reluctantly and only because he expected this would lead to the grant of money he needed. It did not do so. Instead, the House of Commons went on to attack his religious policy, and, when he tried to dismiss them, the members did something without precedent: They refused to disband. While several members forcibly held the speaker in his chair so that the session could continue, the House of Commons passed three resolutions. These did not have any legal force but did express the opinion of the Commons on the central issues of religion and taxation. The resolutions made it clear that anyone who introduced innovations in religion, or who advised the levying or paying of Tonnage and Poundage, was to be considered a "betrayer of the liberties of England and an enemy of the same."[12] An angry and probably frightened House of Commons was showing a new willingness to confront the king.

Charles was no less angry than the leaders of the House of Commons but wished to avoid any more confrontations. In addition, he wanted to show that he could rule without parliament if he had to do so. In fact, eleven years were to pass before he called another, a period during which he collected disputed taxes such as Tonnage and Poundage without the customary authorization. His agents also sought out new extraparliamentary sources of revenue, examining old records to find forgotten or neglected laws so that he could fine those who had unwittingly violated them. Thus, heavy penalties were imposed for breaking the medieval Forest Laws, for failing to take up the honor of knighthood, or for committing some other obscure offense. He also revived Monopolies (indirect taxes on trade), even though they were so unpopular that they had been renounced by Elizabeth I. Finally, Ship Money (a wartime levy on port towns to support the navy) was imposed as a peacetime tax that had to be paid by inland areas as well. All these measures were unpopular, but it was dangerous to resist them. Those who did so were prosecuted, often in Prerogative Courts like Star Chamber, which were particularly responsive to the king's wishes and where the accused did not enjoy the protections of the common law. By such infuriating and frightening expedients Charles was able to raise large sums of money—but only at the cost of alienating many of his important subjects, including members of both the gentry and the peerage.

Of course, some individuals did resist. The best-known case was probably that of John Hampden in 1637. Hampden was a wealthy and respected member of the gentry who refused on principle to pay a small sum in Ship Money, and his prosecution aroused tremendous interest in the country. The royal judges did rule against him, but by such a narrow margin (seven to five) that the verdict was perceived as a moral victory for him and a defeat for the king. Yet such incidents did not really change anything. As long as the king could raise enough money to finance his government, he would not call a parliament. And without a parliament there was no place for his opponents to come together and make themselves heard in an effective way. In the end it was not domestic resistance but rebellion—in Scotland—that finally brought an end to the royal experiment in personal rule.

The Stuarts were monarchs not merely of one but of three distinct realms, each with its own cultural, religious, and political characteristics. Calvinist Scotland was virtually independent, whereas Catholic Ireland was subordinated to the crown and English parliament in important ways, but neither realm was happy with English dominance. Religion was a particularly touchy matter, because, as Conrad Russell has pointed out, each realm possessed "a vigorous minority who preferred the system of the other country to their own."[13] When national and religious issues merged, the combination was dangerously volatile. Thus, when Charles decided to impose Anglican Arminianism on Scotland he was embarking on a perilous and provocative policy. By 1638, his actions had induced Scots of all classes to join in the National Covenant, which was a display of support for their Calvinist and Presbyterian church. They also raised an army and prepared to uphold their cause by force of arms. Faced by rebellion and the threat of invasion, Charles was compelled to raise an army of his own, something he could not afford to do without parliamentary assistance. Of course, given the state of English public opinion, calling a new parliament was risky, but he counted on traditional English hatred of the Scots to rally the members to his side. When he did call a parliament, he also tried to conciliate the members by promising to redress longstanding grievances once the necessary money bills had passed. Unfortunately for him, the members were more fearful of royal absolutism than of a Scottish invasion, and they did not trust even the most solemn of the king's pledges. The result was much passionate debate but not a single penny of assistance. After three weeks, Charles gave up and dismissed the body.

Following the failure of the so-called Short Parliament, the king turned to a variety of desperate expedients designed to avoid the necessity of calling another. He tried to raise loans and (on the advice of the earl of Strafford) considered bringing Catholic troops from Ireland. He even summoned a Council of Peers to York, hoping it would authorize taxes. Nothing worked. With the Scots occupying portions of northern England, and with no money in the treasury to raise a new army, Charles had to sign the Treaty of Ripon. Under its humiliating terms he was to pay £850 per day to support the invaders and also allow them to occupy the counties of Durham and Northumberland until they received their money. Only another parliament could raise the money he now needed, and in November 1640 the body that would be known as the Long Parliament assembled at Westminster.

The Long Parliament and Reform

The Scottish intervention in English politics, so disastrous for Charles, was a great advantage to his political opponents. John Pym, an astute and ruthless politician who had risen to leadership in the Short Parliament, correctly appraised the situation. He understood that the Scots were not his enemies and that their presence, which had compelled Charles to call a new parliament, would force the king to cooperate with that body once it was in session. Pym, who had served in the House of Commons since 1614, was a firm opponent of arbitrary power and royal absolutism. He had helped to pass the Petition of Right in 1628 and had rallied the members against the king's religious and political policies. When the Long Parliament assembled in November 1640, he immediately emerged as a major leader and would continue in that position until his death in 1643.

However, even in this new climate, so favorable to Pym and his colleagues, no one at first dared attack the king directly. Instead they struck at surrogates such as Archbishop Laud and Thomas Wentworth (the earl of Strafford), the advisers who had helped Charles formulate and carry out his unpopular policies in church and state. Strafford was tried in parliament and sent to the block in May 1641. The king, who had promised that he would not allow him to "suffer in his person, honor or fortune," signed the bill condemning the earl to death.[14] Laud too was condemned, although he was not executed until 1645. Parliament also moved to dismantle the financial and political machinery that had made personal rule possible. A Triennial Bill was passed to make sure parliaments would have to be called at least once every three years. Star Chamber and the other Prerogative Courts were abolished. Henceforth, the king would have to rely on common law courts and juries that afforded more protections to the subjects and were not so easily influenced by him. Parliament also swept away or banned the financial devices by which Charles had raised money independently during the eleven years of personal rule. Tonnage and Poundage was authorized at long last, but only for two months at a time. Finally, in order to make sure that Charles would not be able to interfere with the process of reform, a law was enacted that said that this particular parliament could not be dismissed without its own consent.

With few able advisers, no money, and no party of his own in parliament, Charles was helpless to resist this spate of legislation. Thus, by August 1641, parliament had secured most of the reforms envisaged in its long years of struggle with its Stuart monarchs. Gone were most of the extraordinary powers English monarchs had gained under the Tudors. Henceforth, the king could not fund his government unless parliament authorized taxes and could not enforce his rule without the support of juries and the common law courts. He had even lost, at least with regard to this particular body, his traditional right to dismiss parliament at will. This remarkable reformation, a revolution in its own right, had been accomplished by the political nation peacefully, legally, and within the bounds of the Ancient Constitution. Although parliament would go on to make greater and more revolutionary changes, this settlement (reluctantly but legally accepted by the king) would survive the Civil War and Interregnum and become the basis of a restored Stuart monarchy in 1660.

Up to this point, parliament had been united. Not only was there unity of purpose and strong leadership within the House of Commons, but both Houses were also cooperating through a system of joint conferences. The king, in contrast, was isolated, unable to decide upon a coherent policy, and without managers who could control events in parliament. Charles had no distinguishable group of royalists to take his side within the House of Commons and not much organized support elsewhere. What active supporters he could muster were chiefly among his courtiers, officials, and a few great merchants of the City of London who had an interest in royal loans, taxes, or financial policies. Yet, as king, Charles did retain important advantages. His opponents could argue that he was poorly advised or even that he was acting wrongly, but they had to accept that as king he was head of the state; its officials were his servants, its policies his policies. To oppose the king systematically was to be disloyal. There was no place in the constitution, as it was then understood, for formed opposition (organized, ideological, and permanent) or for political parties. Of course, there had always been practical opposition, but, as in the case of the barons who had forced Magna Carta upon King John, that opposition had tended to be temporary and to center around specific grievances. Only as major constitutional questions emerged and became the focus of political debate had this begun to change. However, old ideas lingered, and even among Charles's triumphant opponents in the Long Parliament there was a desire for familiar constitutional forms and comfortable fictions.

Within the framework of those fictions and without formal organization, attitudes of opposition showing common characteristics and interests had developed over the years. For example, the term "Country Party," or "Country Interest," was being used by the 1640s to describe those who generally distrusted courtiers and the court, opposed "popery," and supported the liberties of the subjects as the gentry understood them. Although not everyone who held these views was a Country Party member, the term described a body of men with political and familial ties who already cooperated sporadically in their localities. Probably, such opposition was possible because these men were not radicals or reformers but rather were deeply conservative. Although desiring to redress specific wrongs, they had no wish to effect general change in a system from which they benefited as much as the king. Yet the political situation itself was changing, and national issues were emerging that would defy traditional solutions and around which new loyalties would begin to coalesce.

The Grand Remonstrance of November 1641 became such an issue. Designed by Pym and his colleagues to solidify opinion within the Long Parliament and to rally opinion in the country at large, this measure reiterated familiar grievances. Only on religion did it take a radical position, proposing to abolish the episcopacy altogether. The Remonstrance was rejected by political moderates who were satisfied with what had already been achieved, as well as by those who supported the Anglican church or were unwilling to destroy an ecclesiastical system that supported traditional social and political hierarchies. The Remonstrance passed in spite of this opposition but only by a narrow margin of eleven votes (159 to 148). This result showed the growing divisions in parliament rather than the solidarity for which its leaders had hoped.

The crumbling and partial disintegration of parliament's united front should have afforded an opportunity for the king to form a royalist party that would give him a base of support. All Charles had to do was wait, stress the constitutionality of his position, and demonstrate that he intended to abide by the new restrictions on his power. Instead, he followed the advice of his wife and a group of hotheaded, hardline courtiers and decided on a military coup. Violating the most sacred rights and privileges of parliament, he went to the House of Commons in 1642 with a body of soldiers to arrest, on charges of high treason, five of its leading members. They had been warned and so escaped, but even in failure he had done terrible and lasting damage to his cause. In the short term, parliamentary moderates were forced back into alliance with their more radical colleagues. In the long term, his actions showed that no matter how solemn his promises and agreements, he could never be trusted to abide by them. From now on his opponents would demand safeguards for his behavior, and, because they could not trust him, they would never consider them strong or binding enough to allay their fears.

This breakdown of relations, which was a serious matter in itself, also affected other issues. Of major importance was the problem of Ireland, where in October 1641 a rebellion had erupted among the Roman Catholic population. English settlers were massacred, and stories of atrocities that circulated in London and the country at large put great pressure on parliament to act. In order to take action, an army would have to be raised, but leaders of parliament feared that the king would use it against them. Pym's solution was legislation that would place control of the military in the hands of parliament's nominees rather than men chosen by the king. But the king would never agree to this violation of his traditional rights, and without his approval the bill could not become a statute. Determined to have their way, the leaders of the House of Commons looked about for a precedent and found one in the Ordinance, a kind of law that in the past had been created by the king alone. Turning the procedure on its head, parliament now used it to make law without the king. And although the Militia Ordinance never received royal assent, it was treated as though it had full legal authority.[15] This was clearly unconstitutional, but it did break the stalemate created by the king's ability to veto any piece of legislation by withholding consent, and it enormously increased parliament's institutional power and freedom of action. With passage of the Militia Ordinance in March 1642, parliament had taken its first direct step into revolution.

WAR AND REVOLUTION

By January 1642, the king no longer felt secure in a capital dominated by parliament and its vociferous crowds of supporters. He left London for Hampton Court and was at York during the debates on the Militia Ordinance. The two sides were drawing apart, although communications did not immediately break off and parliament did present proposals for settlement—the Nineteen Propositions—in May 1642. These demanded not only that Charles accept the Militia Ordinance but that he also relinquish much of his power over civil government and the church. Parliament believed it needed such guarantees to secure the settlement it had already achieved, but Charles rejected them in early June, writing that in terms of real power they would have left him "but the Picture, but the sign of a king."[16] By July 1642, military preparations were under way, and at Nottingham on July 22 the king raised his standard and summoned all loyal subjects to his aid. This marked the formal beginning of England's Civil War, and, thereafter, with restive officers on each side and expensive armies in the making, events moved steadily from words into action. In October at Edgehill the first battle was fought. It was a royalist victory, although not a clear or decisive one. The real war had begun.

Terrible as it was to be, this final split between king and parliament and the growing certainty of war did at least bring Charles the assistance and the followers he needed. The so-called Court Party, such as it was, had fallen apart, and many of the hardliners had fled overseas. Their places were taken by disillusioned moderates who had been forced into the royalist camp by the growing radicalism of parliament's leaders. More than one-third of the members of the House of Commons and almost one-half of the peers joined the king and became the base of a new Royalist Party. However, the support of such men was neither absolute nor unquestioning. They wished to preserve the monarchy—but a monarchy restrained and limited by all the recent reforms. In short, these were constitutional royalists who desired a compromise settlement rather than a decisive military victory that would restore Charles to absolute and unfettered authority. And as there were also men of moderate views on the parliamentary side, the hardliners in both camps were at first unable to have their way.

Ambiguity seemed to characterize most relationships at the beginning of this war. Even in parliament, members were anxious to preserve a fiction of loyalty to the old system if not to the king. Thus, the doctrine of the King's Two Bodies enabled them to separate the real and fallible man they opposed from his public legal entity (the crown or the King-in-Parliament), which, in a sense, they supported. At the local level, such myths were less necessary, and men chose sides because of local loyalties, politics, and relationships. Ancient traditions also exerted a powerful influence, and if some men were drawn to the king, others supported parliament as the embodiment of national political rights. Thus, opinion in the country was divided, with royalists and parliament-men existing in every county, many towns, and even within some families. Generally, however, more remote agrarian areas of the west and north tended to side with the king, whereas the east and populous south as well as most urban centers, including London, were for parliament.

National issues did matter, although ordinary people were usually more engaged by religious than by constitutional causes. Elections for the Long Parliament in 1640 had aroused intense interest, even among those who did not belong to the traditional political nation, and popular attention did not wane. Indeed, it intensified as the session continued, and the general populace (at least that of London and its environs) joined in the political process. Tradesmen and apprentices, even crowds of women, gathered at Westminster to demonstrate and petition on behalf of policies they approved or disapproved.[17] This politicization alarmed many political moderates as well as those persons primarily concerned about property and social order. Radicals and activists, however, quickly learned to use popular demonstrations against their opponents. Threatening mobs that intimidated the House of Lords had helped ensure Strafford's condemnation in May 1641. Crowds had also demonstrated in favor of the Grand Remonstrance and of abolishing the episcopacy. The radical democrats, called Levellers by their enemies, were to become particularly skillful in exploiting such opportunities. Whether these interventions were organized and controlled by the political leaders in parliament is unclear, but Presbyterians and Independent ministers (who headed self-governing Protestant congregations) as well as Leveller agitators did mobilize followers for political purposes.

Activism, both political and religious, was also at work in the parliamentary army, where it found considerable scope and was to express itself in ways dangerously destructive to constitutional order—although this danger took some time to show itself. Initially, both armies were raised in similar fashion and were similar in composition. Whether for the king or parliament, great men recruited their tenants, local units were raised in traditional ways, and the ranks were filled out with conscripts. As for the commanders, generals were usually peers, officers were gentlemen, and the lower ranks drew in shopkeepers, apprentices, farmers, tenantfarmers, and laborers as well as the jobless and criminal. Later, as religious policy became more of an issue, the parliamentary forces took on a different tone and religiously motivated men were attracted to their ranks, although zealots were never a majority. Nevertheless, a community of belief did bond units together and helped give the army as a whole a sense of purpose.

Yet religion was also a dividing force and soon began to create a dangerous separation between the civil and military authorities. In 1643, when the war was not going well for parliament, its leaders had purchased Scottish military support by committing the nation to an officially established Presbyterian church.[18] The policy was one to which the Independents could not agree. Having rejected a coercive Arminian Anglican church, they had no intention of submitting to a Presbyterian one. These Independents were never a majority, but their numbers in the army were growing, and the fact that they included men of influence, like General Oliver Cromwell, ensured that their demands for religious toleration would be heard. In addition, although Independency was primarily religious in its aims, it overlapped with another group within the army and parliament—those hardliners who had begun to demand decisive military victory.

By 1644, parliament was under considerable pressure to fight the war to a conclusion. Problems of army organization, weakness in policy, and failures of command could no longer be ignored, and two major actions were taken. First, parliament ordered a reorganization of the army. That task would be carried out by Cromwell himself, along lines he had already pioneered in his own regiment. The result was the New Model army, an effective and highly motivated fighting force that within one year had smashed the king's army at Naseby (June 1945) and won the war. Second, parliament passed the Self-Denying Ordinance, pushed through by Cromwell and his allies, which separated military from civil command by compelling members of parliament (except for Cromwell himself) to resign their commissions. On the positive side, this legislation rid the army of most of the highly placed Presbyterian officers, reduced political conflicts, and allowed the military to get on with the war. In addition, it gave parliament's leaders breathing space to deal with their political and financial problems. On the negative side, time would show that these actions had fatally undermined civilian authority by depriving it of direct control over the military, which was by now becoming increasingly powerful.

Oliver Cromwell, the man who had played such an important part in these events, was a typical gentry landowner and member of the Country Party. A Calvinist in religion, his belief that he belonged to the spiritual elect gave him great confidence once he was convinced that God had approved his actions. In parliament, where he had served since 1628, he allied himself with Pym, and when war broke out he raised a cavalry regiment that he himself trained. An excellent organizer and firm disciplinarian, he was also a strong and inspiring leader who led his troops to one of parliament's first great victories, at Marston Moor in 1644. Although as a mere gentleman he could not aspire to the highest command and was subordinate first to the earl of Manchester and later to Sir Thomas Fairfax, Cromwell nevertheless became the most important and influential army commander. It was a preeminence he deserved and would hold throughout his career. He also exercised great influence in parliament, where he supported Independency and religious toleration. Deeply and instinctively conservative on political issues, he was a pragmatist in achieving his aims. Above everything else, Cromwell desired to make a settlement of the nation within the framework of the constitution.

Although the war continued for a time, any real possibility of royalist military victory had ended with Charles's defeat at Naseby in June 1645. By April 1646, with England lost, he turned to the Scots, hoping they would back him against parliament. But it was a vain hope and a foolish gamble. Scotland and its church were now secure, parliament's leaders were allies, and what the Scots wanted was to collect their money and go home. Instead of assisting the king, they handed him over to parliament in January 1647 and received in return some of what was owed them under the Treaty of Ripon. Yet, even with his army gone, his advisers scattered, and himself a prisoner, Charles was not wholly disheartened or helpless. He was still king, and the political struggle continued. From this point onward, however, he would depend on negotiation and intrigue to attain his ends. Such intrigue would be made easier by parliament's own political problems, which were emerging in the wake of its victory. Having won the war, its leaders found that they faced a new army (their own), which they had no means of controlling and which was increasingly alienated by parliament's Presbyterian religious policy.

The solution they chose was to rid themselves of the army. A few troops would be needed for garrison duty, and others could be re-formed in a new force that could be shipped off to Ireland. The remainder would be given a small portion of their accrued back pay and sent home. The plan was clever but not clever enough. If some of the soldiers were at odds with parliament because they were Independents, all were united in demanding from it their back pay. The soldiers also understood that, once disbanded, they would have no way of obtaining any concessions. Accordingly, in April 1647, eight of the ten cavalry regiments, the elite of the army, took action. They chose representatives they called Agitators to present their grievances to their officers. The infantry immediately followed their lead. Unwittingly, parliament had turned its army into an independent political force.

THE LEVELLERS AND DEMOCRATIC REFORM

Leaders of parliament such as Denzil Hollis, a hardline political Presbyterian who also headed the group seeking peace, were committed not only to a Presbyterian national church but to negotiations with the king. They hoped to reintegrate Charles into the political system as a means of conferring legitimacy on their feeble and unpopular regime. Not everyone in parliament agreed with these aims, and a key group in this opposition was composed of Independents, who were present in the House of Commons but were even more strongly represented in the army outside parliament. Of course, Independents were primarily concerned with obtaining religious toleration for themselves from government, but this was a process that was bound to draw them into politics. In fact, politics was a natural extension of their interests and activities. Independent congregations provided many opportunities for members to join in administration, even to select or elect ministers. Such experience, and their belief in a spiritual elite that superseded the traditional social hierarchy, inclined them toward practical democracy and made them receptive to ideas such as those proposed by the Levellers.

The Levellers were the most important of the radical political groups to spring up during this period. G. E. Aylmer has called them "the first democratic political movement in modern history" and notes that their activities were characterized by "radical journalism and pamphleteering, ideological zeal, political activism, and mass organization."[19] Rather than abolishing property and abolishing social distinctions as their enemies charged, they were democrats who desired that "all alike may be leveled to and bounded by the law."[20] Leveller ideas grew out of popular Puritanism and (like Independency) out of a radical conception of the Calvinist spiritual elite. As John Sanderson has pointed out, Levellers subscribed to an "ascending theory" of authority rather than the descending one that characterized monarchy.[21] They believed that authority resided in the people and was lent to accountable magistrates who were supposed to exercise it for the public benefit. In their view, God had given human beings natural rights, which included freedom of thought and of religious belief as well as the right to participate in their own governance. Consent and participation by the people made a government truly legitimate. The Levellers did not support mixed monarchy, not even a mixed monarchy limited and guaranteed by parliament; they also opposed the House of Lords and aristocratic privilege in general. Their aim was "a secular republic characterized by a substantial degree of social and political equality."[22] Yet, like so many other politicians of the period, they needed to retain connections with England's historic constitutionalism. Thus, they drew upon the idea of the "Norman yoke," claiming (incorrectly) that Leveller ideas were older and more binding than those of a monarchy that had been imposed upon free English people by a foreign tyrant (William the Conqueror) and his lords.

The Levellers, more than most groups, were defined by their leaders, of whom the most important were John Lilburne, William Walwyn, and Richard Overton. Like Cromwell, Lilburne and Walwyn were members of the gentry, although being younger sons they did not inherit any land under the doctrine of primogeniture. Instead, they were apprenticed in the City of London, which was then alive with Puritan ideas. Lilburne became a brewer, and Walwyn prospered as one of the Merchant Adventurers. Overton, a printer and bookseller, seems to have been of lower social status but was intelligent and well-read. The most prominent member of this little group was Lilburne, who had a taste for controversy, real dramatic flair, and a natural combativeness that led him to quarrel with almost everyone in authority. Flogged through London at the tail of a cart, and often imprisoned, he was a man impossible to ignore. Hot-tempered and warmhearted, Lilburne more than any of the others had the power to attract men into a popular movement. But his difficult and idiosyncratic personal qualities made him a fatally disruptive leader for the long term.

Although Leveller ideas circulated widely in London and in the army, the group never had a large following in the country at large. That, however, was true of most of the groups engaged in national politics. Indeed, a mass following would not have been necessary if the Levellers had won the army to their cause. By 1646–1647, this did not appear to be impossible, because the military, particularly the common soldiers, had good cause for discontent. Nevertheless, support among the officers was needed if this discontent was to be turned into effective political action. The key to success was Cromwell, who combined unique prestige in the army with influence in parliament. He himself sympathized with Independency and with the soldiers' grievances, but he was unwilling to disturb the traditional social order. Thus, even though he and the Levellers agreed on such issues as religious liberty, he was suspicious of their democratic political aims. Cromwell still hoped to resolve the nation's political problems within the existing system and to do so in a parliamentary way. "[What] we gain in a free way," he was to explain, "it is better than twice so much in a forced [way]. . . . That [which] you have by force I look upon it as nothing."[23]

CROMWELL AND THE ARMY

Cromwell supported the idea of parliament but was not unreservedly committed to the current body, which he knew to be religiously intolerant and hostile to the well-being of its own soldiers. At the same time, although sympathetic to the grievances of the soldiers, he worried about a possible breakdown of discipline and was determined to keep control of the military in politically safe hands. Therefore, in June 1647, he and other high-ranking officers joined the ordinary soldiers in a Solemn Engagement in which they pledged not to disband until parliament had redressed their complaints and made a satisfactory settlement in church and state. The Engagement also created a political entity, the Grand Council of the Army, to determine what the settlement should be. This body was composed of the commanders and higher-ranking officers (the Grandees), plus two lesser officers and two ordinary soldiers from each regiment (the Agitators). The structure, which gave officers larger numbers and greater influence, was representative rather than democratic and was designed to tame religious and political radicals in the ranks while still giving them a voice in the proceedings. The arrangement did not wholly succeed, and the Declaration of the Army, presented to parliament on June 15, 1647, contained many radical ideas and attitudes.

Indeed, the document began by claiming that the army possessed a special right to speak for the people, because it was "not a mere mercenary army, hired to serve any arbitrary power of a state, but called forth and conjured by the several Declarations of parliament to the defence of our own and the people's just rights and liberties."[24] The Declaration also called upon the current parliament to dismiss itself as soon as possible and demanded that frequent parliaments be summoned thereafter. In the meantime, the body should be purged of corrupt members and of all those who had opposed and defamed the army.

The position of the parliamentary leaders in this crisis was an unhappy one. They had never represented the temper of the country, where high taxes, shortages, economic dislocation, and residual loyalty to the old system—plus some outright royalist feeling—formed a potentially dangerous background to national politics. London, it is true, did offer support, because there Presbyterianism was a strong and well-organized force. Yet London itself was divided and increasingly a focus for Leveller agitation. The parliamentary leaders could find little comfort even in parliament, facing as they did a more and more vocal minority that pressed the claims of Independency and the army.

Under such circumstances compromise was difficult if not impossible. When an attempt was made to conciliate the army in June 1647, angry crowds inspired by the Presbyterians gathered outside the parliament house and forced the members to rescind their concessions. So menacing was the situation that fifty-seven members of the House of Commons, eight peers, and the speakers of both houses fled London and joined General Fairfax in his camp. Soon thereafter his troops occupied London. It was claimed that the soldiers were there to preserve the independence of parliament, but their first act was to restore all those members who were friendly to themselves. In the short term, army intervention did bring peace and order, but it also created a dangerous precedent and emphasized the fragility and instability of the national government.

Amid these shifting political currents, the position of Cromwell and the other Grandees was almost as difficult as that of the parliamentary leaders. Although Lilburne was in prison, he and other London Levellers were in constant touch with sympathizers in the army. There, in the lower ranks, pamphlets circulated and Leveller ideas were eagerly discussed. Ingenious Agitators also made recruiting visits to military units outside London, set up a printing press, and established a communications network. Critics feared such activities were imperiling army discipline and might lead to mutiny and social and political chaos. So far Cromwell and the other moderate officers had managed to keep the army united and under their own control. They had contained and limited radical ideas by joining with those in the lower ranks, by identifying themselves with certain of their interests, and by leading the activists where they wanted to go—only not too far and not too quickly. In such stressful circumstances, it is not surprising that the Grandees began to look about for a safer and more stable settlement, one that would lead in a comfortably familiar direction. While continuing to participate in the Grand Council of the Army, the army leaders also opened negotiations with the king.

For them, restored royal government, with guaranteed toleration for Protestants, was an attractive solution, but it would work only if the king could be kept to his bargain. One means to ensure this was to put things down in black and white in a written constitution. The plan for such a constitution was sketched out by Cromwell's son-in-law, General Henry Ireton.[25] Carefully moderate, filled with checks and balances, it offered a little something to all the major players. The king would be given his throne but would be supervised by parliament, which would appoint his ministers and control the military for a period of ten years. Parliament, for its part, would be made more responsive through immediate new elections and biennial parliaments. To make sure that parliamentary sessions took place but did not become perpetual, each was to last for at least 120 days but no longer than 240 days. In place of the old Privy Council chosen by the king, there would be a new Council of State, which would supervise foreign policy and the militia. Although the franchise would not be altered, seats were to be redistributed to ensure more equal representation. The gentry were also conciliated by making the offices of sheriff and justice of the peace elective, an arrangement that would give them more control of local government. Religion was to be settled in an official Episcopal church, but it was one without coercive authority, thereby ensuring practical toleration for other Protestants. Even the royalists, readmitted to their political privileges after five years, were treated with moderation. Only the Levellers received nothing of substance, although they did favor a redistribution of parliamentary seats.

Ireton's plan was shown to the king and presented to the army council for discussion. Charles, who was himself negotiating secretly with parliamentary Presbyterians and with the Scots in hopes of getting even better terms, gave no immediate answer, but neither did he reject it out of hand. Meanwhile, the Levellers had responded with their own ideas for a constitutional settlement. These were defined in two main documents and in a variety of pamphlets but most importantly in the extraordinary debates that took place at Putney between October 28 and November 1, 1647. In these meetings participants examined not only specific proposals but also fundamental constitutional principles.[26] The position of the Grandees and army conservatives was most ably presented by Ireton and was essentially that of his constitutional proposal. Outstanding among the Leveller speakers was Colonel Thomas Rainsborough.[27]

The core of Leveller belief was the contractual nature of government. As Rainsborough put the matter, "Every man that is to live under a government ought first by his own consent to put himself under that government."[28] Under this concept the people and not the monarch or the aristocracy were the source and foundation of law. In addition, as republicans, the Levellers favored frequent parliaments, equitable distribution of seats, and manhood suffrage or something very close to it. In contrast to these democratic ideas, Ireton took a position that was more traditional for someone of his class. He appealed not to natural law or abstract right but to the "civil constitution of this kingdom which is original and fundamental, and beyond which I am sure no memory of record does go."[29] In his view, participation and the franchise ought to be confined to those who had a fixed interest in the nation, that is, those who possessed property.

The Putney debates thoroughly alarmed army leaders, because they revealed both the strength of the Levellers and the subversive nature of their democratic ideas. Cromwell and the other Grandees speedily dissolved the army council, sent the Agitators back to their regiments, and, when disorders broke out, suppressed them with ruthless vigor. This would have been the logical time to turn to the king—had he not himself forestalled such an action by making terms with the Scots. In return for his promise to suppress Independency and establish Presbyterianism for three years, the Scots had agreed to invade England and restore him to his throne. True to their promise, the Scots invaded England in June 1648, but this time they were defeated by Cromwell and the New Model army. All this left the English Presbyterians, who still controlled parliament, in a position that was more unpopular and more thoroughly discredited than ever.

Ideas about divine right had brought the Stuart monarchs into difficulties. Now, on the strength of its victories, the army, which had appointed itself champion of the people's rights and liberties at Putney, began to think of itself as a special instrument of divine will. Such a mind-set did not make for conciliating attitudes either toward the king or toward those leaders of parliament who had negotiated with him during the war and were still trying to do so. Indeed, on both sides, belief in divine guidance was inimical to true political interaction. In December 1648, army leaders dispatched troops to clear away the obstructionists and compromisers, leaving a tiny Rump of the Long Parliament numbering some fifty members. This Rump then proceeded to try the king and execute him on January 30, 1649, events that, considering their unprecedented nature, proceeded with surprising speed and smoothness. Within a few months, before the startled and not necessarily approving eyes of the nation, the old system was swept away, monarchy and the House of Lords abolished, and the government converted into a republic—the Commonwealth and Free State of England.

To the last, the king maintained that he stood for the freedom and liberty of the people of England and for its fundamental laws. Those, as he was still explaining on the scaffold, consisted of "having of government those laws by which their life and their goods may be most their own. It is not for having share in government . . . that is nothing pertaining to them. A subject and a sovereign are clear different things."[30] But other and different ideas were finding a place in the English political consciousness—and not just among radicals such as the Levellers. Many agreed when, at Charles's trial, the prosecutor proclaimed that a king "is but an officer of trust" and condemned him for breaking the (as yet unspecified) "contract and bargain made between the king and his people."[31] The question was whether and in what way these new ideas would become part of the Ancient Constitution.

THE INTERREGNUM

J.G.A. Pocock has suggested that the grip of history on the English mind was so strong that "the past could only be rejected by a reinterpretation of the past."[32] Yet, during this period, in certain important respects the past was never rejected at all. This was true of constitutional ideas such as the belief that representation conferred legitimacy upon a government, its institutions, and its actions. In justifying its right to try the king, parliament had asserted, "The People are under God the original of all just power; [and] ... the Commons of England in parliament assembled, being chosen by and representing the People, have the supreme power in this nation."[33] This did not, however, imply any commitment to democracy in the sense of rule by *all* the people. Even in this formulation the real emphasis was upon representation and its agency, parliament. Indeed, for Cromwell and the Grandees, as for most men of property, democracy involving universal male suffrage and majority rule did not fit within the proper framework of government. Furthermore, without the support of members of what continued to be the political and social elite, no reform could hope to succeed.

All this was obscured in 1649 by the dismantling of royal government, which seemed to open the way to even more dramatic change and encouraged the blossoming of a variety of groups, each with a political agenda of its own. Some were religious zealots, but others were political activists, among whom the Levellers were most important. Leveller agitation and proselytizing had never in fact ceased, and their agents continued to propagandize in London and in the army. Such groups looked with dissatisfaction at the new government, which, in spite of its name, was only the purged remnant of the Long Parliament plus an executive Council of State headed by Cromwell. So makeshift an arrangement was it that even supporters of the republic expected the Rump to dissolve itself and move quickly to call a new general election.

That did not happen. Not only were the Rumpers unwilling to give up the security of their safe seats, but they also saw no reason to do so. They believed themselves to be the only properly constituted government and the guardians of the new commonwealth. It was also unclear how any new parliament ought to be constituted and who should be permitted to vote. If the traditional franchises were used, then royalists and royalist sympathizers would certainly be chosen, and even if they were barred, the new body would almost certainly replicate the factionalism of the old unpurged one. In addition, it was clear that in those circumstances groups such as the Independents were unlikely to get much support, which would spell trouble for the future of toleration. Given these considerations, it must have seemed almost a public duty for the Rumpers to perpetuate themselves in office, either by eliminating general elections altogether or by structuring them so as to ensure their own reelection.

This was not at all what Cromwell and the army had intended. He had already dealt with troubles within army ranks by putting down a new Leveller insurrection and effectively destroying that movement as a political force. Yet, parliament

would not put its own house in order. It would not enact reforms the army officers requested, and it would not prepare for new elections. Instead, the members
prepared a bill that would have allowed them to continue permanently in office.
Under its terms, new members would have been recruited individually, and no
general election would ever have been needed. This was more than Cromwell and
his fellow officers could tolerate. On April 20, 1653, he went to the House and dissolved the Rump by force. "You are no parliament, I say you are no parliament,"
he told them bluntly, "I will put an end to your sitting," and he ordered his soldiers to turn them out.[34] He also dismissed the Council of State. Because this left
England without any legitimate government, the country would have to be ruled
for the time being by a new Council of Officers, which was, of course, headed by
Cromwell.

These actions, more arbitrary than any Charles had ever attempted, were a symbol not so much of the strength of Cromwell and the army as of their weakness.
The officers had acquired a dangerous taste for intervening in politics. Experience
thus far, however, had shown that although the army could purge and destroy, it
could not create new institutional arrangements that had the legitimacy of those
it had overthrown. Furthermore, the ancient, indisputably legitimate parliament,
even in its purged and desiccated form, had proved to have remarkable staying
power. As one of its members had told Cromwell, "Sir, you are mistaken to think
that the parliament is dissolved; for no power under Heaven can dissolve them but
themselves: therefore take you notice of that."[35]

Cromwell now faced the problem of re-creating government and, even more
difficult, of endowing it with the elusive quality of legitimacy. He did not choose,
as the Levellers would have done, to broaden its elective base. Although, like other
Englishmen, he believed in the power of participation to confer legitimacy, this
was balanced by his determination to maintain order and protect the religious
Independents. His daring solution, implemented in 1653, was the Nominated
Parliament (also known as the Parliament of Saints), in which participation was
determined not by the traditional qualifiers of property and social status but by
spiritual merit.[36] The embodiment of the religious elect, this body would surely
enjoy God's blessing and success in its labors—or so Cromwell imagined.

The idea was attractive but its implementation proved difficult. A body characterized by inward spiritual qualities was hard to identify. In the end, nominations
were submitted by various churches and from the counties. The Council of
Officers then selected 144 persons that it deemed suitable. These included members from Scotland and Ireland. When the new parliament assembled on July 4,
1653, it chose the thirty-one member Council of State, although the Council of
Officers continued to control the army. Both councils were dominated by
Cromwell acting as head of state. This Nominated Parliament has sometimes been
dismissed as a collection of insignificant and impractical religious cranks, and it
is true the body did include a number of religious minorities such as
Congregationalists and Baptists. Many of those men did lack political experience,

but among them were also members of the lesser gentry, substantial merchants, and, most importantly, at least nineteen men who had already served in the Rump. If the social makeup of this group was slightly downscale from the old parliament, its members were nevertheless perfectly respectable, and most of them fitted within existing ideas of the political nation.

Cromwell, who had expected God to bless the spiritual elite at work in the Nominated Parliament, was deeply disappointed by its actual proceedings. The members were hardworking and did enact a number of useful and sensible reforms, such as those establishing civil marriage and civil registration of births and deaths. Their attempts to simplify the common law, however, were impractical, and their attack on tithes and lay patronage in the church was unpopular with the gentry, whose rights would have been affected. Cromwell and the gentry conservatives in the army were prepared to accept neither. Within the new parliament, already divided between the politicians and the religious zealots, a plot was hatched by Cromwell and the politicians. Going early to the House on December 12, 1653, the politicians quickly enacted an abdication agreement returning power to Cromwell. Then they dismissed themselves.

The Nominated Parliament had lasted less than six months and had been, as Cromwell admitted to a later parliament, "a story of my own weakness and folly . . . done in my simplicity."[37] It was an experiment that had failed to catch the enthusiasm of anyone aside from a few religious enthusiasts. The fact that the members had been summoned directly, rather than elected, also weakened any claims to legitimacy that the body might have possessed. In any case, the experience taught Cromwell a valuable lesson. He would not attempt such an experiment again. Instead, his subsequent efforts to create an acceptable government would bring him closer and closer to the old traditional electoral and institutional arrangements, until at last he would virtually re-create monarchy—although with a Lord Protector instead of a king.

The chief innovation of the period after 1653 was a written constitution, known as the Instrument of Government, which was drawn up by General John Lambert. Like Ireton's plan, the Instrument incorporated extensive checks and balances. There was an executive composed of a Lord Protector, who was assisted and balanced by a Council of State with members appointed for life. Parliaments had to be held at least every three years and sit for at least five months. Members were to be summoned from Scotland and Ireland, and a more equitable distribution of seats was designed to give representation to newer population centers. In order to produce a body that would be economically secure, responsible, and sympathetic to the interests of the army, the number of county members was increased to a majority, and only those persons worth £200 were permitted to vote. Religion was settled in a national Episcopal church with no coercive authority, thus giving toleration to religious minorities. Altogether, the Instrument was an intelligent attempt to create stability and balance in government. Unfortunately, however, there was one force in the country that no constitution could check and for which there was no possible balance: the army itself. Military power had to remain with the Lord Protector, because, no matter how it was disguised, force was now the real basis on which government rested.

In December 1653, Cromwell was installed as Lord Protector under the terms of the Instrument. The newly elected parliament met at the beginning of September 1654. Its first task was to ratify the new constitution, but, to the dismay of the protector and his council, it refused to do so. The members rejected the Instrument as invalid, arguing that it had been created by those who had no legal or constitutional standing. Instead, they claimed supreme authority for parliament alone. Clearly, this was not the body of loyal and supportive country gentlemen for which Cromwell had hoped. In fact, almost 100 of them had been members of the Long Parliament, and at least forty were unbending republicans. In spite of this, Cromwell at first attempted conciliation. He agreed to accept some changes as long as the basic principles of the new constitution were preserved, including the principle of religious toleration. Ninety members refused to accept even these limitations and were ejected from the House. When the remainder attempted to limit toleration and began to tamper with the military, he decided to dismiss them and did so in January 1655. The Instrument had not been approved, and England was still without a legitimate government.

By re-creating the essentials of a traditional parliament, Cromwell had also re-created its conflict with the army, an army that, since the Putney debates, had taken on a dangerous political dimension of its own. Not only had it assumed a special place in the body politic, but it had also come to think of itself as more representative than parliament and to believe it had a better right to speak for the people as a whole. This was clearly not the view held by the first parliament under the protectorate (1654), which regarded itself as the rightful successor to earlier parliaments of indisputable constitutionality and as the true repository of legitimacy and sovereignty. The two claims were, of course, irreconcilable, and trouble was bound to follow. When the members of parliament stubbornly refused to ratify the Instrument, Cromwell dismissed them.

Parliamentary opposition to army interference in the political process led, of course, to more intervention. A second Protectorate Parliament was elected, but before it was permitted to meet in September 1656, Cromwell had it purged of 100 members who were thought likely to cause difficulty. Initially this was successful. In an amended version of the Instrument (April 1657), its members invited Cromwell to restore the old bicameral constitutional system with himself as king.[38] This new constitutional proposal was politically attractive, and although opposition from his fellow officers kept Cromwell from taking the title of king, he did adopt the other provisions. The House of Lords was resurrected as the second house, with a membership of between forty and seventy life peers chosen by Cromwell. The Council of State was based upon the old Privy Council, with members also chosen and dismissible by the protector. There was an established church with toleration for Protestant minorities. In addition, the protector was given what Charles had never been able to achieve: an independent income large enough to cover the ordinary costs of government and the military. All in all, these changes enhanced the protector's power and configured it in a way that was closer than any other of the institutional experiments of the Interregnum to the traditional shape of the Ancient Constitution. The members extracted a price for the settlement, however, one that showed they shared the political ideas of their parliamentary predecessors: The protector had to guarantee the ancient liberties and privileges of parliament and agree that henceforth he would not exclude properly elected members.

In practice, this meant that all those who had been excluded had to be admitted to the session that met in January 1658 under the new arrangements. The results were not the positive ones for which Cromwell had hoped. He had rewarded many of his most loyal and helpful colleagues by promoting them into the new second house, and this diminished his support in the House of Commons, where the formerly excluded members were vigorously pressing their republican views. Led by these republicans, the lower house reasserted its claim to exercise all the powers and privileges of the old House of Commons. The members attacked the new version of the House of Lords, demanded a unicameral legislature with sovereign power, and reached out for popular support in London and the army. With army discipline again in danger, Cromwell acted swiftly and decisively. Once more he dismissed a parliament and with bitter words acknowledged the failure of his constitutional efforts: "If this, I say, be the effect of your sitting . . . I think it high time that an end be put to your sitting and I do declare to you here that I do dissolve this parliament. Let God judge between you and me."[39]

The date was February 4, 1658. On September 3, 1658, Cromwell died, and when his firm hand was removed, the political situation steadily deteriorated. A new election was called, employing the old franchises dating from 1640 (although royalists were barred). When parliament assembled, however, it was immobilized by conflicts with the military. Richard Cromwell, who had succeeded his father as protector, resigned when the officers demanded a pure republic with no single person at the head of it. Yet even his resignation did not solve the political problem. In April 1659, this parliament too was dissolved, and the old Rump of the Long Parliament was recalled by the officers, only to be dismissed in its turn when it proved fractious. The parliamentary army in England was now rent by faction, but there was a force in Scotland that was still strong and united—the army of occupation commanded by General George Monck.[40] He marched south, forced recall of the Rump as it had been before the purge of December 1648, and also came to an accommodation with the royalists, who had been watching these developments with renewed hope. Charles II issued a declaration promising amnesty to all but the Regicides (those who had signed his father's death warrant), security of tenure for land transfers, and liberty for tender consciences. By this time, the Rump had been constrained to dissolve itself, and elections on the old unrestricted franchise had produced a royalist parliament. That royalist parliament invited Charles II to return to England, and on May 29, 1660, the king entered London amid joyous celebrations. He had come not by military victory but peacefully and constitutionally to reclaim his throne. The revolution was over.

CONCLUSION

The English Revolution of the mid-seventeenth century did not establish fully democratic institutions, and it is difficult to see how it could have done so. There were proponents of political democracy, the Levellers, who did show remarkable foresight in their program, but they had little support in the country and virtually none from the all-important gentry. In spite of foreign intervention from Scotland and the influence of economic and demographic factors at both the national and international levels, the heart of English politics remained stubbornly local and traditional. The country interest had nothing to gain from democracy and a great deal of practical importance to lose. Indeed, the Leveller talent for agitation that gave that group so much temporary significance also aroused fears and alienated men of property. Such ideas seemed to threaten the natural order and to undermine those social and political assumptions about property and hierarchy that—even more than formal governmental laws and institutions—served to hold society together. The republican and democratic ideas of the Levellers simply did not fit into the existing framework of constitutional tradition and experience.

No government of the Interregnum could free itself from the past, as that past was then understood. The English Revolution, although it can be interpreted in many different ways, testifies above all else to the enduring power of ideas, such as representation, when they are rooted in practical experience and held by a variety of persons who are not necessarily participants in the existing political nation. The gentry guided and limited the revolution, but they did not absolutely determine its direction and outcome. People outside of parliament and beyond the old boundaries of the political nation also played a part. England did not move further toward popular democracy because most people did not wish it and could not imagine it doing so. The same experience and mind-set made army authoritarianism unacceptable. Legitimacy, when all is said and done, involves a people's feelings about the rightness and naturalness of a particular government, and for the English, legitimacy depended on the idea of constitutionality. It is true that the governments of the Interregnum did not have such useful devices as an independent judiciary, which could resolve conflicts between the executive and legislative elements, and that they lacked an accepted procedure for reconfiguring themselves without dissolution. Such deficiencies, however, were not enough to destroy the new political experiments. Those experiments failed because of something much more fundamental—the sense that they were not the ancient, familiar, natural, lasting, legitimate, and lawful constitutional government of the nation.

In the last analysis this was a revolution that never escaped the control of the gentry. Radical ideas and proposals were thrown up but never pursued to a point that endangered traditional social stability. Divided although it was on political issues, this elite shared social values, economic interests, and a belief in the existence of a basic constitutional framework within which acceptable political activity ought to take place. A stabilizing but also a limiting influence, this community of ideas tended to reduce the significance of other distinctions. On the king's side, hardliners of the Court Party had pretty much disappeared as a force prior to the beginning of the war, and moderate constitutionalist defectors from parliament shaped the Royalist Party. In parliament's camp, the moderate-versus-radical division was similarly clouded, in this case by religion. Thus, Cromwell, who might be described as moderate in his basic political views, took the radical side in religious matters by supporting Independency and toleration.

In practice, moderates tended to play a more important role on both sides than did hardliners or radicals. There were two crucial factors. The first was the presence of a strong constitutional tradition that was accepted by most of those with political input (even those outside the customary political nation). This prevented wide acceptance of republican and democratic ideas, and it also helped control and limit change and prevent mob rule and mass violence. The second was the absence of political parties, which would not begin to develop until the end of the seventeenth century. The idea of a loyal opposition did not yet exist; therefore, opposition had no traditional basis, in turn making political activity, accountability, and wider participation difficult. In short, a new system could not be constructed on the ruins of previous institutions, because even when monarchy was eliminated the rest of the constitutional and institutional framework was still in place.

As for leadership, the personal and moral qualities of leaders like Charles I and Cromwell certainly did play a role in determining the course of events. In Charles's case (although practical circumstances, particularly the impoverishment of monarchy, pushed him into illegal and unpopular actions), it was his rigid ideas and political ineptitude that prevented the compromise desired by important politicians on both sides. Among the parliament-men, Cromwell proved to be a remarkably moderate revolutionary. Although as leader he might have followed any number of paths, his continuing aim was to reconstitute traditional constitutional government. And although in the end he failed to make an effective and lasting settlement, he did preserve the ideal of constitutional government, and in so doing he unwittingly prepared the way for restoration of the monarchy.

The outcome of the Civil War and subsequent Interregnum, therefore, was by no means wholly negative. Since the constitution was historical, it could and did assimilate experience and confer respectability with the mere passage of time. In this way, the events and actions of mid-century became the foundation of the more obviously successful Glorious Revolution, which in 1688–1689 firmly and permanently established parliament's preeminent role and made England a limited constitutional monarchy. Such an outcome could not have been foreseen in 1660, when formal terms and limitations were not imposed on the restored Stuart kings. It was Charles II and his brother, James II, who provoked change by attempting to restore all the rights and powers that their father had lost. Their Catholicism and James's adherence to it, not just as a personal belief but as public policy, proved to be the last straw. The English would not accept the Stuart combination of Catholicism and royal absolutism, and, after what they had learned in the events of mid-century, they knew they did not have to do so. Those events, however, had also taught them to detest violent revolution and civil war. Therefore, when James II was compelled to abdicate in 1689, his expulsion from the throne was peaceful and political. The Resolution of the Convention Parliament, which in January 1689 cleared a legal path for the accession of William and Mary, shows how much the political thinking of this period owed, both in its ideas and its ambiguities, to the great struggles of mid-century. The Resolution explained that King James, "having endeavored to subvert the constitution of his kingdom by breaking the original contract between king and people; and . . . having violated the fundamental laws; and having withdrawn himself out of the kingdom; has abdicated the Government; and . . . the throne is thereby vacant."[41]

The revolution of the seventeenth century had failed either to end monarchy or to restore the Stuart concept of kingship, but its events had given Englishmen of all social levels and political persuasions an unparalleled opportunity to learn more about the business of governing themselves. J. H. Hexter has suggested that the lesson learned in that gradual and difficult process was "that their liberties required the survival of representative institutions, and that the freedom guaranteed by those institutions was their highest political priority."[42] This was true also for the English overseas—no matter which side they and their parents had taken on the issues under dispute. At home or in the colonies, men and women would act in terms of what had happened during the period, or at least in terms of what they believed to have happened.

In this way, the English Revolution of the mid-seventeenth century—including the call for toleration for religious sects and familiarity with democratic ideas such as those of the Levellers—did became part of subsequent political development. Historically and experientially, it would play a role in English political life long after the Restoration seemed to bring it to ·a close. Practical toleration of Protestants who did not belong to the established church became a reality in the late seventeenth century, although hatred of "popery" also survived as a potent political force. If republican ideas did not fare so well, at least the representative experience now contained material from the Levellers and other radical thinkers that later movements such as Chartism could draw upon.[43] Ideas had been introduced into English consciousness, horizons broadened, old certainties destroyed, and the crown permanently weakened. With the emergence of political parties in the late seventeenth century, new kinds of political activity would become possible and lead to new ways of making government more effective and yet accountable. The system would even prove to be tough enough and flexible enough to accommodate itself to the emergence of democratic political forces in the late nineteenth and early twentieth centuries. When democracy finally did appear, it would be in a form that had been at least dimly envisaged by some mid-seventeenth-century radicals, revolutionaries, and reformers, although they themselves had not had the power to bring it into being.

CHRONOLOGY

1603–1625	James I
1625–1649	Charles I
1628	Petition of Right
1639–1640	Scottish rebellion ends in Treaty of Ripon
1640	Long Parliament begins
1641	Grand Remonstrance
1642	Militia Ordinance (March); Nineteen Propositions (June)
1645	New Model Ordinance; Self-Denying Ordinance; Battle of Naseby
1647	Putney debates; Ireton's constitution
1648	Scots invade in support of Charles; purge leaves Rump Parliament
1649	Trial and execution of the king; House of Commons abolishes House of Lords and monarchy
1653	Cromwell dissolves Rump Parliament (April); Nominated Parliament (July–December); Cromwell becomes Lord Protector (December)
1654–1655	First Parliament of the Protectorate
1656–1658	Second Parliament of the Protectorate
1658	Cromwell dissolves Parliament (February); Cromwell dies (September)
1660	The Restoration, with Charles II taking the throne
1685	Charles II dies; succeeded by James II
1688	The Glorious Revolution; James II flees and parliament installs William and Mary as joint sovereigns

NOTES

1. J. P. Kenyon, *The Stuart Constitution: 1603–1688* (Cambridge: Cambridge University Press, 1966), p. 328.

2. Peter Laslett, *The World We Have Lost*, 2d ed. (New York: Charles Scribner's Sons, 1971), pp. 23–24.

3. G. E. Aylmer, *The King's Servants: The Civil Service of Charles I* (London: Longmans, 1961), p. 331. He estimated there were 1,500 to 1,800 knights and 7,000 to 9,000 esquires, with the rest mere gentlemen. E. W. Ives, *The English Revolution, 1600–1660* (New York: Harper and Row, 1968), p. 4, says about one man in fifteen belonged to a gentry family.

4. As Tanner points out, a contemporary newsletter (a good source of popular opinion) suggested that the total wealth of the members of the House of Commons was three times that of the House of Lords; J. R. Tanner, *English Constitutional Conflicts of the Seventeenth Century* (Cambridge: The University Press, 1961), p. 90.

5. Goldstone has discussed the wider implications of the population situation. Evidence indicates that between 1500 and 1650 the numbers more than doubled, from 2 million to 5 million; Jack A. Goldstone, *Revolution and Rebellion in the Early Modern World* (Berkeley: University of California Press, 1991), p. 83. A sharp, prolonged inflation resulted from the growing imbalance between the growth of population and agricultural output, perhaps made worse by the debasement of the coinage in the 1540s and 1550s; R. B. Outhwaite, *Inflation in Tudor and Early Stuart England*, 2d ed. (London: Macmillan, 1982), p. 49.

6. All numbers for this period are problematic. Derek Hirst, *The Representative of the People? Voters and Voting in England Under the Early Stuarts* (Cambridge: Cambridge University Press, 1975), p. 105, suggests that by the 1640s the electorate—"licit and illicit"—was much larger than is usually assumed. In a population of 4.5 million with a ratio of males to total population of between 1: 4 and 1: 6, "those capable of voting . . . [by] the early months of the Long Parliament, may have formed between 27 percent and 40 percent of the adult male population." J. H. Plumb believes that in the post-Elizabethan period a new political nation had come into being and that it was "no longer co-extensive with the will of the gentry," although it was certainly not democratic; J. H. Plumb, "The Growth of the Electorate in England from 1600 to 1715," *Past and Present*, no. 45 (1969), pp. 103–107.

7. Norman Cantor, *The English* (New York: Simon and Schuster, 1967), pp. 244–245. They were less eager to point out that Bracton also supported the sovereign power of the king and did not define any sanctions to keep him under the law.

8. Tanner, *English Constitutional Conflicts of the Seventeenth Century*, p. 49.

9. J. D. Gould, "The Price Revolution Reconsidered," *Economic History Review* 17 (1964–1965): 96, 109. Gould points out that the price revolution is no longer accepted so unquestioningly. On population, R. B. Outhwaite says that population was "not the sole determinant of the price level in Tudor and Stuart England, but it looks to be far the most important influence upon it"; R. B. Outhwaite, *Inflation in Tudor and Stuart England*, p. 6.

10. Conrad Russell, "Parliament and the King's Finances," in Russell, ed., *Origins of the English Civil War* (New York: Barnes and Noble, 1973), p. 96. The subsidy had come to be a set sum. Grants were made in multiples of it.

11. The speaker was Charles's chief ecclesiastical adviser, Archbishop Laud, executed in 1645; Charles Carlton, *Charles I: The Personal Monarch* (London: Routledge and Kegan Paul, 1983), p. 226.

12. Tanner, *English Constitutional Conflicts of the Seventeenth Century*, p. 69. ·

13. Conrad Russell, *The Causes of the English Civil War: The Ford Lectures, 1987* (Oxford: Clarendon Press, 1990). Arminianism was felt to be an assault on the national independence as well as on the religious integrity of the Presbyterian Scots.

14. C. V. Wedgwood, *Thomas Wentworth: First Earl of Strafford* (New York: Macmillan, 1962), p. 368. As archbishop of Canterbury, Laud was the most prominent Arminian and

had implemented the king's church policy. Strafford had served as president of the Council of the North and from 1632 as Lord Deputy in Ireland. He was a tough, unpopular administrator who had supported royal power and independence of action. Recalled to assist Charles in England, he was believed to have advised him to act unconstitutionally and to have suggested he import an Irish army to use against his English subjects.

15. Parliament itself was not wholly comfortable about this and in subsequent negotiations with the king continued to try to get him to confirm the Militia Bill/Ordinance and make it a regular statute.

16. The words were those of Charles I in his *Answer* to the *Nineteen Propositions*; John Rushworth, *Historical Collections of Private Passages of State.* . . . (London: Printed by J. A. for Robert Boulter, 1682), I, iii, 728 [NCR Microcard Editions].

17. Brian Manning, *The English People and the English Revolution* (London: Penguin, 1978), p. 26; David Weigall, "Women Militants in the English Civil War," *History Today* 22 (June 1972): 434–438.

18. Ireland was also included in this agreement, a fact that helped fuel the rebellion there and keep it going.

19. G. E. Aylmer, ed., *The Levellers in the English Revolution* (Ithaca, NY: Cornell University Press, 1975), p. 9.

20. John Sanderson, *"But the People's Creatures": The Philosophical Basis of the English Civil War* (Manchester, England: Manchester University Press, 1989), p. 103. The name was one given them by their enemies.

21. Sanderson, *"But the People's Creatures,"* p. 1.

22. Sanderson, *"But the People's Creatures,"* p. 111.

23. Wilbur Cortez Abbot, *The Writings and Speeches of Oliver Cromwell*, 4 vols. (Cambridge: Harvard University Press, 1937), vol. 1, pp. 482 and 483.

24. Kenyon, *The Stuart Constitution*, p. 296.

25. The document was entitled "The Heads of the Proposals" and is reprinted in Kenyon, *The Stuart Constitution*, pp. 302–308. Ireton, a member of the gentry and a member of parliament, served with distinction in the army and signed the king's death warrant. He was deeply concerned about order and the security of property, fearing that extremists would imperil a true settlement of the nation. Less of a pragmatist and more of a theoretician than Cromwell, he died in 1651.

26. The documents were "The Case of the Army Truly Stated" and "An Agreement of the People," both in Don M. Wolfe, ed., *Leveller Manifestoes of the Puritan Revolution* (New York: Humanities Press, 1967), pp. 225–234, 308–310. The Putney debates (also known as the Army debates) are reprinted in C. H. Firth, ed., *The Clarke Papers*, 4 vols. (London: Camden Society, 1891–1901). Excerpts are available in David Wootton, ed., *Divine Right and Democracy: An Anthology of Political Writing in Stuart England* (London: Penguin Books, 1986).

27. Rainsborough, like Lilburne and Walwyn, qualified as a gentleman. The son of a naval officer and member of parliament, he himself served in the navy and later, with distinction, in the army. He was elected to the Long Parliament to replace a member who had died.

28. Aylmer, *The Levellers in the English Revolution*, p. 100.

29. Aylmer, *The Levellers in the English Revolution*, p. 99.

30. C. V. Wedgwood, *A Coffin for King Charles: The Trial and Execution of Charles I* (New York: Macmillan, 1964), p. 157.

31. Wedgwood, *A Coffin for King Charles*, pp. 183, 185. The speaker was John Bradshaw.

32. J.G.A. Pocock, *The Ancient Constitution and the Feudal Law: A Study of English Historical Thought in the Seventeenth Century*, rev. ed. (Cambridge: Cambridge University Press, 1987), pp. 127–130.

33. Tanner, *English Constitutional Conflicts of the Seventeenth Century*, p. 153.

34. Abbot, *The Writings and Speeches of Oliver Cromwell*, vol. 2, p. 643.

35. Abbot, *The Writings and Speeches of Oliver Cromwell*, vol. 2, p. 643. The speaker was John Bradshaw, a member of the gentry and a lawyer who presided over the king's trial and signed his death warrant. He supported Cromwell in the early years of the commonwealth but feared the approach of one-man rule.

36. Cromwell consulted both the millenarian zealot, General Thomas Harrison, and General John Lambert, heir to Ireton's conservative constitutionalism. The Nominated Parliament was a compromise between the two.

37. Abbot, *The Writings and Speeches of Oliver Cromwell*, vol. 4, p. 489.

38. The amended version was entitled *The Humble Petition and Advice*. Under it, Cromwell was even given the right to name his successor, which would have enabled him to create a family dynasty.

39. Abbot, *The Writings and Speeches of Oliver Cromwell*, vol. 4, p. 732.

40. Monck, the son of a poor country gentleman, had been a loyal ally of Cromwell. After the Restoration, he was made the earl of Albemarle and served both as general and admiral.

41. Great Britain, Parliament, *Commons Journals* 10: 14, 15.

42. J. H. Hexter, "The Birth of Modern Freedom," *Times Literary Supplement* (January 21, 1983): 54.

43. Chartism was a working-class political movement that began in the 1830s and proposed a great charter or petition (deliberately reminiscent of *Magna Carta*) demanding, among other things, manhood suffrage, equal electoral districts, and annual parliaments. Although failing in its immediate aims, Chartism did rouse and organize working people for political action. All of its demands (except annual parliaments) were eventually enacted.

SUGGESTIONS FOR FURTHER READING

G. Davies and M. Keeler's *Bibliography of British History: Stuart Period, 1603–1714* (Oxford: The Clarendon Press, 1970) is an indispensable source for anyone beginning research in the period. There are many biographies of major figures such as Charles I and Cromwell; see, for example, Kevin Sharpe, *The Personal Rule of Charles I* (New Haven: Yale University Press, 1992), C. Carlton, *Charles I: The Personal Monarch* (London: Routledge and Kegan Paul, 1983), and P. Gregg, *King Charles I* (London: Dent, 1981). Points of view may be diverse, as in analyses of Cromwell; see Christopher Hill, *God's Englishman: Oliver Cromwell and the English Revolution* (New York: Harper Torchbooks, 1970); M. Ashley, *The Greatness of Oliver Cromwell* (London: Collier-Macmillan, 1957); and A. Fraser, *Cromwell, the Lord Protector* (New York: Knopf, 1973). W. C. Abbott has edited *The Writings and Speeches of Oliver Cromwell* in 4 volumes (Cambridge: Harvard University Press, 1937–1947).

A general collection of printed documents for the period was edited by S. R. Gardiner, *The Constitutional Documents of the Puritan Revolution, 1625–1660*, 3rd ed. (Oxford: Clarendon Press, 1906). The Putney debates from the Clarke Papers were edited by A.S.P. Woodhouse and published as *Puritanism and Liberty: Being the Army Debates, 1647–1649* (London: Dent, 1938). D. Wolfe edited *Leveller Manifestoes of the Puritan Revolution* (New York: Humanities Press, 1967); see also W. Haller and G. Davies, *The Leveller Tracts: 1647–1653* (Gloucester, MA: Peter Smith, 1964). For the other side, see W. D. Macray, ed., *The History of the Rebellion and Civil Wars in England . . . By Edward, Earl of Clarendon* (Oxford: Clarendon Press, 1888); Macray was a leading constitutional royalist of the period. Anyone studying the period should also have some knowledge of the Bible; see Christopher Hill's *The English Bible and the Seventeenth Century Revolution* (London: Allen Lane, 1993).

2

THE UNITED STATES: CREATING THE REPUBLIC

TADAHISA KURODA AND ERWIN L. LEVINE

In national, comparative, and international contexts, scholars frequently categorize the United States as an enduring democracy that has functioned with a written constitution for more than 200 years. The U.S. Constitution and many characteristics that are associated with it—representative government, federalism, separation of powers, checks and balances, the Bill of Rights, independent executive, judicial review, two-party competition, the right to legitimate opposition, and the very idea of constitutionalism—have become part and parcel of what Americans consider to be "democratic" about their political system. The longevity of the Constitution itself seems to demonstrate its viability and appropriateness.[1]

The very durability of the Constitution and the institutions and practices that have grown from and around it, however, create the impression that these were easily invented and implemented by the founders of the republic on behalf of *all* the people. A closer examination of history bursts such an illusion. The varied experiences of England's North American mainland colonies provided the context for the American Revolution and the subsequent era of constitution making that made the United States a political laboratory for republican government. No single date, text, or event can serve adequately to identify the establishment of a democracy where, as Mary Ellen Fischer says in the introduction, (1) "the outcomes of elections or policy formulation are uncertain" but the rules are certain, and (2) "there is an acceptance by all parties of the procedures and an agreement to abide by the results of those processes." It is clear, however, that the Constitution of 1787 marked a critical phase in the development of democracy. Its ratification, implementation, and subsequent evolution involved conflicts that divided Americans as individuals, as members of political parties, and as regions of the country; these conflicts led, over time and often after prolonged struggle, to the inclusion of greater numbers of Americans in the body politic.

This chapter is organized to provide readers with an introduction to the revolutionary and constitution-making eras in American politics and the evolution of new institutions that have become the hallmark of an ever-evolving democracy. To set the context for this introduction, it is important to consider the colonial experience.

THE CONTEXT

British-American colonial societies took root in an environment of complex interchange between and among European and Native American peoples in which war, conquest, technology, trade, and disease played decisive roles. England was a latecomer to the colonial scene in the seventeenth century and struggled to compete with Portugal, Spain, and the Netherlands. Although English policymakers recognized the need to establish colonies for material, political, and religious reasons, lack of economic resources and instability at home made systematic and sustained empire building difficult. They relied on improvisation and opportunism. Some colonies were founded by private enterprises chartered by the monarch, such as the Virginia Company of London and the Massachusetts Bay Company; others by proprietors close to the royal court, as in the case of Maryland and Pennsylvania; still others by the initiatives of settlers themselves, who, like Roger Williams, Anne Hutchinson, and Thomas Hooker, roamed to new areas like Rhode Island and Connecticut. New York became English property by virtue of a successful war against the Dutch, and Georgia was founded as much for philanthropic as for strategic reasons by an act of parliament. As a consequence, the British-American mainland colonies grew from the early 1600s somewhat haphazardly.

Driven by political necessity to settle and develop its colonies, England allowed many kinds of people to emigrate. There were those who left different regions of the British Isles: Puritans who migrated by the thousands during the 1630s to New England, the cavaliers who came to Virginia and the Chesapeake area in the third quarter of the seventeenth century, the Quakers who entered New Jersey and Pennsylvania in the late seventeenth and early eighteenth centuries, and the Anglo-Irish who came in successive waves throughout the eighteenth century to occupy western areas of Pennsylvania, Maryland, Virginia, and the Carolinas. In addition, there were Scandinavians, often Lutheran, who settled along the Delaware River; the Huguenots in New Rochelle and Charleston; the Dutch in New York; and Germans in a great arc from New York through western Virginia. And, of course, there were vast numbers of involuntary immigrants who were shipped across the Atlantic Ocean from Africa as slaves. Each group came with unique customs, religions, family ways, and notions of law and authority. The varieties of religions—mostly but not exclusively Protestant—practiced by the settlers made it extremely difficult for one church to impose itself as the official church for all of them. Except for the articulate and enlightened few, most Americans did not favor religious toleration as a matter of choice, but they had to consider it as a practical necessity.[2]

Colonial society became more heterogeneous as it incorporated new groups of migrants and immigrants, not always peacefully, and these adjustments gave it the feeling of a society that was constantly being remade, not one that was already fully defined. This was especially evident in colonial cities, which were portents of later America. The colonies performed useful economic roles for the British Empire either by providing customers for English goods and suppliers of raw materials for English industry or by serving in multilateral trade relationships with other parts of the empire. Around this imperial economy emerged a landed elite in the Chesapeake and Charleston areas and merchant capitalists in Boston, New York, Newport, and Philadelphia.[3]

By 1750, the British-American mainland colonies in North America each had unique histories, economies, interests, and cultures. They were separated by the Atlantic Ocean from England. Although favorable winds and smooth seas allowed a ship to make that crossing one way in about one month's time, travel, more often than not, took two months. As lengthy and difficult as this voyage was, it was in many ways safer and more reliable than overland routes to the interior and between colonies, for there were few roads, and means of transportation and communications were primitive. This was a time and place where family, friends, and neighbors relied upon personal relationships and face-to-face conversations and not upon impersonal mass media to exchange ideas and feelings. Not surprisingly, therefore, the colonies were not closely linked to each other; what held them together was a habitual and informal deference for the parent country. But the challenges of building homes, cultivating farms, developing trade, providing educational and religious instruction, and establishing political order in a frontier setting also gave British-American colonial men and women the opportunity to develop loyalties to their locale and colony. The diversity of peoples and religions, life in the frontier, and the distance between England and the colonies made it difficult for England to supervise the colonies.[4]

Ironically, England deserves much credit for tutoring the colonists for self-rule. Even as it struggled during the seventeenth century through a civil war and the Glorious Revolution of 1688 to put its political house in order, England permitted representative institutions to develop in British North America. James I allowed the Virginia Company of London in 1619 to establish an elective assembly to assist the governor and councillors. This body became the House of Burgesses, which formed the elected, lower house of Virginia's colonial legislature. This pattern became commonplace in other colonies, all of which had at least one house popularly chosen.

The right to vote derived from the traditional English suffrage qualifications based on property—the forty-shilling freehold. Whereas 15 to 20 percent of adult white males in England satisfied this qualification to vote in parliamentary elections for the House of Commons, as many as 80 percent of adult white males in eighteenth-century Massachusetts and Virginia may have satisfied the same criterion, a result of the much more widespread distribution of property in the colonies than in the home country. Estimates for New York, Pennsylvania, and New Jersey are lower than these but still considerably higher than those for England. Persons with the right to vote did not necessarily exercise their right, because they did not have the time to travel long distances to polling sites to choose among candidates who spoke for similar interests. Many may have been simply indifferent to the outcome of elections—except in times of great public excitement.[5]

Perhaps just as important as the well-established tradition of an elected house in the legislature was colonial control of local government, which operated most directly on the lives of the people. Whether that was oligarchic, as in the county court system of the Chesapeake area, or representative, as in the town governments of New England, colonists themselves served as justices of the peace, sheriffs, constables, and selectmen. These were the officials who preserved law and order, built roads, maintained ferry lines, licensed taverns, provided bounties for the killing of wolves and crows, took care of orphans, and responded to public needs. Service in town and county government provided colonial leaders with a local base from which they frequently moved to the colonial legislature.[6]

Appointment or election to office favored those colonists who had more wealth, better family connections, and greater educational and political experience, for there remained among the politically active citizenry a strong regard for English custom, which assumed there should be a correspondence between those who were at the top of the social and economic orders and those at the top of the political order. Tradition also held that those favored by status had an obligation to serve the larger public and not merely to advance their personal interests. Scholars refer to this belief and practice—that those who were better situated to govern should be chosen to office—as deference. Deference made possible the elite leadership of the revolutionary and constitutional period, but the ideology of the revolution also pushed American society toward political democracy by the time of the Jacksonian Era in the nineteenth century.[7]

The elites, drawn from planters, merchants, lawyers, physicians, publishers, and master craftsmen, were not so well established and not so exclusive as to constitute a hereditary aristocracy closed to newcomers. Economic success and family connections afforded male children of the elites ever-expanding opportunities for formal education at Harvard, William and Mary, Yale, Princeton, Columbia, and other colonial colleges; there were about 3,000 living graduates of these institutions at the time of the American Revolution. Everywhere, they had preponderant influence in town and county government. Their political influence and ambitions were blunted at higher colonial levels, however, by the presence of English authorities, of whom the royal governor was the most important.[8]

Colonial government was therefore representative and had strong elements of local control, and although it was not fully democratic, it had the potential to become more so. Elections in Dedham, Massachusetts, from 1636 to 1736, for example, rarely involved massive turnout of voters, clear division of interests, and candidates running on platforms or identifying with particular parties, and the same kinds of people won time after time. In Virginia, where local officials were appointed, the electorate could only vote for members of the House of Burgesses. Election day in George Washington's Virginia did not conform to modern standards of free and orderly process. Oral voting, not the secret ballot, prevailed; there was only one polling site in each county; and the sheriff had broad discretionary influence in affecting the outcome. And yet, despite these apparent anomalies, the Virginia system produced George Washington, Thomas Jefferson, James Madison, and John Marshall, who were makers of republican institutions in America.[9]

In most colonies, the elected, lower house of the colonial legislature had representatives who had stature in their communities and practical experience in local government. The lower houses gradually acquired control over their own operations: selection of speaker and clerk, determination of disputed elections, and formation of standing committees. Basing their claims solidly upon English constitutional principles, by which the House of Commons operated after 1688, the elected colonial legislatures claimed that taxes were a free gift to the executive granted through the people's representatives and that they were those representatives. Hence, no taxes could be levied without their consent. Relying ultimately upon this power over appropriations, colonial legislatures asserted their influence over public policies of all kinds, in direct contravention of the counterclaims of royal governors appointed by the king. In disputes regarding the sealing of land grants and the payment of the clergy in Virginia during the 1740s and 1750s, the issuance of search warrants in Massachusetts, the seating of a member duly chosen by the people in South Carolina, and the independence of the judiciary in New York during the early 1760s, colonial legislatures made known that they could not be trifled with and ignored.[10]

To a great extent, these elites derived lessons from English history. The struggles to establish parliamentary supremacy against the absolutist claims of the Stuarts and to protect Protestantism against the return of Catholicism in the seventeenth century provided examples of tyranny and of courageous opposition, reflected in various ways in the ideas of James Harrington, Edward Coke, Algernon Sidney, John Milton, and John Locke. After the Glorious Revolution and into the first half of the eighteenth century, English government moved toward greater centralization as monarchs, through royal ministers such as Robert Walpole, found new ways to discipline parliament and to implement public policy through the use of influence, mostly patronage and the distribution of political favors. This period also established close ties between government and finance and saw the rise of great corporate entities (such as the Bank of England), a succession of imperial wars, the building of larger armies, and the resort to higher taxes. Critics of various sorts attacked these tendencies of "court" politics. Identifying themselves as the "country" opposition, writers as diverse as John Trenchard and Robert Gordon (authors of the libertarian anthology *Cato's Letters*), Viscount Bolingbroke, and Catherine Macauley warned of the return of monarchy and the corruption of parliament. Their polemics struck at the close ties between government and England's financial, military, and imperialist forces (a military-financial complex) and urged reforms that favored landed and local interests, frequent elections for the House of Commons, and attention to civil liberties. In spite of their earnest efforts, the country writers lamented their lack of success in arousing complacent English citizens, who were enjoying material prosperity and were seemingly indifferent to the erosion of constitutional liberties. But they gave Americans—themselves engaged mainly in agrarian pursuits, accustomed to decentralized government, and weary of involvement in Europe's wars—a prism through which to view British imperial policy.[11]

The eighteenth century also introduced colonial Americans to the ideas of science and the Enlightenment—whether from English sources, Scottish sources (David Hume, Adam Smith, and Francis Hutcheson), or continental sources (Montesquieu, Voltaire, Diderot, and Count Beccaria). The colonial elite was well attuned to the principal themes of the era: the doctrine of natural laws, the potential for aligning human institutions in accord with such laws, faith in the power of knowledge, skepticism of clerical influence, and the questioning of present-day habits and institutions resting on unexamined assumptions.[12]

It is revealing that Massachusetts lawyer Josiah Quincy provided in his will that his son upon turning fifteen should receive his father's copies of Algernon Sidney's works, John Locke's treatises, Lord Bacon's works, Gordon's *Tacitus*, and *Cato's Letters*. John Adams and Thomas Jefferson acquired similar titles for their libraries. Clearly, within their scope of reading, were classical sources. They were interested in Athens, with its direct democracy and aristocratic culture, and admired Sparta, where citizens sacrificed for the common good, served in volunteer armies, and stressed civic virtues rather than material comfort. But most inspiring of all stood the Roman republic. They studied Roman laws and history, especially through translations of *Plutarch's Lives* and later intermediaries such as Machiavelli and Montesquieu. Here they encountered the heroes who tried to preserve the Roman republic against its enemies. These ideas and examples from the past did not dictate what Jefferson (William and Mary), John and Samuel Adams (Harvard), Alexander Hamilton (Columbia), and James Madison (Princeton) should do in the 1760s, 1770s, and 1780s, but they gave them the vocabulary, metaphors, and terms of debate that informed their attempts to create an independent and republican United States. Americans were able to perform political autopsies on these ancient republics to determine what it was that led to their collapse and death and to search for underlying principles that might maintain the health and constitution of their societies so that they could become *novo ordo seclorum* (new order of the ages).[13]

When parliament, after 1763, began to impose a series of taxes and thereby to raise the prospect of English colonial governors becoming independent of colonial legislative powers over the purse, it unleashed sustained opposition from American elites in the legislatures, who drew upon an accumulated experience in self-government, protected elite interests, claimed to speak for all the people, and were familiar with relevant lessons drawn from history and political thought. The colonial elites began, in conservative fashion, to defend their prerogatives as sanctioned by custom and by English constitutional law and argued that it was the government that was both innovator and violator of cherished principles. From 1763 to 1774, they found that their arguments did not have many sympathetic listeners among the majority in the English royal court. Although William Pitt, Edmund Burke, and other friends of America succeeded in getting specific, obnoxious measures like the Stamp Act and Townshend Acts repealed, they were overwhelmed by the government majority, marshaled by Lord Frederick North, chief minister for George III from 1772 to 1782. That majority adopted an increasingly hard line toward colonial protests.[14]

American leaders also found that legal and peaceful protests, in order to be noticed and to have effect, had to be accompanied by economic sanctions—which created networks of enforcement committees and resulted in limiting the freedoms of colonial citizens. Doing without luxurious imports required the active cooperation of women, whose devotion to home manufactures acquired a political significance; it also reinforced American perceptions that their leaders were acting upon principles and not for material gain. They also discovered that violence perpetrated by the Sons of Liberty and similar groups, acting without warrant from established authority, allowed hitherto inarticulate or inactive colonials to express their views against those deemed to be at fault for causing economic hardships and limiting political freedoms. Such actions raised grave concerns among some leaders about the risks of destroying respect for law and order and of encouraging mobs to turn on colonial leaders themselves.[15]

Until quite late in the process, colonials hoped that they could achieve their goals without breaking away from the empire. For example, James Otis Jr. suggested that colonial protests against taxation without representation could be addressed by parliament granting seats in the House of Commons to colonials. Few on either side of the Atlantic found this an attractive option. Daniel Dulany, John Dickinson, and others in the Stamp Act Congress of 1765, an extralegal gathering of representatives from nine colonies to protest the passage of the stamp tax, sought to distinguish between the powers that parliament rightfully exercised over the colonies, as in the case of the regulation of trade, and those that only the colonists themselves could exercise, as in the case of taxation, but found clear distinctions difficult to sustain. They were struggling with the notion that internal (domestic) affairs belonged to the colonies and external (foreign) affairs belonged to parliament. James Wilson and Thomas Jefferson favored a dominion arrangement in which each colony, like England, owed allegiance to George III and had the right to its own legislature. The legislature of New York, for example, represented the people of New York, just as the parliament represented the people of England; both were united in the monarchy. Meanwhile, the king and parliament perceived in all of these ideas an inevitable colonial drift toward independence, which they sought to nip in the bud. These proposals and counterproposals familiarized Americans with the perplexing questions of what belonged to central government, what belonged to local government, what belonged to both, and what belonged to neither.[16]

The intransigence of the government majority in the House of Commons in the period between 1774 and 1776 gradually eliminated prospects for compromise and accommodation of colonial grievances within the English imperial system. Even though many chose to remain loyal to England—perhaps as many as 60,000 to 100,000 loyalists out of a total population of about 2.5 million in the thirteen colonies took flight to Canada, the West Indies, England, and elsewhere—the colonial leaders opted for independence. These included more radical figures, such as Patrick Henry, George Clinton, Thomas Jefferson, John Adams, and James Madison, and conservatives, such as James Duane, James Wilson, and John Jay. Alexander Hamilton is beyond easy categorization. All were convinced that parliament and the monarchy had exceeded their authority and had forced them to unite in defense of their basic liberties. Significantly, they turned to institutions that had the greatest potential for democratic development—the lower houses of colonial legislatures. Their rhetoric emphasized the duty of these elected assemblies to protect the rights of the people.[17]

EXPERIMENTS IN REPUBLICAN GOVERNANCE

Americans defended their position in favor of decentralized authority by drawing heavily upon the tradition of the so-called country opposition in England and by protesting the resurgence of monarchical influence, the corrupt alliance between government and finance, the use of standing armies, the resort to high taxes, and locust-like government officials. George III and parliament countered that there could only be one sovereign power in any society and that the English constitution since 1688 placed that squarely with King-in-Parliament. Although women, children, and the propertyless in England and colonials in America could not vote, their interests were nonetheless represented in parliament. Parliament was, therefore, the "virtual" representative of all citizens in the empire, who were obligated to obey laws duly passed by the House of Commons, the House of Lords, and the king. Otherwise, anarchy would prevail.[18]

In January 1776, Thomas Paine added fuel to the fire by publishing *Common Sense*, one of the great pamphlets of the revolutionary era. Paine denounced monarchy and thrust colonials toward a republic. What was a republic? Although the term covered a spectrum of possibilities, including societies ruled by princes,

Americans associated it with those societies governed by laws in the making of which representatives elected by the citizenry played a major role. They also accepted the traditional wisdom that republics were best suited for relatively small, homogeneous societies and not for large, heterogeneous ones, which were thought better served by monarchies. Paine wanted to break from England's government, which mixed monarchical, aristocratic, and republican elements (through the king, the House of Lords, and the House of Commons, respectively) and contaminated republican principles. He proposed thirteen republics, each with a legislature elected annually to deal with domestic affairs, and a continental union, with a Congress composed of delegates from the provincial republics to deal with intercolonial and external matters.

The steadily escalating arguments over which side was in the right drove Americans to adopt the very radical position that there was a higher law than the (unwritten) English constitution and that this higher law prevailed at all times and in all places. Relying on a tradition that stretched back through John Locke to Aristotle and Cicero, Americans asserted that this higher law was natural law, a law that existed prior to the formation of society or government. Any legitimate government had to operate in accordance with natural law; a government that violated natural law lost its right to govern. In the Declaration of Independence, Thomas Jefferson identified rights that natural law recognized: life, liberty, and the pursuit of happiness. He insisted that these were inalienable and that government was founded by the consent of the people. George III and parliament had broken the people's trust and had thereby released Americans from their customary obedience to English laws.

The philosophy of natural rights allowed Americans to introduce a trump card to play against the English but injected an egalitarian principle into the debate that others, such as the disenfranchised, the propertyless, women, and blacks, would later draw upon. It also struck Native Americans, such as Thayendanegea (Joseph Brant), as an example of the Americans' base hypocrisy. Although radicals responded enthusiastically to the natural rights doctrine, more conservative revolutionaries expressed worries about where all of this talk about equality would lead.[19]

The Declaration of Independence meant that Americans had to create new governments for nation and states, deriving their legitimacy from the consent of the people expressed through representative legislatures. The Continental Congress, first gathered in Philadelphia in 1774 and consisting of delegates from the separate colonies, became the de facto national government. Out of necessity, it made decisions about the organization of an intercolonial economic boycott of England, the Continental Army under George Washington, and diplomatic missions to European countries. The Second Continental Congress called upon the colonies to establish state constitutions, and between 1776 and 1780 they did so. Each decision further defined who were patriots and who remained loyalist.

On the surface, there were many continuities between colonial and state government. Pennsylvania, which had functioned with a unicameral legislature in previous years, continued this practice under its state constitution of 1776. Virginia's undemocratic county court system hardly missed a beat and retained its self-perpetuating features through the American Revolution all the way to 1851. The state constitutions also shared common features, especially legislative supremacy and suspicion of the executive. Legislatures controlled the purse. In most states, the legislature chose the state governor, who served a short term and had no veto power.[20]

But beneath the surface, the philosophy of the Declaration of Independence and the spirit of revolution introduced conscious republican ideas. In Pennsylvania, for example, the framers of the state constitution favored the one-house legislature as the best way to give voice to the people without the counter-vailing influence of an aristocratic upper house. Those in favor of bicameralism explained that the people consisted of heterogeneous groups, which could not be adequately protected by simple majoritarianism. Both sides argued explicitly for representative institutions, not just for maintenance of colonial precedent based on a royal charter. Everywhere, Americans viewed the role of the legislator differently from the English. Their legislators spoke directly, not virtually, for their voters—at the time, mainly white male property holders—and were expected to reside in the county or district they represented, immediately accountable to the electorate. The legislature, as the heart of republican government, represented society as a whole in miniature and replicated it.

Moreover, suffrage became intimately associated with citizenship. Unlike a monarchy or oligarchy, wherein one or the few determined public policy, a republic depended on the willingness of the people to assume their civic responsibilities, as Spartans and Romans had. The people had to be vigilant and active and keep government in check; there could be no slackers. Finally, state constitutions, unlike the English example, were written documents that could be viewed, read, and understood by all who were literate and not be the exclusive preserve of insiders at court. An active and knowledgeable citizenry required widespread education and access to information, and these in turn meant that the right of people to assemble peacefully, speak their minds, read what newspapers had to publish, and petition government to respond to their grievances followed as necessary complements in a republic. How could young men be properly trained for civic responsibilities unless their mothers were properly educated? asked women like Abigail Adams, Mercy Otis Warren, and Judith Sargent Murray. All of these expectations undermined the tradition of deference and began the process of leveling the playing field over the next several generations—a process that has not yet ended. These subtle changes altered the way existing institutions functioned.[21]

One of the most important innovations in this constitution-making period came from Massachusetts, which had watched as one after another of the other states put together new governments. Its citizens noted that in Pennsylvania, Virginia, New York, and elsewhere legislatures or rump legislatures had performed the task of writing constitutions. They saw dangers in this practice, which reminded them of parliament's power to make and remake the English constitution at will. A constitution should be fundamental law that governs not only the people but also the government itself, including the legislature. If a legislature could make a constitution, it could alter it whenever its interests collided with the existing constitution. Was this not tyranny? Thus, in 1780, Massachusetts invented the constitutional convention, a body separate from the legislature, elected by the people, and specifically empowered to write a constitution, and it instituted the practice of having the final document submitted for ratification to the people of the state. The constitution now had higher status than ordinary law. These significant breakthroughs came not in 1776 but toward the end of a wave of constitution making, during which states served as laboratories testing republican hypotheses.

THE ARTICLES OF CONFEDERATION

The Articles of Confederation, which governed the nation from 1781 to 1789, served as a bridge between the Declaration of Independence of 1776 and the U.S. Constitution of 1787. All three documents put into writing the essential principles upon which American democracy would be based. The Declaration of Independence was the *written* document that established the doctrine of popular consent and the American creed of the inalienable rights of the people. The Articles of Confederation was the *written* document that embodied the principles of state sovereignty, state autonomy, and legislative supremacy—all of which emerged out of the revolutionary period. The Constitution of 1787 was the *written* document that broadened the principle of state sovereignty, retained the principle of state autonomy in a revised form, and extended the principle of legislative supremacy to the doctrine of national supremacy. The common link among all three documents is that each was concerned with the establishment of a harmonious, stable, and orderly society that would also maximize the freedom of the people—although women, slaves, free blacks, and Native Americans were not yet directly included in "the people." Both goals would be achieved by structuring the social and political order, or the *polity,* in such a way that the freedom of "the people" would be advanced, not radically or suddenly and never completely, but advanced nonetheless.

In order for the American Revolution to succeed in establishing democracy, the consent of the people needed to be converted into a legitimate government through the doctrine of natural rights and the principles that it encompassed. (During the twentieth century, newly formed governments of the new nations carved out of wars and the collapse of communism have found that need as well.) The immediate result of that conversion was the Articles of Confederation. The essential problem was how to reckon with the authority and power of the new, postcolonial government that was to become the United States.

There was no great desire on the part of those who provoked the revolution to give up their recently won political power in the states and to establish a strong central government that would merely be a replica of the English government. These advocates of state sovereignty believed that "the greatest gain of the Revolution was the independence of the several states" and the creation of a central government that would be subservient to the states and the state legislatures.[22]

The new government—a confederated republic—was the result of a compact among the separate states, not a compact among the people as a whole. It respected the traditional preference for small republics by upholding state sovereignty, state prestige, and state institutions. George Washington had once called "state sovereignty" a monster, but the American Revolution nevertheless resulted in the affirmation of sovereignty in the states, with power resting with state legislatures, not with a central government that itself had no viable executive office. The following is the preamble to the Articles of Confederation:

> Whereas the Delegates of the United States of America in Congress assembled did on the 15th day of November in the year of our Lord 1777, and in the second year of the Independence of America agree to certain articles of Confederation and perpetual union between the States of Newhampshire, Massachusetts-bay, Rhodeisland and Providence Plantations, Connecticut, New York, New Jersey, Pennsylvania, Delaware, Maryland, Virginia, North-Carolina, South-Carolina and Georgia in the words following. . . . The said States hereby severally enter into a firm league of friendship with each other, for their common defence, the security of their liberties, and their mutual and general welfare, binding themselves to assist each other, against all force offered to, or attacks made upon them, or any of them, on account of religion, sovereignty, trade, or any other pretence whatever.

Contrast that with the preamble to the United States Constitution of 1787: "*We the people of the United States* [emphasis added], in order to form a more perfect union, establish justice, insure domestic tranquility, provide for the common defence, promote the general welfare, and secure the blessings of liberty to ourselves and our posterity, do ordain and establish this Constitution for the United States of America."

Under the Articles, the new nation was a compact among the states that had emerged from colonial status. Under the Constitution, the young states became an extended, or compound, republic that was reunited through the principle of "We the People" (yet not inclusive of *all* people).

The Articles, unlike the Constitution (which followed eight years later), emphasized that each state retained its sovereignty, freedom, and independence from any superior authority. In the Articles, the states were to have ultimate political authority. Ever since the days of the Articles and the early republic that followed, the United States has had as part of its political heritage and culture this question of the relationship of the people to the national government and to the states.

Soon after hostilities broke out with England, the Continental Congress requested the drafting of the Articles of Confederation, under which it could function. The major issues were representation and taxes. The leading author of the Articles was John Dickinson, a moderate who had first sought a settlement inside the British Empire, not outside of it. His November 1776 draft granted significant powers to the new Congress but no taxing power, because there was great hostility to granting such authority to a central government. As the Continental Congress increasingly fell into the hands of more radical delegates, however, Dickinson's plan was reworked, and the Articles submitted for ratification in November 1777 were much altered. In effect, they reflected the methods of operation worked out by the newly independent states in conducting the War of Independence against Britain.

On the question of equal representation of the new states and on the important legislative matters of engaging in war, entering into treaties and alliances, coining money, supplying an army and navy, and appointing a commander in chief of the armed forces, a majority of nine states out of thirteen (rather than a majority of representatives of the states in the Congress) would be required for passage. Thus, a small number of the more populated states would have a veto over the majority of the less-populated states. A minority of states would be able to check the rest, and each state would still be equal in voting power (as is currently the case in the U.S. Senate). On the question of taxation, each state's contribution to the common cause would be based on land values and improvements, not on population. The Articles left to future Congresses the task of finding a formula for the allocation of state taxes to support the new government.

The issues of representation and taxation show that the Articles themselves were born out of the necessity for the society to compromise over state power and state sovereignty. (Individual liberties and rights were not endemic to the era of the Confederation.) The same problems would crop up again in 1787 and would be solved, to some extent, by the U.S. Constitution through equal state representation in the Senate, representation in the House based on population, the three-fifths clause (whereby for purposes of representation and taxation a slave would be counted as three-fifths of a person), and taxation based on population. Slavery, it must be remembered, was not constitutionally prohibited until the Thirteenth, Fourteenth, and Fifteenth Amendments to the U.S. Constitution were passed (in 1865, 1868, and 1870, respectively), and taxation based on income was not allowed until after the Sixteenth Amendment was ratified by the states in 1913.

The states, in the 1781 Articles, bound themselves together in a league of friendship, mutual support, and honor, but there was no national enforcement body for whatever laws were passed by the new Congress. Thus, the Congress had to rely on the states to enforce its laws on individual citizens. Nor was there a national judicial system, except for a Court of Appeals for Admiralty, which was established in 1780.

The major deficiency of the Articles was that the powers granted the Congress were less important than those withheld from it. There was no direct power to tax, and so Congress was dependent on the largesse of the states for money, and Congress was given no power to enforce laws that it had passed. The states, embedded in the doctrine of state legislative supremacy, could do whatever they wanted, with no national judiciary to watch over them either. There was no national uniformity of laws. Congress became a mere rump body, without dignity, without adequate power, without, even, a home. It was compelled to appeal repeatedly to the states before it could even obtain a quorum to approve the peace treaty with England. Many states simply refused to pay their share of the expenses to run the government, and it took eighteen months to collect one-fifth of the taxes due from the states in 1783. National credit was worthless, and foreign nations refused to make commercial treaties.[23]

In 1785, Algiers declared war on the United States; Congress recommended building five ships, but they were never built, and Algiers continued to prey on American commerce for some time. England still refused to carry out the requirements of the Treaty of Paris of 1783, by which it had, among other things, recognized the independence of the United States and ceded claims to lands east of the Mississippi River and south of Canada. It did not evacuate forts in New York and the Ohio Valley and failed even to send a minister to the United States. The central government was despised abroad and disobeyed at home. Eventually, in 1786, the states were asked to pass an amendment (requiring unanimity) entrusting to Congress the collection of revenues from imports. New York rejected the amendment outright, and this veto seemed to destroy the last hope of continuance of national union. Centralists (those who advocated a strong central government) felt frustrated and humiliated that the country they had helped to create appeared to be in jeopardy.[24]

Nevertheless, the Articles were crucial to the evolution of politics in America. They reflected a need for some kind of constitutional framework and thus contributed to the sense of constitutionalism that culminated in 1787, a desire for union, and a need for a national institution of government. The government of the Articles of Confederation fought and won the revolution—no small feat. And the Confederation Congress negotiated a successful peace treaty and enacted the model Northwest Ordinance, which allowed for the admission of new states from existing national territories and provided that these states, once admitted, would enjoy the same privileges as the original thirteen states.

The War for Independence and the immediate postwar difficulties, however, raised troubling issues about the economy, foreign relations, military preparedness, Indian affairs, currency, and the national debt, over which the successful revolutionaries disagreed. The principal fault line divided advocates of state sovereignty from centralists, localists from cosmopolitans, and those in a subsistence economy from those in the market economy. Those wedded to state and local interests often had lives and careers tied to state government, militia service, and provincial interests and included such good revolutionaries as George Mason, George Clinton, and Richard Henry Lee whose understanding of the political world continued to be very much shaped by "country" ideology. They enjoyed strong support among self-sufficient farmers. The centralists and cosmopolitans, by contrast, included many who had been in the officer corps of the Continental

Army (Washington, Hamilton, John Knox), the diplomatic service (John Adams, John Jay, Benjamin Franklin), the committees of the Continental Congress that dealt with finance (Robert Morris, James Madison), and those engaged in the market economy—in sum, those who came to recognize the deficiencies of a decentralized political system in a world of hostile powers as well as the vices of powerful state governments dominated by elected legislatures that responded to popular prejudices rather than to the calls for civic responsibility and sacrifice. Thus, a major split eventually developed among those patriots who had agreed on independence and republicanism in 1776.[25]

As Hamilton pointed out in *Federalist* No. 1, the Articles of Confederation were insufficient to preserve the union, and the union had to be preserved. Just as the Confederation was a natural and pragmatic outcome of the revolutionary movement within the American colonies, so was the convention of 1787 in Philadelphia the natural and pragmatic outcome of the shortcomings of the Confederation. The Articles were, in a sense, a constitutional expression of state legislative supremacy resulting from the Declaration of Independence. The Constitution of 1787 would reflect the need to remedy the deficiencies that emerged in practice from that philosophy. The needs for some sort of centralization, for a stronger national government, and for a national executive branch were becoming obvious.

Those who wrote the U.S. Constitution in 1787 were centralists, although they adopted the label "Federalists" in order to disguise their centralizing desires. They were also political realists, who saw the need to compromise with the political reality of state sovereignty. The Constitution did not eliminate the states, nor did it deny to them *all* their prerogatives. It readjusted the role of the states and the national government by strengthening the national government, and it redefined their relationship by eliminating the Confederation and substituting a federal system. Even so, it then took early action by the U.S. Supreme Court to give this inert document, the Constitution, energy and force.

THE U.S. CONSTITUTION

The U.S. Constitution was written in Philadelphia in 1787 at a convention attended by fifty-five of the seventy-four appointed delegates, thirty-nine of whom actually signed the document. The fifty-five delegates were experienced politicians. Three-fourths of them had been in the Continental Congress, a number had been in state legislatures, eight had signed the Declaration of Independence, seven had been governors of states, and twenty-one were veterans of the War for Independence. A vast majority of the delegates were Federalists, committed to creating a strong, central government with a strong presidency. This small, homogeneous body of men deliberated in secret (something that would be impossible to do in today's society). The members of the convention thus could not play to public opinion during the meetings, something else that would not be possible in the twentieth century.[26]

Many of these delegates were politician-scholars who believed that stability of a society had to be based on the rule of law, not on utilitarian concepts of numerical majoritarianism. Many of them were steeped in the political philosophies of the ancient classics.[27] The delegates hoped "to reconcile the need for a strong [central] government with the demand for much personal liberty and for state and local powers. They could not find in the history of the ancient world any model constitution that might achieve this purpose."[28]

The delegates were very much aware of a major inadequacy of the Articles, a central executive with insufficient power and little authority over the states. They were in Philadelphia to preserve the union and their liberty as well. They sought a system of good government, because they knew that the best was out of reach: As Alexander Hamilton observed in *Federalist* No. 65, "If mankind were to resolve to agree in no institution of government, until every part of it had been adjusted to the most exact standard of perfection, society would soon become a general scene of anarchy, and the world a desert."[29]

Good government required institutional checks against the excesses of direct democracy; it could not simply rely on people to be virtuous. Moreover, an extended, or compound, republic—not merely a league of small republics but an organically unified government over an extensive territory occupied by provincial republics—would ameliorate the clashes that were bound to develop among the diversified and heterogeneous interests of the fledgling United States. In 1787, the nation was "divided by interests and opinions sufficiently diverse to force [the framers] to rise above parochial attachments." The nation had to be made stronger and had to be guided by a centralized government, with an energetic executive, a balanced bicameral legislature (with the states represented equally in the Senate and the people popularly in the House), and an independent judiciary. Such a constitutional framework, with its heavy emphasis on federalism, separation of powers, checks and balances, and indirect elections, would be the means for successfully adjusting relations among individuals and the whole body of people (that is, society in general) and provide "a mechanism for eliciting the superiority of popular government."[30]

The framers sought to preserve the sense of individuality that is everyone's birthright under the doctrine of natural rights. At the same time, they recognized that people were political and social animals who sought individual liberties and rights under the protective cover of other like-minded persons. James Madison's *Federalist* No. 10 (1788), on factions, was a seminal work that clearly recognized the importance of all kinds of interests in the society. In it Madison challenged the prevailing assumption that stable republics were possible only for small, homogeneous populations and asserted that a republic over a broad territory with contending groups offered a better prospect for securing liberty. In the extended republic, people's self-interests had to be guided toward the public good, the late eighteenth century version of "virtue," and that required institutional arrangements that would channel the people's energies and interests toward peaceful compromises.

Thus, the Constitution was born out of conflict and compromises and reflected the varied interests of the separate states and the diversity of the American people. This most delicately balanced document provided a set of procedures to deal with the ongoing conflicts, compromises, and readjustments that people had to make—and must make even today–to live in a civil society.

How much power is compatible with freedom? Whereas too much power allocated to government can threaten freedom, too little can cause government to be entirely ineffective in protecting and promoting national interests. Thus, the question boiled down to the balance of power between state governments and the federal government. Under the old Articles of Confederation, the states had retained a good deal of autonomy, but under the 1787 document, the states had to readjust, giving up some of their powers for the greater national good.

"In the constitutional convention, the spirit of compromise reigned in grace and glory."[31] Representation of the people and the states was to be a mixed bag—indirect election of the president through the electoral college; state legislative appointment of senators (changed to direct elections by the Seventeenth Amendment in 1913) to staggered six-year terms, with each state represented by two senators regardless of the size of the state's population; direct popular election of representatives to the House of Representatives for two-year terms; and an independent national judiciary appointed by the president for life with the approval of the Senate.

Numerical majoritarianism was *not* the guideline for the new republic. To have a free and open society and yet retain a government strong enough to provide security required auxiliary precautions. More important than narrow majorities was the need to create civic consensus. American constitutionalism was an attempt to make popular government work. Hence, the Constitution did not recognize government by simple majority—the Constitution is sprinkled with two-thirds and three-fourths vote requirements for various procedures. In contrast, passage of bills in Congress can be accomplished by a simple majority of those present, which may be less than a majority of the whole number of either house.

Moreover, the framers did not allow for basic civil liberties and civil rights. "We the people" did not mean all the people. When the Bill of Rights was adopted in 1791 as a series of amendments to the Constitution, they were directed as prohibitions against the national government, not the states. Moreover, slaves were noncitizens. Not until passage of the Civil War amendments (the Thirteenth, Fourteenth, and Fifteenth Amendments mentioned earlier), did African Americans theoretically achieve legal rights, and those rights were denied in practice until well into the twentieth century. Women, of course, did not win the right to vote until the Nineteenth Amendment was passed in 1920.

All in all, the framers were aiming for a republican government, not a democracy, in 1787. The framers thought that democracy was anarchical—the Greek word *demos*, to them, did not mean the "people" but rather the "mob," and the mob (that is, the masses) was to be feared for its destructive tendencies. The elitists had made the revolution possible, and they were not about to give up their elitism in 1787, despite the introduction in the preamble "We, the people."

The Constitution was simply not the product of the majority in the country at the time, nor was the Constitution a tribute to democracy and democratic values per se. That would evolve in time with changing social and economic conditions, expansion of territory and population, and increasing pluralism. And, ironically, the people would eventually come to rely on the Constitution as the fundamental law that required a democratic response to those changes as time wore on. In 1787, however, that is not what the delegates to the Constitutional Convention meant, for they were the products of their times and their experiences. The delegates felt that the most important aim of the convention was to set the nation on an even keel, and they believed that the numerical majority of the people was not a stable base for the creation of a balance of power. The base for stability had to be rooted in an institutional framework, whereby power would be checked by power, not necessarily by the people. So much for democracy and majority rule in 1787.[32]

With its adoption, however, the Constitution provided the new nation with the principles and procedures of what would become a democratic government. The Constitution was a unifying document, as carefully spelled out in the preamble, but the framers were still infected with the parochialism of their own state views. The localized nature of the country had deep roots, and every convention delegate was very much a product of the state sovereignty prevalent in those days. Nevertheless, when the convention met, the delegates realized that they were to draw up a document that would govern the country on a national basis.[33]

Essentially, those at the convention were centralists in spirit, seeking to establish a stronger central government than had existed under the Articles. Ironically, only a strong national government through an independent federal judiciary, empowered by the concept of judicial review, could eventually come to interpret the Constitution and the Bill of Rights in this century as protections not only against the national government, but also against the state governments. The Congress would eventually pass civil rights bills in the second half of the twentieth century, and then only after it had been dragged reluctantly into doing so by interest groups in the extended republic seeking new constitutional interpretations of their rights in the judicial system and the legislative process. It would be a long time coming.

In sum, twentieth-century views of democracy were absent from the 1787 convention. Nor was the majority vote concept seen as a safeguard against tyranny. The framers, however, had a conscious design. Indirect elections, institutional separation of powers among the three branches of government, and the institutional division of power between the federal center and the states would be bulwarks against governmental tyranny. Indirect elections of the president and the Senate, in particular, would guard against the excesses of tyranny by the majority.

As Ralph B. Perry has pointed out, "The federal constitution . . . expressed a fear of excesses of revolutionary democracy, and of the mind of the masses. These fears inspired John Adams, Alexander Hamilton, and the other leaders of the Federalist Party; they represented the mood of reconstruction as had Samuel Adams that of revolution." The framers at the convention "represented not only a conservative emphasis on strong government and a delay of the popular will, but also the economic interests of the financial and mercantile classes of the eastern seaboard."[34]

The Constitution was a vague document, saying nothing about political parties, secession, and acquisition of territory; it was hazy about the regulation of commerce and vague about definitions of such terms as the "necessary and proper" clause of Article 1, section 8. Often, the solution was not to have any permanent solution, except the agreement to live by the ground rules and the mechanics, to move slowly via the amending process, and to solve problems on the basis of moderation, compromise, and practicality. The basic law would have to be redefined to suit new conditions. The framers left it to future generations to work out problems as they arose, and the Supreme Court would later take on that challenge with great gusto. The price of this, however, has been "ambiguity, uncertainty, and constant compromise."[35] The *idea* of the Constitution has become as important as the Constitution itself.

The Constitution remains a pragmatic document written by pragmatic politicians. As John P. Roche wrote a number of years ago, the delegates were in a great hurry to have a new government established, and when arguments broke out about definitions, they took refuge in ambiguity. If different framers voted for the same proposition for varying reasons, that was politics. If later generations would be unsettled by the imprecision in language, that would be the problem of later generations and, one might add, the justices of the U.S. Supreme Court. Ambiguity was useful and, of course, has proven to be so as the Constitution has undergone much reinterpretation.[36]

The Federalists wanted a stronger central government, and the only way to obtain it was by engaging in an endless process of give-and-take. For three months they reasoned and cajoled, threatened, and bargained among themselves. The result was a document that the people, by democratic processes in the election of delegates to state conventions for the purpose of ratifying the constitution, indeed could accept. The delegates had done their best to create a diffuse, limited, balanced form of government in which elites such as themselves would fill leading offices. They did indeed lack an overpowering faith in the wisdom and steadiness of the people.[37]

In short, the Constitution was and remains a document that structures the means of governing in a pragmatic manner. Decisionmaking requires consensus. Legislation must walk a tortuous path through both houses of Congress. To be sure, the result is often stalemate or "gridlock." The American mixed government system can be compared, as John Adams might have said, to wrestlers grappling with each other until one has fallen—or until the referee has declared a draw.

STEPS TOWARD DEMOCRACY

The U.S. Constitution of 1787 did not immediately establish a democratic order. Indeed, as Stanley Elkins and Eric McKitrick have pointed out, "'democracy' [did] not emerge as a fully legitimate cultural value in America, commanding more or less universal approval, until the 1830s, with the appearance of a national system of mass political parties." When the states approved the Constitution in 1789, there was as yet no "functional democracy" in any contemporary sense. Despite the historical setting in the prerevolutionary and revolutionary eras we have described thus far, it would take much more time for the republic to broaden its democratic base.[38]

During the struggle to ratify the Constitution, Antifederalists had warned Americans of the absence of a Bill of Rights to protect the states and individual citizens from the assaults of an invigorated central government. When the first Congress under the Constitution proposed a set of amendments and the requisite three-fourths of the states ratified them in 1791, Antifederalists could more easily reconcile themselves to the new system, which had been made safer by their contributions. Americans saw that the constitutional system could correct mistakes and overcome omissions; nevertheless, the road ahead would not be smooth.

Americans had yet to acquire sufficient faith in their institutions and in the political processes that those institutions guaranteed. Having created the nation by a revolution that relied on mass demonstrations and extralegal organizations such as committees of public safety, the Sons of Liberty, and the Continental Congress, Americans—especially those who did not control the newly created institutions—resorted to direct action to shape or resist policy. Thus, in 1786, residents of western Massachusetts, feeling that their legislature and governor taxed them too heavily to pay creditors, rose up behind Captain Daniel Shays, a Continental Army veteran, in a rebellion against the state government. That this government acted in accordance with the Massachusetts Constitution, prepared by a convention and ratified by the people, did not restrain the Shaysites. Even after the U.S. Constitution had been ratified and the Washington administration had taken office, farmers in western Pennsylvania, many of them of Anglo-Irish background and accustomed to resisting outside authority of any kind, refused to abide by a tax upon whiskey levied by the Congress. In the Whiskey Rebellion, they defied Washington, Secretary of the Treasury Hamilton, and the new system. Both rebellions were suppressed; the rebels fled to the interior, beyond the reach of duly constituted authorities. Eventually, economic development and experience would teach the citizens of the new republic to play the democratic game through political parties and make elected officials and representative institutions attend to their interests.[39]

The founders had a low opinion of political parties held together by patronage and political favors—the very qualities that revolutionaries had found obnoxious among the king's ministers and members of parliament. They believed that parties stirred the worst kinds of partisanship, distorted debate, aroused public passions, and elevated themselves above the national interest. In spite of such negative views, the decisions of the Washington administration, particularly in regard to Hamilton's fiscal policies (funding the national debt and assuming the state debts, a national bank, protective tariffs, and excise taxes) and a foreign policy that favored Great Britain over revolutionary France, gradually brought about a division between the party in power, the Federalists, and the party in opposition, the Republicans.

Hostility deepened as each party tended to view its own actions as legitimate and denounced the opposition's alleged subversive activities. Every battle seemed to involve ultimate principles; every departure from one's own philosophy appeared to endanger the republic. In 1798, Federalists in Congress cracked down on dissent by adopting the Alien and Sedition Acts in seeming defiance of the Bill of Rights, and Republicans in the Kentucky and Virginia legislatures adopted resolutions urging the states to refuse to enforce those odious measures. When Federalists lost the national election in 1800 to Thomas Jefferson and the Republicans, some of them threatened to reject the outcome of a free election and to urge their states to secede. When Republican Presidents Jefferson and Madison pushed the United States toward war with Britain (it eventually came about in 1812), many Federalists refused to cooperate. The sharpness of political infighting and the mistrust of the opposition took years to overcome, but in due course Americans came to recognize that political parties were useful institutions to mobilize the citizenry around candidates, issues, and political philosophies and that they were necessary institutions to help bridge the separation between central and state government and among the presidency, the Senate, and the House of Representatives at the nation's capital.[40]

Political leadership played a major part in giving the United States time to build confidence in its institutions. Thus, George Washington used his enormous personal prestige (charisma, if you will) to encourage cooperation between Hamilton and Jefferson, emphasized merit rather than partisanship in the appointment of public officials, and proclaimed neutrality in the war between the English and the French and their allies. He also made the decision not to seek a third term in 1796 and to give his blessings to those chosen to succeed him in a free election. He did not die in office and leave a crisis of political succession for others. Federalist John Adams, the succeeding president, sought to shield the United States from war with France by relying on diplomatic initiatives, which many people believe damaged his chances for reelection by relieving the rival Republican Party of direct association with an enemy of the United States in time of war. As president, Thomas Jefferson tried to promote consensus by declaring that "We are all Federalists, We are all Republicans" at the start of his administration.[41]

Leadership of an institutional sort would also come from John Marshall and the U.S. Supreme Court. During the first dozen years of its existence, however, the Court did not establish itself as an important branch of the central government.

It had little business and behaved in a way not too differently from the political branches. For example, John Jay, the first chief justice, served for six months as acting secretary of state and later accepted a diplomatic mission to negotiate what became the controversial Jay Treaty. He even ran for governor of New York in 1792 without resigning from the bench—and lost; then, in 1795, he resigned to become governor of that state. The justices delivered their opinions *seriatim* and thereby publicized internal divisions. Only during the long tenure of Chief Justice John Marshall (1801–1835) would the Court emerge as a third branch of government, and the case of *Marbury v. Madison* would be crucial in this transition.

Seventeen prominent members of the Constitutional Convention of 1787, three-fourths of the leadership at the convention, at one time or another asserted that "the Constitution secured to courts in the United States the right to pass on the validity of acts of Congress."[42] In *Federalist* No. 78, Hamilton stressed the importance of the right of the courts to declare unconstitutional acts of Congress[43]

> Interpretation of the laws is the proper and peculiar province of the Courts. A Constitution is, in fact, and must be regarded by the judges as a fundamental law. It must therefore belong to them to ascertain its meaning, as well as the meaning of any particular act proceeding from the legislative body. If there should happen to be irreconcilable variance between the two, that which has the superior obligation and validity ought, of course, to be preferred; or in other words, the Constitution ought to be preferred to the statute, the intention of the people to the intention of their [legislative] agents.

These views were put to the test in *Marbury v. Madison* in 1803 during the presidency of Thomas Jefferson, Hamilton's arch enemy and leader of the Republican opposition to the Federalists.

Three loyal members of the Federalist Party, including William Marbury, had been appointed to minor posts as justices of the peace in the federal District of Columbia by President John Adams almost at the close of his administration. Secretary of State John Marshall failed to deliver the commissions to the three people, even though the commissions had been duly signed before Jefferson assumed office. When Jefferson became president, he instructed his new secretary of state, James Madison, not to deliver the commissions to the three Federalists.[44]

In 1789, the first Congress had passed the Judiciary Act, establishing the judicial system under the Constitution. Section 13 authorized the U.S. Supreme Court to issue "writs of mandamus . . . in cases warranted by the principles and usages of law, to any courts appointed, or persons holding office, under the authority of the United States." Marbury now sought to compel Madison to deliver his commission by seeking a writ of mandamus directly in the Supreme Court.

Speaking for the full Court in 1803, Chief Justice John Marshall, who had been appointed to that position by John Adams, agreed that the plaintiffs were indeed entitled to their commissions and should have legal redress. But the remedy to obtain that legal redress was not through a writ of mandamus from the Supreme Court as the Judiciary Act of 1789 stated. According to Marshall, the law giving Marbury the right to seek a writ of mandamus immediately in the Supreme Court was unconstitutional and therefore void. Why?

The Judiciary Act of 1789 gave the Supreme Court authority to issue a writ of mandamus under original jurisdiction. In other words, a person aggrieved could go directly to the Supreme Court. The original jurisdiction of the Supreme Court, however, is spelled out in Article 3, section 2 of the Constitution. The Congress cannot add to original jurisdiction, Marshall argued, without amending the Constitution. The Court found the relevant part of the Judiciary Act of 1789 unconstitutional and claimed the "constitutional" right to overturn an act of Congress based on the national supremacy clause (Article 4, section 2) and Article 3, which extends federal judicial power to "cases and controversies" arising under the Constitution.

The importance of the *Marbury* case cannot be overstated. Marbury gave judicial review a foothold that was to enhance national power as opposed to state power. Even though the Court did not use judicial review to strike against the Congress again until 1857, judicial review would become an important tool of the Court after the Civil War.

The doctrine of judicial review has been effectively and more frequently used against state power, as in the important decisions of *McCulloch v. Maryland* (1819) and *Gibbons v. Ogden* (1824). In the first case, the Supreme Court ruled unanimously that the federal government had the right to establish a national bank and that a state could not tax such a federal instrumentality and thereby threaten to destroy it. In the second case, the Supreme Court ruled that the interstate commerce provisions of the power of Congress in Article 1, section 8, and a federal law regulating coastal commerce took precedence over a New York state law that contradicted national authority. By 1824, then, the doctrine of state legislative supremacy that had emerged from the War of Independence no longer prevailed routinely. In both cases, Marshall and his judicial colleagues, appointed by both Federalist and Republican presidents, interpreted national (what we now call federal) powers broadly and state powers narrowly. Marshall's doctrine of "judicial nationalism" went hand in hand with Hamilton's emphasis on national as opposed to state power. Judicial review became a deeply rooted concept in American jurisprudence. Most, but not all, of the judicial review decisions made today are not of laws passed by Congress but of laws passed by the states, and most of these, of course, deal with civil liberties and civil rights as they relate to the Bill of Rights. Thus, the Court stands as guardian of certain democratic values on behalf of numerically weak groups and unpopular causes when they come under attack by both federal and state legislatures, which are likely to pay greater attention to numerical majorities.[45]

Meanwhile, the president was also playing a more important role. During his administration (1829–1837), Andrew Jackson assumed the role of spokesperson for the nation. Chosen by the electoral college, which represented both states and the people and behaved in accord with the wishes of political parties, Jackson vetoed bills passed by the Congress and challenged Supreme Court decisions. He excelled at defining political issues such as patronage, internal improvements, Indian removal, and the national bank in ways that fostered the perception that he was the representative of the people, the working classes, and democracy. He put his opponents on the defensive as advocates of aristocracy, special privilege, foreigners, and Indians. Jackson's positions became the positions of his party (the Democrats), and both president and party exploited symbols, nicknames, and new techniques for winning support: Jackson was "Old Hickory," and hickory canes became the popular rage; the donkey, a stubborn and hardworking common animal, became the Democratic Party's mascot; barbecues, parades, and public rallies became commonplace; and inflated campaign oratory the norm.

The opposition Whig Party learned to play the electioneering game just as well, and the public responded. As many as 75 to 80 percent of the eligible voters voted in presidential contests during this era. The Democratic candidate won in 1836, 1844, and 1852; the Whig candidate prevailed in 1840 and 1848, clearly establishing that each party was capable of winning and losing and coming back from defeat to win again. The process of contesting elections and abiding by the results became part of the political culture. When seven southern states withdrew from the Union in 1860–1861 in response to the election of Abraham Lincoln on an antislavery platform, President Lincoln could appeal to the nation to rely on the ballot, not the bullet, to settle national issues and could expect that many Americans would agree with him. Indeed, they went to war to preserve the Union and the Constitution.[46]

The institution of the Congress also evolved from its beginnings in 1789. At first, states adopted different methods for electing their representatives to the House. Connecticut, for example, resorted to the election of their representatives at-large, so that the numerical advantage that Federalists enjoyed in the state could be leveraged into winning all the seats. Most states, however, moved to single-member districts as the method most consistent with the American idea of direct representation for the legislature. The Congress discussed great issues of war and peace, public land policy, taxation and embargoes, and even slavery, and its decisions showed the influence of public opinion. As constitutional reform at the state level headed toward universal manhood suffrage and as competition among rival parties heated up, the size of the voting public for congressional, state, and local elections increased. Citizens could now vote at neighborhood polling sites. Elections for local and state officials became more frequent and related to the elections for Congress and president through the actions of political parties. Those unhappy with government action or inaction organized and competed within the rules set by the Constitution and the emerging two-party system.[47]

It helped that the economy during the 1790s showed visible improvement over its uncertain status during the 1780s. The onset, in 1793, of a prolonged war among European powers led to sharp increases in American exports, and American merchants made huge inroads into the carrying trade. The invention of the cotton gin by Eli Whitney made short-staple cotton the new export crop of the South. Meanwhile, investments in turnpikes, canals, steamboats, and, eventually, railroads—primarily by the private sector and by state and local governments—provided the infrastructure for expanded agricultural production and for industry, as much for the domestic as the international market, throughout the first half of the nineteenth century. Reduction in transportation costs, equivalent to the reduction of tariff barriers, had the effect of enlarging markets and increasing competition, allowing more efficient producers to prevail over lesser ones. Financial intermediaries, such as state banks, grew dramatically after 1812 and extended credit to farmers and entrepreneurs. New technology in printing increased the speed and decreased the cost of printing newspapers, pamphlets, and books; and, by 1850, telegraphy made communication across the continent almost instantaneous. Outside of the South and the undeveloped areas of the North, impersonal media and impersonal communications established themselves as elements of a modernizing ethos, which raised questions about traditional practices, such as southern slavery and the subordinate role of women. Territorial expansion and the forced removal of Native Americans—popular measures among voting Americans—allowed for absorption of a growing population and access to the raw materials of the interior. An influx of immigrants (including Catholics)—33 million between 1815 and 1914—provided talent and labor; it also added to tensions within an already diverse society. The developing national market economy, given constitutional sanction by John Marshall's Supreme Court in *Gibbons v. Ogden*, allowed greater numbers of Americans to become reconciled to and even to become advocates and defenders of the Constitution and the political system.[48]

The United States did not have to write a national constitution, create new institutions, develop a market economy, and extend political rights to all adult citizens at the same time. In the revolutionary and early national period, Americans brought forth a republican ideology, applied it creatively to establish a compound republic over an extensive territory, invented the constitutional convention, federalism, and the presidency, and opened the way to democracy—an enviable record of achievement. But democracy required time and space for the evolution of institutional procedures, such as judicial review, and the creation of parallel organizations, such as political parties. Gradually and sometimes grudgingly, politicians and citizens acknowledged that organized opposition, based on free speech and a free press, could be legitimate. It was fortunate that the new system could deliver—or at least take credit for—economic benefits. Finally, the United States profited from the end of the Napoleonic wars in 1815, after which the dangers of intervention posed by great powers in its affairs subsided for almost a century. It could devote its resources to internal development, with marginal concern for events in Europe, Asia, and Africa and with little in the way of taxes to fund a defense budget. Even so, Americans had to fight many political battles and a civil war before they considered broadening the idea of democracy to include numerous immigrant groups, women, African Americans, Native Americans, and others during the nineteenth and twentieth centuries.

In retrospect, Americans of the late eighteenth century clearly drew upon their historical experiences and took advantage of their particular historical circumstances. They set forth the ideal of natural rights as the credo for the United States and crafted the Constitution and Bill of Rights, prescribing the general rules guiding and restraining governments and citizens alike. In so doing, they did not establish democracy but laid the foundation upon which democracy could be built, brick by brick.[49]

CHRONOLOGY

1607–1732	Founding of the thirteen mainland British colonies that became the United States
1688	The Glorious Revolution in England
1754–1763	The French and Indian War
1763–1774	Imposition of taxes and other imperial measures on the colonies by parliament
1765	Stamp Act Congress
1774	The first Continental Congress gathers in Philadelphia
1776	Thomas Paine's *Common Sense*; the Declaration of Independence
1776–1780	First round of state constitutions written
1783	The Peace of Paris
1781–1789	The Articles of Confederation govern the new nation
1786	Shays' Rebellion in western Massachusetts
1787	The Philadelphia Constitutional Convention
1787–1788	Publication of the *Federalist Papers*, written pseudonymously by Alexander Hamilton, James Madison, and John Jay
1788	The U.S. Constitution is ratified by nine states
1789	The first Congress and president are elected
1789	Congress passes the Judiciary Act
1791	The Bill of Rights (the first ten amendments) approved; the first Bank of the United States chartered
1801	Republican Thomas Jefferson elected president
1803	*Marbury v. Madison*; the Louisiana Purchase
1819	*McCulloch v. Maryland*; the Panic of 1819
1824	*Gibbons v. Ogden*
1825	Erie Canal opens

NOTES

1. J. R. Pole, "Historians and the Problem of Early American Democracy," *American Historical Review* 67 (April 1962): 626–646; Robert R. Palmer, "Notes on the Use of the Word 'Democracy,' 1789–1799," *Political Science Quarterly* 68 (June 1953): 203–226; Richard Buel Jr., "Democracy and the American Revolution: A Frame of Reference," *William and Mary Quarterly*, 3d ser., 21 (April 1964): 165–190; and Martin Diamond, "Democracy and the Federalist: A Reconsideration of the Framers' Intent," *American Political Science Review* 53 (March 1959): 52–68.

2. Bernard Bailyn, *Peopling of British North America: An Introduction* (New York: Alfred A. Knopf, 1986); David Hackett Fischer, *Albion's Seed* (New York: Oxford University Press, 1989); Howard Mumford Jones, *America and French Culture, 1750–1848* (Chapel Hill: University of North Carolina Press, 1922); Philip D. Morgan, ed., *Diversity and Unity in Early North America* (New York: Routledge, 1993); Gary B. Nash, *Red, White, and Black: The Peoples of North America*, 3d ed. (Englewood Cliffs, NJ: Prentice-Hall, 1992).

3. Gary M. Walton and James F. Shepherd, *The Economic Rise of Early America* (Cambridge: Cambridge University Press, 1979).

4. Richard D. Brown, *Modernization: The Transformation of American Life, 1600–1865* (New York: McGraw-Hill Ryerson, 1976); Clinton Rossiter, *Seedtime of the Republic* (New York: Harcourt Brace, 1953); Sidney Mead, "The Rise of Denominationalism," *Church History* 23 (December 1954): 291–320; Bernard Bailyn, *The Origins of American Politics* (New York: Alfred A. Knopf, 1967); Michael Kammen, *People of Paradox: An Inquiry Concerning the Origins of American Civilization* (New York: Alfred A. Knopf, 1972).

5. Chilton Williamson, *American Suffrage from Property to Democracy* (Princeton: Princeton University Press, 1960), is authoritative for the mainland colonies and the United States. Scholars are much less precise about the extent of suffrage in eighteenth-century England. For example, Jack P. Greene and J. R. Pole, eds., *The Blackwell Encyclopedia of the American Revolution* (Cambridge, MA: Blackwell Reference, 1991), includes several essays that discuss the subject. W. A. Speck's entry, "The Structure of British Politics in the Mid-Eighteenth Century," at page 4, says that in 1700 one in four adult men could vote, according to the most generous estimates, and that over the eighteenth century, population growth and "erosion of franchise in some constituencies" reduced eligibility "quite significantly." The entry by Donald S. Lutz, "Consent," at page 635, estimates that the voting electorate in England in the late eighteenth century was 5 to 6 percent and that "the electorate in America was about ten times the percentage of the male population, as it was in England." Finally, Rosemarie Zagarri ("Suffrage and Representation," p. 652) claims that "in seventeenth-century elections in England, no more than one-fifth of the adult male population could vote."

6. Robert A. Gross, *The Minutemen and Their World* (New York: McGraw-Hill Ryerson, 1976); Charles S. Sydnor, *Gentlemen Freeholders* (Chapel Hill: University of North Carolina Press, 1952).

7. Robert Shalhope, *Roots of American Democracy* (Boston: Twayne Publishers, 1990).

8. Beverly McAnear, "College Founding in the American Colonies, 1745–1775," *Mississippi Valley Historical Review* 42 (June 1955): 24–44.

9. Kenneth Lockridge, *A New England Town, the First Hundred Years, 1636–1736* (New York: W. W. Norton, 1970); Sydnor, *Gentlemen Freeholders*.

10. Jack P. Greene, *The Quest for Power: The Lower Houses of the Assemblies in the Southern Royal Colonies, 1689–1776* (Chapel Hill: University of North Carolina Press, 1963).

11. H. Trevor Colbourn, *The Lamp of Experience: Whig History and the Intellectual Origins of the American Revolution* (Chapel Hill: University of North Carolina Press, 1965); Bernard Bailyn, *The Ideological Origins of the American Revolution* (Cambridge: Harvard University Press, 1967); John Murrin, "The Great Inversion, or Court Versus Country: A Comparison of the Revolution Settlements in England (1688–1721) and America (1776–1816)," in J.G.A. Pocock, ed., *Three British Revolutions: 1641, 1688, 1776* (Princeton: Princeton University Press, 1980), pp. 369–453.

12. Henry F. May, *The Enlightenment in America* (New York: Oxford University Press, 1976); Eric Foner, *Tom Paine and Revolutionary America* (New York: Oxford University Press, 1976); Carl Bridenbaugh and Jessica Bridenbaugh, *Rebels and Gentlemen: Philadelphia in the Age of Franklin* (New York: Oxford University Press, 1962).

13. Meyer Reinhold, *Classica Americana: The Greek and Roman Heritage in America* (Detroit: Wayne State University Press, 1984), pp. 94–109; Howard Mumford Jones, *O Strange New World, American Culture: The Formative Years* (New York: Viking Press, 1967), pp. 227–272.

14. Edmund S. Morgan, *The Birth of the Republic, 1763–1789* (Chicago: University of Chicago Press, 1956).

15. Pauline Maier, *From Resistance to Rebellion* (New York: Alfred A. Knopf, 1972); Edward Countrymen, *A People in Revolution* (Baltimore: Johns Hopkins University Press, 1981).

16. Randolph G. Adams, *Political Ideas of the American Revolution* (Durham, NC: Trinity College Press, 1922); Samuel H. Beer, *To Make a Nation: The Rediscovery of American Federalism* (Cambridge: Harvard University Press, 1993).

17. Robert R. Palmer, *The Age of Democratic Revolutions* (Princeton: Princeton University Press, 1959), vol. 1, pp. 185–206.

18. Bailyn, *Ideological Origins*; Jack P. Greene, *Peripheries to Center* (Athens: University of Georgia Press, 1986).

19. Carl Becker, *The Declaration of Independence* (New York: Alfred A. Knopf, 1942). Many contemporaries believed that the Declaration only claimed that Americans as a group had the same right to self-government as the English people did. But already some saw in the Declaration of Independence a commitment to equality among Americans themselves. In later times, Stephen Douglas spoke for the former, Abraham Lincoln for the latter. See Wilmoore Kendall, "Equality: Commitment or Ideal," *Intercollegiate Review* 24 (Spring 1989): 25–33; Garry Wills, *Lincoln at Gettysburg* (New York: Simon and Schuster, 1992).

20. Benjamin F. Wright, *Consensus and Continuity* (Boston: Boston University Press, 1958).

21. Mary Beth Norton, *Liberty's Daughters: The Revolutionary Experience of American Women, 1750–1800* (Boston: Little, Brown, 1980); Gordon S. Wood, *Creation of the American Republic, 1776–1787* (Chapel Hill: University of North Carolina Press, 1969).

22. Merrill Jensen, *The New Nation: A History of the United States During the Confederation, 1781–1789* (New York: Alfred A. Knopf, 1950), p. 424.

23. Morgan, *Birth of the Republic*, pp. 113–128. For a spirited defense of government under the Confederation, see Merrill Jensen, *The New Nation*, especially part 5, pp. 347–421.

24. Stanley M. Elkins and Eric McKitrick, "The Founding Fathers: Young Men of the Revolution," in *Political Science Quarterly* 76 (June 1961): 181–216.

25. Cecelia M. Kenyon, "Men of Little Faith: The Anti-Federalists on the Nature of Representative Government," *William and Mary Quarterly*, 3d ser., 12 (January 1955): 3–46; Jackson Turner Main, *Political Parties Before the Constitution* (Chapel Hill: University of North Carolina Press, 1973).

26. For a lively discussion of the 1787 convention, see Forrest McDonald, *The American Presidency: An Intellectual History* (Lawrence: University Press of Kansas, 1994), pp. 160–181. His chapter also contains an excellent bibliography on the convention in its extensive footnotes.

27. Forrest McDonald, *The Intellectual World of the Founding Fathers*, paper delivered as the Sixteenth Jefferson Lecture in the Humanities, Washington, DC, May 6, 1987, and his *American Presidency*, pp. 12–159.

28. Russell Kirk, "What Did Americans Inherit from the Ancients?" *Intercollegiate Review* 24 (Spring 1989): 46.

29. *The Federalist* No. 65 (New York: Random House, 1937), p. 428.

30. Beer, *To Make a Nation*, pp. 381, 383, 386.

31. Catherine Drinker Bowen, *Miracle at Philadelphia* (Boston: Little, Brown, 1966), p. xii.

32. Thomas Dye and L. Harmon Ziegler, *The Irony of Democracy* (Monterey, CA: Brooks/Cole Publishers, 1987).

33. Bowen, *Miracle*, p. 4.

34. Ralph Barton Perry, *Puritanism and Democracy* (New York: Vanguard Press, 1944), pp. 131–133.

35. Morton Borden, ed., *The Antifederalist Papers* (East Lansing: Michigan State University Press, 1965).

36. John P. Roche, "The Founding Fathers: A Reform Caucus in Action," *American Political Science Review* 55 (December 1961): 799–816.

37. Roche, "The Founding Fathers," pp. 799–816; Clinton Rossiter, *1787: The Grand Convention* (New York: W. W. Norton, 1987), pp. 257–273.

38. Stanley Elkins and Eric L. McKitrick, *The Age of Federalism: The Early American Republic, 1788–1800* (New York: Oxford University Press, 1993), p. 451.

39. David P. Szatmary, *Shays' Rebellion: The Makings of an Agrarian Insurrection* (Amherst: University of Massachusetts Press, 1980); Thomas P. Slaughter, *The Whiskey Rebellion: Frontier Epilogue to the American Revolution* (New York: Oxford University Press, 1986); McDonald, *The American Presidency*, pp. 147–151.

40. Richard B. Hofstadter, *The Idea of a Party System: The Rise of Legitimate Opposition in the United States, 1780–1840* (Berkeley: University of California Press, 1969); Paul Goodman, "The First American Party System," in William Nisbet Chambers and Walter Dean Burnham, eds., *American Party Systems* (New York: Oxford University Press, 1967), pp. 56–89; Lance Banning, ed., *After the Constitution: Party Conflict in the New Republic* (Belmont,CA: Wadsworth Publishing, 1989); Elkins and McKitrick, *Age of Federalism*.

41. William Nisbet Chambers, *Political Parties in the New Republic, 1787–1809* (New York: Oxford University Press, 1963), uses the Weberian model of traditional, charismatic,

and rational/legal authority to frame this study of political parties. See also James Thomas Flexner, *Washington: The Indispensable Man* (Boston: Little, Brown, 1969); Stephen G. Kurtz, *The Presidency of John Adams: The Collapse of Federalism, 1795–1800* (New York: A. S. Barnes, 1957); Marshall Smelser, *The Democratic Republic, 1801–1815* (New York: Harper and Row, 1968).

42. Edward S. Corwin, *The Constitution of the United States of America: Analysis and Interpretation* (Washington, DC: U.S. Government Printing Office, 1953), p. 556.

43. Corwin, *Constitution*, p. 558.

44. Donald O. Dewey, *Marshall Versus Jefferson: The Political Background of* Marbury v. Madison (New York: Alfred A. Knopf, 1970); Richard E. Ellis, *The Jeffersonian Crisis: Courts and Politics in the Young Republic* (New York: Oxford University Press, 1971); Francis N. Stites, *John Marshall: Defender of the Constitution* (Boston: Little, Brown, 1981); R. Kent Newmyer, *The Supreme Court Under Marshall and Taney* (Arlington Heights, IL: Harlan Davidson, 1968); John A. Garraty, ed., *Quarrels That Shaped the Constitution* (New York: Harper and Row, 1964).

45. F. Thornton Miller, *Juries and Judges Versus the Law: Virginia's Provincial Legal Perspective, 1783–1828* (Charlottesville: University Press of Virginia, 1994), argues that in Virginia, and perhaps in the rest of the South, the states' rights tradition lived on.

46. Richard P. McCormick, "Political Development and the Second Party System," in Chambers and Burnham, eds., *American Party System*, pp. 90–116; Robert V. Remini, *The Jacksonian Era* (Arlington Heights, IL: Harlan Davidson, 1989); Richard B. Hofstadter, *The American Political Tradition and the Men Who Made It* (New York: Alfred A. Knopf, 1948), pp. 45–67.

47. Douglas J. Amy, *Real Choices/New Voices: The Case for Proportional Representation Elections in the United States* (New York: Columbia University Press, 1993).

48. Stuart Bruchey, *The Roots of American Economic Growth, 1607–1861: An Essay in Social Causation* (New York: Harper and Row, 1968), Stanley Lebergott, *The Americans: An Economic Record* (New York: W. W. Norton, 1984), and George Rogers Taylor, *The Transportation Revolution, 1815–1860* (New York: Holt, Rinehart, and Winston, 1951), address economic changes; Richard D. Brown, *Modernization*, pp. 122–158, and his *Knowledge Is Power: The Diffusion of Information in Early America, 1700–1865* (New York: Oxford University Press, 1989), pp. 160–196, 218–244, Nancy F. Cott, *The Bonds of Womanhood: "Women's Sphere" in New England, 1780–1835* (New Haven: Yale University Press, 1977), Carl F. Kaestle, *Pillars of the Republic: Common Schools and American Society, 1780–1860* (New York: Hill and Wang, 1983), and James M. McPherson, *Ordeal By Fire: The Civil War and Reconstruction* (New York: Alfred A. Knopf, Inc., 1982), pp. 5–22, discuss modernization.

49. Gordon Wood, *The Radicalism of the American Revolution* (New York: Alfred A. Knopf, 1992).

SUGGESTIONS FOR FURTHER READING

Excellent anthologies that survey the spectrum of interpretations of the American Revolution and the constitution-making era include George Athan Billias, ed., *The American Revolution: How Revolutionary Was It?* (Fort Worth, TX: Holt, Rinehart, and Winston, 1990); Stephen G. Kurtz and James H. Hutson, eds., *Essays on the American*

Revolution (New York: W. W. Norton, 1973); and Gordon S. Wood, ed., *The Confederation and the Constitution: The Critical Issues* (Boston: Little, Brown, 1973). Peter S. Onuf, "Reflections on the Founding: Constitutional Historiography in Bicentennial Perspective," *William and Mary Quarterly* 46 (April 1989): 341–375, is a brilliantly written review of recent studies of the Constitution.

Bernard Bailyn and Gordon S. Wood sparked scholarly debate about republican ideas and institutions with their influential studies in the 1960s. Bailyn's *The Ideological Origins of the American Revolution* (Cambridge: Harvard University Press, 1967), and *The Origins of American Politics* (New York: Alfred A. Knopf, Inc., 1968), argue that the makers of the American Revolution saw the events of their day from a republican tradition that emphasized civic responsibilities and civic virtues against the corrupting influences of consolidated political authority in alliance with military power, financial interests, and personal ambition. Wood followed with a monumental study of republican thought, *The Creation of the American Republic, 1776–1787* (Chapel Hill: University of North Carolina Press, 1969). In "A Symposium of Views and Reviews," in the *William and Mary Quarterly*, 3d ser., 44 (July 1987): 550–640, contributors assessed Wood's republican synthesis. They made clear that Bailyn and Wood have not converted everyone. Scott Douglas Gerber, *To Secure These Rights: The Declaration of Independence and Constitutional Interpretation* (New York: New York University Press, 1995), offers a recent critique and an alternative conceptual framework based on natural law.

To examine relevant documents, students may look to Merrill Jensen, ed., *Tracts of the American Revolution, 1763–1776* (Indianapolis, IN: Bobbs-Merrill, 1967); J. R. Pole, ed., *The American Constitution for and Against: The Federalist and Anti-Federalist Papers* (New York: Hill and Wang, 1987); and Michael Kammen, *The Origins of the American Constitution: A Documentary History* (New York: Penguin Books, 1987).

Recent studies well worth examining are Samuel H. Beer, *To Make a Nation: The Rediscovery of American Federalism* (Cambridge: Harvard University Press, 1993), which examines the origins of federalism; Stanley Elkins's and Eric McKitrick's magisterial *The Age of Federalism: The Early American Republic, 1788–1800* (New York: Oxford University Press, 1993), which offers a comprehensive interpretation of the new regime established by the adoption of the Constitution; Michael Lind, *The Next American Nation: The New Nationalism and the Fourth American Revolution* (New York: The Free Press, 1995), which suggests that national identity has changed radically over time; and Forrest McDonald, *Novus Ordo Seclorum: The Intellectual Origins of the Constitution* (Lawrence: University Press of Kansas, 1985), which completes a series that began with two earlier studies on the Constitution.

See the endnotes for additional sources on particular topics.

3

GERMANY:
INTO THE STREAM OF DEMOCRACY

ROY H. GINSBERG

Who and what had the most influence in crafting German democracy, and under what domestic and international conditions did democratization occur? The Basic Law—or constitution—of the 1949 Federal Republic of Germany (FRG) bears the imprints of German democrats and the Allied governments who occupied the western zones of Germany. German democrats sought to draw on and improve upon the country's antecedent—though elusive—liberal strands, and the Allied governments sought to ensure that a democratized Germany would never again imperil Europe. Scholars debate the extent to which democratization was primarily a consequence of either Allied or indigenous action. We can never be certain, but the democratic transition did occur under Allied auspices in close coordination with German democrats, and it did result in the longest period of democratic government in German history.

For victor and vanquished alike, democratization was a response to the abuse of power by Adolf Hitler and the National Socialists (Nazis) following the demise of the Weimar Republic. The Nazis had manipulated Weimar's democratic constitution to gain and then abuse power, and postwar West Germany was then faced with the challenge of devising new methods to ensure that the laws upholding democracy would never again be used to bring it down. The surviving leaders of the prewar liberal German political class, including such anti-Nazi luminaries as Konrad Adenauer and Kurt Schumacher, proclaimed the merits of democratic governance, and in the end West Germans themselves would solidify democracy.

Many German leaders took their initial cues from Allied authorities, however, and an activist Allied occupation policy was critical to the establishment of the new Bonn Republic. The Allies demanded changes in German political practices, punished top Nazi elites, and installed a democratic political class. These steps to enforce positive change contrasted sharply with the policies of revenge or apathy chosen by the World War I victors, which had contributed to the Weimar Republic's demise. Indeed, international political and economic conditions in the wake of World War II heavily influenced the course of West German democratization.

At first, the Western Allies were in no rush. They assumed that democratization would occur over a long period, and they initiated a harsh occupation, which included an ambitious search for, and punishment of, Nazi officials. However, the coming of the cold war unexpectedly hastened the unification and independence of the western zones, shortening the occupation and democratic incubation periods. As the Soviets barred democratization in the eastern zone and the Western Allies feared Soviet hegemony over a unified Germany, the West backed off previous commitments to keep Germany whole. The establishment of a democratic republic in the west became a geostrategic priority—a bulwark against the spread of communism. By 1949, Germany had become a victim of the cold war and was divided into two states: one communist—the German Democratic Republic (GDR) in the east—and one democratic—the FRG in the west.

Although international political conditions hastened the creation of the FRG, domestic and international economic conditions were conducive to—perhaps instrumental in—the democratic transition and consolidation. Without the FRG's economic miracle, or *Wirtschaftswunder*, coupled with the wider economic recovery of Western Europe in which millions of Germans and Europeans enjoyed substantial increases in their standards of living following the ravages of depression and war, the Bonn Republic might have suffered the consequences of economic turmoil that had contributed to the fall of the Weimar Republic. The unprecedented prosperity of the 1950s enabled many citizens to associate economic well-being with democracy and helped put Germany into the stream of democracy after the war.

AUTHORITARIAN AND LIBERAL TRADITIONS: GERMANY BEFORE 1918

Germany experienced authoritarian rule in the Confederation (1815–1870) and in the Second Empire (1871–1918) until the Weimar Republic was established in 1919. During these years, however, some liberal inroads were made that provided the Weimar Republic with a legacy—albeit partial and weak—of democratic behavior. In the early nineteenth century, for example, when the German states were dominated by Napoleonic France, Prussian serfs were freed and elements of self-government were permitted in Prussian cities. Such democratic reforms vanished, however, with Napoleon's defeat in 1814.[1] The 1815 Congress of Vienna ended Napoleonic rule and tied thirty-eight Germanic states in a loose German Confederation.

The Confederation was dominated by conservative rulers who blocked the kinds of liberal reforms that were occurring elsewhere in Western Europe. The Confederation's legislature (Federal Diet)—comprising appointees from the member states—coordinated common policies but was not empowered to legislate. It was used to "suppress the liberal-national movement whenever it lifted its head."[2] For a short time following the liberal revolution that engulfed Europe and Germany in 1848, the German princely rulers agreed to permit an all-German constituent assembly, the Frankfurt Assembly, to be convened to draft a liberal constitution. Elections to the Assembly—the first truly representative German body—were based on universal male suffrage. In the end, however, the princes feared liberalism and dissolved the parliament. The states remained authoritarian, yet some liberal reforms persisted (e.g., the election of a liberal majority to the lower house of the Prussian parliament was tolerated by the crown).[3] The Prussian state dominated the Confederation, engineered a pan-German customs union, or *Zollverein*, beginning in the 1830s, and successfully pressed for political union, which took the form of the German Empire (or *Reich*) in 1871.

Authoritarianism coupled with federalism and a small dose of democracy were provided for by the new constitution. The various states, or *Länder*, had internal autonomy and administered federal law, but their princes, not the citizens, were sovereign. A few liberals found their way into some of the *Länder* parliaments but they had little power. The central *Reich* organs were responsible for foreign affairs and defense. Federal laws were binding on all citizens. *Länder* princes were represented in the lawmaking, Prussian-dominated Federal Council (*Bundesrat*). Delegates were appointed and instructed by the twenty-five *Länder* governments.

The Prussian king was *Reich* emperor or *Kaiser* (head of state) and appointed (and dismissed) the chancellor (head of government), irrespective of the legislature; thus the chancellor was responsible to the emperor. The *Kaiser* also influenced the passage of legislation because he could rely on the Prussian vote in the *Bundesrat*. With elections based on universal manhood suffrage, the Federal Diet or *Reichstag* was the only democratic representative body, but it was a "strangely democratic island in an authoritarian environment."[4] Its consent was required for legislation and the federal budget, but the *Reichstag* controlled neither the *Reich* ministries nor the chancellery—both were subject to imperial appointments. Since the *Reichstag* had no hold over the head of government and had little control in terms of *Reich* policy, political opposition in the parliament was "pointless."[5]

The *Reich* allowed but controlled political parties: for example, the Social Democratic Party of Germany (SPD); the Center (Catholic) Party; and the National Liberal Party. Fearful of the rise to power of the workers, Chancellor Otto von Bismarck suppressed the SPD after 1878. Although democratic liberalism did not exist nationally, a "democratic sphere of life" flourished at the local level: "Towns were a breeding place of democracy."[6] The strains between authoritarianism and liberalism continued until World War I broke out. With Germany's defeat in World War I, Kaiser Wilhelm II abdicated in 1918, and the empire was replaced by the Weimar Republic.

DEMOCRACY AND TOTALITARIANISM: 1918–1945

The Weimar Republic (1919–1933) was born out of the empire's defeat. Following elections, a constitutional assembly adopted a democratic constitution in 1919. Bad luck stalked Weimar even though its constitution was among Europe's most progressive.[7] Stigmatized by the Versailles Treaty's harsh and humiliating settlement imposed by the victorious Allies, particularly France and Britain, Weimar remained weak and divided at home and isolated abroad. The international depression that hit in 1929 fueled extremist/nationalist fervor, particularly helping the Nazis (the National Socialist German Workers' Party), which under Hitler exploited both nationalist and economic grievances. The Nazis' percentage of the parliamentary vote increased from 2.6 percent (twelve seats in the 577-seat *Reichstag*) in the 1928 elections to 18.3 percent (107 seats) in 1930 and to 37.8 percent (230 seats) in 1932. Within months of Hitler's appointment as the chancellor of Germany in 1933, all opposition was eliminated, the republic was overthrown, Germany abrogated its commitments under Versailles, and the Third Reich (1933–1945) was instituted. (It was Hitler's invasion of Poland that triggered World War II in 1939; Germany was defeated by Allied forces in 1945, the Third Reich collapsed, and the victorious Allies occupied Germany and set up military governments.)

Weimar's constitution had provided for a federal democratic republic that wove together strands of liberal ideas from Germany's political past. Civil liberties were codified, and women were given voting rights. The *Reichsrat*—upper house of parliament—consisted of deputies who were appointed by parliamentary governments of the *Länder*. The *Reichstag*—lower house—consisted of delegates popularly elected from party slates on the basis of pure proportional representation.[8] The *Reichstag* had lawmaking and budgetary powers and could give consent to, or force the resignation of, the chancellor and/or individual ministers. The chancellor was head of cabinet and ran the federal government.

The president, popularly elected (for a seven-year term) and politically independent of the *Reichstag* (members there were elected to four-year terms), had significant defense and foreign policy powers. The constitution gave the president the power to appoint or dismiss chancellors and government ministers. Under emergency conditions (Article 48), the president could suspend basic rights, dissolve parliament, call for new elections, and issue decrees, as long as a cabinet minister or the chancellor countersigned such actions. Because the cabinet was responsible to the parliament, presidential actions were designed by the crafters of Weimar's constitution to have parliamentary support. However, as it turned out, the president could simply ignore a divided, weak, and acquiescent *Reichstag*. The latter had the power to revoke presidential decrees but could also demur.

What went wrong with Weimar? The republic faced huge difficulties, including a political culture torn between liberalism and authoritarianism, the punitive measures of the Versailles Treaty, the hostility or ambivalence of the Western powers toward the new German democracy, and the impact of the depression. These problems became insurmountable when combined with the built-in constitutional flaws of the new democracy.

The founders gave too much power to the presidency, an office designed to guard—not undermine—the constitution. The president was expected to stand above parochial politics. In reality, however, power accrued to President Paul von Hindenburg because the *Reichstag* remained divided and coalition governments lasted only a few months or less. With constant government turnovers, there was a vacuum of political leadership. Parliament was quick to bring down governments but took no responsibility to ensure the formation of successor coalitions. By the early 1930s, the president was ruling by decree and dismissing or appointing chancellors on his own. Ironically, his emergency powers under Article 48 opened the way to dictatorship when, in fact, they were designed to protect democracy. Thus, Weimar failed to produce a balance between the parliament and the president because the executive was given too much power. In the end, the chancellor was responsible to the president, not parliament. Representative democracy suffered and then died.

Political parties pursued highly parochial interests and the body politic splintered into small, ungovernable pieces. Weimar operated like a "caricature of the politics of the Kaiser's Germany in which each group had a vision of national interest which it identified wholly with its own exclusive concerns."[9] Cooperation to form stable coalitions eluded the political parties. There were no catch-all parties to articulate and manage diverse interests, reflecting the absence of an ideological consensus. The communists and Social Democrats were unable to form a coalition of the political left strong enough to counter attacks from the right. As in 1848, the left and center—Weimar's SPD and its allies, the Center Party and the Democratic Party—scared off segments of the middle class, fearful of a socialist revolution, into the hands of nationalist extremists. Groups that had suffered financially from hyperinflation in the 1920s were receptive to Nazi rhetoric. Thus, the Social Democrats were forced to work in coalitions with the right extremists. The aristocracy, the military, industrial and employer interests, and the Protestant church all supported political parties that condoned, and later supported, the Nazi assault on democracy.[10]

An electoral system based on pure proportional representation allowed a number of small political parties into the *Reichstag*, including such reactionary and antidemocratic groups as the Nazis. Fringe parties on the far left and far right won a handful of votes and gained seats in the *Reichstag*. Even a few seats meant power in a fragmented, multiparty parliament. The major political parties depended on the smaller ones to make up parliamentary majorities to form coalition governments. Since small parties could consent to participate in the formation of a government, they could also pull out, causing the government to collapse. Pure proportional representation therefore magnified the power of small parties in ways that contributed to governmental instability. In the 1930 *Reichstag* elections, for example, fourteen small parties gained representation (nine received between three and thirty seats). None received 5 percent of the total vote, yet these parties participated in decisions and formed and brought down governments.[11]

The irony is that proportional representation was designed to enhance democracy but instead contributed to a surge in the number of parties, making governance highly problematic and opening the door to abusive practices of extremist groups. The FRG would fix this fundamental flaw, but for Weimar, pure proportional representation was too much democracy for too weak a democratic system.

In the end, Weimar's leaders were able to do too little to create a "national and republican iconography."[12] Weimar rejected the old but found it difficult to create a new political culture: Governments tended to avoid political confrontation and clung to the ideal of a united nation even when faced with a polarized and divided people. Entrenched authoritarian elites and their ideas were not expunged from the bureaucracy and economy: In the end, the legacy of traditional conservatism prevailed.[13]

International politics also plagued Weimar. The Versailles Treaty dictated a harsh settlement to a new democratic regime that was made to pay for the mistakes of its authoritarian predecessor. Allied policy was either hostile or ambivalent toward the fate of the new democracy. To avoid occupation or dismemberment, Weimar's founders were forced by ultimatum to sign the Versailles Treaty on June 16, 1918, thus forever associating Germany's humiliation in defeat with the new democracy. Germany was forced to accept blame for starting World War I, cede borderlands and overseas colonies, accept severe military restrictions, and pay excessive war reparations. Nationalist extremists charged the democrats with sacrificing German interests, charges that eroded the republic's legitimacy.

The Allies' harsh punishment and isolation of Germany—it was prohibited at first from joining the League of Nations—failed to take into account a valuable history lesson: Upon the defeat of France in 1815, the victorious Allies did not impose an unduly harsh settlement. France was allowed to retain its basic prewar territorial integrity, and occupation troops and war reparations were removed three years after the war ended. Although the Allies sought to ensure that France would not be in a position again to threaten the wider peace, the country was spared humiliation and was quickly able to take its place as a great power. The Allies thus recognized that they needed France to maintain the overall balance of power. Imperial Germany failed to remember this lesson of balance-of-power politics when it humiliated France in the Franco-Prussian War of 1870–1871, annexed French provinces, and otherwise imposed an unduly harsh settlement.

French revenge was played out in the harsh settlement imposed on Germany after World War I, and German revenge against France was played out in the Nazi invasion of France in 1940.

The victorious World War I Allies were not committed to Germany's democratic transition during the interwar years: France was hostile, Britain aloof, and the United States isolationist. The absence of the United States from both the League of Nations and the implementation of the Versailles settlement left Weimar to face the wrath of historical European hatreds. Unlike the situation after World War II—when the Western Allies would physically occupy entire zones, put democratic reforms into effect, seek to purge leaders of the disgraced old regime, and oversee and approve the drafting of a democratic constitution—Weimar's inexperienced, outnumbered, and outmaneuvered democrats were left alone to face hostility at home and abroad. The harsh results of Versailles were compounded by the 1929 depression, which caused widespread economic misery as inflation and unemployment soared out of control—conditions seized upon with glee by the Nazis. In 1930, the Nazi Party, buoyed by proportional representation and widespread economic misery, began to exceed the electoral support of the SPD.

The end of Weimar came on January 30, 1933, the day von Hindenburg replaced the previous chancellor with Hitler. Although the Nazis were the largest party in the *Reichstag*, they did not have a parliamentary majority. Thus, Hitler at first presided over a coalition government. His party was in control of key government ministries—the Prussian police and the propaganda agencies—that aided him in his subsequent coup. Article 48 enabled him (with Hindenburg's support) to issue emergency decrees to arrest and silence his opposition. The Nazis still did not receive sufficient support to form a government without coalition partners in the March 1933 parliamentary elections. However, the *Reichstag* soon passed the Enabling Act with the support of all major political parties but the SPD, turning its powers over to Hitler and his cabinet. Within a few months, Hitler was ruling by decree and had outlawed opposition. The Nazi victory was achieved by default rather than by revolution.[14]

Hitler moved quickly to eliminate his opposition, using imprisonment and death, and shut down the *Reichstag*. By July 1933, all *Länder* and federal institutions and schools were purged of non-Nazis, and free trade unions and open political parties were eventually outlawed. Hindenburg's death removed the last obstacle to Hitler's full control, as he merged the offices of chancellor and president to complete his coup. The persecution leading to the annihilation of the Jews and others followed. Hitler and his supporters then went on to terrorize and imprison German Jews, Gypsies, and homosexuals, branding them internal enemies, and in 1942 they embarked on the "Final Solution"—the systematic elimination of European Jewry—and the elimination or mass murder of other ethnic groups disdained by the Nazis under their occupation.

Between 1935 and 1939, Hitler remilitarized the Rhineland, rearmed Germany, and annexed Austria, all in contravention of Versailles. In 1939, he invaded

Czechoslovakia after having promised France and Britain in the 1938 Munich Agreement that he would not do so if they agreed to permit him to take the Sudetenland. The Western powers' policy of appeasement to avoid war ultimately failed, and they declared war on Germany following Hitler's invasion of Poland on September 1, 1939, thus beginning World War II. Hitler's invasion of Russia in 1941 soon required Germany to fight a two-front war. Defeats in Russia during 1942–1943 and the arrival of the Americans and the Allies from the south and west in 1943–1944 (the Italian campaign and the invasion of Normandy) then forced the Germans to retreat. They faced defeat in 1944, and in 1945 the Allies triumphed; Hitler committed suicide as Russian and Allied forces closed in on his Berlin headquarters.

DESTRUCTION AND RENEWAL: ALLIED OCCUPATION, 1945–1949

The major wartime Allies—the United States, the United Kingdom, and the Soviet Union—were unable to agree on how to govern Germany after its surrender on May 8, 1945. At the February 1945 Yalta Conference, they had agreed to divide Germany into occupation zones once it had been defeated. The capital was to be moved to Bonn and the former capital, Berlin, would also be divided into three occupation zones. At war's end, the Soviets occupied the eastern part of Germany, the Americans and British the western part. France was later given an occupation zone carved out of the two western zones, and the three Western Allies also controlled sections of Berlin, far inside the Soviet zone. At the July–August 1945 Potsdam Conference, there was no agreement on how to construct a new German polity; thus, military governors continued to retain sovereignty in each of the occupation zones. The Soviets wanted a unified, centralized, and neutralized Germany, which the Americans feared would be susceptible either to Soviet hegemony or to a resurgence of Nazi power. The Americans and British wanted a federal republic with power divided between central and state governments. The French, not present at Potsdam, preferred strong *Länder* and a weak national government, no doubt reflecting their interests in maintaining control and influence in the Saar and Ruhr regions.

The Potsdam participants did agree to treat Germany as a single economic unit and to establish an Allied Control Council to oversee interzonal transport, finance, industry, and foreign trade. Each occupier was permitted to extract war reparations from its own zone; however, the Soviets were permitted to extract certain reparations from the western zones as additional indemnification. All agreed to disarm the military (demilitarization), to try to punish Nazi leaders and officials for war crimes (denazification), to reeducate the masses and reorient the political culture in the ways of democracy (democratization), and to strip Germany of the industrial capacity to wage war (decartelization). Despite postwar meetings that attempted to solve the German problem, no peace treaty ever ended the war and provided for Germany's future. Such a treaty came only when the old wartime Allies relinquished their residual occupation rights and confirmed the unification of the two Germanies in the November 1990 Paris Charter.

Heavy on the minds of the Western occupation powers in 1945 was the need to avoid the mistakes of the victorious Allies in their treatment of the Weimar Republic in 1919. This time, Allied occupation policy oversaw and approved the drafting of a new democratic constitution, provided substantial economic reconstruction aid, and created a framework for regional economic integration and reconciliation—all crucial factors in the founding of the new Bonn Republic. Still, any hope that the wartime Allies would reach an accord on the future of Germany was dashed by the growing differences between Washington and Moscow over each other's European actions.

The Basic Law was formulated rapidly. Once the Western Allies determined that a relationship based on mutual trust was not possible with the Soviets, the crucial steps leading to West German statehood began.[15] In London on June 4, 1947, the foreign ministers of the United States, Britain, France, Belgium, the Netherlands, and Luxembourg recommended the terms of the political framework under which the western occupation zones were to unify into what would become the FRG and asked the minister-presidents of the *Länder* in those zones to form a Parliamentary Council to draft a constitution. In Bonn on September 1, 1948, the Parliamentary Council, whose members were chosen by *Länder* parliaments, produced a draft subject to the foreign ministers' overall guidelines, after having made several revisions based on compromises among members and between members and the military governors. On May 12, 1949, the military governors approved the final draft. All the *Länder* (save Bavaria) approved the Basic Law. The Occupation Statute, establishing the terms of Allied occupation rights in the new state, entered into force. On May 23, 1949, the Parliamentary Council ratified the Basic Law, and on August 14, 1949, the first parliamentary elections were held.

Impact of International Politics and Economics

Within a year of Potsdam, cooperation among the wartime Allies unraveled, with dire implications for Germany. The forced merger in 1946 of the Social Democrats with the Communist Party in Soviet-occupied East Germany mirrored a trend throughout Eastern Europe: the forced consolidation of communist rule. These moves help to explain why the Western Allies sought to unify their occupation zones into a single West German state despite the Yalta and Potsdam commitments.

In 1946, the British and Americans concluded that: war reparations and deindustrialization were bound to impoverish Germany and lead to political instability and thus ought to end; the separate zones were not economically viable and ought to be integrated; and interzonal monetary union and the elimination of trade barriers would hasten economic reconstruction and thus contribute to democratization. Concerned about the high cost of subsidizing their zone while the Soviets were squeezing war reparations not only out of their own zone but out of the western zones as well, the U.S. military government of the U.S. zone of occupation ceased deliveries of reparations to the Soviet Union in spring 1946.[16] By 1948, the British and American zones were brought together in an economic and monetary union.

For their part, the Soviets were horrified by Western monetary union, which they viewed as inconsistent with the wartime Allies' policy of keeping Germany whole in lieu of a final settlement. Their response, the land blockade of West Berlin from June 1948 to March 1949, was met by a massive U.S. airlift of food and medicine to the beleaguered West Berliners. The U.S. aid endeared the Americans and the West to a generation of Germans who saw them as their defenders. The Soviet threat gave the West Germans and Western Allies a common enemy around which to press for a West German state. Soviet actions put democratization in a positive light in contrast to the totalitarianism of the East. The blockade was an important factor in the creation of the Federal Republic of Germany (also known as the FRG or West Germany) in 1949. The Soviets responded immediately with the creation of the German Democratic Republic (the GDR or East Germany). Thus, the German nation was divided into two hostile states—victims of the cold war.

The 1947 Truman Doctrine (U.S. offers of military assistance to countries under communist threat) and the 1948–1953 Marshall Plan (U.S. economic aid to hasten reconstruction and thus strengthen the European democracies against communism) were implemented with the idea that an independent, democratic, and economically reconstructed West German state would form the western bulwark against the spread of Soviet power in Europe. Marshall Plan aid was contingent on the Europeans and West Germans working cooperatively to plan and coordinate economic reconstruction projects. In the Organization of European Economic Cooperation (OEEC), the United States—impatient with centuries of European wars induced by nationalism—attempted to cultivate peaceful ties. The cold war and U.S. economic aid were powerful inducements to change. Marshall Plan aid coupled with the German economic miracle brought widespread prosperity to many West Germans. Economic growth helped Germany in its democratic transition in ways never afforded to Weimar.

The FRG became a charter member in the 1951 European Coal and Steel Community (ECSC), a coal and steel common market that took the regulation of the coal and steel industries—heavily concentrated on the Franco-German frontier and critical to any war effort—out of the hands of national authorities and placed them under supranational control. ECSC anchored West Germany in a democratic community that grew first into the European Economic Community in 1957 and then into the European Union in 1993. In addition, it validated the FRG's democratic transition in ways never envisioned during the interwar years.

The U.S. government played a crucial role in the launching of the ECSC, strongly pressing French and German politicians, industrialists, and workers to overcome mutual fears, go beyond the tired politics of Franco-German hostility, and create a new and lasting peace.

The 1950 Korean War prompted the United States and its allies in the North Atlantic Treaty Organization (NATO) to beef up their defenses in Europe by rearming the FRG. No one contemplated unilateral rearmament. Instead, West Germany would rearm as a member of the West European Union (the 1948 collective self-defense pact of the United Kingdom, France, and the Low Countries) and NATO. In exchange for abrogation of the Occupation Statute—the removal of occupation forces from all of the FRG (except West Berlin), and thereby the return of nearly all aspects of sovereignty to the West German state—the Germans were pressed to forswear the manufacture or attainment of nuclear weapons. NATO troops replaced occupation troops as West Germany was brought into the political and military framework of the Western powers. These actions precipitated a Soviet response: the creation of the Warsaw Treaty Organization with East Germany as a member. The two Germanies thus were placed on the front line of the bipolar cold war world.

These new postwar institutions anchored West Germany's democratic transition to a community of European and Atlantic democracies, contributing to democracy's success in contrast to Weimar's isolation. The FRG sought and received its western neighbors' acceptance. The subsequent process of European integration and German democratization became symbiotically linked and have remained so to the present. European integration permitted Germany to resume its place in Europe without frightening its neighbors and disturbing the peace.

Impact of the Allied Occupation

Western occupation policies and the ways in which the occupiers worked with democratic German political leaders set the stage for the drafting and approval of the Basic Law in 1948–1949. The Western Allies were insistent that Germany should not be permitted to rise again to imperil Europe, that Germany would have to exist under new constraints, and that the German people would have to reorient their political culture toward liberal and democratic practices. Ten aspects of Allied policy paved the way for the democratic transition, and all provide insights into how foreign influence was crucial in shaping and securing German democracy.[17]

First, the wartime Allies agreed at Potsdam to permit supervised local and *Länder* elections and governments. As a result, in the western zones, democracy was reestablished at local levels between 1945 and 1949, actively encouraged by the Western Allies. Initially, however, politicians, including the minister-presidents of the *Länder*, were appointees of the occupation authorities, and there were many instances where the occupation governments imposed their will, for example, by insisting on liberalization of the press and the establishment of an independent radio system—alien ideas to the authoritarian traditions of the German media.

Second, the redrawing of the *Länder* borders by the victorious Allies was deliberately crafted to weaken historic divisions and create new loyalties. For example, the Allies eliminated the old Prussian state from postwar German geography—a state that had dominated the empire, helped bring down Weimar, and then provided a stronghold for Hitler's *Reich*. Third, but closely related, the policy of demilitarization removed Prussian militaristic traditions from postwar Germany, traditions that had permeated German political culture since the eighteenth century. Whereas the Prussians had dominated the federal structure in the empire and Weimar, the federal order created in 1949 was based on equality among the constituent states. Germany developed a post-Prussian—and thus nonhegemonic—federal order, a necessary ingredient in the country's democratic transition.

Fourth, a harsh occupation policy proved unrealistic. Although U.S. President Franklin D. Roosevelt and Treasury Secretary Henry Morgenthau first sought severe treatment to send a message to Germany to mend its ways, the urgency of feeding, sheltering, and reunifying families, rebuilding infrastructure, and setting up local and regional governments by Allied-approved democrats so dwarfed the occupation governments' capacities that such an approach proved impossible. A more pragmatic occupation strategy thus evolved. To democratize Germany, the Allies needed to develop a constructive and supportive relationship with German democrats: In short, 1945 was not going to be a repeat of 1919.

Fifth, as early as 1946 it had become clear to Britain and the United States that the separate occupation zones were not economically viable. A divided, deindustrialized, and weakened Germany would pose far-reaching problems for Germany and Europe. An economically impoverished Germany would be neither conducive to democratization, nor able to form a bulwark against the spread of Soviet power. Therefore, Germany's western neighbors formed a collective self-defense pact in 1947, in part as a hedge against a resurgent Germany—a testimony to the fears that economic misery in Germany could unleash undesirable reactionary political forces. In addition, Britain and the United States concluded that economic reconstruction in their zones required the elimination of trade and monetary barriers in order to create a large single market; thus, they called for a single currency (the deutsche mark), which was achieved by 1948; this became a precursor to political union the following year. Economic integration of the western zones was seen as a means to safeguard stable democratic government.

Sixth, the democrats who sought to build popular support for the Bonn Republic benefited from the Allied presence. Aside from the humiliation of occupation, the period between 1945 and 1949 afforded political parties the opportunity to form and identify themselves as the legal opposition to the occupiers—a move accepted by the Western Allies. Parliamentary democracy was strengthened in response to, and sometimes in protest against, Allied demands, for the Western

Allies authorized the reorganization of political life one step at a time, licensing political parties and permitting local and regional elections—all under Allied supervision.

Thus, seventh, the Western Allies could keep Germans who were strongly anti-Nazi from dominating the reconstruction effort. This decision helped the Germans to reconstruct their political order without one group seeking retribution against another, a feature of the 1920s that had helped destroy Weimar. In addition, as democrats sought to create their own independent political movements, they could blame the occupiers for postwar problems rather than point to internal scapegoats or be subject to public ire themselves. Weimar had had no foreign democratic forces occupying the country to safeguard against antidemocratic behavior or shoulder the blame for hardships.

Eighth, gradual political reconstruction had merit. There were four years (1945–1949) for the transition to democracy to begin and six years (1949–1955) for the transition to be consolidated under Allied occupation before sovereignty was largely transferred back to the FRG and the occupation troops withdrawn. The West Germans were eager to be rid of their occupiers, but the foreign presence served as a safety net, giving Germany time for a gradual evolution from dictatorship to occupation to representative democracy, and this was a key to successful democratization—a luxury not afforded to Weimar.

Ninth, whereas Weimar's democrats had been blamed by the opposition for acceptance of the Versailles terms, the unconditional surrender of the Third Reich had its advantages for postwar democrats, because no one could assert that Hitler's army had been stabbed in the back by democratic groups. The 1949 government could not even be blamed for postwar scarcities: Many Germans associated their social and economic problems with the occupiers, but they associated the FRG with the economic miracle.

Tenth, wholesale denazification was soon abandoned in favor of reeducation. The Western Allies, especially the United States, had agreed that political reorientation would start with repudiation of the Nazis, and already the Nazis' defeat was a first step in discrediting them. Although the United States had begun with the idea of collective guilt—that all Germans bore responsibility for Nazi atrocities and should experience the effects of defeat as a means to educate them—this policy of punishment was soon viewed as having an adverse affect on the creation of a new democratic order. Indeed, the Allies soon realized that too many Germans were linked to the Nazis for there to be sufficient human resources to investigate, try, and punish millions of individuals on a systematic and objective basis without undermining the democratic transition.

Ultimately, the Allies decided to engage Germans in democracy rather than prompt them to equate democracy with a witch hunt, and so they identified and worked with an active minority of individual German politicians who went on to lead the German people.[18] Many Germans were hostile to the efforts to impose collective guilt, and some considered themselves victims of Nazism. Charges of selectivity and shoddy evidence began to turn denazification into a highly divisive issue. In the end, many Nazis either were not tried or were given light sentences and other mild punishments, then rehabilitated and released. The German judiciary in particular was left unscathed by denazification; indeed, the same jurists who earlier had sent the Nazis' opponents to their deaths were in positions to mete out punishment to Nazis or their collaborators in ways many have considered much too lenient.[19] This failure of denazification proved unacceptable to Nazi victims, but the Allies chose pragmatism over idealism.

Indeed, although the Allies did impose certain requirements, the Germans were given considerable room to develop their own constitutional ideas. The 1949 Occupation Statute, for example, restricted some aspects of internal lawmaking as well as many areas of foreign policy and defense policy. On other issues, however, the occupation governments relented, as during the winter of 1949, when the Western Allies accepted several SPD demands in order to hasten agreement on West German independence at the time of the Berlin crisis. Moreover, in many instances the Allies insisted on a point—for example, the federal form of government—that the Germans had planned to include anyway.

Impact of German Leaders and Political Parties

In 1945, there were scores of political and intellectual leaders and thousands of followers of Weimar democratic groups who had "somehow weathered the storm and were . . . rallying to rebuild society and state." They "rose from the catacombs of concentration camps and other hiding places"[20] to play key roles in the drafting of *Länder* constitutions, the evolution of the institutions of local and *Länder* governments, and the reconstituting of political parties—all authorized by the occupation authorities.[21] Two luminaries left indelible marks: Konrad Adenauer, of the Christian Democratic Union (CDU), and Kurt Schumacher of the Social Democratic Party (SPD.) Adenauer was the first chancellor and Schumacher the first opposition leader of the FRG in 1949. Each set the pace for the return of political pluralism in a healthy and workable form.

Echoes of Germany's troubled past marked the events that led to the revival of political parties. All three major parties had roots in the Confederation and empire but had been outlawed in the Third Reich: the CDU and its Bavarian affiliate, the Christian Social Union (CSU); the SPD; and the Free Democratic Party (FDP). Whereas their predecessors had appealed to limited constituencies—a key element in the defeat of Weimar's Social Democrats and centrists by the Nazis—their reincarnations deliberately appealed to wider electoral segments as "catch-all parties." Catch-all parties (sometimes called umbrella parties) as well as a new electoral system that kept extremist parties with small electoral shares from gaining legislative seats helped reduce the number of national political parties to just three by the 1960s. The CDU/CSU began to appeal to both Protestants and

Catholics, and the SPD, by 1959, reached out to constituents beyond its traditional labor union base. The smaller FDP played a special role as a balancer, a potential coalition partner that could moderate the policies of either large party.

Government and opposition quickly developed a healthy confrontational relationship that had eluded Weimar. The first government, a CDU-CSU-FDP coalition, was confronted by a vibrant and vocal opposition in the SPD. The SPD blamed the government for the country's problems and maintained that the SPD could handle them better, but it accepted an opposition role nonetheless. The government in turn blamed domestic ills on foreign occupation.[22] Adenauer proved to be a powerful force for democratization and independence. Father figure to millions after the war, he had been president of the upper house of the Prussian legislature and mayor of Cologne. Harassed and incarcerated by the Nazis, he was reappointed by the British to his former post in Cologne, elected chairman of the Parliamentary Council in 1948 (the body charged by the Allied foreign ministers to draft a new constitution), and became chancellor in 1949.

When the British Labor government dismissed him from his mayoral post within months of his appointment, Adenauer charged the occupiers with favoring the SPD. He then began to devise ways to give his CDU a policy identity separate from other political groups. He was adept at carving out a CDU party program in economic and foreign policy separate from that of the SPD. CDU support for a "social market economy," that is, market liberalization coupled with socially responsible government intervention, contrasted with the SPD's planned economy and proposals for nationalization, which for many came too close to the Soviet model. CDU foreign policy stressed strong cooperation with France and the West. This led to membership in Western economic and security institutions and, as a consequence, to the end of Allied occupation and the attainment of nearly all elements of sovereignty by 1955. Schumacher opposed CDU policies, claiming that Adenauer accepted a divided Germany and pandered to foreign interests. Political pluralism—with clear alternatives for the voter—had arrived in Germany.

During his time in the Parliamentary Council, Adenauer pressed for a constitution that benefited from hindsight: "In rebuilding Germany we want to learn from . . . [past] mistakes, including the errors of the Weimar constitution. We want to keep in mind specific German traits, and finally we want to avoid being unduly influenced by present conditions." He also pressed the Western Allies for an occupation statute to delineate the rights and duties of conquerors as well as conquered: "Just as the vanquished have duties they have rights too."[23] Thus was created the 1949–1955 Occupation Statute under which the Allies would retain rights to intervene in domestic and foreign affairs even after West German independence in 1949.

On behalf of the Parliamentary Council, Adenauer and the military governors communicated over various draft articles of the future Basic Law. In order to attain independence and sovereignty for his country, Adenauer had to walk a tightrope between the Allies and the SPD. The latter rejected Allied demands for any changes in the draft and for any limits placed on German sovereignty. Adenauer insisted that it was better to compromise with the occupation powers to create an imperfect Basic Law that promised sovereignty and an end to occupation, rather than to postpone statehood indefinitely. Indeed, he believed that by working with and not openly opposing the Allied military governors, and by accepting the Occupation Statute, there would be a gradual evolution toward the realization of full German sovereignty.[24] Eventually, Adenauer's policy would pay off: In 1955, the Occupation Statute was abrogated, and the FRG achieved nearly all the attributes of a sovereign state.

Kurt Schumacher, an SPD leader with close ties to the trade unions Hitler sought to eliminate, was arrested and imprisoned in 1933 and tortured at Dachau. Schumacher emerged at war's end as a nationalist and patriot who opposed collaboration with East or West. He refused to work with the Soviet communists after they forced the East German Social Democrats to merge with the East German communists—a merger that sounded the death knell for democratic government in the East. In 1946, he was elected SPD chairman at the first postwar party congress. Although he lost the race for chancellor in 1949, he then served the cause of democracy as the republic's first opposition leader. Having suffered for his beliefs by opposing Hitler, Schumacher denounced Western efforts to impose collective guilt on the Germans.[25] For example, he labeled Adenauer "the chancellor of the Allies" and was expelled from a *Bundestag* session in 1952 when he described the European Defense Community (EDC)—which the Adenauer government agreed to join before the EDC treaty was aborted in 1954—as "a naked celebration of the victory of a clerical coalition over the German people. . . . Whoever agrees to the [EDC treaty] stops being a good German."[26]

Schumacher was also a forceful player in the Parliamentary Council's deliberations on the drafting of the Basic Law. Schumacher wanted a strong, centralized state to run a socialist-based economy. In 1949, he announced that the SPD would not accept the draft Basic Law unless its demands for a more centralized state were met. He also opposed the interference of the Allied powers in West German affairs through the Occupation Statute—yet before his death in 1952, he criticized Adenauer for actions to secure the end of the occupation.[27]

After Schumacher's death, his party began to undertake reforms culminating in the 1959 Bad Godesberg Declaration. At a party conference in Bad Godesberg, the SPD, under the leadership of Willy Brandt, accepted the principles of a social market economy and integration with the West. It sought to expand its electoral base of workers to include a broader representation of the German electorate and accepted membership in Western economic and military institutions. By 1966, the party had gained sufficient support to join its first postwar government in coalition with the CDU/CSU, and in 1969, the SPD for the first time headed a coalition with its own chancellor, Willy Brandt. Despite his many failed policies and his inability to win a majority of voters to his side, Schumacher will be remembered for providing the new republic with an independent and forceful opposition and moral leadership.

CRAFTING THE NEW DEMOCRACY: PROVISIONS OF THE BASIC LAW

One hundred and one years after the 1848 liberal revolution and sixteen years after the fall of Weimar, the Basic Law was ratified. The mistakes of Germany's political past weighed heavily on the minds of the founders, and they were determined to avoid making the same errors again. Unlike the Weimar Constitution, the Basic Law forbade behavior and actions designed to destroy the state. Unlike the empire and Weimar, the FRG was crafted as a fully federal system in that the *Länder* were given the power to legislate in all areas other than those relegated to the federal government or those under concurrent jurisdiction as defined by the Basic Law. Thus, a workable balance was created between federal and *Länder* governments, allowing local autonomy but reserving sufficient powers at the center for viability.

Basic Rights and the Notion of a Militant Democracy

Civil liberties and civil rights are hallmarks of the Basic Law, but, unlike Weimar, the FRG does outlaw behavior and actions designed to destroy the state, thus making it a "militant democracy," capable of strong action to defend itself against its enemies.[28] Already in 1946–1947, the *Länder* constitutions included measures to protect basic rights but also measures to deny those rights to any person or group that sought to endanger the democratic order—in other words, they established "militant democracies." The Parliamentary Council then took a similar approach in the Basic Law: Basic rights such as freedom of speech, press, or assembly may be forfeited and political groups outlawed if they endanger the democratic order or the FRG's existence.

Nevertheless, rights are prominently incorporated into the first nineteen articles of the Basic Law. In contrast, basic rights were merely appended to the Weimar Constitution, where they were subject to change by parliamentary acts. The *Reichstag* even altered the constitution by passing laws, such as the 1933 Enabling Act, without changing the constitution's original text. The Parliamentary Council, however, required that any modifications would have to be incorporated into the text of the Basic Law, thus precluding enactment of extraconstitutional laws. Examples of rights in the Basic Law that responded to the legacy of the Nazis are found in Table 3.1.

The Parliamentary Council also declared unalterable essential parts of the Basic Law, such as the dignity of man, the inviolability of human rights, the sovereignty of the people, the federal structure, the subjection of legislation to the constitu-

TABLE 3.1 Selective Basic Rights Provisions of the Basic Law

Article	Provision	Role of Legacy
Article 1	Dignity of man is inviolable and its respect/protection is duty of the state	Nazis grossly violated the dignity of non-Aryans and non-Nazis
Article 2	Right to life and the inviolability of each persons freedom	Nazis killed 6 million Jews and many other ethnic/disadvantaged opposition groups
Article 3	Equality before the law: discrimination prohibited over parentage, race, faith, origin, language, or religious or political opinion	Nazis discriminated against people in all areas under Article 3
Article 4	Undisturbed religious practice guaranteed: no one may be compelled to render war service involving arms (Article 12a provides for substitute service)	Nazis destroyed Jewish synagogues; Nazi conscription was enforced
Article 5	Censorship is outlawed	Nazis controlled all media
Article 6	Every mother may claim protection/assistance from the community; illegitimate children have same opportunities as legitimate ones	Nazis discriminated against non-Aryan mothers and children
Articles 8 and 9	Freedom of peaceful assembly and of association guaranteed	Nazis outlawed unauthorized groups and assemblies, including non-Nazi trade unions and political parties
Article 13	Inviolability of the home unless pursuant to the law	Nazis forced entry into homes

TABLE 3.1 (continued)

Article 16	No one can be deprived of citizenship unless pursuant to a law; right of asylum guaranteed	Nazis stripped Jews and others of their citizenship, forcing many to escape abroad if possible
Article 17	Right of appeal to the Federal Constitutional Court if any person believes his/her rights have been violated	No such appeal allowed during the Nazi era
Article 18	Whoever abuses basic freedoms to attack the democratic order forfeits those rights as determined by the Federal Constitutional Court	There was no independent and free judiciary during the Nazi era to protect the republic against its enemies

tion, and the subjection of the executive and the judiciary to the law. Finally, in response to the Nazis' mass executions, the Basic Law prohibits capital punishment.

Electoral and Party Systems

To give democracy a better chance, the framers of the Basic Law deliberately rejected a number of features from the Weimar Constitution. For example, they created an electoral system in which half of the deputies in the *Bundestag* are elected on the basis of proportional representation and the other half, on the basis of single member districts, in which the successful candidate must win a plurality of votes. Under proportional representation, the voter selects a party slate, and the winners represent a political party; in single-member districts, the voter chooses a candidate from a specific election district, and the winner represents that constituency. Each German citizen thus casts two votes, one for a party and one for an individual candidate.

No electoral system is perfect. Pure proportional representation failed in Weimar when it gave small parties a chance to gain parliamentary representation and produced a fragmented multiparty system. Single-member districts discriminate against smaller parties that may have support nationwide but cannot win a plurality in any one district. The framers of the Basic Law in 1949 tried to avoid the pitfalls of either electoral system. Later, to restrict the number of parties still further and keep extremist parties out, the 1956 Federal Election Law required parties to poll at least 5 percent of the national proportional representation vote or win three electoral districts. As a result of these restrictions, the FRG has had a "two and one-half" party system, as either the CDU/CSU or the SPD, usually in coalition with the tiny FDP, has been able to form a government at the federal level.

Executive, Legislative, and Judicial Powers

Again in response to the Weimar experience, the framers took deliberate steps to weaken the presidency. The federal president, as head of state, has neither the popular mandate nor the political power of his Weimar predecessor. He is elected by a Federal Convention of representatives from the federal and *Länder* parliaments for a five-year term and may be reelected once. In contrast to his Weimar predecessor, he may not dismiss the chancellor, he has no independent emergency powers, and he is not commander in chief of the armed forces. The Basic Law gives these powers to the federal chancellor and the government, who are indirectly accountable to the people because they must obtain and keep majority support in the *Bundestag*. The Basic Law bestows mainly symbolic and ceremonial powers upon the president.

The president does appoint the federal chancellor, but that individual must be confirmed by a majority in the *Bundestag*. If the nominee fails to obtain a majority, the parliamentary parties propose another candidate, but any candidate must obtain majority support. Thus, the appointment power is largely honorific unless the parliament is unable to reach agreement on forming a new government. In that case, the president has significant influence in aiding the formation of a new government. Although the president may have a party affiliation, this officeholder is expected to rise above parochial politics and consider the good of the nation as a whole.

Real power under the Basic Law resides in the federal chancellor. Thus, the legitimacy of the head of government and the other ministers is rooted not in the presidency, as it was in Weimar, but in the legislature. The majority party or coalition of parties in the *Bundestag* must support the chancellor and the government in order to pass legislation and remain in power. Only the chancellor can appoint or dismiss individual ministers. The chancellor forms and heads the government and is responsible for formulating and executing general policy. The majority of bills originate in the federal government, which is headed by the chancellor and his cabinet. The chancellor may dissolve parliament at any time and call for new elections by asking the president to do so. The chancellor is commander in chief during wartime, and the minister of defense is commander during peacetime. The chancellor heads the federal bureaucracy.

Article 67 of the Basic Law empowers the *Bundestag* to remove the chancellor through a "constructive" vote of no confidence, that is, only if the majority of *Bundestag* members simultaneously elect a successor and submit a request to the president for the dismissal of the chancellor. The president must comply with the request and appoint the person elected. This puts the onus of responsibility on the *Bundestag* to reach a consensus on a new head of government first, before dismissing the existing one. This "constructive" vote of no confidence contrasts sharply with the *Reichstag*'s regular votes of no confidence in sitting governments during the Weimar years when the *Reichstag* had failed to accept responsibility for providing a successor to a government that it failed to support. The absence of a constructive vote of no confidence in Weimar led in time to a presidential form of government followed by the Nazi coup. Only rarely in the FRG's history has a sitting government been subjected to a successfully orchestrated constructive vote of no confidence (the first was in 1972). As a result, coalition governments have been more stable and yet responsive to parliament.

The Basic Law does not provide for the removal of individual ministers from the chancellor's cabinet by a vote of no confidence. If the *Bundestag* is unhappy with one or several ministers, it must vote no confidence in the whole government. This has avoided the problem in Weimar of attempts to diminish the chancellor's authority by censuring a member of his own government.

The crafters of the FRG set up two chambers, the *Bundesrat* and the *Bundestag*, both with precedents going back to the empire and Weimar. As the upper house, the *Bundesrat* was designed to provide for the interests of the *Länder* and to be a counterweight to the central government. The *Bundesrat* has the right of legislative initiative and must approve any laws that directly affect the specific rights reserved by the Basic Law to the states (e.g., education, police matters, and state finances). The *Bundesrat* also must approve any laws affecting *Länder* borders, proposed constitutional amendments, and national emergencies. Its members are appointed by the executive branches of the *Länder*, and they vote on the basis of instructions from their home governments. In contrast, the party-based *Bundestag* deputies are elected by the people. All bills must be passed by the *Bundestag* before they become federal law, and *Bundestag* members may question government ministries in written and oral form. The *Bundestag* elects the federal chancellor and supplies the government with a working majority.

In sum, the *Länder* are represented in the *Bundesrat*, and the people are represented in the *Bundestag*. The central government must take into account the interests of the states, and the states must submit to the requirements of the central government in order to provide for the security and well-being of the federation. For the first time in German political history, a constitution substantially increased the powers of parliament and also gave the *Länder* a strong voice in national decisionmaking, thus contributing to a healthier balance between executive and legislative authority and between state and central authority than had been achieved in previous German federations. The wartime Allies dissolved the Prussian state in 1945, thus removing a long-standing impediment to democratic federalism, and the newly created *Länder* provided for a much more balanced collection of individual states than had existed during the previous century.[29] The *Länder* are competent in all fields other than those of exclusive and concurrent jurisdiction as defined by the Basic Law.

The Federal Constitutional Court also acts as a counterweight to central authority. One-half of the federal judges are elected by the *Bundestag*, the other half by the *Bundesrat*. Following a U.S. suggestion, the concept of judicial review was embodied in the Basic Law. Thus, the Federal Constitutional Court, much like its U.S. Supreme Court counterpart, is given the sole power to review the constitutionality of all laws. The Federal Constitutional Court interprets the Basic Law in jurisdictional disputes between constitutional organs or between the Federal and *Länder* governments; it decides on the constitutionality of laws; it rules on the forfeiture of basic rights by individuals and on the constitutionality of political parties; and it acts as an appeals court for disputed elections to the *Bundestag* and as a high court to try the president if impeached.

Conclusion: Germany's Democratic Transition

In its democratic transition, Germany did not suddenly discover democratic practices for the first time: As the Basic Law was being drafted, the founders drew on the limited democratic experiences of the empire and on the mistakes of Weimar for lessons and insights. The Bonn Republic derived from the empire its federal form, bicameral legislature, and liberal suffrage rules. Even though the *Kaiser's*

Germany discriminated against parties, the FRG's three main political parties originated in the empire. In addition, the empire's Federal Council was a forerunner of today's *Bundesrat* and its *Reichstag,* of today's *Bundestag.*

The 1949 Basic Law can also trace some of its features to Weimar, especially to the mistakes made in the Weimar constitution. In the Bonn Republic, presidential powers were drastically reduced, and the chancellor became the dominant political figure. His power relative to the *Bundestag* increased with the introduction of the constructive vote of no confidence, but he remained responsible to the legislature rather than to the president. Civil liberties were protected against legislative infraction, yet the democracy was allowed to defend itself against internal enemies.

The weakness of Weimar's political parties and the Nazi antiparty dictatorship had discredited democratic politics and political parties. Cabinet crises, minority governments, and strong antiparliamentary groups had paralyzed Weimar's party system, and thus the new or revamped postwar parties faced a skeptical and disaffected electorate. Nevertheless, leading parties in the post-1949 *Bundestag* have proved capable of broadening their support and shaping the coalitions necessary to form governments as pure proportional representation was replaced by a system that has made it very difficult for fringe parties to gain parliamentary representation. In addition, strong leaders such as Adenauer and Schumacher helped to create a viable, yet competitive, party system that gave voters credible alternatives. Thus, the Bonn Republic's party system has supplied the foundation for a stable democracy.[30]

Article 21 of the Basic Law stipulates that political parties may be freely formed, but their internal organization must conform to democratic principles, and they must publicly account for the sources of their funds. In exchange for meeting these requirements, parties that succeed in winning *Bundestag* seats receive substantial federal funding. Such support testifies to the commitment to independent political parties and their function in the democratic order. There are limits to their freedoms, however, in a "militant democracy": Parties that seek to impair or abolish the democratic order, or jeopardize the existence of the FRG, are unconstitutional. Two such parties were banned by the Federal Constitutional Court— the right-wing Socialist *Reich* Party in 1952 and the German Communist Party in 1956.

The quality of German political culture since the 1960s has been "entirely different" from what it was at the beginning of the republic and "even further removed from that of Germany in the Weimar period."[31] Education of German youth about the atrocities of the Nazis and the merits of a democratic republic has helped to replace the public detachment from politics in the 1950s with a new acceptance since the 1960s of Germany's past actions and its new democracy. In 1958, for example, the *Länder* set up a central office of ministers of justice to track down Nazi criminals, and in 1969, a federal law eliminated the statute of limitations on prosecutions for acts of genocide. During the late 1950s and 1960s, trials of Nazi death camp officials and others brought to light for millions of Germans the various Nazi atrocities in ways more effective than when the occupation authorities revealed such truths.[32] Although German judges have tended to apply very lenient sentences to those found guilty of war crimes, the trials themselves proved to be of educational value to many young Germans. Periodic desecration of Jewish cemeteries and the painting of swastikas on synagogues from the 1950s to the present have revealed lingering anti-Semitism. However, such actions have generally remained isolated, have not formed an overall pattern, and are met by widespread public condemnation. "The Bonn Republic, unlike its predecessor, has built up a reserve of cultural support which should enable it to deal with . . . future issues of the quality and extent of democracy at least as effectively as other Western democracies."[33]

One concern to students of German politics is the fear that the commitment to democracy may be predicated on economic prosperity. What would happen to German democracy if a 1930s-style depression occurred again? The question is virtually impossible to answer, but Germany's democratic institutions and practices do seem stable and firmly rooted. The economics and finance ministries and the independent *Bundesbank*, for example, are strongly committed to controlling inflation as a matter of policy (a legacy of Weimar's periods of hyperinflation), and there are other built-in procedures that make a full-scale depression very hard to envisage short of an international catastrophe. German democracy weathered various economic recessions during the 1970s and 1980s and today, in the 1990s, appears to be surmounting the huge financial and social costs of integrating 17 million East Germans into the FRG. The economic hardships associated with unification have stirred some racist rhetoric and violence, mostly leveled against non-Germans, but, as in the case of the public's response to isolated instances of anti-Semitism, racial and ethnic violence is immediately and widely condemned in the media.

The Basic Law makes Germany a militant democracy, which means that it provides for the defense of democracy from internal enemies. In retrospect, the self-defense provisions of the Basic Law have helped to protect and strengthen the new system, giving the FRG time and needed safeguards to establish itself. Removing the disgraced members of the old guard from the highest levels of public office through trial and public pressure was a necessary precondition for the democratic transition. At lower levels, however, in order to break with past political practices and inform citizens of the merits of the new order, gradual reeducation in the end proved more successful than the initial attempt to undertake a massive witch hunt for the rank-and-file functionaries of the old regime. The FRG thus tried to complement the removal of antidemocratic elements from the highest levels of politics with the education of citizens about the merits of democratic government.

Finally, an activist international presence was very helpful to indigenous German democrats; the former brought expertise, experience, and assurance to embolden the latter. International reconstruction aid was also a necessary ingredient as it enabled the FRG to gain internal legitimacy by pointing to new economic growth and development. Germany's democratic transition might have been doomed without an improvement in the economic picture for the majority of citizens. Also, the acceptance of the new democracy by neighboring democratic states helped to restore the FRG's international standing and credibility. Membership in the European Community and NATO enhanced the FRG's economic and physical security, helping to stabilize and validate democratic transition and consolidation. Democracy needs a secure regional environment within which to take root. Thus, the postwar international isolation and humiliation imposed on Weimar was avoided after World War II. The FRG's democratic successors to the Nazis were not made to pay for the mistakes of the previous regime.

German democrats drew on the country's democratic legacy, however withered and weak, and took advantage of public revulsion against the authoritarian past. A blend of international democratic standards promulgated by the Western Allies and indigenous experience with democracy worked well for the transition. Over time, the active role of outside democrats in the transition declined as homegrown democracy took root and German democrats took over. In sum, the Germans overcame enormous odds and international and domestic skepticism to establish a democracy in their country despite its authoritarian past.

CHRONOLOGY

1815–1870	German Confederation
1848	Liberal Revolution foiled
1871–1918	German Empire
1919–1933	Weimar Republic
1933–1945	Third Reich
1939–1945	World War II
1945–1955	Defeat of Germany, Allied Occupation, Reconstruction, and cold war
1945	Division of Germany; Allied occupation
1945–1949	Democracy at local levels of government established in western zones
1948	Economic and monetary union of western occupation zones; creation of Parliamentary Council of German democrats to draft constitution
1948–1949	Soviet blockade of West Berlin; U.S. airlift
1949	Basic Law and Occupation Statute entered into force; independence of Federal Republic of Germany declared; first parliamentary elections held; Konrad Adenauer elected chancellor

1950s	*Wirtschaftswunder* (the economic miracle)
1951	Entry into European Coal and Steel Community
1955	Occupation Statute abrogated; occupation forces withdrawn; admittance into the North Atlantic Treaty Organization
1958	Entry into European Economic Community and European Atomic Energy Community
1969	Election of Willy Brandt as first Social Democratic Chancellor
1989	Fall of Berlin Wall
1990	Unification of East and West Germany; removal of residual Allied occupation rights

Notes

1. William Carr, *A History of Germany, 1815–1985* (London: Edward Arnold, 1987), p. 4.

2. John H. Herz, *The Government of Germany* (New York: Harcourt Brace and World, 1972), p. 39.

3. For a useful overview of the 1848 revolution, see Carr, *A History of Germany*, ch. 2.

4. Herz, *The Government of Germany*, p. 43.

5. Herz, *The Government of Germany*, pp. 40–46.

6. Walter Stahl, ed., *The Politics of Postwar Germany* (New York: Praeger, 1953), p. 9.

7. For a good description of the rise and fall of the Weimar Republic, see Harold James, *A German Identity, 1770–1990* (New York: Routledge, 1989), ch. 5.

8. Proportional representation is an electoral system in which the number of parliamentary seats a political party receives is roughly proportional to the number of votes it receives in the election. The more seats a party receives the more influence it has over decisions and government formation.

9. James, *A German Identity*, p. 127.

10. Herz, *The Government of Germany*, pp. 52–55.

11. When a party drops out of a coalition government, the government falls, at which time either parliamentary parties attempt to form a new coalition that commands a majority, or new elections are held. Weimar's governments often lasted only a few months.

12. James, *A German Identity*, p. 122.

13. Herz, *The Government of Germany*, p. 51.

14. Herz, *The Government of Germany*, p. 60.

15. For an excellent review of this process, see chs. 2–5 in Peter H. Merkl, *The Origins of the West German Republic* (New York: Oxford University Press, 1963).

16. John F. Golay, *The Founding of the Federal Republic of Germany* (Chicago: University of Chicago Press, 1958), pp. 6–13.

17. Many of these insights are from James, *A German Identity*, pp. 177–181.

18. Herz, *The Government of Germany*, pp. 71–73.

19. Alfred Grosser, *Germany in Our Time: A Political History of the Postwar Years* (New York: Praeger Publishers, 1971), ch. 2.

20. Merkl, *The Origins of the West German Republic*, p. 20.

21. Carl-Christoph Schweitzer et al., eds., *Politics and Government in the Federal Republic of Germany: Basic Documents* (Leamington Spa, Engl.: Berg, 1984), ch. 1.

22. James, *A German Identity*, p. 183.

23. Konrad Adenauer, *Memoirs, 1945–1953* (Chicago: Henry Regnery, 1965), p. 103.

24. Adenauer, *Memoirs, 1945–1953*, p. 134.

25. Lewis Edinger, *Kurt Schumacher: A Study in Personality and Political Behavior* (London: Oxford University Press, 1965), p. 183.

26. James, *A German Identity*, p. 182.

27. Edinger, *Kurt Schumacher*, p. 185.

28. For further explanations of how the Basic Law provides for a "militant democracy," see Grosser, *Germany in Our Time*, pp. 82–85.

29. Uwe Thaysen, *The Bundesrat, the Länder, and German Federalism* (Washington, DC: American Institute for Contemporary German Studies, 1994), pp. 7–8.

30. Walter Stahl, ed., *The Politics of Postwar Germany* (New York: Praeger, 1953), p. 13.

31. William E. Paterson and Gordon Smith, eds., *The West German Model: Perspectives on a Stable State* (London: Frank Cass, 1981), p. 167.

32. Grosser, *Germany in Our Time*, pp. 217–218.

33. Paterson and Smith, *The West German Model*, p. 167.

SUGGESTIONS FOR FURTHER READING

Among the most useful and comprehensive works that cover the political development of Germany from the Confederation to the Bonn Republic, are: William Carr, *A History of Germany, 1815–1985* (London: Edward Arnold, 1987), and Harold James, *A German Identity, 1770–1990* (New York: Routledge, 1989). Notable works that cover Germany's democratic transition include John H. Herz, *The Government of Germany* (New York: Harcourt Brace and World, 1972); Walter Stahl, ed., *The Politics of Postwar Germany* (New York: Praeger, 1953); Peter H. Merkl, *The Origins of the West German Republic* (New York: Oxford University Press, 1963); John F. Golay, *The Founding of the Federal Republic of Germany* (Chicago: University of Chicago Press, 1958); and Alfred Grosser, *Germany in Our Time: A Political History of the Postwar Years* (New York: Praeger, 1971). Frank A. Ninkovich's *Germany and the United States: The Transformation of the German Question Since 1945* (Boston: Twayne, 1988), offers readers insights into the role of the United States in Germany's democratic transition. A useful collection of primary sources associated with the transition and consolidation years may be found in Carl-Christoph Schweitzer et al., eds., *Politics and Government in the Federal Republic of Germany: Basic Documents* (Leamington Spa, Engl.: Berg, 1984).

Konrad Adenauer's *Memoirs, 1945–1953* (Chicago: Henry Regnery, 1965), and Lewis Edinger's *Kurt Schumacher: A Study in Personality and Political Behavior* (London: Oxford University Press, 1965), offer invaluable insights into the formidable contributions Adenauer and Schumacher made to Germany's democratic transition.

Works that analyze Germany's democratic consolidation include Uwe Thaysen, *The Bundesrat, the Länder, and German Federalism* (Washington, DC: American Institute for Contemporary German Studies, 1994); William E. Patterson and Gordon Smith, eds., *The*

West German Model: Perspectives on a Stable State (London: Frank Cass, 1981); and Lewis J. Edinger, *West German Politics* (New York: Columbia University Press, 1986). Two new works on postwar Germany worthy of attention are: Noel Annan, *Changing Enemies: The Defeat and Regeneration of Germany* (New York: HarperCollins, 1995), and Peter Pulzer, *German Politics, 1945–1995* (New York: Oxford University Press, 1995).

4

JAPAN: FOREIGN OCCUPATION AND DEMOCRATIC TRANSITION

STEVEN A. HOFFMANN

DISCREDITED NORMS AND POLITICAL OPPORTUNITY

Japan's current parliamentary democratic system appeared when Japanese society was in a condition of partial anomie, or normlessness. The disastrous final stages of World War II, Japan's 1945 surrender, the beginning of foreign occupation, and the disarmament, demolition, and abolition of Japan's entire military system helped to discredit the militarism and extreme nationalism that had shaped the nation's political culture in the 1930s and 1940s. This absence of certain norms or values was particularly difficult for the Japanese, whose culture prescribes a rigid code of rules for each social situation. Defeated and under foreign (mainly U.S.) occupation from 1945 until 1952, the Japanese found themselves in a situation for which "social conditioning had provided no preparation."[1]

The preceding governmental system, led in the early 1940s by representatives of the military forces and civilian politicians prepared to interact with them, had been hierarchical. Sitting on top of a regulated society, the government had claimed that Japan was one large family with the divine emperor (at that time, Hirohito) at its head. One of the regime's central values was *kokutai* (national polity). The term encompassed the idea that the nation was organically tied to the monarchy and that sovereignty ultimately lay in the emperor's hands. Since 1868, Japanese governments had emphasized what might be called a sense of "traditional homogeneity,"[2] in part to counter the perceived threat posed by Western imperialism.

By the early 1940s, the Japanese government customarily maintained a sense (and reality) of permanent crisis, demanded public acquiescence, and persecuted dissent.[3] Yet, in a number of ways this was not a totalitarian regime but rather an oligarchical regime. "State institutions, while powerful, were not comprehensive in their activities, leaving many critical functions to private or civil society." Power was not centralized in one individual. The supremacy of the emperor was mainly a matter of formal constitutional legality; decisionmaking power was usually exercised by other persons acting in his name. The so-called Imperial Will was actually the consensus (ratified by the emperor and usually shared by him) of those few persons whose leadership of informal factions and military and civilian institutions, such as the cabinet and the supreme commands of the military services, placed them near the throne. The emperor himself exercised the right to question that consensus to make sure of its soundness and consistency and had room to indicate personal preferences and take some initiatives, particularly where consensus was still lacking. Cabinets were coalitions reflecting estimates of the relative strengths of political and military institutions and leaders. These estimates were made by palace officials and other advisers to the throne who wanted the cabinet to represent coalitions of elite groups that they "believed desirable for 'coping with the trends of the time.'" The palace officers and other advisers were also the persons mainly responsible for "negotiating cabinet coalitions into existence."[4]

Japanese prime minister General Hideki Tojo, whose cabinet chose to go to war with the United States, cannot be called a dictator comparable to Germany's Adolf Hitler or Italy's Benito Mussolini. He "was more the representative of the military clique that had maneuvered itself temporarily to the top." Informally, the political system had contained a "welter of rival groups" that competed with each other and formed "complex alignments and contractual obligations ramifying in various directions. . . . " Those alignments constituted "an overlapping and interlocking web." Even the controlled "Tojo election" of 1942, held when the war in the Pacific was already under way, provided only an 80 percent majority for the parliamentary candidates endorsed by the military, "a far cry from the virtually unanimous votes that truly totalitarian regimes characteristically muster."[5]

But Japan's prewar and wartime regimes had been profoundly antidemocratic. In 1940, a state-sponsored mass organization had been organized to bring Japan's multiple political parties into one body. The dominant ideology was semifascist, if not wholly so. Advocated mainly by members of the army officer corps (who often came originally from families in the economically depressed rural countryside of the 1920s and 1930s), it xenophobically decried decadent Western influences that were supposedly having deleterious effects on Japan. From the militarist perspective, a country with "puritanical, Spartan-like, native virtues" was in danger of becoming "a profit-mad, materialistic, compliant lackey of the West." To save Japan from this degrading fate, militarists called upon patriotism, nativism, Shintoism, Pan-Asianism, dreams of regional economic autarky, and other elements with great fervor. In pursuit of their ideology, militarists in the army high command had advanced their power by taking advantage of intimidation and assassination incidents staged by persons even more extreme in their views, by exploiting attempts at putsches, and through "artificially created war emergencies."[6]

A fateful step had been the 1941 appointment of Tojo as prime minister by Emperor Hirohito, who had acted on the advice of the influential Marquis Koichi Kido, who then held the politically active post of Lord Keeper of the Privy Seal in the palace bureaucracy. Kido hoped that "Tojo might try to restrain the militarists," and Tojo apparently tried initially to find a diplomatic alternative to war with the United States.[7] But he ultimately opted for war.

By the end of 1944, however, the course of the war had allowed some moderate personages of rank and distinction who had survived politically to maneuver the army extremists "out of power."[8] Although the Japanese state was still run by an oligarchical dictatorship, it contained institutions and practices capable of being used later within a democratizing process. Among them were a parliament, a cabinet, elections, and a constitutional monarchy.

CRUCIAL INDIVIDUALS: GOALS, SKILLS, AND CHOICES

Emperor Hirohito

By 1945, Hirohito's training and experience had inhibited him in his role as constitutional monarch, even though he had been politically active on various occasions during his presurrender career. He had been kept informed of the 1941 decisions that led to war, and he may have known about the plan for the Pearl Harbor attack and "even made suggestions about how to carry it out"[9]; yet he probably could not have changed the war policy even if he had opposed it. The emperor ultimately played an important role in the Japanese government's decision to accept the Allies' 1945 terms of surrender, acting to resolve an impasse in the cabinet and in the Japanese government.[10]

According to General Douglas MacArthur, the supreme U.S. commander during the occupation, one of Hirohito's concerns at their first meeting, on September 27, 1945, was to "bear sole responsibility for every political and military decision made and action taken" by the Japanese people in "the conduct of war."[11] He allegedly made this statement even though it implied that a death sentence might ultimately be passed on him. MacArthur reportedly demurred and indicated his desire that the emperor guide the Japanese people in carrying out occupation orders. If the story is accurate, this was a taste of what the U.S. commander's policy would be: to use the emperor to legitimize occupation policy and any new governmental system that the occupation would produce. The monarchy, an institution that had served to sanctify an authoritarian system, could now help to legitimate a democratic one. In addition, it could ultimately be used by Americans, and by those Japanese who were so inclined, to claim that a political and even spiritual continuity existed between the old political system and the new one.

Hirohito's own main postwar goal was to preserve the *kokutai* principle, which placed the throne at the center of any Japanese political system and preserved his own dynasty. But he was also ready to provide legitimacy to political reform. In his meeting with MacArthur, he had promised full compliance with the declaration of policy issued by the leaders of the Allied powers at the Potsdam conference a short time earlier.[12] Among other things, that declaration had spoken positively of "strengthening . . . democratic tendencies" in Japan and had set the goal of having Japan ruled by a responsible government that would be established by the demonstrated will of Japan's people.[13] The occupation would be terminated only after such a government was in place and other goals of the declaration had been attained.

On New Year's Day, 1946, the emperor issued a rescript formally renouncing the living-god status that tradition and governmental indoctrination had accorded to him. The initiative that produced the rescript may originally have come from one or more American occupation officials who perceived such renunciation as being compatible with U.S. policy. Certain foreign individuals were involved in the drafting, editing, and translation processes, but so were the Japanese prime minister and other key Japanese personages, including the emperor himself. The emperor's commitment to the rescript was sincere, at least partly because the rescript allowed him to preserve the traditional notion that he was descended from Shinto gods, even if he himself was not one of them.

The portion of the rescript most heavily stressed in public by MacArthur's General Headquarters (GHQ) stated that "the ties between us and our people have always stood upon mutual trust and affection. . . . They do not depend upon mere legends and myths. They are not predicated on the false conception that the emperor is divine and that the Japanese people are superior to other races and fated to rule the world."[14]

As such, it caused no negative campaign in the press or public in part because at least some of Japan's people had never regarded the emperor as a supernatural and omniscient figure. Despite the veneration accorded to him by state-sponsored Shintoism, to them he had been a man, even if endowed with some greater degree of divinity than other human beings. Nevertheless, the rescript was politically significant: "It practically eliminated the possibility of the emperor myth ever being revived as an instrument of reaction. It facilitated uninhibited public discussion of the constitutional problem of sovereignty."[15]

One version of events has Hirohito making clear his position on the matter of sovereignty when the Japanese cabinet agonized, in early 1946, over a new U.S.-authored draft constitution, which, legally, was an amendment to the so called

Meiji Constitution of 1889.[16] That draft defined the emperor as merely the symbol of the state and national unity in a political system based on popular sovereignty. When Hirohito allegedly discussed the draft constitution with then Prime Minister Kijuro Shidehara on February 22, the emperor's endorsement was "decisive" in securing the government's support, at least in the view of one source.[17] When Hirohito was consulted by Shidehara on the night of March 5, 1946, he reportedly backed the most "thoroughgoing" draft yet produced from intense discussions in Tokyo between the Japanese and U.S. sides. He also publicly sanctified the draft constitution via another imperial rescript, which contained a key statement: "It is . . . my desire that the Constitution of our empire be revised drastically upon the basis of the general will of the people."[18]

Among the democratizing actions Hirohito was prepared to undertake was a campaign of tours of inspection and other public appearances, which were designed to "humanize" the emperor even further and place him in contact with the people.[19] Although the inspiration for this activity seems to have come from one or more of MacArthur's officials,[20] the shy emperor assumed a public role that was unusual and difficult for him, even if it allowed him some more public freedom. It also enabled him to court the Japanese people, work against calls for his abdication, and increase his value to the U.S. occupation administration.

If Hirohito can be said to have possessed distinctive personal skills, perhaps the most salient were his flexibility, his sensitivity to political realities, and his apparent ability to convince MacArthur of his personal honor and sincerity.[21] In addition, he commanded important resources including the authority to surrender and to dissolve Japan's armed forces. Finally, he had sufficient legitimacy to share some of it with the occupation administration and with a new political system. Hirohito thereby made it possible for both the occupation and the political reform processes to proceed without violent resistance.

Shigeru Yoshida

Other than the emperor, the most important Japanese figure in Japan's transition to democracy was the man who served as prime minister during much of the occupation and continued to hold that post for some time after. In Japan, Shigeru Yoshida has "taken on luster as a leader who stood up to General Douglas MacArthur, . . . was able to mitigate the harsher features of the occupation, . . . [and who helped pave] the way for a favorable peace settlement."[22] That luster probably adds some legitimacy today to the system he helped to create a half-century ago.

Yoshida's relationship with MacArthur was neither puppet nor opponent. In a culture that values *sempai-kohai* (senior-junior) relationships, he and the supreme commander formed "a kind of partnership between a senior and a junior." Prepared to do more than accept occupation orders passively, Yoshida served "as a filter through which important policies and orders passed, [and] on occasion he offered advice about how problems should be handled." Just as importantly, the management of "key government operations" and parliamentary maneuvers, undertaken in conformity with occupation policy, was left to him.

Yoshida had a prewar and wartime résumé that (on balance) probably gave him some political advantages in the postwar setting. His was an aristocratic (*samurai*) background, but he himself was raised in a family atmosphere of business acumen, wealth, internationalism, and pro-British sentiment. A product of Japan's most elite university (Tokyo University), he had married well, becoming son-in-law to a politically influential personage (Count Nobuaki Makino, son of Toshimichi Okubo, one of the founders of modern Japan). Yoshida's father-in-law was the holder of important posts during the course of his career, including that of Lord Keeper of the Privy Seal (1925–1935), and was well known for being pro-Western in some of his views.

A career diplomat, Yoshida himself had been nominated for the post of foreign minister in 1936, but his appointment was rejected by army leaders. He had been Japan's ambassador to the Court of St. James (1936–1938) and probably had even earlier gained an admiration for "the British political system, with its parliamentary politics and combination of aristocratic and democratic traditions." He had retired from his regular diplomatic career in 1939, although he would engage in informal diplomacy thereafter and would become a paramount figure in Japanese foreign affairs after the end of the war.

As a person, Shigeru Yoshida was far more acerbic, opinionated, independent-minded, testy, and stubborn than the term "diplomat" might suggest. Having privately opposed the prewar Anti-Comintern Pact (which made Japan Germany's ally), he later worked to prevent a war he thought Japan could not win, although he did propose that the British Empire and the United States compromise with the Japanese government concerning Japan's aggressive policies on the Asian mainland (in other words, practice at least partial appeasement). Near the end of the war, in early 1945, he helped a former prime minister, Prince Fumimaro Konoe, prepare a peace memorandum to the emperor; for this and other reasons he was arrested by the Kampei Tai—the military police, Japan's equivalent of the Gestapo. He was subjected to intense interrogation while incarcerated but was released after U.S. bombing of the Tokyo area struck two of the prisons in which he had been held. His prison experience gave Yoshida "a halo of martyrdom that made him a symbol of resistance to militarism ever after."[23]

Yoshida made his commitment to democracy evident in his earliest meeting with MacArthur. Speaking as foreign minister, he responded to one of the general's customary lectures with "a little speech of his own," arguing:

"Democracy" had swept through Japan after World War I. Political parties had carried democracy to such an extreme that military men hesitated to appear in public. But the situation had changed when the Depression began in 1929, giving rise to Nazism, fascism, and communism. In Japan support for the military increased. Yoshida said democracy takes time to develop and needs an affluent country in which to thrive.[24]

In the English-language version of his memoirs, Yoshida wrote that his time as prime minister in the postwar Japanese government might have been easier "had we found our own aims to be diametrically opposed to those of the occupation." Instead, "the difficulties experienced by both sides sprang mainly from the fact that our aims were the same." If the occupation authorities provided the impetus for reform and progress, Yoshida's government did what it could to shape "the final form that was given that impetus" by expressing its own views.[25] Yoshida's conservatively independent frame of mind, which persisted whether he was in or out of power, constituted one reason why his relationship with the important Government Section (GS) of the U.S. occupation administration was one of conflict, at least at certain times.

Yoshida did have some goals that were very much his own. Apparently, one was "to maneuver so as to utilize the power of the occupation to his advantage"; another was to pack his political protégés advantageously into his party's machine.[26] Others seem to have been to protect the emperor and to correct the "ignorance" of men within MacArthur's headquarters so as to prevent or alter mistaken actions.[27] Although careful observers of his career might challenge his alleged self-description as a "good liberal," he professed opposition to both the extreme right and the extreme left in Japanese politics. His apparent desire was "to bring to Japan a moderate, two-party system in which the party of the left would resemble the British Labour Party." He may well have also longed to re-create the internal Japanese power structures that had preceded the rise of the militarists, that is, those found in the Meiji and Taisho periods of modern Japanese history. In the foreign policy sphere, Yoshida was committed to achieving a good peace treaty for Japan, the signing of which would end the occupation, and to returning Japan to a respected place in international affairs "as a partner of the Western powers." To him, such an outcome would constitute the restoration of Meiji and Taisho Japan's "traditional diplomacy."[28]

His view of the occupation administration was sophisticated. With some justification, he differentiated and sought to maneuver between the "real soldiers" in the U.S. General Headquarters and others, particularly in the higher ranks, whom in his memoirs he called "civilians . . . though in uniform . . . who had, until their arrival in Tokyo, been lawyers, salesmen in department stores, editors of provincial newspapers and so on." He strongly favored the soldierly group because they were "more practical" and (like him) apprehensive of social unrest, disorder, and communism in Japan. In Yoshida's view, the civilian-based participants were "idealists" overly concerned with "trying to speed the work of democratizing Japan as planned."[29]

New to being in a central position in politics, Yoshida was "a shrewd observer and quick learner,"[30] skillful in taking advantage of the "extraordinary circumstances" offered by the occupation, such as the U.S.-dictated "purge" of some "veteran" politicians from political life.[31] He also became skillful in dealing with MacArthur and the GHQ administration, once he learned how loosely organized MacArthur's administration was and that "staff sections often disagreed."[32]

Yoshida was politically maladroit in certain ways but proved adept at arousing support within the Japanese political system for the new "MacArthur" constitution and in securing the necessary implementing legislation. At a later opportune moment (late 1948–early 1949), he also demonstrated political skill by successfully campaigning publicly "to win more freedom of action for the government and build up the self-respect of the people." In the election of January 23, 1949, his party won an absolute majority in the lower house, "one of the few times in Japanese history that a party won so sweeping a victory."

Yoshida played an important role in leading a conservative political party that later (despite some resistance from Yoshida and from his personal political faction) combined with another conservative party to produce the so-called Liberal Democratic Party (LDP), Japan's dominant party from the mid-1950s to the 1990s. One of the ironies of the newfound Japanese democracy, however, may have been the way in which Yoshido's political career was forced into decline, and his prime ministership eventually ended, prior to the formation of the LDP. He was pressured, in part, by resentment in Japanese political circles against his "one-man rule." Accusations made against him, including "dictatorial tactics and abuse of the Diet [the Japanese parliament]" and having "toadied to the United States at the expense of Japan's sovereign integrity," were also part of the complex process that eventually removed him from center stage in 1954.[33]

Douglas MacArthur

General Douglas MacArthur's official title while he oversaw the U.S. occupation of Japan was Supreme Commander for the Allied Powers (SCAP), an acronym also given to his command post in the occupation administration and, sometimes, to his entire headquarters staff. MacArthur actually occupied two posts, each in a different chain of command. As commander in chief, Far East, he was responsible to the Joint Chiefs of Staff (JCS) in Washington, and as SCAP he was nominally accountable (by 1946) to an international oversight body called the Far Eastern Commission (FEC). He would "switch hats" to help preserve his autonomy, although at all times he remained answerable, theoretically at least, to four U.S. government officeholders: the chairman of the JCS, the U.S. Army chief of staff, the secretary of war (later called the secretary of defense), and, ultimately, the U.S. president. His authority, as outlined to him by President Harry Truman in a statement prepared by the U.S. Departments of State, War, and Navy, was "supreme." In fact, "control of Japan" was to be exercised by him "through the Japanese government," but only "to the extent that such an arrangement produces satisfactory results." Both the emperor and the Japanese government were subordinate to him. If necessary, MacArthur could bypass that government and could enforce his orders "by the employment of such measures as [he deemed] necessary."[34]

Broad policymaking guidelines as well as a number of explicit instructions were given to MacArthur through a series of U.S. government documents provided to him or his staff. But he was consulted or given prior information about the policies described in many (if not all) of those documents. The Potsdam Declaration of July 26, 1945, issued by the World War II victors, provided some guidance as well, although that document's ambiguities and "disagreement between the [former] belligerents as to [its] meaning" made such guidance quite limited. In the final analysis, MacArthur exercised an enormous amount of personal discretion. Very much a political general, he believed that policy for Japan "should for the most part be made in Tokyo rather than in Washington." During his military career, MacArthur had shown "a penchant for repeated conflicts with his superiors, especially civilians."[35] That behavior would enhance his authority while he served as SCAP—but would ultimately end his career in Japan.

MacArthur did not agree with Yoshida that Japan's militarist phase had been an aberration, a temporary break from major trends in Japan's recent past. For MacArthur (and for U.S. policy planners in general, at least initially) the structure of Japan's social and economic system was the root of what U.S. statesman Dean Acheson called Japan's "will to war." As MacArthur explained with some hyperbole after his term as SCAP had ended, Japan "had evolved a feudalistic system of totalitarianism which had produced results which were almost like reading the pages of mythology."[36]

The supreme commander's commitment to Japan's democratization during the occupation seems to have been based largely on dogmatic ideological and religious conviction, self-confidence, ethnocentrism, his earlier family and personal participation in U.S. colonial domination over the Philippine Islands, and ambitions he entertained toward becoming president of the United States. He was convinced that the U.S. "democratic way of life" should flow into the mental, moral, and physical vacuum created by Japan's "collapse of faith." But he was equally convinced that democracy was a concept flexible enough to "take on a Japanese form."[37] His ideas on how to inculcate democracy into Japan were later summarized in his memoirs this way:

> First destroy the military power. Punish war criminals. Build the structure of representative government. Modernize the constitution. Hold free elections. Enfranchise the women. Release political prisoners. Liberate the farmers. Establish a free labor movement. Encourage a free economy. Abolish police oppression. Develop a free and responsible press. Liberalize education. Decentralize the political power. Separate church from state.[38]

These were the programs he administered with varied degrees of consistency and success and with varied (and not always positive) implications for the development of Japanese democracy.

But the supreme commander had still other goals. In consonance with a central tendency that existed in the plans formulated earlier in Washington, he wanted the emperor on the throne and not included among the war criminals set for trial. To do otherwise, he argued, would cause all "government agency" to break down in Japan as well as the disappearance of "all hope of introducing modern democratic methods." He also placed a high priority on preserving domestic peace and tranquillity—law and order—throughout the occupation and was particularly concerned about unruliness and violence that he associated especially with Japan's communists.[39] The mounting tensions of the cold war during the later years of the occupation led both the U.S. government in Washington and MacArthur's SCAP administration in Tokyo to give greater importance to the goal of making Japan an "economically self-supporting, politically stable American ally in the struggle against communism in Asia."[40] The ultimate adoption of this goal and the seeming decline in U.S. democratic reformist zeal that accompanied it were part of a policy that a number of commentators have called the U.S. occupation's "reverse course."[41]

Among the skills MacArthur put to good use in Japan was his ability to construct and maintain the role of charismatic leader. Using various personal, publicity, and news devices available to him and his administration, he projected traits that many Japanese found appealing. Among them were his idealism, "his messianic pose and turn of phrase" as well as "his 'Jovian image of decisiveness and absolute authority,' and his 'dedication to duty . . . imperious aloofness and lordly graciousness.'"[42] Something of a MacArthur cult seems to have developed in Japan during his tenure there, although the extent of its spread among Japanese citizens, for whom "food, clothing, and shelter"[43] were major concerns, is not clear. The supreme commander enhanced his image by having his U.S. Army kitchens help feed people and by providing food for distribution by the Japanese government. He reportedly made "public announcements whenever food-laden ships were about to arrive at Yokohama or Kobe."[44]

Another important skill seems to have been MacArthur's ability to be heard in Washington. His persuasiveness in written and other communications, his decisive actions in Japan, his stubbornness to the point of refusing to implement a policy he opposed, all combined to produce a formidable presence in absentia. He could influence the formation of policy back home and block, modify, or delay the implementation of Washington (or Allied) initiatives in Japan. Furthermore, he could keep "occupation policies from becoming embroiled in American politics, as happened with China policy."[45] Of help to him, surely, was his personal standing with the U.S. public as a major military figure, especially after his larger-than-life role in World War II. He would have been aided as well by his political connections in Washington and elsewhere in the United States, by his politically conservative reputation, and by the impressions (both positive and negative) he made on military and political colleagues. Even after his military setbacks in Korea in late 1950, MacArthur was still a "fearsome figure" to the Joint Chiefs of Staff.[46]

Among the additional skills MacArthur demonstrated in Japan was an apparent ability to convince the Japanese government that he was the authentic representative and voice in Japan of the will of the United States and its allies. Yet another skill lay in his handling of internal Japanese politics, allowing him to work constructively, and with only a small amount of overt friction, with a series of Japanese prime ministers and other politicians and to steer the development and implementation of policy through them.[47] Among the top Japanese politicians, a thriving but highly controlled process of multiparty politics seems to have functioned under MacArthur's peculiar combination of tutelage, heavy-handed intervention, and benign neutrality.

Perhaps the most important strategic choice MacArthur made was to structure this new political process by means of a constitution introduced early in the occupation. As the Government Section saw it, a basic problem was "whether to permit and encourage the slow growth of local democratic institutions and political maturity and at some later time to advise the development of an organic law that would merge and reflect the new institutions, or to promote the early and drastic overhaul of the basic law and then build on that new foundation."

In choosing "immediate constitutional revision," MacArthur (and GS) reasoned that the gradual and natural course would be too slow and could not guarantee that "a reactionary cabinet, privy council or Emperor would not, overnight, wipe out all the gains that might be achieved." Accomplishing constitutional revision immediately would supposedly provide "the Japanese people" with a "goal" and would result in a "solid foundation on which to build."[48] In the end, an important cadre of Japanese politicians and officials gained experience in functioning under such a constitution before the occupation ended in 1952.

One of MacArthur's personal contributions to democratizing Japan came with his dismissal by President Truman in 1951. It was an unintended and ironic contribution. Although his dismissal brought MacArthur popular sympathy in Japan, it also constituted an object lesson to Japan of "civilian control over the military" in the U.S. political system. The comparison could easily be made between MacArthur—with his independence of action in Korea and his seeming desire to extend the Korean War into China—and the aggressive behavior of Japanese officers on the Asian mainland in the 1930s. The political management dimensions of the two episodes of military behavior were very different.[49]

JAPAN'S NEW INSTITUTIONS AND PROCEDURES

The executive and legislative institutions of postwar Japan derive some of their legitimacy from their prewar origins, some from their association with the new 1947 constitution, and some from other sources like the benediction of the emperor and the cooperation of a democratic-minded Japanese public. Most of these institutions are not really new (whatever their formal-legal paternity) but continuations of old ones. What has changed are their powers and roles, their relative positions, and the inability of certain institutions like the army high command to serve as centers of power any longer. They also operate within the context of a constitution containing civil rights provisions that are more extensive than those found within the U.S. Constitution.

Under the 1947 constitution (known as the "MacArthur constitution"), the office of the emperor still exists, but "his role did not change as much as that of those around him." Gone are prewar institutions and power bases that served to make the palace a separate locus of power, such as the office of the Lord Keeper of the Privy Seal. All aristocratic titles are abolished, excepting those of the emperor's immediate family. Sovereignty no longer officially rests with the emperor but is constitutionally assigned to the Japanese people and nation. The 1947 constitution allows the emperor such roles as formally "appointing the prime minister . . . convoking the Diet[, and] receiving foreign ambassadors."[50] But these are ceremonial functions only and allow him no discretion. As the state "symbol" rather than "chief of state," his political role "is even weaker than that of the British monarch."

The Meiji political system had given the emperor decree powers extensive enough to have him share lawmaking responsibility with the parliament, but the postwar constitution makes clear that the Diet is now technically supreme. It is the "highest organ of state power" and the state's "sole" lawmaking organ. The lower house (the House of Representatives) must stand for election at least once every four years, sooner if it is dissolved. A more complicated but equally regular election process determines the party makeup of the upper house (the House of Councillors).

Although the cabinet is responsible to parliament, the prime minister and cabinet together exercise "supreme executive authority." This is a British-style cabinet system, which differs from the prewar system wherein "the cabinet was not responsible to the legislature . . . [and] the legislature had no power either to select a prime minister or dissolve the cabinet." The MacArthur constitution makes the cabinet clearly answerable to parliament in a number of specific ways. For example, all members of the cabinet must be civilians. The prime minister and a majority of the other cabinet members must have seats in parliament. The Diet elects the prime minister, and the government will fall if the lower house approves a no-confidence motion or "rejects a confidence resolution." The cabinet must either resign soon after such an event or dismiss the lower house within ten days, stage an election, and then resign just after the new Diet opens.

In the prewar political system, electoral "strength was but one element in the struggle for political influence," with "economic power, military strength, administrative autonomy, and proximity to the emperor" being elements of at least equal significance.[51] The cabinet had competed not just with the institutions of the palace and certain informal advisers to the emperor but also with the "Army and Navy Chiefs of Staff . . . and the Supreme War Council."[52] After the 1947 constitutional change, parties—and their fortunes in elections, in parliament, and in the cabinet—became crucial.

The Process of Institutional Reform

A recurrent theme in the U.S. government's wartime and immediate postwar planning for Japan had been the desire to induce the Japanese to institute democratic political reform on their own initiative. It would be best if U.S. guidance or oversight of the reform process were circumspect and indirect. A related theme, found in at least one planning document, was that a plainly directive U.S. (and Allied) role would cost the reforms considerable support and acceptance.[53]

Yet MacArthur felt compelled to become overtly directive for a number of reasons. Among them was his concern for safeguarding the person and the utility of the emperor. Another was the failure of the cabinet-appointed Japanese committee on constitutional revision, headed by Dr. Joji Matsumoto, to go beyond merely "touching up" the earlier Meiji Constitution. Although inadequate communication between the Japanese government and SCAP may have been part of the problem, the committee's thinking was in line with the opinion of Japanese conservatives at that time, including Yoshida. The committee felt that abuse of the Meiji Constitution by the militarists had taken place and that this constitution and its principles (like the emperor's sovereignty) were not fundamentally flawed. Matsumoto's group was also working within a Japanese legal tradition that emphasized utilitarian "interpretation and application" of existing legal codes rather than major revision.[54]

Any list of reasons for MacArthur's quick action must also include his anticipation of external interference and even pressure from the Far Eastern Commission (FEC). An eleven-nation body, the FEC had recently been established to enable the World War II Allies (and not just the United States) to take part in making policy for Japan. By early 1946, MacArthur "was concerned that if he did not act swiftly, the new FEC might soon tie his hands" so far as constitutional matters were concerned. Participating in the FEC was the Soviet Union. MacArthur felt pressured, too, by the fact that a general election for the lower house was scheduled for April 10, 1946. He wanted that election to constitute an unofficial plebiscite on any drafted constitutional changes.[55]

After being persuaded by one or more members of his staff that he possessed the requisite legal authority, MacArthur, on or about February 3, 1946, decided to entrust to SCAP's Government Section (headed by Brigadier General Courtney Whitney) the task of producing a draft constitution. MacArthur wanted that draft based on certain points:

> (1) the emperor is at the head of the state, (2) war as a sovereign right is abolished and is renounced by Japan "even for preserving its own security. No army, navy, or air force is authorized" and (3) the feudal system is abolished, and the rights of peerage, except those of the emperor's family, would not extend beyond the lives of those now holding them. Finally, the budget would be patterned after the British system.

Members of the GS staff, including General Whitney and his deputy, Colonel Charles Kades, then used MacArthur's instructions, a Washington document known as SWNCC-228, and other sources to write a basic constitution. After MacArthur approved it (with one change) on February 11 or 12, Whitney presented copies to Japanese officials including Foreign Minister Yoshida and Minister of State Matsumoto at a meeting held on February 13. Among the thoughts conveyed by Whitney (and possibly by other Americans) at the meeting was the idea that the SCAP model draft should be adopted "in order to save the emperor from [possible] trial as a war criminal." Although that idea may have been communicated "as friendly advice," Matsumoto reportedly perceived it as a threat. Whitney also warned that if the SCAP draft was not sponsored by the cabinet "MacArthur would present it directly to the people [before the forthcoming election]." He seems to have added that the people "were already dissatisfied with the published version of the Matsumoto draft. The cabinet had a reactionary reputation and, to save itself, it had best adopt this draft constitution."[56]

The Japanese government then sought a compromise path with the Americans, but ultimately felt that the effort was generally unsuccessful. When Prime Minister Shidehara went to MacArthur for advice, MacArthur himself referred to the matter of safeguarding the throne and mentioned the severity of opinion toward Japan within the FEC.[57] After intensive discussions between Japanese representatives and GS officers, the cabinet decided on March 5 and 6 to accept a text that differed in no major way from the original SCAP draft except for providing for a bicameral Diet with an elected upper house rather than a unicameral Diet.

The members of the cabinet felt that they had no other alternative. Beyond their concern for the emperor, they assumed that failure to subscribe to the latest text would result not only in its publication, but also in its probable support by the Japanese newspapers. They further anticipated that "the cabinet would [then] have to resign in favor of a leftist government that would support the document."[58]

A major effort was mounted to present the new constitution publicly as a Japanese creation. In keeping with a requirement in the Meiji Constitution that "the initiative right" of constitutional amendment lay with the emperor and that presentation to the Diet had to be by "imperial order," the emperor's rescript on the subject was made public by the Japanese government on March 6, along with the substance of the draft constitution. MacArthur's own public announcement spoke of the "decision of the Emperor and Government of Japan to submit to the Japanese people a new and enlightened constitution which has my full approval." MacArthur's "Civil Censorship Detachment" prohibited Japan's press from referring to the proposed constitution as something authored by officials of the occupation.[59]

Even in his memoirs, published in 1964, MacArthur claims that he had not forced a constitution on Japan since he had not ordered the Japanese to accept it.

That claim was "closer to deception than to inaccuracy." The truth was suspected and rumored rather quickly, if not fully known, at least among journalists and other politically connected persons in Japan. On March 8, 1946, the *Asahi* newspaper welcomed the new "epoch-making Peace Constitution" but commented editorially that the Shidehara cabinet probably had not been "capable of drafting it single handedly. It must have been made possible by [the] strong advice of SCAP."[60]

Once the emperor had begun the process of providing procedural legitimacy for the constitution, SCAP and the Japanese government sought to continue that process. The first postwar election for the lower house of parliament took place on April 10, 1946, with many more voters eligible to participate than in the past, because the franchise had been extended to women for the first time and because the voting age had been lowered from twenty-five to twenty. MacArthur thought that the election outcome signified support for the constitution (apparently because the communists—the only party to oppose the constitution vocally—had done poorly). By the end of April, Yoshida was prime minister for the first time, the result of a complicated round of postelection political maneuvers that included intervention and machinations by the United States among influential Japanese political figures. Yoshida and a special minister then spent much time during the summer of 1946 providing explanations to the Privy Council and to both houses of the Diet, which created special committees to go over the various issues. Finally, the constitution was formally approved on October 29, 1946.

Although Diet dissidence probably was reduced by SCAP's commitment to keep Japanese politicians associated with the militarist era out of parliament and public office generally, parliamentary deliberations on the constitution were wide-ranging and covered important matters. While dealing with the emperor's status, Yoshida and other government spokesmen made comments depicting "the emperor and the people [as possessing] sovereignty together." Such language constituted a reversion to the old *kokutai* concept, one dimension of which had been the idea that a powerful spiritual tie made the emperor and the people one entity. The Yoshida government's view elicited negative responses in Japan, among them a challenge from the president of Tokyo University, who had recently received an appointment to what was then the upper house of parliament, the House of Peers. But Yoshida had evidently sought to appeal to people for whom *kokutai* and "family state" still had some resonance, even though he also agreed to a GS demand that the constitution's preamble contain a clear statement that "sovereignty rests with the people."

The Diet's review of the draft constitution produced some amendments. One of the more important alterations, likely to appeal to conservatives, was hardly noticed in Japan at the time but proved to be a source of great controversy after the end of the occupation. Article 9, the passage that renounced war as an option for the future Japan, was altered by adding phrases that "seemed to limit Japan's renunciation only to war as a means of settling international disputes: war for other sovereign purposes, such as self-defense, would not be prohibited." Immediate controversy may have been prevented by the position taken by the Yoshida government during the 1946 constitutional debate, that position being "that Article 9 banned armament even for defense." But the Japanese government, in cooperation with the U.S. government, later asserted the right of Japan to defend itself under the constitution and created the so-called Self-Defense Forces.

The advocacy of the constitution to parliament by Yoshida and his allies in 1946 may have "erased many of the doubts and frictions" that SCAP methods had produced earlier. More flexibility by GS after the draft constitution had been made public may have had an impact as well. According to one estimate, GS "accepted some eighty to ninety percent of the Japanese government's suggested revisions of the text" (apart from the preamble). A decision taken by the FEC may also have been helpful in producing this result. The commission decided to advise the Japanese government, through MacArthur, that the Diet should later review the constitution again and amend it, not less than one year but no more than two years after the constitution had come into effect. This FEC decision "may have mitigated some of the feeling of pressure in Japan," even though the decision would never be implemented by the Japanese government. Despite overwhelming approval of the constitution by the Diet, however, a supplementary resolution to the Constitutional Revision Bill passed by the lower house expressed members' dissatisfaction with certain "aspects of the procedure and substance of the constitutional reform."[61]

After 1946, the constitution was not amended again despite considerable prorevision sentiment within Japan's conservative political camp during the 1950s. Among the things that conservatives wanted during this period were amendments that would enhance the emperor's status and make clear the legality of Japan's new Self-Defense Forces, which were in reality new armed forces. A commission created by the Diet in 1956 finished a massive investigation of the constitution by 1964; the commission's majority favored partially amending a constitution it regarded as imposed on Japan by the occupation. "By this time, however, conservative strength among the voters and in the Diet had substantially declined, and the Liberal Democrats did not have the two-thirds majorities in the houses of the Diet and the simple majority among the voters needed to amend the constitution. No proposals for amendment were, therefore, introduced."[62]

Important among the factors producing general acceptance of the constitution in Japan was its linkage to peace, which may have appealed to the strong sense of pacifism that apparently existed in certain quarters in postwar Japanese society. Democratization also appealed to people who were disillusioned by events and prepared to reject the hierarchy, bureaucracy, and arrogance associated with the old ruling elite.[63] Some other reasons for the constitution's acceptance were closely related to long-term elements in Japan's culture and history. In Japan, ideas or thought-systems imported from abroad, like Buddhism, had been grafted onto indigenous ones, then assimilated to the point where they became Japanese. This process was especially likely to continue in the period of defeat immediately after World War II, a time of popular "idealism and risk-taking."[64] However incompletely the Japanese public may have understood democracy at that moment, both the elites and the masses could perhaps respond positively to a proposed constitution that on its face conformed "to the best standards of a true parliamentary democracy."[65]

More cynical interpretations might point out that the Japanese government, which wanted to preserve "as much of the ancient regime as possible," could not help but understand that complete cooperation with SCAP would produce an end to the military occupation. The public, at first concerned about food and somewhat apathetic toward politics despite the idealism it may have felt, surely wanted security and political stability—and was seemingly prepared to seek both within the potentially democratic political system that was already functioning by 1947. During the latter stages of the occupation period, when U.S. and Japanese economic policies and the economic stimulus provided by the Korean War produced accelerated economic recovery, most Japanese were rewarded for their adherence to constitutional democracy. A limited degree of international rehabilitation associated with the successful conclusion of the 1951 San Francisco treaty to end the war (in conjunction with the formation of the United States–Japan cold war military alliance) constituted a further reward for Japan, as did the official end of the occupation in 1952. Nevertheless, many Japanese from the political left to the political right felt that their country had achieved only "subordinate independence"; Japan was, in their view, an economic and military dependent of the United States in the cold war setting.[66]

Here was one likely source (among others) of the strong sentiment for revision of the constitution, especially its war-renunciation provision, expressed by many conservative political figures toward the end of the Yoshida era and immediately after it. Not all of this sentiment was directed toward amending the constitution in limited and minor ways. One type of revisionism advocated the complete rewriting of the 1947 constitution to conform to Japanese traditions. Because of its mainly "ideological and emotional appeal," such extreme revisionist thinking enjoyed only a brief period of limited popularity in Japan. Other sources of extreme revisionist opinion included the return of former purgees to political life, the personal ambitions of prewar bureaucrats and politicians opposed to Yoshida and his faction, resentment at the imposition of a constitution by the United States, and real ideological differences within conservative ranks, mainly between politicians (often former bureaucrats) of the prewar and postwar generations. Constitutional revision was a publicly stated goal of the LDP when it was created in 1955.

Since the early 1950s, however, Japanese nationalism "has been much more pragmatic than emotional," and many people within the general population of

Japan were "positively antagonized" by the "tune of the extreme revisionists." It was a tune closely associated with prewar bureaucrats, and the negative public reaction to it indicated "the psychological gap" that existed "not only between pre-war and postwar generations but also between the bureaucratic elite and masses." Support within the LDP for extensive revision declined as the lack of public support for it was perceived, as pragmatism and realism prevailed, as the prewar elements in the party ranks declined in influence and numbers over time, and as faction politics within the LDP raised the specter of "intra-party disunity and conflict with opposition parties" over the issue. By the early 1960s, the party was advocating only limited constitutional revision. Not until 1995, however, did the party abandon its "decades long [official] call for the establishment of an 'independent constitution'" and pledge instead to seek a dialogue with the public on the broad scope of a proper constitution for modern Japan.[67] This move seemingly implied that the party would no longer hold an official position that sounded more radical than its real policy.

The LDP's 1995 action took place during a time of considerable discussion of the revision issue in newspapers, public opinion polls, and other public forums. The Gulf War in the Middle East and a recent, highly destructive earthquake in Japan helped to raise critical questions about apparent constitutional restrictions on the government's abilities to respond to the problems of the 1990s. Other issues were given considerable publicity by an influential conservative newspaper (*Yomiuri Shimbun*) that published its own proposed new draft constitution. Amid a general recognition that the existing constitution was forced upon Japan by the United States some form of constitutional change seemed possible as the twentieth century closed, but the tenor of the public discourse in Japan indicated that the democratic principles and institutions of the current constitution were likely to be affirmed rather than undermined.

SOCIAL GROUPS AFTER 1945:
PURGES AND REWARDS

The key decisionmaking groups in the regime that ruled Japan just prior to and during World War II had been leaders of the armed services, party politicians, big business leaders, and bureaucrats, along with the emperor's privy council and such extraconstitutional advisers to the emperor as court officials and the so-called senior statesman (*jushin*). After 1945, the party politicians, bureaucrats, and men from big business became the Japanese ruling groups; the rest had been excluded from power. Other groups empowered by occupation reforms included unions, intellectuals, teachers, and leaders of parties in seemingly perpetual opposition to cabinets dominated by conservatives. These groups had little chance to rule the new political order yet nonetheless became staunch defenders of democratic practices and the 1947 constitution. No longer endangered by political persecution and permitted the exercise of political rights, they could become new and effective countervailing forces against the conservative old guard.[68]

The political importance of the "purge" instituted by the U.S. occupiers cannot be overemphasized. It was clearly designed to eliminate from Japan's political life, at least temporarily, persons who were not necessarily criminals but who shared responsibility for the nature and policies of the old regime. Although the postwar Japanese state was ostensibly responsible for the purge, it was in truth demanded and supervised by officials in SCAP. Opening Japan to new leadership was clearly one of SCAP's goals.

Anyone who had been purged was forbidden to occupy public office, a term that was broadly defined. It covered not only employment by the government and elective positions in any "public organization," but also included "all teaching and administrative positions in both public and private educational institutions and the higher editorial and executive positions in newspapers, magazines and other media of mass communication. [It] . . . was further broadened to include executive positions in some two hundred or so designated business corporations."

Whole categories of people were "automatically" excluded from public offices, including former officers in the regular armed forces, former participants in "military police or naval police or secret intelligence organizations," and holders of "important official posts in occupied territories." Excluded too, not automatically but frequently, was any person who had allegedly "shown himself to be an active exponent of militant nationalism and aggression."

Because the purge was carried out over an extended period rather than at once, persons active in party politics under the occupation could suddenly find themselves sidelined. Yoshida would never have become prime minister after the 1946 election without the purge policy of SCAP, which suddenly retired Ichiro Hatoyama, the head of the leading political party and the favorite for the prime ministership. Upon learning that he had been purged, Hatoyama approached Yoshida about taking his (Hatoyama's) party post, at least temporarily, and with it the prime ministership.

Whatever hidden power those purged might still have exercised behind the scenes after their involuntary withdrawal, they tended, as time passed, to get "left behind in the backwash of rapid new developments." Some, like Hatoyama himself, managed to come back eventually, but most of the civilian returnees who "were important enough to have been purged" were relatively elderly men, incapable "of catching up and competing with the vigorous new generation." Even though purged party politicians were probably the group that eventually recovered most successfully from the purge episode (when compared to their military or bureaucratic compatriots) these "ex-purgees . . . made no more than limited headway against the resistance of the new generation of politicians . . . [with] a vested interest in the new order." Some former purgees were instrumental in removing Yoshida from the prime ministership in 1954, and some of his successors as prime minister were men who had returned from the purge. But, broadly speaking, former purgees in party politics were not inclined to destroy democracy in Japan. Moreover, the typical depurged politician could assimilate himself better into the new democratic environment than could the typical depurged administrator or soldier. That was probably because such politicians had experience in electoral and party politics.

Just as important as the readiness of party politicians to function according to democratic rules during and after the occupation was the return of political parties to a central position in the political system. Nevertheless, as was the case before 1945, the politics of political factionalism remained important. The kind of factional maneuvering that took place within postwar conservative parties in existence before 1955 continued later within the faction-ridden ruling party (the Liberal Democratic Party). Therefore, Japanese prime ministers, who must seek the consensus position within the cabinet, have often been weak, and their cabinets can be unstable. They must often rely heavily, as must the nation, on the services and skills of the bureaucracy.

Bureaucrats in postoccupation Japan have had good reason to favor multiparty democracy. "Largely spared" by the purge, Japan's "civilian career officers in the central ministry bureaucracies" lost little if any power in the transition to democracy. Indeed, the bureaucracy probably now has more political influence than it did before and during the war. In the political system prior to surrender, the bureaucracy's role was restricted whenever the cabinet itself wielded relative strength or "was controlled by a strong superior power like . . . the militarists." Because postwar cabinets have often been weak, however, and because the Diet initially lacked experience, "the bureaucracy has continued [its] traditional tendency to assume effective power by default." This tendency was evident during the mid-1990s, as the political party system became more competitive and prone to coalitional instability after years of one-party rule.[69]

FOREIGN MODELS AND
THE INTERNATIONAL ENVIRONMENT

The U.S. occupation of Japan clearly constitutes a case of a distant great power facilitating another country's transition to democracy "by support, by intimidation, [and] . . . by taking sides in an internal struggle."[70] It used other methods as well. Yet the democratic political system of Japan was not a direct copy of the U.S. system, primarily because both Americans and Japanese apparently saw the necessity for some degree of continuity with earlier trends in Japanese history. One of those trends had been the evolution toward democracy that Japan had experienced from 1868 to the 1920s. Whereas Japan's Meiji Constitution of 1889 was "an idealized version of Prussian constitutional absolutism,"[71] Japan's parliamentary system, by the 1920s, had shown a marked inclination "to evolve in the direction of the British example."[72] Broadly speaking, occupation policy was to continue that evolution.[73]

Nevertheless, the occupation authorities made attempts to incorporate some U.S. principles into Japan's political system. One of them was a separate judicial system that included a supreme court empowered to subject all legislation to "constitutional review." This particular attempt to Americanize Japanese politics was not too successful. In the words of one observer:

> The Japanese judicial system . . . has largely returned to what can be considered a nat-ural outgrowth of the prewar system, and the supreme court exercises its review pow-ers with great circumspection. It does protect individual rights from bureaucratic maladministration, but it attempts not to upset actions of the Diet or involve the courts in the administration of law in the American style.[74]

Another form of U.S. intervention in Japanese political life, one that was appar-ently more successful, commenced after the occupation ended. A recent report discloses that money was provided by the U.S. Central Intelligence Agency (CIA) to Japan's Liberal Democratic Party and to its members during the 1950s and 1960s. This operation, which, apparently, was phased out in the early 1970s, resembled at least one other cold war program: the secret support given by the United States to Italy's Christian Democratic Party after World War II. In Japan, the CIA also infiltrated the major opposition party (the Japan Socialist Party), which it suspected of "receiving secret financial support from Moscow, and placed agents in youth groups, student groups and labor groups." CIA intervention can perhaps be given slight credit for some important structural features of Japanese democracy, foreign policy, and security policy, including LDP "one-party rule," close Japanese governmental ties with Washington, and the maintenance of U.S. military bases in Japan.[75] But the CIA's role should not be overstated, as many fac-tors combined to produce these results.

THE JAPANESE VERSION OF DEMOCRACY

The kind of indigenization of the new political system that took place during the occupation and after was far more important than any CIA influence. Indeed, the appearance of a distinctly Japanese version of parliamentary democracy does much to explain the long-term survival of democracy in Japan. That version has been favored by its elite practitioners, although with various reservations and desire for revision and reform. Some reforms were recently instituted by Japan's political leaders and parliamentarians—who thereby demonstrated to a reform-minded public their continued commitment to democracy.

Two strikingly Japanese features of the system were, until 1994, the electoral system for the lower house of parliament (the House of Representatives, the more powerful of the two houses) and the persistent salience of factionalism, that is, the interplay of informal cliques of politicians. These two features stood apart from the constitution but were linked to each other to an extent.

Elections to the lower house (until late 1994, when the electoral law was changed) were accomplished in a fashion "unlike that of any other major Western democracy, but . . . similar to [Japan's] prewar system."[76] Indeed, this system, with some variation, had been in use since the 1920s (although the 1946 election may have been an exception). As of 1994 the number of seats in the lower house belonging to each voting constituency ranged from two to six, depending on the population size of the constituency. But the seats were not distributed very equitably across the 129 constituencies, because rural constituencies were markedly overrepresented. The voter cast only one vote, for an individual candidate rather than a party list. The candidate receiving the highest number of votes received one of the seats belonging to that constituency, another seat went to the candidate receiving the second highest vote count, and so on until all the seats available to the constituency had been won.

This distinctive electoral method (along with other causes) produced interesting political consequences. For example, a large party like the LDP could run more than one candidate in a given constituency, and those candidates competed against each other as well as against the candidates put forward by other parties. In addition, the voter was encouraged to focus on individual candidates and the service each could provide to the constituency rather than on party, policy, or ideology. A candidate therefore could maintain a local bloc of reliable supporters (a *jiban* or *jimoto*), as was the case in the prewar party system, and/or create a more formally organized support association (a *koenkai*) to work on garnering and maintaining strength among voters. Such personalized support groups for individual politicians became part of the larger factional groups to which Diet members, at least within the larger parties, usually belonged. The fact that a candidate could be elected "in a five-member constituency with as little as 10 percent of the total votes [made] . . . it easy for small parties, for factions within large parties, and for individual candidates with a personal base of support, to be elected."[77]

Encouraging the appearance and persistence of factions was the candidates' need for substantial campaign funds, sometimes for use against same-party candidates whose policy positions differed little (if at all) from their own. One of the funding sources could be the faction leader. A faction had often been instrumental in securing a candidate's nomination by the party. Persons elected to the lower house with LDP endorsement usually took up or continued roles as members in one of the five "major factional lineages" into which the party was usually divided during its history or one of the smaller ones that have existed from time to time.[78]

This electoral system changed in 1994, however, after corruption scandals and party realignment created a favorable atmosphere for reform. One widely used argument for abandoning the old electoral system was that candidates' needs (and that includes incumbents) for large amounts of money for reelection to lower house seats constituted a potent source of corruption. Another argument was that the old electoral method supported the existence of factions, which supplied money to their own candidates. Factions "have long been criticized as a hotbed for money politics and a principal cause of opaque policy-making procedures." The new lower house voting method is intended to reduce the personalized competition among candidates, their local support bases, and their factions and to create greater interparty competition over substantive policy issues.

Under the new system, each voter has two votes. One vote is cast for an individual candidate to fill one of the 300 seats elected from single-member districts, like those found in Britain or the United States. In addition, the voter opts for a political party (and not a candidate) within one of the eleven very large multimember districts that together, like the single-member districts, cover the entire country. Two hundred seats will be filled by election from these large districts; the lower house will therefore contain 500 members instead of the 511 it contained previously. Parties will compete against one another within any large district, the seats available to that district going to each winning party via a proportional representation method.

In keeping with the spirit of reform, and at the behest of the 1994 LDP party president, the LDP factions publicly pledged to disband—at least to the extent of closing their offices, dropping their special names, and refraining from holding any further faction meetings. Nevertheless, the faction system will probably continue, because LDP factions can transform themselves into "policy study groups" and can maintain "personal offices."[79] Moreover, certain other procedural and extraconstitutional factors, which sustained the role of faction in Japanese party politics in the past, are likely to do so in the future. Among them are the methods employed in selecting the membership of the cabinet, whenever the LDP has participated in it, and filling important posts within the LDP's own internal organization. A good example is the progression of methods by which the president of the LDP (who is usually Japan's next prime minister) has been chosen. A candidate (often a faction leader himself) has needed support from his own faction, and factions have usually maneuvered in competition and alliance with each other.

Even if all the procedural sources of Japanese factionalism are eliminated in the future (and that is rather doubtful), there are cultural sources as well. Japan's factions (at least within the LDP) generally are not based on ideology or policy differences but on political self-interest and personal loyalty. Personal hierarchical obligations between leader and followers, and between seniors and juniors, along with the importance of group participation, are all strong themes in Japanese society and culture. It is hardly surprising that they should infuse political life as well and that democratic politics in Japan should operate in ways with which political practitioners are socially familiar.

The role of the Japanese bureaucracy also represents the indigenization and social assimilation of a democratic system. One leading observer has noted:

> [The] tradition of bureaucratic dominance is stronger in Japan than in any other contemporary democracy. . . . Civil and military bureaucrats were the direct heirs of the samurai "oligarchs" who carried out the Meiji Restoration in 1868. They were well entrenched before the political parties began to gain influence in the early twentieth century, and they regained dominance when party politicians subsequently proved unable to run Japan effectively.[80]

Structurally, the postwar Japanese democratic system allows bureaucrats major influence on policy to an extent hardly imaginable, at least in the United States. A U.S. president appoints hundreds of officials to enable him to oversee and supervise the United States federal bureaucracy. In contrast, the Japanese prime minister makes relatively few such appointments, and even these appointees have little power. Therefore, he has little supervisory capacity. Japanese politicians also lack the large staffs and other sources of expertise, separate from the civil service, that are available to the U.S. president and to members of the U.S. Congress. Japanese bureaucrats are seldom deprived of their jobs for rejecting or attempting to undermine a prime minister's policies.

Bureaucrats in two organizations with considerable power over Japanese economic policy in the postoccupation era—the Ministry of International Trade and Industry (MITI) and the Ministry of Finance—have acquired "an unshakable confidence" in their "ability to look after the nation's interests better than the people themselves or the representatives they elected." This remains true even though the competence of the finance ministry has been seriously questioned in Japan in recent years, the result of banking and stock problems. The confidence of these officials is explained in part by the fact that for several decades the MITI bureaucrats and their collaborators elsewhere could be said to have designed and implemented an industrial policy that "turned Japan into an economic superpower."[81]

The view that an indigenized version of democracy exists in Japan is controversial. Some argue that Japan is really being run by a "ruling triad," a "cohesive and stable political elite" from the bureaucracy, big business, and the LDP. Most variants of this model see the politicians serving as "'supreme ratifiers' of the bureaucracy's policies" and acting "to insulate the bureaucracy from pressure by political and interest groups so that it can autonomously implement policies fostering high economic growth." Although somewhat popular in Japan, this so-called "Japan Inc." model is either extreme or long out of date, challenged by a "growing consensus" among observers that the Japanese political process is currently "more fragmented or sectionalized than it is cohesive or unified." An extreme version of this latter interpretation appears in the writings of journalist Karel Van Wolferen, who claims that Japan's political system is so fragmented that it cannot make decisions in its own best interest. He calls it a "government without a top." Like the Japan Inc. model, Wolferen's views contain elements of truth but are too simplified.[82]

JAPAN'S TRANSITION TO DEMOCRACY: INTERPRETATIONS AND OUTCOMES

Modern scholarly literature contains a variety of interpretations in regard to the postwar period in Japan. Some interpretations place most weight on the U.S. role and on its supposedly positive results, but there is also a left-revisionist approach that portrays the U.S. occupation as less than a triumph for Japan and the United States and questions the value of Japan's version of democracy. Another approach holds that Japan probably would have become democratic on its own: After militarism and its devotees had been discredited by cataclysmic military defeat, the evolution toward democracy clearly under way by the early twentieth century would have continued once the militarist aberration was over. Of course, discourses on the subject of the establishment of democracy in Japan can undoubtedly combine these alternative approaches (and others) in many ways.

Interpretations that give primacy to the U.S. role and judge that role favorably tend to stress the goals, choices, skills, and actions of individuals and groups during the time of transition and show the old regime to have been manifestly incapable of reforming itself via any sort of natural evolution. Thus, the occupation becomes an important disjuncture in Japanese history. Writing in this vein, a Japanese scholar focusing on the 1947 constitution remarks, "Among the political leaders of Japan in the immediate postwar era there existed neither the intent nor the capability to draft so liberal and so democratic a document. Had the new constitution not been imposed from above . . . it would not have come into existence."[83] Such interpreters nevertheless see acceptance of the postwar democratic system in Japan as a matter of choice, despite its origination in coercion. The system takes root, they argue, substantially because many people (or the people as a collectivity) rationally perceive themselves to be better off, emotionally respond to liberation from various sorts of earlier oppression, and are open to learning from past disaster. The Japanese elite and Japanese people were also prepared to accept MacArthur's authority and make use of the political system associated with him, in the absence of alternative authority and in a highly insecure time.

A left-revisionist interpretation, by way of contrast, is likely to focus on the limited extent to which the postwar occupation authorities succeeded in being reformist. The reformist impulse of the occupation is said to have been modified and in some ways vitiated by the "reverse course" after 1947–1948 and by opposition from Japan's conservative postoccupation government. The cold war, which helped to produce the reverse course in Japan, is said to be a key element in the international political setting, along with Washington's commitment to Japan's economic recovery and to the advancement of the international capitalist order. Such revisionist views criticize structural/institutional continuities in Japanese politics, such as the retention of the emperor and the bureaucracy, that fostered the dominance of conservative policymakers. The occupation administration, they argue, relied too heavily on presurrender Japanese institutions. Left-revisionists also emphasize the eventual convergence of U.S. policy with Japanese conservatism.

The overall political outcome of Japan's postwar transition process, according to the most important contemporary left-revisionist scholar, John Dower, was the "reconsolidation of a paternalistic, albeit more liberal, state" integrated into "the global anti-communist camp." Thus, postoccupation Japan has been a limited capitalist democracy in which the defense of democratic reform has been left mainly to "the progressive and radical forces." These forces, or groups, had firmly supported U.S. initiatives early in the occupation, but, after U.S. policy changed, came to be among the occupier's "severest critics." Both the conservative and progressive forces in Japanese postwar politics, says Dower, "had prewar roots and reflected tensions starkly evident in the prewar society." Some significantly different features of the postwar polity, and some of the most important outcomes of the democratization process, he says, are "the [substantial] size of the [progressive] opposition [to the conservatives], its diversity and articulateness, and its ability to exist without fear of crass government repression."[84]

The interpretation holding that Japan would probably have become democratic on its own and that the occupation episode in Japanese history merely served as the "catalyst [but] not creator" of Japanese democracy is a view that Japanese conservatives like Yoshida would surely find congenial. A prominent U.S. scholar, Edwin O. Reischauer, has argued that "on the whole the Japanese political system . . . would probably have been much the same sort of parliamentary democracy it is today, even without the strong occupation efforts to produce this result." The kinds of political behaviors found in elections and in the way the Diet functions now would be "much the same," because they "are clearly the natural outgrowth of the political habits already well established by the 1920s." In addition, the political parties that Reischauer observed (he wrote this particular essay in the early 1980s) were, he claimed, "for the most part simply the continuation of prewar political groupings."

Once military government had been discredited by the outcome of the war, "the obvious alternative . . . for most Japanese was some form of parliamentary democracy . . . except for the possibility of a dictatorship by the right or left." Progress toward democracy might well have been "slower and less certain," and the Meiji Constitution would very possibly have undergone "revision and reinterpretation" rather than being replaced by something new. Conceivably, more "unclarities and anomalies" would have remained in the political system than is now the case. For example, theoretical sovereignty would still lie in the hands of the emperor. But the real situation, even on this issue, would be much as it is now, with actual sovereignty lying elsewhere.

Reischauer implies that dictatorship might have been possible without such strong U.S. pressure and control. Indeed, simple failure by the occupation authorities "to maintain orderly political procedures in the early postwar years" probably would have contributed to the eruption of "open conflict" between the Japanese progressive left and conservative right. He guesses that such a conflict would have resulted in "initial victory" for the left, followed by "a crushing reaction of the right." But contemporary Japan is, Reischauer concludes, "much more the result of Japanese skills and past experiences together with general world conditions [after World War II] than it is the product of any significant American planning." Even though the occupation speeded up certain developments in Japan, it is other social, economic, military, and cultural experiences and skills found in Japan, and the postwar international situation outside Japan, that should be most heavily weighted when explaining Japan's democratization process and its outcomes.[85]

Any synthesis of these alternative approaches, even a rough one, demands careful consideration of both continuities and discontinuities from prewar Japan. The reform proposals of Japan's wartime and immediate postwar governments, proposals that predated those of the occupation regime, "give us some indication of what postwar changes would have been like had the occupation authorities not had the last word." Continuities are visible in those earlier proposals, but they were different enough from those of SCAP as to require the conclusion that "the occupation mattered enormously."[86] The ledger is therefore more heavily weighted on the side of the discontinuities. Certain reforms would not have been possible without the occupation army, including the idea that the emperor's role should be merely symbolic and the development of the new constitutional order. The latter reform required not only a new constitution but also such measures as "the abolition of the special police, the end of anti-leftist legislation . . . and respect for fundamental human rights." These changes reduced the ability of conservative politicians to suppress the leftist forces. Despite continued conservative and bureaucratic dominance, left-of-center parties and social groups would now have a greater voice and a more legitimate place in the Japanese political game than they had attained in the 1920s and 1930s.[87]

Besides providing a greater role in political life to the Japanese left wing (a condition that developed further after 1993 with cabinet representation for the socialists for the first time since 1947), the new constitutional order is structurally different from its predecessors in other crucial ways. The military is out of politics, as are the emperor and the pre-1947 extraconstitutional loci of power. Parliamentary votes of no confidence will force cabinets to resign. Democratic practices are now institutionalized, and parties and factions influenced by public opinion share the center of the political game with the bureaucrats. The bureaucracy is now at least technically subject to parliament's policymaking controls and to either the ruling party or ruling interparty coalition. Rarely are the bureaucrats "capable of acting contrary to the majority of elected officials in parliament. . . . [Their] power lies within the arena of preferences set by the parliamentary majority."[88] These are very broad preferences, however, rather than matters of detail, and the power of the bureaucrats may be rising as recent elections "have become more volatile"[89] in their outcomes while coalitions and majorities behind them have become unstable.

In the last several decades, civil liberties, especially press freedom, have been firmly planted in the political culture, and the government-guided educational system and other forms of socialization now try to replicate that political culture within each new generation. Moreover, postwar Japanese conservatives—both politicians and bureaucrats—have, over time, become quite different from their prewar and wartime brethren. In addition to their democratic experience, their desire to keep Japan in a respectable place among the industrial democracies seems to guide their actions. Their focus on economic growth through international trade rather than militarism favors continued democracy, even though Japan's trade surpluses have ultimately brought diplomatic conflict to the international capitalist order.

Japan may be a far-from-perfect democracy, but the skills, goals, and actions of the major occupation decisionmakers and their Japanese counterparts did play a crucial role in producing a real democracy.[90] They did so in a sociopolitical, economic, and cultural context that prepared Japanese practitioners of democracy to adapt it, indigenize it, and (some decades later) undertake further reform of it. In addition, the regularization and routinization of democratic political thought and behavior that began during the U.S. occupation, and the sharing of power and broadening of political participation that began at the same time, are by now major outcomes of Japan's transition to democracy. Still another major outcome is the development of a culturally specific style of Japanese democracy with which most elite practitioners of politics can feel comfortable, as can the press and public, assuming the recently demonstrated capacity for reform is sustained in the troubled times that seem to lie ahead. These outcomes of Japan's democratic transition have in turn become major prerequisites for Japanese democracy's continued existence.

CHRONOLOGY

| 1889 | Japan's "Meiji" Constitution promulgated |
| 1890 | First Diet (parliament) elected and convened |

1889–1920s	Evolution of Japan toward democracy
1920s and 1930s	Economic problems and then depression in Japan
1930s to August 1945	Japan's militarist-fascist period
1941	Japan attacks Pearl Harbor and enters World War II
August–September 1945	Japan surrenders to the Allied forces, ending World War II; American occupation of Japan begins under the leadership of General Douglas MacArthur
September 27, 1945	General MacArthur and Emperor Hirohito meet for the first time
January 1, 1946	"New Year's Day Rescript" of the emperor (formal renunciation of his divine status)
March 6, 1946	The Japanese government publicly announces the substance of a new constitution
April 10, 1946	Japan holds first postwar general election for parliament
May 22, 1946	Shigeru Yoshida becomes prime minister for the first time
October 7, 1946	New (MacArthur) constitution approved by parliament; takes effect in 1947
1951	MacArthur dismissed from his post in Japan by President Harry Truman
1951	San Francisco Peace Treaty concluded between Japan and World War II opponents; takes effect in 1952
1952	American occupation of Japan ends
1954	Last Yoshida term as prime minister ends
1955	Creation of the Liberal Democratic Party (LDP), the dominant party of Japan until 1995
1994	Reform of the Japanese electoral system

Notes

1. Kazuo Kawai, *Japan's American Interlude* (Chicago: University of Chicago Press, 1960), pp. 4–6.

2. Toshio Nishi, *Unconditional Democracy: Education, and Politics in Occupied Japan* (Stanford: Hoover Institution Press, 1982), pp. 8, 18–22; Kawai, *American Interlude*, pp. 44, 71.

3. Nishi, *Unconditional Democracy*, pp. 18–19.

4. Foregoing quotations and material from T. J. Pempel, *Politics and Policy in Japan: Creative Conservatism* (Philadelphia: Temple University Press, 1982), p. 14 (quotation); Richard B. Finn, *Winners in Peace: MacArthur, Yoshida, and Postwar Japan* (Berkeley: University of California Press, 1992), p. 26; David A. Titus, *Palace and Politics in Prewar Japan* (New York: Columbia University Press, 1974), pp. 105–106 (quotations), 187, 298–323; Kawai, *American Interlude*, pp. 48, 55; and Herbert P. Bix, "The Showa Emperor's

'Monolgue' and the Problem of War Responsibility," *Journal of Japanese Studies* 18(2) (1992): 345–347. For an explanation of the "Imperial Will" concept, the competition to have influence over it, and how it could differ from, and yet be linked to, the emperor's "personal will," see also Titus, *Palace and Politics*, pp. 6, 47, 49, 54–57, 95, 284, 298–303, 315–323. I have tried to reconcile some of the contradictory impressions provided by these sources.

5. Kawai, *American Interlude*, pp. 48 (quotation), 55, 115 (quotations), 119.

6. Kawai, *American Interlude*, pp. 43–44, 48.

7. Finn, *Winners in Peace*, pp. 26–27.

8. Kawai, *American Interlude*, p. 48.

9. Quotations and material are from Finn, *Winners in Peace*, p. 26.

10. Finn, *Winners in Peace*, p. 326; Kawai, *American Interlude*, p. 79; Carol Gluck, Historian, Columbia University, Television Interview, Arts and Entertainment Network, August 10, 1995.

11. Direct quotation of emperor's words from Douglas MacArthur, *Reminiscences* (New York: McGraw-Hill, 1964), pp. 287–288. Another account indicates that the emperor also offered to abdicate "in due course"; Tetsuya Kataoka, *The Price of a Constitution: The Origins of Japan's Postwar Politics* (New York: Crane Russak, 1991), p. 26. Kataoka takes his material from the official U.S. government documentary series *Foreign Relations of the United States* 6 (1945) (Washington, DC: U.S. Government Printing Office, 1969), p. 627. A summary of the meeting by Hirohito's translator fails to support MacArthur's account; no mention is made of Hirohito's statement of responsibility for the war. MacArthur's quotation may be unreliable. See John W. Dower, *Japan in War and Peace: Selected Essays* (New York: The Free Press, 1993), p. 345. But for indications that the quote was consistent with a readiness by the emperor to use the language of self-sacrifice when it suited him, see Daikichi Irokawa, *The Age of Hirohito: In Search of Modern Japan* (New York: The Free Press, 1995), pp. 3, 30, 76–77, 93–99, 124–126.

12. Finn, *Winners in Peace*, p. 24.

13. Finn, *Winners in Peace*, p. 30 (source of quotation), and Kawai, *American Interlude*, pp. 59–60.

14. About the decisionmaking and quotation, see Finn, *Winners in Peace*, pp. 63–64. But see also Irokawa, *Age of Hirohito*, pp. 126–127, and Herbert Bix, "Showa Emperor's 'Monologue,'" pp. 320–321.

15. Kawai, *American Interlude*, pp. 72–79, 84 (quotation).

16. Finn, *Winners in Peace*, pp. 99–100.

17. Finn, *Winners in Peace*, p. 100.

18. Nishi, *Unconditional Democracy*, p. 122. Another version of these events argues that the emperor was actually reluctant to assent to the new constitution because it deprived him of all political powers. This source also claims that the emperor, after some procrastination, finally (on March 5, 1946) yielded in only the most formal sense while responding to a set of fears, one being that he might be forced to abdicate. See Herbert Bix, "Inventing the 'Symbol Monarchy' in Japan, 1945–1952," *Journal of Japanese Studies* 21(2) (1995): 337–340.

19. Kawai, *American Interlude*, pp. 84–87 (quote); Finn, *Winners in Peace*, p. 64.

20. Irokawa, *Age of Hirohito*, pp. 101–102; Bix, "Symbol Monarchy," pp. 345–346.

21. See MacArthur, *Reminiscences*, pp. 287–288; Finn, *Winners in Peace*, pp. 27, 100; Nishi, *Unconditional Democracy*, pp. 54, 122; Kawai, *American Interlude*, p. 83.

22. The material on Yoshida in this section and quotations are taken from Finn, *Winners in Peace*, pp. 324, xviii, 217–218, 19–23.

23. Finn, *Winners in Peace*, p. 21; see also Dan Kurzman, *Kishi and Japan* (New York: Ivan Obolensky, 1960), pp. 206, 214.

24. Finn, *Winners in Peace*, p. 23.

25. Shigeru Yoshida, *The Yoshida Memoirs* (Boston: Houghton-Mifflin, 1962), pp. 128–129.

26. Kawai, *American Interlude*, p. 114.

27. Yoshida, *Memoirs*, p. 58 (quotation); Finn, *Winners in Peace*, pp. xvii, 22.

28. Finn, *Winners in Peace*, pp. 217, 313, 248–250, 20; J. W. Dower, *Empire and Aftermath: Yoshida Shigeru and the Japanese Experience, 1878–1954* (Cambridge: Harvard East Asian Monographs, Harvard University Press, 1979), p. 277.

29. Yoshida, *Memoirs*, pp. 43–45, 53–55.

30. Finn, *Winners in Peace*, p. 111.

31. Kawai, *American Interlude*, p. 114.

32. This and following quotations are from Finn, *Winners in Peace*, pp. 111, 191, 216; see also pp. 105, 114–119, 213, 215, 216.

33. Finn, *Winners in Peace*, pp. 191, 216–217 (quotations); "one-man rule" is from Kawai, *American Interlude*, p. 114; other quotations and material are from Dower, *Empire and Aftermath*, p. 276; see also Kurzman, *Kishi and Japan*, pp. 263–264, 278–284.

34. Kataoka, *Price of a Constitution*, p. 52 (quotes); Nishi, *Unconditional Democracy*, pp. 34, 308; William Manchester, *American Caesar: Douglas MacArthur, 1880–1964* (New York: Dell, 1979), p. 550.

35. Howard B. Schoenberger, *Aftermath of War: Americans and the Remaking of Japan, 1945–1952* (Kent, OH: Kent State University Press, 1989), pp. 46 (direct quotation from MacArthur), 48 (quotation), 50; on MacArthur's discretionary authority, see Nishi, *Unconditional Democracy*, p. 35; see also Robert E. Ward, "Presurrender Planning: Treatment of the Emperor and Constitutional Changes," in Robert E. Ward and Yoshikazu Sakamoto, eds., *Democratizing Japan: The Allied Occupation* (Honolulu: University of Hawaii Press, 1987), pp. 1–41; on the Potsdam Declaration, see Kataoka, *Price of a Constitution*, pp. 16–24, 39.

36. Dower, *Empire and Aftermath*, pp. 277–278.

37. Nishi, *Unconditional Democracy*, pp. 42, 68; see also Schoenberger, *Aftermath of War*, pp. 40–89 passim.

38. Nishi, *Unconditional Democracy*, pp. 41, 310.

39. Nishi, *Unconditional Democracy*, pp. 54–55 (quotations), 65–66, 68, 139.

40. Schoenberger, *Aftermath of War*, p. 74.

41. Schoenberger, *Aftermath of War*, pp. 71–75, 81–84 (quotation); but see also Robert E. Ward, "Conclusion," and Yoshikazu Sakamoto, "International Context of the Occupation," in Ward and Sakamoto, *Democratizing Japan*, pp. 405–414 passim, 60–64.

42. Manchester, *American Caesar*, pp. 556–558; "messianic pose" is from Edwin O. Reischauer, *Japan: The Story of a Nation*, 4th ed. (New York: McGraw-Hill, 1990), p. 188; "imperious aloofness" is from Kawai, mentioned in Manchester, p. 556.

43. Finn, *Winners in Peace*, p. 115.

44. Nishi, *Unconditional Democracy*, pp. 62–63.

45. Finn, *Winners in Peace*, pp. 207, 209; see also Nishi, *Unconditional Democracy*, pp. 73–79, 273–274; Theodore McNelly, "Induced Revolution," in Ward and Sakamoto,

Democratizing Japan, pp. 63–64; China policy reference is from Reischauer, *Story of a Nation*, p. 187.

46. Manchester, *American Caesar*, pp. 652–653, 678.

47. See Finn, *Winners in Peace*, pp. 111, 170–173, 207–209, 211–212.

48. All quotations (from a SCAP document) are from Nishi, *Unconditional Democracy*, p. 111.

49. Finn, *Winners in Peace*, p. 289; see also Saburo Ienaga, *The Pacific War, 1931–1945* (New York: Pantheon, 1978), pp. 58–74.

50. See Bradley Richardson and Scott Flanagan, *Politics in Japan* (Boston: Little Brown, 1984), pp. 39, 40, 46, 47; and "The Constitution of Japan," appendix to Theodore McNelly, *Politics and Government of Japan*, 2d ed. (Boston: Houghton-Mifflin, 1972).

51. Pempel, *Politics and Policy in Japan*, p. 34.

52. Richardson and Flanagan, *Politics in Japan*, p. 46.

53. Robert E. Ward, "Presurrender Planning," in Ward and Sakamoto, *Democratizing Japan*, pp. 19–23; see also Finn, *Winners in Peace*, p. 91.

54. Nishi, *Unconditional Democracy*, p. 126; Hideo Tanaka, "The Conflict Between Two Legal Traditions in the Making of the Constitution of Japan," in Ward and Sakamoto, *Democratizing Japan*, pp. 107, 110–113 (quotations), 117.

55. Finn, *Winners in Peace*, p. 89 (quotation); Kataoka, *Price of a Constitution*, p. 35; Courtney Whitney, *MacArthur: His Rendezvous with History* (New York: Knopf, 1956), pp. 248–249; see also MacArthur, *Reminiscences*, p. 300.

56. McNelly, "Induced Revolution," in Ward and Sakamoto, *Democratizing Japan*, pp. 79, 82 (quotations); Whitney, *MacArthur*, pp. 246–252; Finn, *Winners in Peace*, pp. 91–98; confirmation of the McNelly account, in slightly different language, can be found in Kataoka, *Price of a Constitution*, pp. 37–38.

57. Nishi, *Unconditional Democracy*, p. 121; and Yoshida, *Memoirs*, pp. 132–135.

58. McNelly, "Induced Revolution," in Ward and Sakamoto, *Democratizing Japan*, p. 83 (quotation); Nishi, *Unconditional Democracy*, p. 120.

59. McNelly, "Induced Revolution," in Ward and Sakamoto, *Democratizing Japan*, pp. 83–84.

60. Nishi, *Unconditional Democracy*, pp. 122–123; see also Kawai, *American Interlude*, pp. 51–53.

61. Preceding paragraphs and quotations are from Finn, *Winners in Peace*, pp. 107–111, 114–121; Kataoka, *Price of a Constitution*, p. 39; McNelly, "Induced Revolution," in Ward and Sakamoto, *Democratizing Japan*, pp. 85, 92, 94–99; Yoshida, *Memoirs*, pp. 143–144; and Ward, "Conclusion," in Ward and Sakamoto, *Democratizing Japan*, p. 418; for an unfavorable view of the Yoshida government's role, see Kawai, *American Interlude*, pp. 62–70.

62. McNelly, "Induced Revolution," in Ward and Sakamoto, *Democratizing Japan*, pp. 99–100.

63. Nishi, *Unconditional Democracy*, pp. 135, 137; on importance of peace to the emperor and Yoshida, see Finn, *Winners in Peace*, pp. 120–121.

64. Nishi, *Unconditional Democracy*, p. 136.

65. Kawai, *American Interlude*, p. 55.

66. "Ancient regime" and cooperation with SCAP references are from Nishi, *Unconditional Democracy*, p. 4; "subordinate independence" and related material are from Dower, *Empire and Aftermath*, pp. 370–372.

67. Material and quotes on constitutional revision from H. Fukui, "Twenty Years of Revisionism," in D. F. Henderson, ed., *The Constitution of Japan: Its First Twenty Years, 1947–1967* (Seattle: University of Washington Press, 1968), pp. 41–70; *Kyodo Economic Newswire* (Kyodo News Service), December 16, 1994, May 5, 1995.

68. Kawai, *American Interlude*, p. 9. Much of the material and all quotations in the following section are from Kawai, *American Interlude*, pp. 91–92, 95, 96; see also Finn, *Winners in Peace*, pp. 109–111.

69. Civilian "career officers" reference is from Tetsuya Kataoka, "Introduction," in Tetsuya Kataoka, ed., *Creating Single Party Democracy* (Stanford: Hoover Institution Press, 1992), p. 4; prewar and postwar comparison is from Kawai, *American Interlude*, p. 116; see also *New York Times*, January 16, 1994, and February 27, 1994.

70. See the Introduction to this volume.

71. Nishi, *Unconditional Democracy*, p. 135.

72. Kawai, *American Interlude*, p. 111.

73. Edwin O. Reischauer, "The Allied Occupation: Catalyst Not Creator," in Harry Wray and Hilary Conroy, eds., *Japan Examined: Perspectives on Modern Japanese History* (Honolulu: University of Hawaii Press, 1983), p. 339.

74. Reischauer, "The Allied Occupation," p. 339.

75. *New York Times*, October 9, 1994.

76. Ellis Krauss, "Politics and the Policymaking Process," in Takeshi Ishida and Ellis Krauss, eds., *Democracy in Japan* (Pittsburgh: University of Pittsburgh Press, 1989), p. 41. The term *indigenization* is borrowed from Sakamoto, "International Context," in Ward and Sakamoto, *Democratizing Japan*, p. 65.

77. J. A. A. Stockwin, "Political Parties and Political Opposition," in Ishida and Krauss, *Democracy in Japan*, p. 99.

78. Krauss, "Politics," in Ishida and Krauss, *Democracy in Japan*, p. 46.

79. Material on the 1994 changes is from *Japan Times Weekly International Edition*, April 11–17, 1994, January 2–15, 1995; *New York Times*, January 29, 1994; *Japan Economic Newswire* (Kyodo News Service), November 24, 1994 (quotations), December 20, 1994 (quotation); *Daily Yomiuri*, November 25, 1994; Jiji Press Ticker Service, January 31, 1994; *South China Morning Post* (Hong Kong), January 31, 1994; Seizaburo Sato, "The Recruit Affair: Criticizing the Critics," *Japan Echo* 16: 3 (1989): 43.

80. John Creighton Campbell, "Democracy and Bureaucracy in Japan," in Ishida and Krauss, *Democracy in Japan*, p. 114.

81. *New York Times*, April 10, 1994; and see Campbell, "Democracy and Bureaucracy in Japan," in Ishida and Krauss, *Democracy in Japan*, pp. 130–133.

82. Kenji Hayao, *The Japanese Prime Minister and Public Policy* (Pittsburgh: University of Pittsburgh Press, 1993), pp. 7–14. Hayao quotes from Karel Van Wolferen, "The Japan Problem," *Foreign Affairs* 65 (Winter 1987): 289; see also Van Wolferen's book, *The Enigma of Japanese Power: People and Politics in a Stateless Nation* (New York: Alfred A. Knopf, 1989).

83. Rinjuro Sodei, "A Question of Paternity," in Wray and Conroy, *Japan Examined*, p. 353; for this type of interpretation, see also his entire article, pp. 352–356, and the Finn and Nishi books, cited in this Notes section.

84. J. W. Dower, "Reform and Reconsolidation," in Wray and Conroy, *Japan Examined*, pp. 343–351; for full-scale left-revisionist works, see Dower's *Empire and Aftermath*, especially pp. 275, 367–369, and Schoenberger's *Aftermath of War*, cited earlier.

85. For these arguments, see Reischauer, "Catalyst Not Creator," in Wray and Conroy, *Japan Examined*, pp. 335–342.

86. Eiji Takamae, "Some Questions and Answers," in Wray and Conroy, *Japan Examined*, pp. 357–363; following quotations are from same source.

87. See Stephen S. Large, "The Patterns of Taisho Democracy," and George O. Totten III, "Japan's Political Parties in Fascism, Democracy and War," both in Wray and Conroy, *Japan Examined*, pp. 177–178, 266–267, respectively.

88. T. J. Pempel, "Prerequisites for Democracy: Political and Social Institutions," in Ishida and Krauss, *Democracy in Japan*, pp. 30–31.

89. Takeshi Ishida and Ellis Krauss, "Democracy in Japan: Issues and Answers," in Ishida and Krauss, *Democracy in Japan*, p. 13.

90. See T. J. Pempel, "Prerequisites," in Ishida and Krauss, *Democracy in Japan*, pp. 17–37.

Suggestions for Further Reading

The major contemporary research sources on the creation of Japan's form of democracy include: R. E. Ward and Y. Sakamoto, eds., *Democratizing Japan: The Allied Occupation* (Honolulu: University of Hawaii Press, 1987), and Tetsuya Kataoka, *The Price of a Constitution: The Origins of Japan's Postwar Politics* (New York: Crane Russak, 1991). A good introduction to the left-revisionist historical viewpoint is Howard B. Schoenberger, *Aftermath of War: Americans and the Remaking of Japan, 1945–1952* (Kent, OH: Kent State University Press, 1989). Any list of primary sources should include: *Supreme Commander for the Allied Powers: The Political Reorientation of Japan, September 1945 to September 1948*, Report of the Government Section of SCAP, 2 vols. (Washington, DC: Government Printing Office, 1949).

The important memoirs and biographies of postwar political actors include: Douglas MacArthur, *Reminiscences* (New York: McGraw-Hill, 1964); Shigeru Yoshida, *The Yoshida Memoirs* (Boston: Houghton-Mifflin, 1962); J. W. Dower, *Empire and Aftermath* (Cambridge: Harvard University Press, 1979); and Daikichi Irokawa, *The Age of Hirohito* (New York: The Free Press, 1995).

Among the valuable scholarly sources on the current Japanese political system is Takeshi Ishida and Ellis Krauss, *Democracy in Japan* (Pittsburgh: University of Pittsburgh Press, 1989). One controversial book has interpreted Japanese politics as lacking any decision-making center: Karel Van Wolferen's *The Enigma of Japanese Power* (New York : A. A. Knopf, 1989). Wolferen's view counterbalances another extreme interpretation, which holds that political decisions in Japan are made by a cohesive power elite. A recent book that acknowledges these extremes but is not trapped by them is Kenji Hayao's *The Japanese Prime Minister and Public Policy* (Pittsburgh: University of Pittsburgh Press, 1993).

Politically sensitive suggestions for revising Japan's current constitution, made by one of Japan's leading newspapers (especially in November 1994), can be found in the *Daily Yomiuri* via Mead's Lexis-Nexis service. Other Japanese newspapers and news services are also available on Lexis-Nexis. The weekly newspaper *Japan Times* and such valuable journals as *Japan Echo*, *Asian Survey*, and the *Journal of Japanese Studies* are usually found in college or university libraries.

5

Argentina:
The Melancholy
of Liberal Democracy

ALDO C. VACS

After more than fifty years of political turmoil that earned Argentina a well-deserved reputation as one of the most unstable countries in the world, a new period of democracy was inaugurated by elections in 1983. More than a decade later, to the surprise of many observers, this democratic experience had not been interrupted by a military coup. In 1989, for the first time since 1916, power was peacefully transferred from an elected president to another who represented the main opposition party. A third democratic contest in 1995 resulted in the reelection of the incumbent president. Meanwhile, the armed forces, which during a half-century had deposed all elected presidents, remained subordinated to the civilian authorities. Political groups that in the past had tried to gain power through unconstitutional means such as military coups or revolutionary violence have engaged in the construction of political parties able to compete in a liberal democratic environment. Public opinion polls indicate that, unlike what happened in the past, a large majority of the population supports a democratic regime and rejects any attempt to overthrow the elected authorities.

Although these auspicious developments stand in stark contrast to the instability characteristic of traditional Argentine politics, clearly there is a wide gap between the idealistic expectations that accompanied the return to democracy in the early 1980s and the political realities of the 1990s. The democratically elected administrations of Raúl Alfonsín (1983–1989) and Carlos S. Menem (1989–1995; 1995–1999) reneged on many of their electoral promises and gradually limited popular participation in the decisionmaking process. And although the basic elements of a liberal democracy have been preserved, the electoral pledges of fostering income redistribution, social justice, and participatory democracy have been replaced by the application of neoliberal economic policies, a decline in social services, and the concentration of power in the executive branch.

The concepts of liberal democracy and neoliberalism as used in this chapter have specific meanings that do not always resemble the usage common in the United States. As used here, *liberal democracy* refers to a political regime characterized by political pluralism, division of powers, periodic elections, party competition, majority rule with constitutional limitations, protection of certain citizens' rights—such as freedom of speech and the press, right of assembly, and right to own private property—separation between the public and private spheres, and publicity of state actions. *Neoliberalism* refers to the contemporary revival of classic economic doctrines that advocate free market and free trade economic policies and reject the intervention of the state in the economy. This laissez-faire approach is currently followed by most Latin American governments calling for market, trade, and foreign investment liberalization, privatization of state enterprises, deregulation, market-determined interest and exchange rates, moderate taxation, fiscal discipline, elimination of subsidies, reduction of social expenditures, and thorough respect for private-property rights.

Argentina's transition to democracy and the process of consolidation of liberal democracy are part of a trend that has affected most Latin American countries since the early 1980s. During the last decade and a half, the military authoritarian regimes that prevailed in most countries in the region have been replaced by civilian democratic governments. Although national differences resulting from diverse political, social, economic, and historical experiences can be pointed out, it is apparent that currently the political and economic commonalities largely exceed the variations. In all cases, the transition to democracy was detonated by the economic crisis of the early 1980s. In all cases, the authoritarian rulers were succeeded by liberal democratic governments committed, in different degrees, to implement free market economic policies to replace the traditional state-centered strategies pursued in the past. In most cases, the transition led to situations in which power was concentrated in the executive and limits were imposed on congressional and popular participation in the decisionmaking process. Usually this trend was accompanied by the rise of such personalistic leaders as Víctor Paz Estenssoro in Bolivia, Fernando Collor in Brazil, and Alberto Fujimori in Peru who, after promising income redistribution and progressive social change, switched to the implementation of neoliberal policies. From this perspective, the Argentine case is a specific illustration of a general trend that engulfed all of Latin America; thus, many of the analytical observations presented here apply, with slight modifications, to other countries in the region.

In this chapter I will examine the political and socioeconomic circumstances that led to the reemergence and gradual consolidation of liberal democracy in

Argentina. The first section contains an interpretive analysis of the country's development throughout this century in order to highlight the causes of political instability and the rise of democracy in the 1980s. The second section examines the main domestic and international factors that facilitated the current amalgamation of liberal democracy and neoliberal economic policies into a relatively stable political-economic configuration. The remaining sections analyze the evolution of the two constitutional administrations since the transition to democracy, focusing on the constellation of political forces, socioeconomic developments, and institutional arrangements that help to explain why and how Argentine liberal democracy has survived for more than ten years.

Modern Argentina: Economic Decline, Social Conflict, and Political Instability

The Argentine cycle of political instability inaugurated in 1930 was characterized by a succession of weak civilian administrations followed by increasingly authoritarian regimes that reached their repressive climax with the 1976–1983 military government.[1] In retrospect, this last authoritarian regime represented the culmination of a protracted process of political decay correlated to the incapacity of successive governments to reverse the country's economic decline. Political stability from the 1870s to 1930 had been associated with the continuous prosperity generated by Argentina's insertion into the world economy as a supplier of grains and beef and an importer of manufactures, particularly to and from Great Britain.

In these favorable circumstances the political system evolved, through a process of co-optation, from an oligarchic regime controlled by the landed elites to a mass democracy that incorporated the middle sectors and portions of the organized working class. This transformation led to the electoral rise to power of the Radical Party (Unión Cívica Radical, or UCR), which satisfied the demands of its middle- and low-income supporters by implementing moderate income redistribution policies without trying to introduce structural changes. The Great Depression of the 1930s marked the end of this period of stability as the export-import model of growth—characterized by exporting a few primary products and raw materials to the developed countries and importing manufactures from them—collapsed due to falling prices and demand and growing protectionism. The struggle for economic shares among different socioeconomic groups intensified, leading to the Argentine elites' reassertion of their prerogatives, first through the use of the military and afterward through fraud and coercion.

However, the attempt to re-create a liberal economic model and oligarchic political system failed as Argentina as well as other Latin American countries began to experience a process of import-substitution industrialization in which locally produced manufactures replaced those imported from developed nations.

Active state intervention erected protectionist tariff barriers and subsidized industrial production through cheap credit and energy supply, tax breaks, and low-priced raw materials and facilitated the growth of industrial entrepreneurial and working classes. In the mid-1940s, this process culminated in the rise to power of Juan D. Perón, who was supported by a populist coalition made up of organized labor, industrialists, and military and civilian middle-class groups that favored state intervention, rapid industrialization, income redistribution, and the nationalization of strategic economic sectors. Populist policies were relatively successful in promoting economic growth and political stability until the early 1950s, when economic stagnation required a change in economic strategy. The adjustment program—which included measures to reduce the growing balance-of-payments deficits, incentives for foreign investment in order to attract new capital and technology, and stabilization plans aimed at reducing inflation—affected the nationalistic and redistributionist premises of populism and led to the weakening and collapse of the Peronist regime in 1955.

Afterward, a succession of military and civilian governments engaged in a series of unsuccessful attempts to restructure the Argentine political and economic systems.[2] Notwithstanding the different origins and ruling styles of these political regimes, all of them practiced exclusionary or repressive policies toward important sectors of the population, particularly against the supporters of Peronism and leftist groups. At the same time, however, these governments maintained state intervention in the economy while trying to shift the country's industrialization strategy in a new direction. Relative protection and support for local producers were combined with incentives for foreign investment and financial loans. There were also attempts to promote exports (especially of manufactures), foster international competitiveness, and modernize the most dynamic sectors of the economy.

These policies failed, in part as a result of international and domestic economic factors such as the relative scarcity of foreign investment, global recessions, unfavorable trade and financial trends, infrastructural deficiencies, inflationary pressures, hard currency shortages, and state mismanagement. To a large extent, however, the failure of these developmentalist attempts was also related to the continuous presence in Argentina of social and political actors and behaviors that had fostered the rise of populism and that were able to outlast the decline of the economic conditions in which they thrived. Populism had left as its legacy a "high organizational density" (labor unions; middle-class organizations; industrial, agricultural, and commercial associations; state bureaucracies; and military pressure groups) that even during authoritarian periods "allowed the formation of 'distributive coalitions' . . . able to block, through multiple vetoes, the organizational capacity of a new social regime of accumulation" while reinforcing the conditions for economic decline and political ungovernability.[3] The fight among well-organized socioeconomic sectors for preserving or augmenting their respective shares of a dwindling economic pie focused on the state, seen as an instrument for the attainment of sectoral goals, and led to economic crises, social conflict, increasing governmental paralysis, and military coups.

The 1976–1983 military regime was inaugurated after several of these abortive attempts had shown the infeasibility of trying to break this impasse while these distributive coalitions continued to operate. Determined to attack the causes of this stalemate in a radical manner, the authoritarian rulers believed that the unrestrained use of force combined with the loosening of free market forces—up to then fettered by the existence of an interventionist state and a semiclosed economy—would create the conditions for renewed economic growth. These measures would restore social discipline and destroy the socioeconomic and political bases for the emergence of populist and corporatist experiments.[4] The distributive coalitions would perceive the futility of trying to influence public policies in their favor because the market, and not the state, would assume the role of allocating resources and distributing income. This would eliminate one of the main causes of the high levels of social and political mobilization that had destabilized previous governments. After this transformation occurred, the military and their civilian allies envisioned the establishment of a semiauthoritarian political regime in which some form of restricted elections would be authorized without jeopardizing stability.

However, the military regime failed to attain these political-economic goals for a number of reasons, including the restrictions imposed by the armed forces on the economic team's ability to reduce military budgets and privatize state enterprises, the application of misguided exchange and monetary policies, the persistent refusal of the economic agents to modify their expectations and behavior in the expected direction, and the unfolding of adverse international conditions.[5] In the face of growing domestic economic problems, foreign-debt crisis, and political opposition, the military split into opposing factions. One group led by General Eduardo Viola—appointed president in March 1981—tried to moderate the liberal economic orthodoxy while establishing closer ties with conservative and provincial parties in order to co-opt their support. Another group led by the commander in chief of the army, General Leopoldo F. Galtieri, opposed any kind of political opening and counted on the backing of the civilian supporters of neoliberal economic programs. Galtieri overthrew Viola in December 1981 and attempted to solve the crisis by increasing repression while simultaneously trying to attract popular nationalistic support through the recovery of the Falklands/Malvinas Islands, occupied since 1833 by Great Britain and claimed by Argentina.[6] This tactic worked briefly, but, after the surrender of the Argentine forces on the archipelago, Galtieri was forced to resign and his successor, General (Ret.) Reynaldo Bignone, lifted the ban on political activities and called for elections to ease popular unrest.

The military was forced to transfer power amid internal turmoil and international isolation. However, through brutal repression and the application of neoliberal economic policies, the military had succeeded in changing Argentina's socioeconomic structure, reducing the power of organized labor, and atomizing the middle sectors. The military's policies had also strengthened some leading capital sectors (made up of horizontally diversified and vertically integrated domestic economic groups and foreign corporations linked to the local and export markets) while weakening other economic groups (which specialized in a single activity and produced for one specific market).[7] As a result, the Argentine society that emerged from the authoritarian period was much more fragmented than the organizationally dense one that before 1976 had facilitated the development of the distributive coalitions. The military regime had been unable to complete the restructuring of Argentina by consolidating a market economy and instituting a conservative political regime, but it had generated the conditions in which a neoliberal project of political-economic transformation had a chance to be implemented in a democratic context for the first time since the 1930s.

THE SURPRISING MERGER OF LIBERAL DEMOCRACY AND ECONOMIC NEOLIBERALISM

In Argentina, the exhaustion of the import-substitution industrialization model and the parallel decline of the populist experience marked the beginning of a series of political-economic experiments intended to reestablish conditions for economic growth, social peace, and political stability. By 1983, it had become clear for many influential actors, including upper- and middle-class groups as well as sectors of the military, that even though authoritarian regimes could implement with mixed success some neoliberal policies they could neither complete the application of the program nor guarantee in the long run the maintenance of this economic approach. The continuity and deepening of the neoliberal restructuring required the establishment of political structures and procedures able to legitimize the economic model, secure its survival during periods of social and economic strain, and replace the arbitrary and unpredictable authoritarian regimes with a system of formal rules and procedures that would allow rational calculations on the part of the socioeconomic agents. The 1976–1983 regime had failed to attain these goals, and this failure had led to growing political instability as the economic crises escalated, forcing the military to transfer power to an elected civilian government and jeopardizing the continuation of the neoliberal program of structural transformation.

The influential groups that benefited from these policies recognized that without adequate political underpinnings the free market model that they favored was doomed to fail. However, they rejected as unrealistic or dangerous the demands for structural socioeconomic change and broadened participation advocated by populist and leftist political groups. The populists were accused of supporting the forms of state intervention that led to the economic, social, and political crises of the 1960s and 1970s. The leftists were denounced for advocating redistribution and participatory approaches that would lead to growing stalemate and democratic breakdown.

At the same time, the merger of political and economic liberalism began to be seen by the weaker and less affluent sectors of Argentine society as the only realistic approach to improve their plight. The collapse of the earlier democratic distributionist and semiauthoritarian populist experiments, the tremendous suffering caused by the authoritarian rulers as well as their ultimate failure in overcoming the country's structural deficiencies, and the simultaneous awareness of the crumbling of the socialist experiences in other parts of the world all helped to generate this perception.

In the international realm, the trend toward economic liberalization was reinforced by a global surge of transnationalization and interdependence in the 1970s and 1980s that prompted the development of a global capitalist political economy. Individual states, however, were severely limited by their growing incapacity to control or modify the nature and outcomes of free market interactions that affected economic, social, and political developments within and across national boundaries.[8] In the case of Argentina—and Latin America as a whole—the pressure for the application of neoliberal programs was reinforced by the endorsement by influential policymakers of the so-called Washington Consensus, which advocated the implementation of free market policies.[9]

However, the application of unrestrained liberal economic policies can in turn generate social and political unrest. In the absence of adequate state intervention, self-regulating market economies allocate the cost of economic transformation unequally among different socioeconomic groups and generate hardship for substantial segments of the population, which could react in ways that threaten the economic balance. To guarantee the stability of the free market system, it is necessary to introduce a value-rational element of belief in its validity (legitimacy) that is normally obtained from its association with liberal democracy.[10]

The basic features of liberal democracy—a government whose legitimacy rests on a claim to represent the citizenry; individual consent; equality before the law; separation between the private and public domains; majority rule with constitutional limitations; competitive periodic elections; the possibility of citizens' participation as voters and candidates; and guarantees for the freedoms of expression, assembly, and organization[11]— were acceptable for the elites as long as these basic features provided the necessary legitimacy to the political economic model and were not used to restrict property rights, interfere in the market, or re-create populist and redistributionist experiences. Moreover, liberal democratic governments might be more inclined or better prepared than authoritarian ones to apply effectively such neoliberal policies as reducing public expenditures (particularly military budgets), promoting trade liberalization favoring consumers over specific groups of producers, obtaining support for privatization and deregulation decisions, and reducing uncertainty concerning the respect for property rights by enforcing the rule of law and eliminating the element of arbitrariness present under authoritarian regimes.

This notion of liberal democracy pervaded the Argentine transition and was shared by substantial sectors of the population—including upper-, middle-, and even low-income groups—who began to link democracy and markets with an underlying notion of efficient allocation of resources, power, and wealth, respectively. Elections were seen as the mechanism through which citizens would convey their political choices by selecting their government, whereas the market was regarded as the mechanism through which consumers would express their economic preferences by exchanging goods and services. Liberal democracy and free markets were seen as mutually reinforcing mechanisms that would create adequate conditions to foster political freedom and economic prosperity.[12] In this political-economic arrangement, however, the preservation of the free market establishes the boundaries of what are considered permissible policies as well as the appropriate level of political participation. These restrictions are also reflected in the features of the political leaders who emerge during the period of liberal democratization. These leaders are skillful political operators and tacticians. They do not have, or they rapidly discard after election, strong ideological ascriptions and campaign platforms. Rather, they embrace neoliberal economic strategies, rely on technocratic experts, and try to demobilize the population by emphasizing the leader's role, the advantages of delegative authority, and the need for passive consent.

Some concern over the long-term stability of this political-economic configuration is justified, especially when considering the strength and durability of the commitment to democracy by different groups in Argentine society—as well as in other postauthoritarian societies. Domestic support for democracy depends on a number of variables such as the degree of devastation brought about by the authoritarian rulers and the intensity of the population's revulsion against these regimes, the depth of the popular belief in the legitimacy of democracy, the lack of feasible political-economic alternatives, the existence of a favorable international climate, the ability of democratic administrations to establish effective institutional arrangements and to preserve peace and order, the existence of representative political parties, and other conditions. But besides these political factors, a crucial element that ensures the stability of liberal democracies is the majority's support for its distinctive socioeconomic features, namely private property, free markets, consumer sovereignty, and minimal state intervention in the economy.

The critical problem is that if this support is mostly based on the expectation of material benefits—that is, on the belief that a market economy would generate prosperity and that, in the long run, most of the population would partake in the benefits resulting from economic growth—it can ebb if these hopes are lost. If, on the one hand, the expectations of economic and social progress held by low- and middle-income sectors are dashed by a continuous incapacity of the market system to generate adequate rates of economic growth and more satisfactory income distribution patterns, there would be growing pressures to abandon some of the basic tenets of liberalism and to implement more interventionist state policies to redistribute income, promote employment, and improve social services. On the other hand, if these attempts to introduce structural changes appear imminent or get under way, powerful domestic socioeconomic groups and foreign actors might revert to their old fears of popular participation as conducive to state intervention in the market and restrictions on private profits and property rights. What has held true in regard to Eastern and Central Europe in the early 1990s is also applicable, with slight modifications, to Argentina and other nascent liberal democracies in Latin America:

> The transition to [or deepening of] free market economies involves, at least in the short run, drastic measures resulting in the aggravation of economic dislocations and hardship for large segments of the population. The rhetoric of social justice, however, has been deeply engraved in people's minds in all state-socialist societies [as well as in redistributionist and populist capitalist systems] and therefore unemployment, decreasing living standards and new market-induced inequalities represent a potential source of conflict and division which may decisively modify the strength and capabilities of political actors and affect the extension of citizenship and the creation of truly democratic institutions.[13]

If a situation were to emerge in which the political and economic sides of the liberal democratic equation no longer complement each other—for instance if parties opposed to the neoliberal policies were to come to power and maintain their electoral promises or were able from the opposition to hinder the application of these policies—the commitment of powerful international and domestic groups to economic liberalism might take precedence over their allegiance to political democracy. This situation might result in antidemocratic moves and, depending on the correlation of forces, in further limitation of popular participation and growing concentration of power in small groups; in a serious deterioration of the regime's capacity to maintain control over the economic, social, and political circumstances; or in the breakdown of democracy.

THE ALFONSÍN YEARS: POLITICAL DILEMMAS, ECONOMIC VACILLATIONS, AND EXECUTIVE ISOLATION

In Argentina, the consolidation of a stable liberal democracy that exhibited a definite commitment to complete the neoliberal economic restructuring started by the authoritarian regime was a gradual and often wavering development that began to unfold under the Radical administration of President Raúl Alfonsín (1983–1989). The Alfonsín years represented a transitional stage in which the clash between the remnants of the old structures and practices and the emerging liberal ones was still intense. This resulted in an approach that hesitatingly progressed toward more exclusionary policymaking practices; this approach never completed its course in a number of policy areas, leading to growing political and social conflicts and economic crisis.

In the economic realm, the trend was toward increasing concentration of the decisionmaking power in the hands of technocratic and politically isolated economic teams. This exclusionary approach was justified by arguing that the economic crisis required swift and decisive action that could be hindered by previous consultation with different groups, when in fact the democratic legitimacy and popular support for the administration empowered it to make autonomous decisions. Thus, the successive economic packages were designed in secrecy, disclosed suddenly to the population, and sometimes enacted by decree, ignoring congressional prerogatives. However, once the policies had been announced, the Radical government tried to encourage socioeconomic coordination among industrialists, business, agricultural producers, and labor through the creation of corporatist institutional mechanisms or through state-led negotiations with different sectors.

After their 1983 victory, the Radicals initially tried to fulfill their electoral promises by implementing a Keynesian economic program expected to facilitate economic growth and a moderate redistribution of income through a general agreement on wages and prices, state intervention to promote investment and exports, and reduction of payments on the foreign debt.[14] The attempt collapsed after a few months amid growing inflation, capital flight, stagnation, and socioeconomic conflict. The weakened state inherited from the military lacked the capacity to control key economic variables or to bring about a coordination pact among the socioeconomic sectors that either dominated the market (financial speculative institutions and large economic groups) or preferred to fight for their economic shares in a traditional way (labor, middle-income sectors, small and medium farmers, and industrialists). As a result, the original economic program was discarded and replaced in June 1985 by a "heterodox" plan that combined liberal stabilization measures (raises in public tariffs and taxes, cuts in public expenditures, privatization, monetary stringency, devaluation, and new currency pegged to the dollar) with unorthodox ones (a wage and price freeze, deindexation, and fixed real interest rates). Initially, this plan succeeded in stabilizing the economy and improving the government's popularity, thus helping to secure its victory in the congressional elections of September 1985. However, in 1986, the distributive struggle and the pressures on the administration coming from different sectors intensified, and the governmental attempts to satisfy some of these demands led to contradictory policies that undermined the economic plan.

The Radical government was unable to reduce the influence of Peronist labor leaders.[15] In 1984, a bill intended to guarantee democratic union elections and minority representation and to reduce the power of the traditional Peronist officials was defeated in the Argentine Senate. The Peronist-led General Confederation of Labor (Confederación General del Trabajo, or CGT) obtained legal recognition and organized several general strikes in opposition to the economic policies. Some labor leaders considered the CGT actions unnecessarily confrontational and began to negotiate with the government. As a result, one of the members of the moderate group was appointed minister of labor, and the administration sent to Congress legislation that satisfied some labor demands, including collective bargaining, social services provided by the unions, and the protection of trade union rights. However, the 1987 congressional elections, in which the Radicals were defeated by the Peronists, showed that the political gambit of incorporating moderate labor leaders into the administration had failed to increase its popularity, and they were asked to resign. Afterward, the traditional lines of battle between labor and government were once again clearly drawn. As the economic situation worsened, real wages declined, social services deteriorated, delays in salary payments multiplied, and unemployment grew, creating fertile conditions for labor conflicts, including general strikes, particularly as inflation led to a rapid decline of real wages.

Following a similar pattern, Alfonsín's military and human rights policies fluctuated between responding to popular demands by bringing human rights violators to trial and reacting to military revolts by pardoning most of them. Ultimately, these vacillations led to the loss of civilian support without completely satisfying the armed forces.[16] Alfonsín came to power with a program that called for the reorganization and modernization of the armed forces, the depoliticization of the institution, and the establishment of the principle of civilian supremacy as well as the investigation, trial, and punishment of those responsible for the human rights violations committed between 1976 and 1983. Initially, the military budget was reduced and a law for the protection of the constitution and democracy was promulgated (the latter included severe sanctions for those trying to overthrow the constitutional authorities). A commission was created to investigate the fate of *los desaparecidos* (the "disappeared ones") and the state terror practices implemented by the military government. A presidential decree ordered the prosecution of the members of the military juntas, and they were convicted in late 1985.

However, faced with growing manifestations of military discontent, Alfonsín tried to lessen the unrest by limiting the number of officers under judicial investigation. A bill was passed that lifted any penal action against any members of the military who had been involved in state terrorist activities if they were not indicted within sixty days after the promulgation of the law. Encouraged by this concession, military groups continued to press the administration. In April 1987, after a revolt led by Colonel Aldo Rico, Alfonsín endorsed a bill that removed criminal liability from any action committed by members of the military when obeying orders from superiors.

Growing popular dissatisfaction with these policies and increasing socioeconomic problems led to a resounding defeat of the administration and victory of
the Peronists in the congressional and gubernatorial elections of 1987, with the
UCR losing control over the lower house and in a number of important
provinces. Meanwhile, facing a new inflationary upsurge and an intensification of
the distributive struggle, Alfonsín moved in a more orthodox economic direction
and announced measures intended to open and deregulate the economy, privatize
public enterprises, reduce the size of the state, and cut public expenditures.
Nevertheless, these policies fell short of satisfying the demands made by business
groups, which considered them insufficiently liberal and no longer trusted the
ability of the government to implement any stabilization program. The measures
were also rejected by the working and middle-income sectors that experienced an
abrupt drop in their real wages and salaries.[17] The voluntary agreements between
the government and the industrial and commercial associations temporarily to
freeze prices in exchange for a governmental promise to reduce fiscal expenditures
and the money supply, freeze public tariffs, and maintain the exchange rates finally collapsed in early 1989. The agricultural sector refused to sell foreign
exchange and organized lockouts. There was a speculative run on the dollar in the
financial sector. Labor unions organized mobilizations and strikes demanding
wage raises. The International Monetary Fund (IMF), World Bank, and foreign
banks refused to disburse new funds. The industrial and commercial sectors fostered price increases. The government failed to control the fiscal deficit.[18]

Discontent inside the armed forces reemerged when Rico led a new revolt that
was quelled by the army command in January 1988. Military hardliners continued
to conspire, and another mutiny erupted in December 1988, led this time by
Colonel Mohammed Seineldín, known for his extreme anticommunist and
nationalistic views. The rebels demanded an amnesty for soldiers prosecuted for
human rights violations, government vindication of their actions during the
"dirty war," the removal of the army high command, the appointment of a new
leadership who supported their demands, and an increase in military expenditures. The revolts, although defeated, represented a serious blow to the authority
of the Radical administration, which was forced to meet some of the rebels'
demands after their surrender to guarantee the loyalty of the rest of the armed
forces.

Alfonsín's capacity to overcome military pressures was further eroded when, in
early 1989, a senseless attack organized by a leftist group against a military garrison was defeated only after a violent armed confrontation.[19] This event reinforced
the position of the military, which took the opportunity to denounce the existence
of an antimilitary conspiracy backed by leftist and human rights organizations
with the acquiescence of the administration. After the attack, Alfonsín announced
the creation of a National Security Council with military representatives to advise
the president on the handling of subversive activities and a Domestic Security

Committee whose military members were allowed to gather domestic intelligence at presidential request.

In this context of economic, social, and political disarray, a Peronist victory in the general elections of May 1989 was predictable. Two figures emerged as the main contenders in the Peronist internal dispute: Antonio Cafiero, governor of Buenos Aires and president of the Peronist Party (officially the Party of Justice—the Partido Justicialista or PJ), and Carlos Menem, governor of La Rioja and the first-vice-president of the PJ. Cafiero controlled the political machine of the PJ at the national level and counted on the backing of several Peronist governors (particularly those of the most developed provinces), a group of moderate union leaders, and a large number of national deputies and senators. Menem was endorsed by a number of governors from the less-developed provinces, some deputies and senators, and a smaller group of labor leaders. Cafiero's program called for nationalistic and redistributionist economic policies, the defense of democracy, and moderate opposition to the Radical administration to reassure the middle class. In contrast, Menem's much more populist and nationalistic rhetoric appealed to the symbols of Peronist folklore and sentimentality to secure the support of the traditional grassroots members of the PJ. Menem's approach proved to be successful, first in the primary election in which he defeated Cafiero, then in the presidential contest in which he secured close to 52 percent of the votes against 39 percent gathered by the Radical candidate, Eduardo Angeloz.

In the days following the May 1989 election, the progressive paralysis of the Alfonsín administration combined with the misgivings concerning Menem's vague economic and social promises to worsen the crisis. Frantic attempts made by the administration to reach an agreement with the Peronists to manage an orderly transition and obtain support for economic stabilization measures failed. The already high inflation was replaced by hyperinflation (which climbed to 80 percent in May and 120 percent in June 1989), detonating a social explosion with violent demonstrations and looting of supermarkets and food stores that led to the declaration of a state of siege in late May. Finally, Alfonsín announced that, considering the critical juncture and the impossibility of reaching an agreement with the coming administration, he had taken the decision of resigning as of June 30 to facilitate Menem's early inauguration.

The Alfonsín administration had failed to meet some of the crucial challenges of governance: adequately managing the economy, guaranteeing social peace, and eliminating the sources of political instability. This failure can in part be attributed to the inability of the Radical administration to follow steadfastly a policy course aimed at completing the transformation of the Argentine model of social accumulation. By attempting to pursue a middle course between Keynesian and neoliberal strategies, between state intervention and free market policies, between social coordination and technocratic fiat, and between inclusionary and exclusionary policymaking, the Alfonsín administration ended in alienating crucial domestic and foreign economic, political, and social actors and in fostering the formation of the broadest possible hostile coalition.

The vacillating course followed by the Alfonsín administration resulted in a gradual decline in the level of direct and indirect participation by Congress and civil society in the decisionmaking process but fell short of attaining the degree of concentration of power and exclusion necessary to secure the stability of a liberal democratic regime and to impose a neoliberal economic program. It would remain for the Menem administration, taking advantage of the acute crisis left by the Radical administration and the weakening of important sectors of civil society, to complete the unfinished neoliberal restructuring and create the conditions for the stability of liberal democracy in Argentina.

THE MENEM YEARS: CONSOLIDATING LIBERAL DEMOCRACY

Menem's rise to the presidency was the culmination of a process that started with the internal political reorganization of Peronism after the defeat suffered by the PJ in the 1983 elections.[20] Before and during the presidential campaign, Menem appealed to the traditional populist themes of income redistribution, social justice, and economic independence, promising huge salary raises and a productive revolution that would result in the re-creation of the economic prosperity and abundance associated with the first Peronist administration (1946–1952). At the same time, however, Menem discreetly contacted representatives of powerful economic groups, giving them assurances that his economic policies would not affect their interests and offering them important positions in his cabinet if he were elected.

After his inauguration, the new president surprised many of his followers and adversaries alike by not only embracing but even deepening the neoliberal course followed by his predecessors. The application of this "bait-and-switch" tactic meant that the promises made during the electoral campaign were forgotten and replaced by a free market program to be implemented by some of the most representative figures of Argentina's elites. Top executives of the holding company Bunge & Born, for example, were appointed in the economic ministry in a complete reversal of the traditional Peronist hostility toward this diversified transnational economic group.[21] The turn was completed with the appointment to other economic posts of conservative and traditionally anti-Peronist representatives of orthodox economic ideas. The Menem administration's initial measures shaped a severe program for economic stabilization and structural adjustment aimed primarily at containing hyperinflation. This involved a devaluation and the elimination of subsidies; the lifting of restrictions on foreign investment; reduction of public expenditures and tax reform to attain a balanced fiscal budget; and privatization of several state enterprises.

However, the gradual implementation of neoliberal measures attempted in the first few months of the Menem administration was not successful. After a while, inflation grew, interest rates skyrocketed, the local currency lost value, and capital flight resumed. In the opinion of Menem and his closest advisers, it was necessary to implement more drastic and radical free market policies to restructure the economic system and prevent a new economic crisis. In December 1989, to accomplish this task, Antonio Erman González was appointed minister of economy. González had belonged to Menem's group of closest advisers since the early 1970s, and his loyalty to Menem was unquestioned. Neither a member of the ruling party (González belonged to a conservative faction of the small Christian Democratic Party) nor representative of any important socioeconomic organization, González was able, with presidential support, to isolate himself from political and sectoral pressures to check or halt the liberalization program. González eliminated state controls on the private sector, privatized most state enterprises, lifted tariff barriers, and reduced the size and expenditures of the public sector. This program helped to cut inflation, stabilize the exchange rate, and reduce capital flight. At the same time, these measures also adversely affected the quality and availability of essential services (including health, education, and justice) and had a regressive impact on the distribution of income, increasing poverty and reinforcing the growing concentration of income and wealth already in evidence during the Alfonsín years.[22]

In early 1991, a number of circumstances, including charges of corruption, renewed inflation, less than expected fiscal revenues, and the rise of the dollar, all indicated to Menem the convenience of replacing González with another figure able to deepen the application of the neoliberal program. González was appointed minister of defense; the up-till-then minister of foreign relations, Domingo Cavallo, was appointed minister of economy. Cavallo—a Harvard-trained economist, former president of the Central Bank during the last military government, and former Peronist congressional representative in 1987–1989—strongly advocated economic liberalization and an outwardly oriented strategy of growth instead of the traditional Peronist approach based on state intervention and the expansion of the domestic market.[23]

Cavallo's economic package—the so-called Convertibility Plan—completed the neoliberal turn: A new currency was created, the peso, freely convertible in dollars at a parity rate of 1:1; the more rapid privatization of public enterprises and a debt-for-equity plan accompanied massive dismissals in the public sector; and taxation reform and further opening of the economy were promised. A comprehensive executive decree deregulated most of the economy, established a free market environment lifting regulations on transportation, professional and commercial activities, import and export trade, financial transactions, collective bargaining, and social security arrangements, and abolished most official regulatory agencies. The use of an executive decree to modify or eliminate more than forty different laws was justified by the government for reasons of need and urgency, but this explanation was rejected by the opposition, which argued that congressional approval was necessary. Nevertheless, legal challenges to the validity of the decree were turned down by the courts, and the measures were swiftly implemented.

Cavallo's neoliberal economic policies succeeded in accomplishing some impressive results: Inflation was contained, the economy grew at a significant rate, privatizations moved forward, the rate of exchange remained the same, and capital inflows increased. At the same time, however, the program reinforced the trends toward regressive income distribution, concentration of wealth and oligopolization of the economy, and increased unemployment. It also facilitated imports and hindered exports, leading to a growing trade deficit. By December 1992, foreign support for the government's policies was reflected in the final agreement reached with the creditor banks to reschedule the foreign debt; that resulted in the incorporation of Argentina into the Brady Plan, a U.S.-sponsored initiative unveiled by Treasury Secretary Nicholas Brady in 1989 that offered the indebted countries a debt reduction by private bank and World Bank and IMF loans in exchange for implementing further liberalization measures such as privatization, deregulation, lifting of tariff barriers, and removal of restrictions on exchange markets, foreign investment, and financial flows.

Although in the early stages the government lost some senatorial and provincial races, support for the economic stabilization program increased gradually and helped to generate a Peronist victory in the 1991 congressional elections. More important yet, the Menem administration's neoliberal policies produced a number of structural, market-oriented transformations that would be difficult, if not impossible, to reverse: The interventionist state and distributive socioeconomic coalitions that had been the basis of the populist and developmentalist experiences of the past were no longer viable.

During this period, organized labor, often defined as the "backbone" of Peronism, suffered tremendous setbacks, resulting in splits and an unprecedented weakening of the labor movement.[24] Peronist labor organizations had participated in the electoral campaign, supporting Menem and enhancing his reputation as a leader able to prevent the repetition of labor strife that had shaken the country under Alfonsín. Some labor leaders, however, had refused to forgo the possibility of strikes under a Peronist administration and were severely criticized by Menem loyalists. After the inauguration, these union loyalists were appointed to important positions in the administration and formed a group that elected a CGT executive council composed exclusively of pro-Menem union leaders.

The continuous trend toward economic liberalization worsened labor problems. Support for the privatizations was absent among employees in the public sector who were threatened by dismissals. In the private sector, however, the trade unions were reluctant to engage in a direct confrontation with the government and employers during a recession. Perceiving these divisions and the generalized weakness of the labor movement, the administration refused to budge and reacted forcefully against its opponents, dismissing state workers, imposing obligatory conciliation in conflicts in the private sector, and recognizing the progovernment branch of the CGT as the only one with legal status. A bill limiting the right to strike of public and private workers employed in health services, public utilities, telecommunications, public transportation, education, and justice administration was sent to Congress; after Peronist and opposition representatives refused to pass it, the measure was enacted by presidential decree in October 1990. Afterward, new executive measures were enacted, weakening even further labor's capacity to challenge the neoliberal policies: New rules for collective bargaining decentralized the negotiation process and eliminated state intervention; labor contract laws were modified, making it possible for employers to change the conditions of work, fringe benefits, and wages; wage and salary raises were tied to increases in productivity; and new legislation limited the capacity of the trade unions to control the institutions that provided health and recreation services for workers, traditionally the main source of patronage and funds for organized labor. Labor opposition to these measures was ineffective, and the attempt to create a Peronist, labor-based political alternative to Menem failed.

While the taming and weakening of organized labor was under way, the hesitation of the Peronist Party to champion the shift toward neoliberalism also resulted in successful governmental attempts to gain control over its structures. The president of the party and governor of Buenos Aires province, Antonio Cafiero, and his supporters, after losing the presidential primaries, called for unity and stated their solidarity with Menem but suggested the wisdom of a more gradual economic transformation that would preserve some traditional Peronist social policies. In exchange, Menem's political operatives repeatedly accused Cafiero and the party leadership of opposing the administration and demanded their resignations. In mid-1990, due to the opposition of pro-Menem Peronist factions associated with non-Peronist parties, a provincial constitutional reform supported by Cafiero was overwhelmingly defeated by the Buenos Aires electorate. As a result, Cafiero and his supporters resigned their party positions, and Carlos Menem was elected the new president of the party. Menem, in turn, asked for a leave of absence and appointed his brother, Senator Eduardo Menem, the acting president of the party.[25] Afterward, the party machine remained under the tight control of the administration and supported without exception all executive policy initiatives. Support for the PJ rose or declined according to fluctuations in the popularity of Menem and his associates, and the success of his economic policies in generating stability was translated into solid electoral support for the party in congressional elections. Attempts by Peronist groups opposed to Menem to maintain some influence inside the party failed, and some of them left the organization to create a leftist coalition, the Frente Grande (Big Front).

The government's actions had shattered the chances of labor and intraparty opposition but, at the same time, disarticulated and weakened two pillars of its popular support: the organized labor movement and the Peronist Party. The problem of gaining support for the administration's program was compounded by the fact that the shrinking of the state precluded traditional clientelistic practices, such as offering jobs or services to the low- and middle-income sectors of the population. Faced with this decline in support and mobilization capacity, the Menem administration began to search for a new constituency among the middle- and upper-class groups that approved Menem's turn toward neoliberal policies. The administration's conservative shift was also encouraged by the collapse of several Peronist provincial administrations amid accusations of corruption and mismanagement, leading to the revival of traditional provincial parties or the emergence of new conservative parties. Expecting that these parties would be able to win some elections, Menem distanced himself from the bankrupt Peronist administrations and emphasized the support offered by these provincial parties to his neoliberal economic program in order to cement new alliances.

The concentration of decisionmaking power in the hands of the executive branch was apparent also in its human rights and military policies.[26] Early on, the Menem administration explored the possibility of obtaining congressional approval for an amnesty bill that would benefit the military as well as members of the former Peronist guerrilla organization, Montoneros, who were imprisoned or indicted. When this proved impossible, Menem issued presidential pardons to those military officials and civilians sentenced or indicted for human rights violations and politically motivated crimes, at the same time lifting the sanctions applied to those involved in failed military rebellions during the previous administration. And although reducing the armed forces' budget and privatizing military enterprises, the administration tried to cement good relations with the high command by authorizing the armed forces' participation in the planning and execution of antisubversive operations, granting them moderate salary raises, and earmarking the proceeds from the sale of military properties for the modernization of the armed forces.

These tactics reduced the margin for maneuver of the hardline military sectors, and they split into two groups. One, led by Rico, opted for leaving the army and establishing a right-wing nationalistic political movement to participate in elections; another group, led by Seineldín, continued to operate inside the army trying to attain control and pressure the administration. In late 1990, Seineldín and his supporters revolted and, for the first time, real combat took place between troops loyal to the army command and a group of rebels who finally surrendered. This defeat was followed by the punishment of those involved in the mutiny, but in order to reduce tensions Menem pardoned the former members of the military juntas and other high officers incarcerated for their responsibility in the human rights violations committed during the 1976–1983 period. Although internal military friction was not completely eliminated, the defeat of the rebels, the pardons, and the promotion of more professionally oriented officers to positions in the high command quelled the possibility of new revolts and considerably reduced the chances of military pressures on the administration.

Regarding the judicial system, the Menem administration tried to prevent any intervention of the judiciary in the policymaking process and to limit the courts' ability to perform their oversight role.[27] The nomination and appointment of judges sympathetic to the administration eliminated many of the potential obstacles to the use of executive power to implement controversial economic, labor, social, and foreign policy initiatives. This process culminated in the enactment of a law that increased from five to nine the number of Supreme Court justices. The packing of the high court with Menem loyalists prevented any judicial opposition to the administration's policies and perfected the process of concentration of power in the executive that had been completed in other areas.

In the foreign policy realm, Menem opted for a pragmatic approach, discarding the nationalistic, nonaligned, and autarkic elements of the traditional Peronist "Third Position" in foreign policy while favoring Argentina's unconditional alignment with the United States.[28] The administration gave proof of this resolve by refusing to condemn the U.S. invasion of Panama, announcing its intention to accept nonproliferation safeguards for the Argentine nuclear program, discontinuing its missile project, withdrawing from the nonaligned movement, fostering a rapprochement with the United Kingdom, and sending ships and troops to the Persian Gulf during the crisis there. Many of these presidential initiatives were criticized by the domestic opposition as violations of Argentina's sovereignty, abandonment of its traditional neutrality, and unconstitutional measures that should have been approved by the Senate. Nevertheless, a decisionmaking style characterized by its secrecy and lack of consultation continued to prevail in foreign policy amid the ineffective complaints of different groups.

The main opposition party, the UCR, remained in disarray, unable to block Menem's initiatives or to elaborate alternative programs. The preeminence of Peronism was confirmed in the congressional elections of September 1993 in which it obtained 43 percent of the votes (against 30 percent for the Radicals) and was able to win nine extra seats in the lower house. Interpreting these results as a confirmation of his popularity, Menem renewed his campaign to amend the constitution, which, at the time, did not allow presidential reelection. In December 1993, negotiations between Menem and the president of the UCR, Alfonsín, resulted in an agreement in which the UCR, in exchange for supporting the reform, obtained the president's promise to replace three pro-Menem Supreme Court justices with less-partisan personalities and a commitment to support constitutional provisions intended to limit executive power, create the post of chief of cabinet responsible to Congress, shorten mandates, reform the judiciary, and reinforce controls on the administration. This pact cleared the way for Congress to call for a constitutional reform.

Although both Peronist and Radical shares of the vote declined in the April 1994 constitutional assembly elections, they still gained a substantial majority in the convention. The constitutional reform was completed and approved in August 1994. It included among the new provisions the possibility of presidential reelection and thus cleared the way for Menem's candidacy to a four-year term in the May 1995 elections. In these elections, the electorate showed a clear preference for political and economic stability. Menem obtained close to 50 percent of the vote, followed by the candidate of a center-left coalition with 29 percent; the UCR finished a distant third, with less than 17 percent of the vote. At the same time, the Peronists gained an absolute majority in the lower house and preserved their control over the Senate and most provinces.

It is too soon to tell, but given these conditions the implementation of the 1994 constitutional amendments designed to check presidential power—such as the creation of a chief of cabinet and some supervisory agencies responsible to Congress—may not have the expected consequences. In practice, by retaining control over the party, its congressional representatives, most governors, and the judiciary, Menem may very well be able to pursue in his second administration the same elitist approaches and exclusionary policies that characterized his first term. Moreover, the decline of the main opposition party, the relative fragility of the center-left coalition, and the weakness of the socioeconomic organizations reinforce this impression, making it difficult to foresee in the near future greater popular participation and the rise of more representative institutions.

Conclusion: Prospects for Argentine Liberal Democracy

Assessing all these developments, it is possible to conclude that the consolidation of liberal democracy in Argentina under Menem represented the culmination of a number of embryonic developments that were already in evidence during the Alfonsín administration. Since 1983, most of the procedural features of democracy have been preserved, including periodic elections, party competition, and majority rule with constitutional limitations. However, there was only limited political uncertainty concerning electoral results for the parties, and candidates with chances of success were those that supported the existing political-economic arrangements or wanted to introduce minimal reforms. The rules of the political and economic games left room for some degree of uncertainty concerning who would win or lose, but this competition was limited by such factors as the immutability of the market economy and the preeminence of market interactions in setting the conditions for the distribution of wealth, income, and prestige; the stricter separation between state and civil society; the dominant role of professional politicians; and the generalized preference for pragmatic solutions.

All of this was reinforced by the consolidation of a clear split between two disparate political moments and logics. In the preelection moment, parties and socioeconomic organizations were subordinated to the political leaders and played a mobilizing role, catering to as many particularistic interests as possible in order to generate a personalistic mandate. In the postelection moment, the logic of governance and administration prevailed. "Apolitical" technocrats were appointed. Successful attempts to demobilize the population took place in order to transform the electorate into an atomistic aggregation of individuals with no shared group interests. The autonomous role performed by political parties and socioeconomic organizations in the mobilization and articulation of interests and conveying of demands was rejected. Passive consent and the efficacy of delegative authority were extolled.

As a result, growing emphasis was placed on the merits of apoliticism, efficiency, and technical solutions. The role of parties and socioeconomic organizations as mediators between civil society and the state was ignored. Political apathy increased and direct relations between the personalistic leader and the population were promoted. Ideological and programmatic appeals became negligible while personalistic approaches proliferated. This approach was favored by elected politicians, businessmen, and bureaucrats as well as by large portions of the population that indicated a growing preference for personalistic leadership, disregarding the ideological, organizational, or representative features of the parties and candidates.

The liberal democracy that has emerged in Argentina seems to confirm the validity of Joseph Schumpeter's interpretation of the modern democratic method as an "institutional arrangement for arriving at political decisions in which individuals acquire the power to decide by means of a competitive struggle for the people's vote" but in which the citizens do not decide among policy options or participate actively in the decisionmaking process.[29] When confronted with the rise of tensions between market forces and popular demands, the Alfonsín and Menem administrations turned to solutions that, without eliminating the democratic features of the regime, represented a consistent effort to reduce organized political participation, concentrate political power in the executive branch, establish direct relations between personalistic leaders and the masses, and intensify, when necessary, the use of legal yet repressive methods.

The basic features of a liberal democracy were preserved, but a number of initiatives were enacted to limit the participation or influence of organized political and socioeconomic groups in the decisions. The role of mediator between civil society and the state traditionally assigned in a mass democracy to the political parties was limited by subordination of the parties to personalistic leaders, lack of consultation, co-optation of technocratic and extraparty actors, and use of direct forms of communication between the leader and the population that thwarted the parties' traditional functions. A similar process affected the socioeconomic organizations—both labor and capital—which were weakened, subordinated, and co-opted and whose roles as articulators and representatives of interests were ignored by establishing relations with prominent actors rather than with institutions.

With different degrees of success, both Alfonsín and Menem tried to concentrate most of the decisionmaking power in the executive branch, especially to facilitate the application of economic policies aimed at strengthening the free market system. Repeated attempts were made to exclude Congress from meaningful participation in these decisions and to prevent the judiciary from exercising control over them. There were also successful initiatives, particularly under Menem, to curtail certain rights and freedoms (strikes, collective bargaining, unionization, access to mass media, publicity of state actions) while opposing any expansion of the remaining ones. The use of legal yet repressive measures to deal with challenges from the opposition forces intensified, and the roles of the military and the security forces in domestic affairs—despite promises made at the beginning of the democratic period to reduce them to a minimum—were enhanced.

This trend was facilitated by certain features of Argentina's political evolution and institutional structures.[30] Historically, the executive branch has dominated the legislature and the judiciary, which have often been unable to act as effective counterweights to the power of the president. The Argentine Constitution grants presidents considerable power by making them chiefs of state and government, assigning them the leadership of the armed forces and foreign relations, giving them a large degree of control over provincial governments, and establishing a number of conditions under which presidents can temporarily rule by decree. Furthermore, the dismissal of Congress and the removal of judges by successive authoritarian regimes have diminished the role and prestige of the parliamentary and judicial institutions. Finally, elected presidents have many times been charismatic individuals as well as the founders or uncontested leaders of the majoritarian political parties. This has facilitated the subordination of congressional delegations to presidential will and denied Congress an independent legislative role. A similar fate has affected the judicial branch, as many elected administrations removed or appointed judges for political and clientelistic considerations or ignored judicial decisions with which they disagreed.

Under Menem, other specific economic and political circumstances strengthened the unilateral decisionmaking capacity of the executive and eased the implementation of the neoliberal program. The Peronist tradition of personalistic leadership helped to concentrate power in the hands of a charismatic president and to exclude other actors from the decisionmaking process. In addition, the hyperinflation of 1989 generated among a substantial portion of the population a strong longing for economic stability that superseded any propensity to demand the implementation of economic and social policies that could unleash, according to the administration, a new inflationary surge.

Associated with all these developments was a characteristic style of political operation that can be categorized as neopopulist, insofar as it retained some of the characteristics of traditional populism while introducing new organizational, representative, and programmatic features.[31] From traditional populism, this new political style retained such features as the existence of a personalistic leader who appeals directly to a diverse mass of followers, many of whom had become unrepresented or anomic due to social, economic, and political transformations that created new actors or disarticulated old identities. In this sense, both Alfonsín, in an embryonic form, and Menem, in a more mature manifestation, fit the populist mold: Both of them attempted to build a personalistic leadership based on direct contact between leader and followers. They tried, with different degrees of success, to bypass the existing organizations and to establish a direct relationship with the new groups created by the neoliberal policies (self-employed and nonunionized workers and industrialists and financiers) as well as with those whose political identity had been shattered by the political-economic transformations (disenchanted organized workers, frustrated middle-class sectors, disgruntled members of the old agricultural, industrial, and commercial elites).

The new version of populism, however, differs from the old one not only because it rejects the statist, nationalistic, and redistributive aims and embraces a free market, pro-Western program of capitalist accumulation, but also because it rejects the corporatist approach typical of traditional populist experiences. Thus, Perón's populism favored the creation from above of a series of socioeconomic and political organizations subordinated to the state that would converge, in an organic manner, into an "organized society" where conflict would be eliminated. In contrast, Menem—and, to a lesser extent, Alfonsín—promoted the disintegration or neutralization of these institutional actors while trying to establish a direct relationship between the leader and members of the population considered as individuals. The expectation was that from this "atomized society," out of a myriad of competing individual interests and actions—as in a classic liberal utopia—economic prosperity and political order would finally emerge.

Finally, it should be underscored that Argentina's tradition of corporatism resulted in a misleading paradox: In assigning to the state a central role in socio-economic and political terms, it helped to create the conditions for the destruction of organized opposition to the neoliberal project and to facilitate the effective implementation of policies intended to reduce the state's intervention in the economy and its capacity to implement redistributionist economic and social policies. State power allowed Alfonsín to manipulate and co-opt some political and socioeconomic actors and allowed Menem to shatter and subdue political parties and socioeconomic organizations that had been established and nourished by the state and remained dependent and subordinated to it. In both cases, there was a trend toward concentration of power in the executive branch, especially in the techno-bureaucratic economic teams. Under Alfonsín, this trend toward executive predominance met the resistance of remnants of autonomous political and socioeconomic actors and suffered from internal vacillations, leading to growing presidential isolation and impotence. Under Menem, executive predominance was bolstered by the existence of critical circumstances—hyperinflation, social explosions, and political disarray within the opposition—that offered the executive branch the opportunity and resources necessary to impose its will on Congress, parties, and socioeconomic organizations.

In conclusion, the structural transformations completed in Argentina since 1983, with the consequent atomization of civil society and the strengthening of the executive capacity to enforce neoliberal policies, have made it highly probable that liberal democracy combined with an exclusionary neopopulist policymaking style will remain largely unaltered. The legitimacy of the liberal democratic regime has become indisputable, and its prospects for long-term stability are considerable. Nevertheless, although this triumph of liberal democracy has guaranteed respect for basic civil liberties and prevented the repetition of the brutal authoritarian experiences of the past, it also has brought about a degree of melancholy and political disenchantment as citizens perceive the limitations of a regime that does not leave room for the fulfillment of the idealistic expectations about political participation and socioeconomic transformation that accompanied the early stages of this transition to democracy.

CHRONOLOGY

1810	Creole provisional governmental Junta replaces Spanish authorities
1816	Declaration of Independence
1816–1829	Civil wars between federal and centralist groups
1829–1852	Period of authoritarian control by Juan Manuel de Rosas
1853	National constitution, molded on U.S. presidentialist system, is adopted
1853–1861	Sporadic civil war between Buenos Aires elites and provincial leaders
1862–1880	Consolidation of oligarchic regime led by agroexporting Buenos Aires elites
1880–1916	Economic prosperity generated by export-import growth model and political stability under oligarchic democracy
1916–1930	Co-optative democracy and economic prosperity under middle-class Radical administrations
1930–1943	Military coup, return of oligarchy to power, and beginning of import substitution industrialization
1943–1955	Rise, consolidation of power, and decline of Juan D. Perón and populist regime
1955–1966	Political instability, cycles of military and civilian regimes, and conflict between Peronists and anti-Peronists
1966–1973	Bureaucratic authoritarian military regime in power; urban explosions, guerrilla warfare, and socioeconomic crisis
1973–1976	Return to democracy under Peronist elected government; President Perón dies in office (1974) and is replaced by his wife and vice president, María E. Martínez; growing conflict between guerrilla groups and military
1976–1983	Military regime, "dirty war," and economic crisis; invasion of Falklands/Malvinas Islands and defeat (1982); Military call for elections (1983)

1983–1989	Radical party wins elections; Raúl Alfonsín elected president; growing economic and social problems and rise of Peronism
1989	Peronists win elections; Carlos S. Menem elected president for period 1989–1995; hyperinflation and social crisis
1989–1995	Menem in power; political stability and application of free market economic policies
1994–1995	Constitution amended, including possibility of presidential reelection; presidential tenure reduced to four years
1995	Menem reelected president for period 1995–1999

Notes

1. On Argentina's political-economic evolution see, for example, Juan E. Corradi, *The Fitful Republic* (Boulder: Westview Press, 1985); and David Rock, *Argentina, 1516–1987: From Spanish Civilization to Alfonsín* (Berkeley: University of California Press, 1987).

2. On Argentina's development after 1930, see Guido Di Tella and Rudiger Dornbusch, eds., *The Political Economy of Argentina, 1946–1983* (Pittsburgh: University of Pittsburgh Press, 1989); Mónica Peralta-Ramos, *The Political Economy of Argentina: Power and Class Since 1930* (Boulder: Westview Press, 1992); Guillermo O'Donnell, *1966–1973: El Estado Burocrático Autoritario: triunfos, derrotas, y crisis* (Buenos Aires: Editorial de Belgrano, 1982); and William C. Smith, *Authoritarianism and the Crisis of the Argentine Political Economy* (Stanford: Stanford University Press, 1989).

3. Juan Carlos Portantiero, "La crisis de un régimen: Una mirada retrospectiva," in José Nun and Juan Carlos Portantiero, eds., *Ensayos sobre la transición democrática en la Argentina* (Buenos Aires: Puntosur, 1987), pp. 57–80.

4. See Adolfo Canitrot, *La disciplina como objetivo de la política económica: Un ensayo sobre el programa económico del gobierno argentino desde 1976* (Buenos Aires: Estudios Cedes, vol. 2, no. 6, 1979).

5. See Jorge Schvarzer, *Expansión económica del estado subsidiario, 1976–1981* (Buenos Aires: CISEA, 1981) and *Martínez de Hoz: La lógica política de la política economica* (Buenos Aires: CISEA, 1983); Juan V. Sourrouille and Jorge Lucangell, *Política económica y procesos de desarrollo: La experiencia argentina entre 1976 y 1981* (Santiago, Chile: CEPAL, 1983); and Aldo C. Vacs, "Authoritarian Breakdown and Redemocratization in Argentina," in James M. Malloy and Mitchell A. Seligson, eds., *Authoritarians and Democrats: Regime Transition in Latin America* (Pittsburgh: University of Pittsburgh Press, 1987), pp. 15–42, as well as *The Politics of Foreign Debt: Argentina, Brazil, and the International Debt Crisis* (Ph.D. diss., University of Pittsburgh, 1986), pp. 265–366.

6. See O. Cardoso, R. Kirschbaum, and E. van der Kooy, *Malvinas: La trama secreta* (Buenos Aires: Sudamericana-Planeta, 1983); Oscar Ozlak, ed., *"Proceso," crisis, y transición democrática*, 3 vols. (Buenos Aires: Centro Editor de América Latina, 1984); Vacs, "Authoritarian Breakdown"; and Enrique Vázquez, *La última: Origen, apogeo, y caída de la dictadura militar* (Buenos Aires: Eudeba, 1985).

7. D. Aspiazu, E. Basualdo, and M. Khavisse, *El nuevo poder económico en la Argentina de los años ochenta* (Buenos Aires: Legasa, 1986); Carlos Filgueira, "El estado y las clases:

Tendencias en Argentina, Brasil, y Uruguay," *Pensamiento Iberoamericano*, no. 6 (July–December 1984), pp. 35–61; José Nun, "Cambios en la estructura social de la Argentina," in J. C. Portantiero and J. Nun, eds., *Ensayos sobre la transición*, pp. 117–137; Héctor Palomino, *Cambios ocupacionales y sociales en Argentina, 1947–1985* (Buenos Aires: CISEA, 1987); and Juan M. Villareal, "Changes in Argentine Society: The Heritage of the Dictatorship," in Mónica Peralta-Ramos and Carlos H. Waisman, eds., *From Military Rule to Democracy in Argentina* (Boulder: Westview Press, 1987).

8. On these trends, see Peter Dicken, *Global Shift: The Internationalization of Economic Activity*, 2d ed. (New York: Guilford Press, 1992), and Howard M. Wachtel, *The Money Mandarins: The Making of a Supranational Economic Order* (London: Pluto Press, 1990). Relevant analyses of the transnational processes from the interdependence perspective can be found in Robert Keohane and Joseph Nye, *Power and Interdependence: World Politics in Transition* (Boston: Little, Brown, 1977); and Robert O. Keohane, *After Hegemony: Cooperation and Discord in the World Political Economy* (Princeton: Princeton University Press, 1984).

9. On the Washington Consensus, see John Williamson, ed., *Latin American Adjustment: How Much Has Happened?* (Washington, DC: Institute for International Economics, 1990), esp. pp. 7–38.

10. On the different foundations on which it is possible to build legitimate orders, see Max Weber, *Economy and Society* (Berkeley: University of California Press, 1978), vol. 1, pp. 31–36.

11. Robert A. Dahl. *Polyarchy: Participation and Opposition* (New Haven: Yale University Press, 1971), and G. Bingham Powell Jr., *Contemporary Democracies: Participation, Stability, and Violence* (Cambridge, MA: Harvard University Press, 1982). On the procedural aspects of democracy, see Robert A. Dahl, "Procedural Democracy," in Peter Laslett and James Fishkin, eds., *Philosophy, Politics, and Society,* 5th ser. (New Haven: Yale University Press, 1979), pp. 97–133.

12. For a widely read argument on the connection between liberal economics and political democracy, see Milton Friedman, *Capitalism and Freedom* (Chicago: University of Chicago Press, 1982). For a more philosophical presentation of similar ideas, see F. A. Hayek, *The Constitution of Liberty* (Chicago: University of Chicago Press, 1960). A critically informed analysis can be found in John A. Hall, *Liberalism: Politics, Ideology, and the Market* (Chapel Hill: University of North Carolina Press, 1987).

13. Grzegorz Ekiert, "Democratization Processes in East Central Europe: A Theoretical Reconsideration," *British Journal of Political Science* 21 (Summer 1991): 312–313.

14. For an analysis of the initial economic program of the Radical administration, see Vacs, *The Politics*, pp. 367–393.

15. On the Alfonsín administration labor policies, see Ricardo Gaudio and Andrés Thompson, *Sindicalismo Peronista/Gobierno Radical: Los años de Alfonsín* (Buenos Aires: Fundación Friedrich Ebert—Folios, 1990).

16. On the Alfonsín administration human rights and military policies, see Carlos Acuña and Catalina Smulovitz, *Ni olvido ni perdón? Derechos humanos y tensiones cívico-militares en la transición argentina* (Buenos Aires: Documento de Trabajo CEDES no. 69, 1991); Rosendo Fraga, *La cuestión militar: 1987–1989* (Buenos Aires: Centro de Estudios Unión para la Nueva Mayoría, 1989); Jorge Grecco and Gustavo González, *Argentina: El ejército que tenemos* (Buenos Aires: Sudamericana, 1990); *Felices Pascuas! Los hechos inéditos de la rebelión militar* (Buenos Aires: Planeta, 1990); and Ernesto López, *El último levantamiento* (Buenos Aires: Legasa, 1988).

17. On the evolution of the Radical administration economic policies in a neoliberal direction, see Aldo Vacs, "Argentina," in James M. Malloy and Eduardo Gamarra, eds., *Latin America and Caribbean Contemporary Record, Volume 7: 1987–1988* (New York: Holmes and Meier, 1990), pp. B3–B9; José Luis Machinea, *Stabilization Under Alfonsín's Government: A Frustrated Attempt* (Buenos Aires: Documento CEDES 42, 1990); and William C. Smith, "Democracy, Distributional Conflict, and Macroeconomic Policymaking in Argentina (1983–1989)," *Journal of Interamerican Studies and World Affairs* 32 (Summer 1990): 1–42.

18. William C. Smith, "Hyperinflation, Macroeconomic Instability, and Neoliberal Restructuring in Democratic Argentina," in Edward C. Epstein, ed., *The New Argentine Democracy: The Search for a Successful Formula* (Westport, CT: Praeger, 1992), pp. 35–41.

19. On this attack and its consequences, see Juan Salinas and Julio Villalonga, *Gorriarán, La Tablada, y las "guerras de inteligencia" en América Latina* (Buenos Aires: Mangin, 1993).

20. Menem's political career and activities are discussed in Gabriela Cerutti, *El Jefe: Vida y obra de Carlos Menem* (Buenos Aires: Planeta, 1993); Gabriela Cerutti and Sergio Ciancaglini, *El octavo círculo: Crónicas y entretelones de la Argentina menemista* (Buenos Aires: Planeta, 1991); Alejandra Dahia and Laura Haimovici, *Menem y su entorno* (Buenos Aires: Puntosur, 1989); Pablo Giussani, *Menem: Su lógica secreta* (Buenos Aires: Sudamericana, 1990); Alfredo Leuco and José A. Díaz, *El heredero de Perón* (Buenos Aires: Planeta, 1988); and Oscar Martínez et al., *El Menemato: Radiografía de dos años de gobierno de Carlos Menem* (Buenos Aires: Letra Buena, 1991). For Menem's own presentation of his program and ideas, see Carlos Menem, *La esperanza y la acción* (Buenos Aires: Emecé, 1990), and Carlos Menem and Eduardo Duhalde, *La revolución productiva* (Buenos Aires: Peña y Lillo, 1989). On the evolution of Peronism, see Alvaro Abós, *El posperonismo* (Buenos Aires: Legasa, 1985); Leopoldo Frenkel, *El Justicialismo* (Buenos Aires: Legasa, 1984); and Alejandro Horowicz, *Los cuatro peronismos* (Buenos Aires: Legasa, 1985).

21. See Raul Green and Catherine Laurent, *El poder de Bunge & Born* (Buenos Aires: Legasa, 1989).

22. On the increase in poverty prior to 1989, see Instituto Nacional de Estadísticas y Censos (INDEC), *La pobreza en el conurbano bonaerense* (Buenos Aires: Estudios INDEC No. 13, 1989); and INDEC, *La pobreza urbana en la Argentina* (Buenos Aires: INDEC, 1990). On the distribution of income under Menem, see Alberto Minujin, ed., *Cuesta abajo: Los nuevos pobres* (Buenos Aires: UNICEF/LOSADA, 1992), and Alberto Minujin and Gabriel Kessler, *La nueva pobreza en la Argentina* (Buenos Aires: Planeta Argentina, 1995).

23. See Domingo Cavallo, *Volver a crecer* (Buenos Aires: Sudamericana-Planeta, 1982); and D. Cavallo, R. Domenech, and Y. Mundlak, *La Argentina que pudo ser: Los costos de la represión económica* (Buenos Aires: Fundación Mediterránea/Manantial, 1989).

24. On the situation of organized labor, see the interviews collected in María Herminia Grande, *CGT, 1982–1992: El poder que no fue* (Buenos Aires: Editorial Fundación Ross, 1993).

25. *Clarín*, August 6–12, 1990 (edición internacional).

26. Carlos Acuña and Catalina Smulovitz, *Ni olvido ni perdón?*; Hugo Chumbita, *Los carapintada: Historia de un malentendido argentino* (Buenos Aires: Planeta, 1990); and Rosendo Fraga, *Menem y la cuestión militar* (Buenos Aires: Centro de Estudios Unión para la Nueva Mayoría, 1991).

27. See Horacio Verbitzky, *Hacer la corte* (Buenos Aires: Planeta, 1993).

28. On the Menem administration's foreign policies, see Carlos Escudé, *Realismo periférico: Fundamentos para la nueva política exterior argentina* (Buenos Aires: Planeta, 1992);

and Roberto Russell, ed., *La política exterior argentina en el nuevo orden mundial* (Buenos Aires: FLACSO/GEL, 1993).

29. Joseph A. Schumpeter, *Capitalism, Socialism, and Democracy* (New York: Harper and Row, 1976), p. 269. For an excellent analysis of Schumpeter's ideas, see Richard Bellamy, "Schumpeter and the Transformation of Capitalism, Liberalism, and Democracy," *Government and Opposition* 26 (Autumn 1991): 500–519.

30. On the features of Argentina's institutional political conformation and the presidentialist tradition, see Hector Muzzopappa et al., *Actores e instituciones: Sistema político y constitución en la Argentina* (Buenos Aires: Legasa, 1989); Hilda Sábato and Marcelo Cavarozzi, eds., *Democracia, orden político, y parlamento fuerte* (Buenos Aires: Centro Editor de América Latina, 1984); and Helio Zarini, *Análisis de la Constitución Nacional* (Buenos Aires: Astrea, 1991).

31. On the notion and diverse meanings of populism, particularly concerning its Latin American and Argentine manifestations, see, for instance, Michael L. Conniff, ed., *Latin American Populism in Comparative Perspective* (Albuquerque: University of New Mexico Press, 1982); Carlos de la Torre, "The Ambiguous Meanings of Latin American Populisms," *Social Research* 59 (Summer 1992): 385–414; Rudiger Dornbusch and Sebastian Edwards, eds., *The Macroeconomics of Populism in Latin America* (Chicago: University of Chicago Press, 1991); Lars Schoultz, *The Populist Challenge: Argentine Electoral Behavior in the Postwar Era* (Chapel Hill: University of North Carolina Press, 1983); and Aníbal Viguera, "Populismo y 'neo-populismo' en América Latina," *Revista Mexicana de Sociología* 55 (July-Sept. 1993): 49–66.

Suggestions for Further Reading

There are a considerable number of English-language studies of different periods and aspects on Argentine politics. For a general survey of Argentina's historical development, see David Rock, *Argentina, 1516–1987: From Spanish Colonization to Alfonsín*, 2d ed. (Berkeley: University of California Press, 1987). Among the most interesting analyses of the transition to democracy in the 1980s and its aftermath are the articles included in Edward Epstein, ed., *The New Argentine Democracy: The Search for a Successful Formula* (Westport, CT: Praeger, 1992), and Mónica Peralta Ramos and Carlos Waisman, eds., *From Military Rule to Democracy in Argentina* (Boulder: Westview Press, 1987). Another examination of the most recent transition to democracy can be found in this author's chapter, "Authoritarian Breakdown and Redemocratization in Argentina," in James M. Malloy and Mitchell A. Seligson, eds., *Authoritarians and Democrats: Regime Transition in Latin America* (Pittsburgh: University of Pittsburgh Press, 1987). Attempts to present a comprehensive analysis of the roles played by different groups and institutions in Argentina's contemporary political development include Peter Snow and Luigi Manzetti, *Political Forces in Argentina*, 3d ed. (Westport, CT: Praeger, 1993). Those interested in the political-economic evolution of the country can consult Juan Corradi, *The Fitful Republic: Economy, Society, and Politics in Argentina* (Boulder: Westview Press, 1985), William C. Smith, *Authoritarianism and the Crisis of the Argentine Political Economy* (Stanford: Stanford

University Press, 1989), and Gary Wynia, *Argentina: Illusions and Realities* (New York: Holmes and Meier, 1986). Information on current events is easily available in English through the *Foreign Broadcast Information Service—Latin America* and the *Latin America Weekly Report* as well as the foreign news and business sections of the *Miami Herald, New York Times, Wall Street Journal,* and *Washington Post.*

6

ROMANIA: THE ANGUISH OF POSTCOMMUNIST POLITICS

MARY ELLEN FISCHER

In December 1989, when the communist regime of Nicolae Ceauşescu came to a bloody end, there seemed little hope for establishing a democratic system in Romania. Not only did the country lack many of the socioeconomic and cultural characteristics considered to be prerequisites for democracy by traditional theorists,[1] but major features of the collapse—the type of autocratic rule that preceded the breakdown, for example, and the violent nature of the breakdown itself—also made the chances for democratic consolidation seem remote to transition theorists.[2] Indeed, sporadic violence continued in Romania for almost two years, and the first elections, held in May 1990, offered little choice to voters outside major urban areas. By the end of 1991, however, the first parliament had written a new constitution, and in 1992 the second presidential and parliamentary elections were judged open and fair by most domestic and foreign observers. By then, conflicts had moved from the streets to less violent (but equally contentious) settings: inside parliament, within political parties, among the branches of government, and between the government and various domestic and international actors from trade unions and other interest groups to the International Monetary Fund (IMF), the World Bank, the European Union, and the Council of Europe. By 1995, most observers (transition theorists included) had become more optimistic about the chances for democracy in Romania, although the outcome of the transition still remained in doubt.

To assess the potential for democracy in Romania, we must first examine the precommunist and communist backgrounds that set the stage and gave rise to the pessimism and violence there. Next we shall consider the first six months of transition, including the first elections, to identify the crucial decisions and major actors during this period. We shall then discuss the period from June 1990 to

December 1991, when the first parliament wrote the new constitution and the political unity of the new ruling party began to disintegrate over economic policy and other issues. Our survey of 1992 focuses on elections: local elections held in the spring, the first parliament's struggle over a new electoral law, and elections for parliament and president in September. Finally, we shall examine the period of minority government after September 1992 and evaluate how far Romania had traveled, by mid-1995, toward establishing a democratic political system.

THE BACKGROUND: REASONS FOR PESSIMISM

In Romania, as in much of communist Eastern Europe before 1989, hopes had been raised on a number of occasions that real democratization was imminent, but these expectations were never fulfilled. For example, the Romanians adopted their first constitution in 1866 after the weakening of the Ottoman Empire, and the defeat of Russia in the Crimean War began the process that would allow the country to emerge as an independent state by 1879. Based on the Belgian Constitution of 1831, the Romanian document resembled liberal constitutions in West European states.[3] A bicameral parliament shared power with the first king, Carol I, but the complicated electoral system restricted political influence to the rural and urban propertied classes. In addition, the rapid growth of a new state bureaucracy, modeled on the centralized French administrative system, shifted power from local landowners to administrators in Bucharest, where the king wielded considerable power. After 1886 he usually "could make and unmake governments" with the help of the bureaucracy.[4] King Carol's strategy was to allow the Conservative Party (large landowners) and the Liberal Party (businessmen, professionals, bureaucrats, and small landowners) to alternate in power. In effect, the king, the propertied classes, the government bureaucracy, and party leaders cooperated to protect their mutual interests and to exclude the masses from real political influence.

Their fears of mass participation were not unfounded. At the beginning of the twentieth century, the Romanian kingdom was an agrarian society lacking most of the socioeconomic features traditionally considered prerequisites for democracy.[5] In 1899, only 15 percent of Romanian citizens were literate, and about 17 percent lived in urban areas.[6] The disparity in land distribution between large and small holdings was the greatest in Europe, including Russia: In 1907, over 95 percent of the holdings were crowded onto 40 percent of the land, more than 60 percent of the peasant holdings were below even bare subsistence (3 hectares), another 25 percent were marginal (below 5 hectares), and rural living standards were actually deteriorating.[7]

There is some evidence that Romanian agriculture was beginning to shift toward intensive growth strategies at the turn of the century and that yields were rising, at least on owner-managed larger holdings; thus landlords might, with time, have become "rational capitalist producers."[8] A violent peasant revolt in 1907 and further unrest during World War I, however, led the government after the war to defend the small, inefficient producer with the most extensive land reform in interwar Europe (excluding the Soviet Union). The 1918–1921 reform turned over 40 percent of all arable land to peasant owners and destroyed the political and economic power of the landowning elites and the Conservative Party. Unfortunately, dividing the land into small plots did little to turn Romanian peasants into more efficient farmers and in some ways even delayed the country's industrialization.[9]

The major purpose of the reform, however, was not to improve the social and economic situation of the peasants but rather to prevent them from becoming political radicals. Bolshevism posed a potential threat to Romania's internal stability, as did the ethnic minorities in territories acquired after World War I, which had brought devastating losses in 1916 but windfall profits with the peace treaty, when the small kingdom more than doubled in size and population by the addition of territories: Transylvania, the Banat, and Bucovina from Austria-Hungary; Bessarabia from Russia; and northern Dobrogea (Dobrudja) from Bulgaria. The 1930 census would show that almost 30 percent of the population of the new Greater Romania (*Romania Mare*) was not ethnically Romanian; political unity was therefore threatened by ethnic tensions.

The land reform, however, helped by a new constitution providing for universal male suffrage, did succeed in temporarily pacifying the peasants. The new political system was a parliamentary democracy in form, but—in contrast to parliaments in Western Europe, where governments were created by the legislatures—the Romanian parliament was created by the government. King Ferdinand and the party he chose to form the government (usually the Liberals) used the same techniques that Ferdinand's uncle, Carol I, had developed to control the outcome of elections. In 1922, for example, the Liberals conducted the elections and won 222 of 369 seats in the Chamber of Deputies; in 1926, out of office, they won 16 seats; and the next year, back in power, they won 318 seats.[10] Rather than being accountable to the voters, the elected government in effect united with the king and the civil service to dominate them.[11]

The political confusion following the 1927 deaths of both King Ferdinand and Ion Brătianu, the leader of the Liberals, allowed the National Peasant Party to win the one interwar election (that of 1928) generally regarded as having been free of political manipulation. But accountable democracy was unhappily short-lived; from 1930 until World War II, King Carol II was the dominant figure in Romanian politics, first manipulating the political process as both his father, Ferdinand, and the first Carol had done, then establishing a royal dictatorship.

One of Carol II's major goals for Romania was rapid industrial growth, which was not a new priority for Romanian politicians. Disputes between Liberals and Conservatives before World War I and among Liberals, Social Democrats, and National Peasant leaders in the interwar period had usually focused on how, not whether, to industrialize. Nevertheless, the Romanian elites had never been able to achieve sustained industrial growth. Governments over the years had attempted to encourage the growth of industry, the Conservatives by inviting foreign investment, the Liberals by protecting native industry with high tariffs and heavy taxes on the peasantry. In 1899, about two-thirds of all industrial capital in Romania was foreign, although Liberal protectionist policies would reduce that to 36 percent by 1929.[12] Neither approach brought the hoped-for results: 81 percent of the population of the Romanian kingdom in 1913 was employed in agriculture, and only about 3 percent of the labor force could be counted as industrial workers. World War I then devastated the country, and by 1929 per capita gross material product had barely returned to the levels of 1913.[13]

Carol II did, however, provide strong state support and protection for steel and armaments production in the 1930s, but this still did not translate into benefits for the population. The international depression that started in 1929 cut per capita income by almost 50 percent, and by 1937 this had not yet returned to 1927 levels. Indeed, "Romania was the slowest of the East European states to recover from the ... depression. As late as 1940 the standard of living was estimated to be between 33 and 64 percent lower than in 1916."[14] Romania in 1938 had the highest mortality rate in Europe (except for Spain, which was then in the middle of a civil war) and the highest death rate from pellagra (a condition due largely to malnutrition): "No country in Europe between the two World Wars had conditions of health that were worse than the Romanian."[15] One estimate asserts that Romania's standard of living in 1930 was roughly comparable to that of England in 1648 or France in 1789, and yet the literacy rate was far better—equivalent to the English in 1860 or the French in 1870.[16] After all, the one area in which Romania and East European governments achieved remarkable success during the interwar period was in the spread of mass literacy and opportunities for higher education. Ironically, these educational successes in themselves contributed to instability because the newly literate masses could not only recognize their misery but could also formulate and express demands.[17] Political repression and radical protests intensified in the late 1930s until international pressures and the war intervened.

Carol II was forced to abdicate in 1940 in favor of his young son, Michael, but the boy became king in name only. In reality, Marshal Ion Antonescu instituted a military dictatorship, put down an attempted coup by the Romanian fascist Iron Guard, and ruled Romania as an ally of Germany until 1944. With the powerful Soviet army poised at Romania's eastern frontier, the king took control, arresting Antonescu in August 1944 and changing sides in the war, but this rule was short, as he was forced into exile by the communists in 1947.

THE EARLY COMMUNIST PERIOD: 1945–1965

Once again, after World War II, Romanians were promised democracy and given a new constitution, this time by the Communist Party backed by the Soviet occupation forces, but Gheorghe Gheorghiu-Dej and his colleagues in the communist leadership were intent on using force to create their own version of socialist democracy. This meant, first, the destruction of the former political and economic elites, and second, the creation of completely new political and economic structures aimed at rapid industrialization. With Soviet support, the communists outlawed all other political parties, imprisoned or exiled their leaders, and forced the king to abdicate, in effect creating a replica of the Soviet political system by 1948. Meanwhile, the Communist Party took over the economy and society. A land reform in 1945 destroyed any remnants of the large landowning class, a currency reform in 1947 ruined the middle classes, and in 1948 expropriation of large industrial properties began so that, by 1950, 90 percent of industrial production was state-owned. Between 1948 and 1953 commerce was also taken over: The percentage of privately owned shops dropped from 90 to 14.[18] In this manner the new, revolutionary elites forcibly destroyed the old elites in the name of progress.

The peasants were handled more cautiously, in part because they constituted the overwhelming majority of the Romanian population and in part because the country was already short of food as a result of the war and a subsequent drought. Not until 1949 did a campaign begin to force the peasants into collective farms; there was considerable resistance, and at the end of 1957 private farms still occupied over half the arable land. In 1958, harsher methods were instituted to achieve more rapid results, and by the end of 1962 only 3.5 percent of arable land was in private hands.[19]

Central planning started in 1949, and by 1953 the rate of investment had reached one-third of national income, with over half of the investment funds going to industry and construction, about a tenth to agriculture, and only 3.2 percent to housing.[20] Such coercive measures did produce rapid industrialization—but without higher standards of living. Stalin's death in 1953 brought a period of relative relaxation as more investment went to agriculture, consumer goods, and housing. The emphasis on rapid industrial growth returned in 1955, to be followed by a short burst of popular concessions in lieu of destalinization in 1957.[21] The following year, Gheorghiu-Dej not only renewed the industrialization and collectivization campaigns, but he also persuaded Nikita Khrushchev to end the hated Soviet occupation by withdrawing troops from the soil of his loyal Romanian ally. During the 1960–1965 Five-Year Plan, 74 percent of state investment went into industry or energy development and only 10 percent into light industry and food processing.[22] Khrushchev was not fully supportive of this return to rapid industrialization, however, and friction developed between the Soviet and Romanian leaders. Unaware of the nature of the disagreement, the Romanian population responded with enthusiasm to any signs of discord between Bucharest and the hated Russians. Although Gheorghiu-Dej did not become genuinely popular in Romania, he was able to enhance support for his regime by manipulating Romanian nationalism.[23]

Gheorghiu-Dej died in 1965 after a short bout with cancer. By that time, he had destroyed the pre-1945 Romanian elites and established a new political, economic, and social order based on Communist Party rule and the overriding economic goal of industrial growth. He and his colleagues had distanced themselves to some degree from the Soviet Union, but inside Romania he had used coercion rather than consent to keep himself in power and had achieved high rates of growth by suppressing living standards. Nevertheless, by the mid-1960s his regime had created a number of the traditional socioeconomic prerequisites for political democracy: a literate populace, a transportation and communications infrastructure, an industrial base, health, cultural, and educational facilities, and a system of agriculture in which small plots had been consolidated into large holdings with the potential for efficient utilization. By contrast, the communist elites had eliminated political pluralism, autonomous social groups, private economic activity, and private property ownership, and they had achieved their socioeconomic gains through coercion and depressed living standards.

The Ceauşescu Era: 1965–1989

In March 1965, the party Politburo chose Nicolae Ceauşescu to succeed Gheorghiu-Dej as the new Romanian leader.[24] Ceauşescu had extensive support at lower levels in the party but was surrounded by colleagues in the top leadership who possessed considerably more prestige. At first, therefore, he followed cautious policies, using promises rather than coercion or threats to consolidate his position. He also emphasized Romanian national interests in his foreign policy and gained tremendous popularity in Romania and the West by denouncing the Soviet-led Warsaw Pact intervention in Czechoslovakia in 1968. By the early 1970s, Ceauşescu had strengthened his personal power sufficiently to implement his less popular priorities: the economic model of rapid industrialization through high investment and suppression of living standards, until then associated with Stalin and Gheorghiu-Dej; the centralization and personalization of political power in Ceauşescu and his wife, Elena; and the mobilization of every citizen—in public and private life—to achieve goals that he himself would set.

The plans for Romania's industrialization that were initiated in the 1960s under Gheorghiu-Dej had been even more protectionist than the policies of the Liberals in the 1920s and those of Carol II in the 1930s. Ceauşescu continued and even intensified his predecessor's stress on extensive industrial growth and import substitution. Until the late 1970s, the country experienced a rapid rise in industrial development, some improvement in living standards, and extraordinary successes in foreign policy. But, by the end of the decade, the high rates of growth were falling off and investment mistakes—in petroleum-related industries, for example—had produced a rising foreign debt. Ceauşescu continued to use Romanian nationalism to justify his policies, and he was so xenophobic that he resented deeply any interference in his affairs by foreign banks. In 1979, therefore, he decided to pay off the country's foreign debt, not merely service it. In order to do so, he increased Romanian exports, lowered internal consumption, and reduced imports, even of goods necessary for domestic industries. This drastically reduced Romanian living standards, as food became scarce and restrictions on electricity and heat made homes and public buildings dark and cold. Petroleum rationing meant that private automobiles, which had proliferated during the 1970s as symbols of the regime's economic accomplishments, now sat idle—constant reminders of the imposed hardships. By 1985, Romania's per capita gross national product (GNP) was the lowest of any East European Comecon member,[25] and, on March 31, 1989, Ceauşescu was able to announce the complete repayment of Romania's $12 billion foreign debt.[26]

Romanians compared the food and energy shortages of the 1980s with those they had suffered during World War II, and many privately blamed Ceauşescu. Publicly, however, his personal power remained unchallenged. During the 1970s he had become infallible and omniscient, the center of a leadership cult rivaling those of Lenin, Stalin, and Mao, and the public glorification of Ceauşescu and his wife intensified as the 1980s wore on. Meanwhile, his demands affected the private lives of Romanian citizens in very personal ways. One notorious scheme was his "systematization" program to "rationalize" the geographical distribution of living space. In Bucharest this meant the destruction of large parts of the old town to create grandiose avenues, blocks of apartments, and public buildings. In the countryside, meanwhile, villages were razed and people forced into high-rise apartments, often without water or sewers, to create urbanized citizens who would work nearby in fields or factories. The original idea had promise—to distribute the jobs and social amenities of modern society more evenly throughout urban and rural areas—but Ceauşescu's demand for speed and coercive methods distorted the process into a revolutionary scheme to transform living space in accordance with his ideological priorities. Indeed, Ceauşescu's centralization of political and economic power, his leadership cult, his ideological demands, his use of a monolithic party as well as police terror, and his invasion of citizens' private lives made Romania under Ceauşescu once again totalitarian rather than authoritarian.[27]

An even more widespread violation of privacy, one that people associated specifically with Elena Ceauşescu, was the demand for population growth to supply workers who would fuel economic growth. As early as 1966, abortions and contraceptives were outlawed in Romania, and by the 1980s harsh penalties were enforced against anyone involved in terminating a pregnancy. Women were even subjected to forced gynecological exams to ensure that, if pregnant, they carried to term.[28]

By the last years of rule, Ceauşescu and his wife had engendered the intense hostility of most of the Romanian population. Yet, except for several scattered and ineffective strikes, there was no overt resistance, due largely to Ceauşescu's skills at personnel manipulation and his ubiquitous secret police (the *Securitate*) and its effective methods of intimidation. There were no autonomous social groupings, such as the Roman Catholic Church or the Solidarity trade union movement in Poland, around which political movements could coalesce, and Ceauşescu and the *Securitate* allowed no groups to gain experience in political opposition as Charter

77 was allowed to do in Czechoslovakia. The country was kept isolated from both East and West; during the Gorbachev years, Ceaușescu did not even permit *glasnost* or *perestroika* to contaminate his homeland. Ironically, the autonomy from the Soviet Union that had proved so popular to nationalistic Romanians during previous decades allowed Ceaușescu to ignore Gorbachev's calls for reform after 1985.

Then, in early 1989, six men who had served in the Romanian Communist Party leadership—including several of the most important architects and practitioners of Romania's independent foreign policy in the 1960s—signed a letter of protest and sent it to Ceaușescu and abroad for broadcast into Romania, accusing him of betraying both the nation and socialism. They condemned his systematization campaign, his violations of human rights, and his food exports that threatened the "biological existence" of the Romanian nation; they acknowledged that they risked their lives and liberty in writing, but they felt compelled to do so because "the very idea of socialism, for which we have fought, is discredited by your policy."[29] The public silence of Romanian elites in the face of Ceaușescu's policies had finally come to an end. Nevertheless, he remained firmly in control throughout 1989 as, one by one, the other communist regimes of Eastern Europe collapsed.

Not until December 1989 did the end of communist rule in Romania come quickly and violently, following a series of demonstrations that began in Timișoara and spread to Bucharest. Nicolae and Elena Ceaușescu were forced to flee from angry crowds, but they were soon captured. On Christmas day—tanks and snipers in the streets of Bucharest and other cities had already killed about 1,000 people while the violence continued—the couple was tried and executed by the provisional government. In just over one week Romania had gone from totalitarian dictatorship to chaos with considerable bloodshed. Such a start to the postcommunist transition did not bode well for the future. The literature on democratic transitions tells us that a violent revolution provides the least favorable context for the consolidation of democracy; a negotiated or "pacted" agreement between elites from the previous authoritarian regime and their opponents is much more promising.[30] In addition, traditional theorists who assess the likelihood of a democratic transition by focusing on political, economic, and social prerequisites would have to conclude that Romania in 1990 did not seem to have much chance. Indeed, Ceaușescu had destroyed any remnants of civil society that might have survived the early communist period.

THE TRANSITION BEGINS: DECEMBER 1989–JUNE 1990

The transition to a new government began on December 22, 1989, when Nicolae and Elena Ceaușescu escaped by helicopter—only temporarily, as it turned out—from the hostile crowds in Bucharest. The first six months of the post-Ceaușescu era would start and end with Bucharest in chaos. In December 1989, tanks and snipers fought throughout the center of the city; in June 1990 Transylvanian miners would come to Bucharest en masse to support the new government, beating up demonstrators protesting the outcome of the May elections and sacking the headquarters of opposition parties and the homes of their leaders. During the interim, a series of violent episodes rocked the capital and several other cities. Nevertheless, during these turbulent months a provisional government was established, parties and other political organizations began to operate with the support of a free press, and a president and parliament were elected. In addition, a number of new political figures moved into prominence, most notably the interim president, Ion Iliescu, and prime minister, Petre Roman. Despite the uncertainty, instability, and violence of these first months, both men would retain their positions after the May 1990 elections.

Within hours of the Ceauşescus' narrow escape, a diverse group of individuals had made their way through the crowded streets to the Communist Party's Central Committee building and joined together to form a provisional government, the Council of the National Salvation Front (NSF).[31] The group included communist officials who had fallen out of favor with Ceauşescu or had resigned or retired in protest, intellectual and political dissidents, and some military officers. At first it seemed unlikely that the members of this provisional government would be able to stabilize the situation. Their earliest statements projected weakness, panic, and confusion as they began to try to calm the population and gather support.

They immediately emphasized that the NSF Council did not seek dictatorial power and that its authority and membership were temporary. That very first evening they worked out a program for the immediate future that was a model of both reassurance and ambiguity. It promised to install a democratic, pluralist system of government based on free elections to be held in April; restructure the entire economy (the issue of property ownership was avoided); restructure agriculture and support small-scale peasant production (again the issue of ownership was bypassed); reorganize the educational system; and remove the mass media from the control of "one despotic family," placing all media in "the hands of the people." The NSF Council did not promise privatization, a market economy, a free press, or a reduced role for the state, but the overall thrust of the program implied fundamental change to the population.[32]

The most conspicuous themes to appear in NSF statements in those early days were praise of the armed forces and condemnation of the "tyrant." On December 23, Ion Iliescu, a member of the council, appealed on television to citizens throughout the country to help the army fight the "terrorists" trying to restore Ceauşescu to power.[33] He also was able to report that Nicolae and Elena Ceauşescu had been captured and were under military guard; sporadic fighting would continue until after their executions were announced two days later. The NSF's first decrees were a series of anti-Ceauşescu measures reversing his most hated policies such as the ban on abortions and the systematization program. In addition, stores of food were distributed to stabilize the situation, and the death penalty was abolished so that members of the old regime would not fear retribution and continue fighting. The NSF Council worked feverishly, issuing new decrees and stressing the need for unity and order.

Ceaușescu had been overthrown, but it was not yet clear how many features of the old regime would change. The most frequent public spokesman for the Council was Iliescu, formerly a high official within the Romanian Communist Party (RCP) until he fell out with Ceaușescu in 1971. Soon to emerge at his side as the second prominent advocate for the NSF would be Petre Roman, an engineer and the son of a top RCP and Comintern official from the interwar era. Iliescu, at 59, was a father figure: short and stocky with a receding hairline and a background that was strictly Romanian, except for studies in the Soviet Union during the 1950s. Roman was in his early forties, strikingly handsome, almost boyish, and quite sophisticated and cosmopolitan. His mother was a Spanish Catholic and his father a Romanian Jew; he had earned a doctorate in France and spoke fluent English, French, and Spanish. Whereas Iliescu was quite sensitive to the wants and fears of ordinary Romanians, Roman could communicate effectively with intellectuals and with foreign audiences and governments. The skills of the two men thus were complementary, and they would make an effective team for as long as their partnership lasted (until September 1991). However, being privileged members of the communist elite, they would also be regarded with mistrust by many Romanians, and their vocabulary and speech patterns sounded much like an early Ceaușescu or like Gorbachev at the height of his *demokratizatsia*. Critics called for Iliescu to resign and complained that he was trying to establish another communist dictatorship, although both he and Roman were playing down their backgrounds in the communist *nomenklatura* and portraying themselves as longtime opponents of Ceaușescu.

Calm descended, temporarily, but the streets of Bucharest remained volatile. On January 12, 1990, demonstrators turned violent, calling for restoration of the death penalty to punish those who had collaborated with the "tyrant." The immediate, panicky response from Iliescu and Roman, facing a crowd surrounding them in the streets, was to agree, but they had second thoughts when order returned, and one week later the NSF Council reconfirmed the elimination of the death penalty and placed strict limits on public demonstrations. This action only served to stimulate further protests, however, and on January 23 thousands of people came out to denounce the NSF for its announcement, despite previous denials, that it would place candidates on the ballot to run in the spring elections. The leaders of several opposition parties and their supporters then demanded a more broadly based provisional government and ruling council. Before formal negotiations could take place, however, anti-NSF demonstrations filled the streets, and the next day, January 29, the NSF Council responded by bringing thousands of workers into the city in the first of a series of orchestrated pro-NSF demon-

strations that would take place over the next five months, culminating in the miners' June invasion. Yet on January 29 Iliescu bitterly criticized the opposition
groups and their leaders for initiating the previous day's street violence and for
reneging on an agreement to negotiate privately with the NSF. Both the NSF and
its opponents were learning to manipulate street protests.

Despite the violence and harsh words, the NSF Council and its opponents did
compromise and enlarge the government in early February, renaming it the
Provisional Council of National Unity. Eventually, it included over 250 members
and represented more than thirty political parties including the NSF. Its main task
was planning for the May elections, and the inclusion of NSF opponents had an
important effect on the rules of the game. The original electoral law adopted by
the NSF in late January had provided for single-member, winner-take-all districts
in the parliamentary elections, which would have favored the large, well-organized NSF.[34] After intensive arguments, however, the new Provisional Council
agreed on March 14 to an extremely complicated system of proportional representation in constituencies and no threshold requirement,[35] thus allowing small
parties to enter parliament and fragment the emerging party system. Indeed, it
was made so easy to compete that over seventy parties fielded candidates and
eighteen parties were eventually elected to parliament. Even so, the NSF easily
won a majority of seats in May 1990, and its dominance of the first parliament was
not affected. The precedent of proportional representation was established, however, and would remain in effect for the 1992 elections, with less positive results
for Iliescu supporters as it turned out.

The first time around, however, the election results showed overwhelming support for the NSF. Iliescu could not have known in advance that his victory in May
1990 would be so complete: that he would be elected president with 85 percent of
the vote; that his party would gain two-thirds of the seats in the legislature; that
no opposition party would win more than 7 percent of the vote (the Hungarian
Democratic Union of Romania [HDUR]); or that the newly reorganized "historical" parties from the interwar era, led mostly by Romanian emigrés returning
from abroad, would end up with only 6 percent (the National Liberals) and 3 percent (the National Peasants).[36] Back in March, however, Iliescu had faced a number of worrisome developments.

First, he was compelled to make major concessions to the opposition by including them in the Provisional Council and changing the electoral law. Second, he
was personally threatened by a declaration publicized on March 11 at a huge rally
in Timişoara, the cradle of the December revolution, that was signed by a number of groups complaining that they had not "initiated a revolution against the
communist regime and its entire *nomenklatura* . . . in order to create the opportunity for a group of anti-Ceauşescu dissidents from within the RCP to gain
power."[37] The document also insisted that former communist activists be forbidden to run for parliament or president; this, of course, would have eliminated

Iliescu from political life. The Timișoara demands may have convinced Iliescu and his colleagues to compromise several days later on the electoral law within the Provisional Council, but soon both events were overshadowed by a third dilemma: how to deal with an explosion of ethnic violence on March 19 and 20 in Tîrgu Mureș, where both Hungarians and Romanians were killed and the government's slow reaction was harshly criticized by all sides.[38]

None of these developments favored the NSF in the forthcoming May 20 elections. To compensate, the politically experienced former communists dealt with their electoral opponents by a shrewd combination of force, financial pressure, and propaganda: breaking up or restricting their rallies; supplying NSF candidates and organizations with buildings, communication facilities, paper, printing supplies, and television time while making it difficult for opponents to gain access to same; and playing on the population's fear of change and the unknown and on their nationalism, fear of foreigners, and resentment against returning emigrés who had "deserted" the country during its most difficult years. In addition, television and most of the press outside Bucharest were dominated by the government and its candidates, giving much of the country insufficient information for real choice. This manipulation by the government was reminiscent of precommunist and communist elections in Romania and infuriated the opposition, which had hoped for more after the December events.[39]

The NSF also used its control over public resources to make life easier for Romanians compared to recent years. And although many foreign observers criticized campaign methods, they concluded that the results would have been the same had the campaign been open and fair: "President Ion Iliescu and the ruling National Salvation Front appear to enjoy fervent support among the Romanian people. Many Romanians feel grateful to them for the improvement in food and fuel supplies and the wage increases they have seen since the December revolution."[40] But this report, dated May 30, 1990, went on to warn: "Yet the irregularities will have reverberations into the future. The Front faces an increasingly radicalized opposition which refuses to enter into a coalition with a partner it alleges has engaged in dirty electoral tricks."

Indeed, these first few months would have negative results for some years to come. Although the initial violence in December was important in toppling the old regime and forcing a pact between regime reformers and opponents, the recurring street violence of 1990 became more and more dangerous to the cause of democratic transition. If we divide the Romanian elites into our four standard categories—old regime hardliners; old regime reformers; moderate opponents; and radical opponents—we see that the December events had eliminated the first group—supporters of Ceaușescu—from the top level of the new government.[41] The NSF Council was dominated by the second group, former communists like Iliescu and Roman, liberalizers rather than democrats who wished to reform the old system. Originally, the NSF Council had contained individuals from the third and fourth groups, moderate and radical opponents of the old regime; and although these individuals gradually left the NSF, a few continued to participate in the new Provisional Council. During the first half of 1990, however, many actions of the radicals provoked Iliescu and his NSF colleagues into choosing violence and dirty tricks, and, given their political experiences inside a Leninist party, they turned instinctively to these alternatives. Thus, the NSF's repressive tactics turned even the more moderate opposition into radicals.[42]

The events of June 13–15—when miners descended on Bucharest in response to Iliescu's plea for support against radical protesters—completed the polarization process. The miners terrorized the streets of the capital for two days and ransacked the offices and homes of regime opponents. The violence (and Iliescu's apparent acquiescence) horrified everyone in Bucharest at the time and alienated foreign governments, whose citizens could see the events on television.[43] The election campaign irregularities had been bad enough, but now the images of Iliescu and Romania would be tarnished for months to come, and Romanian politics would be polarized between reformist former communists and a radicalized opposition.

The first elections had been won by the NSF and Ion Iliescu based on a platform that was ostensibly anticommunist but in reality was anti-Ceauşescu.[44] Thus, the first elections differed from the "foundation" elections in other East European countries such as Poland, Czechoslovakia, and Russia, which were essentially referendums on communism. However, like other "foundation" elections, they were "pre-party": [45] The big winner, the NSF, was typical of early postcommunist political formations in that it was a movement rather than a party—a broad assortment of individuals with different political programs—held together by Iliescu's personality and, even more important, by its adherents' fears of the future, the past, and the possibility of chaos.

The NSF had indeed used "dirty tricks" during the election, but its policies nevertheless enjoyed widespread support. Iliescu promised change—that Romania would never return to the policies of Ceauşescu—and he reassured voters that the changes would not be introduced too quickly (as the historical parties and other opposition groups demanded) and ordinary citizens would not be prosecuted for past collaboration with the *Securitate* or other crimes from the Ceauşescu era (also demanded by the opposition).[46] He promised peace, security, order, and an end to uncertainty and violence. Implicit in his campaign was the understanding that the paternalistic state would continue to provide jobs and economic necessities. Iliescu won the election overwhelmingly. Nevertheless, Romania in June 1990 was not yet a democracy but a "plebiscitary autocracy," where the government had been subjected to popular approval through a vote (plebiscite), but where there was little respect as yet for the rights of individuals or groups.[47] Iliescu had won the election but suddenly tossed aside his mandate by inviting the miners to Bucharest—thereby enraging the opposition and unnecessarily antagonizing foreign governments.

POLITICAL LEARNING:
JULY 1990–DECEMBER 1991

Despite this lurching and somewhat ominous beginning, the next eighteen months of Romanian political transition would see significant achievements. A new parliament and government would begin to function and soon faced overwhelming responsibilities, including organizing the new system and drafting a new constitution. First, however, the newly installed politicians would have to deal with more urgent problems.

Economic Decline and Social Unrest

Romania, like other postcommunist systems, was attempting a simultaneous transition of political and economic structures. As the new political processes were beginning to function, the attempt to change from a planned to a market economy was producing inflation, unemployment, and a drop in production. Between the first price deregulation in the fall of 1990 and the end of 1991, for example, the prices of consumer goods increased almost 500 percent and real wages decreased by over 20 percent. Annual inflation rates in 1991–1993 ran about 200 percent. Meanwhile, the gross domestic product (GDP) shrank, industrial production dropped, and labor productivity fell (by 13.5 percent, 21 percent, and 11.6 percent, respectively, from 1990 to 1991).[48] The attempt to create new political processes and institutions therefore must be viewed against this background of disastrous economic decline and frequent threats of violence from various social groups, most notably trade unions, most ominously miners.

During the summer of 1990, as the members of parliament met for the first time and began to work, they tried to deal with these desperate issues of economic reorganization and supply the population with basic necessities in order to prevent further violence. Nevertheless, strikes and protests continued to occur sporadically throughout the fall and winter of 1990, intensifying after price increases were instituted on November 1. Unable to agree on specific economic policies and unwilling to take responsibility for the continuing decline in living standards, parliament voted in mid-November to empower the government for six months to issue decrees on economic reform. In December, there were repeated (but unfruitful) discussions about a government of "national unity" that would draw some of the opposition parties into a coalition. Indeed, the government felt so insecure that it postponed another series of price increases planned for January 1, 1991, and refused to allow King Michael to return from exile in Switzerland for a brief visit, turning him back at the Bucharest airport when he arrived in late December without a visa.

The government that Prime Minister Petre Roman had formed in June 1990 after the elections was composed mainly of highly educated young technocrats, trained in communist Romania but possessing experience in the West and committed to rapid economic reform. The popular protests during 1990 slowed the price reforms, however, and caused disagreement within the ranks of the NSF between those who wished to continue shock therapy for the economy despite popular complaints (these were the people close to Roman) and those concerned about social stability and public support (centered around Iliescu).[49] The NSF and the government nevertheless managed to hold together through most of 1991 and introduced a number of significant changes: a modest land reform in February that permitted some privatization and redistribution but favored cooperative land use; a banking law in March and a foreign investment law in April, both prerequisites for further reforms; and a privatization law in August that promised eventually to distribute 30 percent of state companies to citizens through vouchers in ownership funds.[50] The last three laws created a more favorable climate for foreign investment, but the violence of the previous June lingered in the minds of many potential investors. Meanwhile, another round of food price increases, implemented on April l, 1991, brought still more protests.

Falling levels in production and living standards caused the violence to escalate over the summer, and in September miners once again descended on Bucharest. This time they came to protest yet another series of price increases and demand the resignation of both Iliescu and Roman. Relations between the president and prime minister had become quite strained, and Iliescu surprised Roman by accepting his public offer to resign, in effect making the prime minister the scapegoat for the economic decline. Iliescu evidently did not envisage a slowing of the reforms, however, because as his new prime minister he chose Theodor Stolojan, an economist who had resigned as finance minister in April 1991 because he felt the economic reforms were progressing too slowly.

Stolojan was regarded as a "technocrat," one with special expertise in economics but without any party affiliation. A number of ministers were independents, and Romanian understanding of the separation of executive and legislative powers at that time required any member of parliament who accepted a ministerial post to leave the parliament. Stolojan managed to induce three National Liberals as well as members of two small parties allied with the NSF to join in a coalition government. In doing so, he promised that he would continue rapid economic reforms but would remain in office only long enough to oversee parliamentary approval and popular ratification of the new constitution in 1991 and to organize and administer new parliamentary elections in 1992; he himself, he insisted, would not be a candidate for political office in the future.[51] These promises—all of which he kept—enhanced his prestige and effectiveness. Indeed, Stolojan held Romania together for the next year despite continued economic suffering and divisive campaigns for local and national elections in 1992. Meanwhile, he inspired wide respect for his ability and integrity, and his popularity increased despite the economic hardships that his policies imposed. Nevertheless, he kept his promise to resign after the 1992 fall elections and left the country to take the long-postponed offer of a position at the World Bank.

The Constitution

Even before Stolojan came to office, however, some reasons for optimism were beginning to emerge about the prospects for democracy in Romania. As Stephen Holmes observes, the "optimal moment to draft and ratify a constitution . . . is the period when the memory of autocracy is balanced by the experience of chaos."[52] The drafting of the new Romanian Constitution took place at just such a time, when the memory of Ceaușescu's oppression was "balanced" by the chaos of 1990 and 1991. The drafters wanted to create a document that would ensure both liberty and order, and in the process they looked to a number of contemporary and historical sources for models. They wanted to select structures from successful democratic systems, particularly in Western Europe, and adapt them to the Romanian environment. A constitution, after all, is far more than a mere legal document: "It is also a political, social, and moral foundational instrument that reflects the triumphs and sorrows of a nation's past and its hopes for the future." Thus, those writing the new document looked to Romania's past as well as to foreign examples.[53]

During this process, they made several crucial choices that shaped the new political system. First, Romania would follow the communist precedent established after World War II and continue to be a republic rather than return to a monarchy. Second, Romania would have a semipresidential system modeled in part on the French Fifth Republic, a return to earlier Romanian practices—if we assume that the president's role would resemble that of the king. Third, the state would retain an administrative structure centralized in Bucharest with no provisions for local autonomy or federalism, a system originally borrowed from the French in the nineteenth century; by the late twentieth century this aspect was strongly entrenched in Romanian tradition.

Taken together, these three choices were soundly rooted in Romanian institutional development, but they immediately posed problems for a transition to democracy. For example, the changes made the president the major individual actor in the new system at a time when attitudes toward President Iliescu had already divided society into two hostile camps. People either hated or admired him—few were neutral—and his continued prominence would mean that society would be polarized not only over Iliescu but also over the new constitution. Anyone who sought moderation or compromise would be fiercely attacked from all sides. Another problem was the issue of monarchy. Many of those who opposed Iliescu saw King Michael as the only viable alternative, and so they also opposed a republic, hoping instead that the king would return permanently as monarch— despite polls showing that most Romanians supported a republic. Both of these issues alienated urban intellectuals especially from the new government. A different type of discontent was provoked by the decision to continue the centralized administrative structure and to preserve a unitary system rather than create a federation. This concentration of power in Bucharest was seen by nationalistic Romanians as necessary to defend the unity and territorial integrity of the country, but the decision would produce friction with local officials and would intensify the resentment and fears of the Hungarian minority.

Hungarians made up about 8 percent of the population and had played a major role in the initial demonstrations to overthrow Ceaușescu. They had hoped for special cultural, linguistic, and educational rights in the new Romanian democracy as well as political autonomy in the two Transylvanian counties where they made up a large majority of the population.[54] Ethnic friction appeared early in 1990, however, as the Hungarians' resentment over their harsh treatment during the Ceaușescu period finally erupted in demands for immediate redress of their grievances. Some of their actions in turn aroused the resentment of ethnic Romanians, who resisted special treatment for these neighbors, pointing to historical injustices perpetrated against the Romanian majority in Transylvania before 1918, when the area was ruled by Hungary. The two ethnic groups were geographically intermingled throughout Transylvania, and violence first broke out in Tîrgu Mureș, a city with almost equal Romanian and Hungarian populations. Hungarian demonstrations provoked Romanian counterdemonstrations, and the situation at last exploded in March 1990.

By that time, some Romanian politicians, like political figures elsewhere in the postcommunist world, were already playing on Romanian nationalism to broaden their own political support. Such nationalist demagoguery was by no means new in Romania, having been used quite successfully by many Romanian leaders in the twentieth century including Carol II, Antonescu, Gheorghiu-Dej, and Ceaușescu. In the postcommunist period, Gheorghe Funar, leader of the Party of Romanian National Unity (PRNU) and in 1992 elected mayor of Cluj, the historic capital of Transylvania, initially would be the most prominent of those to base political careers on nationalist and anti-Hungarian hatreds.[55]

Many of the ethnic, social, and political divisions in Romania were reflected in legislative battles over the new constitution, and Romanian nationalism would also prove to be a major factor in shaping the document. Approved in draft form on July 9, 1991, by both chambers voting together as a Constituent Assembly, the constitution was debated throughout that fall—as the miners once again descended on Bucharest and Stolojan formed his new government—and passed in final form on November 21. It was ratified by the population in a national referendum on December 9.[56] Like other postcommunist constitutions, the Romanian version contains detailed provisions not only for civil liberties but also for economic and social rights such as health care, education, unemployment compensation, maternity leave, protection of the handicapped, pensions, and the right to own and inherit property.[57]

In addition, however, the document includes a number of nationalistic features: making Romania "a national state . . . unitary and indivisible" (Article 1.1); establishing Romanian as the official language (Article 13); and failing to guarantee national minorities the right to use their own language in judicial proceedings (a feature of the original draft deleted by the parliament despite the passionate objections of Hungarian members). Moreover, some civil liberties such as inviolability of domicile or access to information may be limited for reasons of "national security," freedom of speech does not extend to "defamation of the country and the nation," and laws imposing unspecified restrictions on "rights or freedoms" are permitted in order to "defend national security."[58] These provisions deeply alienated the ethnic minorities, especially the Hungarians, who felt betrayed and excluded from the new system.

The constitution makes parliament "the sole legislative authority" (Article 58) and rejects the unicameral communist precedent, returning to the historical tradition of a Senate and a Chamber of Deputies. Both are to be elected for four years on the basis of population, however, so there is no clear functional or representational justification for two bodies, and the main result has been a slowing down of the legislative process. If different versions of a law are passed by each chamber and a joint commission fails to produce a common version, both chambers meet in joint session and vote as a single body, each member having one vote. In each chamber, ordinary laws are passed by a majority of those present and voting; statutory laws (on a variety of important issues specified in Article 72), by a majority of the members of each chamber; and constitutional amendments, by two-thirds of the members.[59]

The president is "the guarantor of the country's national independence, unity, and territorial integrity" and "ensures the observance of the Constitution" (Article 79). Elected by the entire population for four years, the president needs the support of a majority of registered voters to be elected in the first round. Otherwise a second round is held between the top two candidates, and whoever receives more votes wins the office. No one can serve for more than two terms (but Iliescu's 1990–1992 term presumably does not count, so he should be eligible for reelection in 1996). The president must rise above partisan politics and not belong to a political party while in office. He selects a candidate for prime minister, appoints the government with the approval of parliament, and appoints and removes ministers on the recommendation of the prime minister. The president has special powers in the areas of foreign policy, defense, and public order and can preside over sessions of the government when such issues are discussed. He may also dissolve parliament if it fails to give a vote of confidence to the government.[60] Once in office, however, the prime minister and the government are responsible only to parliament as long as they can muster a majority to prevent a no-confidence vote. In addition, in contrast to the 1990–1992 rules, the new constitution allows ministers to remain members of parliament.

Other important institutions include the Constitutional Court to consider the constitutionality of laws, actions, and other issues, composed of nine justices appointed to nonrenewable nine-year terms, with the president, the Chamber of Deputies, and the Senate each appointing three of the justices; and the Supreme Court of Justice, whose members are appointed to six-year renewable terms by the president on the recommendation of the Higher Council of Magistrates. Local government officials—including local, city, and county councils and mayors—are elected, but each county has a prefect appointed by the government in Bucharest to administer local services provided by the central government, to oversee any local ordinances, and to suspend—with permission of the courts—any local decree he believes illegal. Prefects can thus be crucial mediators between local and central governments even though their responsibility is to Bucharest, and this can at times produce friction and confusion.[61]

When the new constitution was submitted to parliament, the NSF controlled a huge majority of the votes in both chambers. Nevertheless, the parliamentary debates were at times quite bitter, and over 1,000 amendments were introduced. Of these, 145 were passed, including thirty-nine proposed by opposition deputies or senators. Many changes enhanced the powers of the legislature vis-à-vis the president, the government, or the Constitutional Court; others strengthened individual rights; still others weakened rights guaranteed to national minorities, which, to say the least, was a bitter disappointment for Hungarian delegates. They and almost all of the Liberal and National Peasant delegates eventually voted against the new constitution. Most other parties strongly supported the document, however, giving it 81 percent of the votes, far more than the required two-thirds. The popular referendum on December 9 saw a turnout of 69.1 percent, of whom 77.3 percent voted in favor (53.5 percent of the entire population).[62] The parliament had now completed its task as a Constituent Assembly, and Romania had a new constitution in force.

THE YEAR OF ELECTIONS: 1992

The next task would be the elections of local officials in February 1992 and of parliament and president later in the year. The constitution left the details of elections up to parliament, which had already decided on procedures for the local elections. A draft law on local elections had been introduced by Roman's government in June 1991, and parliament finally passed it in November after imposing a series of major changes.[63] The original version of the electoral law had continued the tradition of mayors appointed from Bucharest and had provided for the election of local and county councillors in single-member districts, "first past the post." Both choices would have given tremendous advantages to the party in power in Bucharest, but controversies within the NSF and pressure from other parties eventually resulted in a series of compromises that enhanced local autonomy.

Mayors were now to be elected by a simple majority of those voting, with a runoff election between the top two candidates if no one gained a majority of votes the first time. Local councillors would be elected in multimember constituencies with proportional representation in which voters would choose a party rather than individual candidates; county councillors would be elected indirectly by local councillors through proportional representation and party lists.[64] Despite these changes, the NSF won a greater proportion of local offices than its share of votes justified. Nevertheless, opposition groups took a number of important mayoral posts—a National Liberal became mayor of Bucharest, for example, and the nationalist Funar took Cluj—and the NSF failed to win a majority of mayors or of councillors nationwide. Indeed, the party-preference results from the local councillor elections gave the NSF 34 percent, the opposition Democratic Convention of Romania (DCR) 33.3 percent, various nationalist parties 8.6 percent, and "floating" parties formerly allied to the NSF 12.1 percent.[65] These results raised hopes among regime opponents that the upcoming national elections would unseat Iliescu and the NSF. By then, however, Iliescu and the NSF would no longer be allies.

Political Parties

By the end of 1991, the spectrum of political parties had become more diversified. The ruling party, the NSF, gradually divided into Iliescu and Roman factions. It split formally in March 1992, shortly after its unhappy showing in the local elections, when Iliescu supporters walked out of the NSF party congress (controlled by Roman) to set up their own Democratic National Salvation Front (DNSF). The major issue dividing the NSF and Iliescu's DNSF ostensibly involved the speed of economic reforms, and the president's reluctance to move too quickly gained him the support of most of the state bureaucracy and industrial workers. Personal animosities, however, were even more important: Friction between Iliescu and Roman before September 1991 turned into bitter enmity after Roman was forced out of the government.

Meanwhile, the splintered opposition was trying to unite, and, after several umbrella organizations formed and reformed, the DCR was established in November 1991. This new umbrella coalition of democratic opposition parties included the two historical parties, the National Peasants (renamed the National Peasant-Christian Democratic Party) and National Liberals, as well as the Hungarian Democratic Union of Romania, the Social Democratic Party, the Romanian Ecological Party, and the Civic Alliance Party (this last composed mainly of intellectuals). Despite the agreement to cooperate, there were significant differences among these parties, based on ideologies, programs, constituencies, and personal rivalries among leaders. What united these groups in the end, however, was a shared antipathy toward Iliescu and his faction within the NSF; after the split in the ruling party, therefore, Roman's NSF would often make common cause with the DCR. Issues on which these opposition parties disagreed most vigorously—in addition to specific economic and social policies—included religion, the monarchy, and nationalism. The last was especially divisive (and eventually would almost destroy the DCR),[66] because all the Romanian groups were strongly pro-Romanian, anti-Russian, and—at least in foreign policy—anti-Hungarian. The HDUR had been profoundly disappointed that its political allies had not supported its protests against the nationalist provisions in the new Romanian Constitution or its proposals for Hungarian autonomy and special cultural rights. In fact, the Hungarian party would decide to run its own candidates in the fall 1992 national elections.

The political opposition also included radical parties outside the Democratic Convention: the Party of Romanian National Unity (Funar's PRNU), extremely nationalistic and anti-Hungarian; the Greater Romania Party, racist (anti-Hungarian, anti-Semitic, and anti-Gypsy) and led by former Ceauşescu syco-phants-turned-fascists; and the Socialist Labor Party (SLP), heir to the Romanian Communist Party. These three small parties reflected that strange combination of left and right radicals—sometimes termed the red-brown (communist-fascist) opposition—so typical in postcommunist party systems. They would begin to play an important role after the 1992 elections, when their support would be crucial to the minority government appointed by Iliescu. Even during 1991 and 1992, however, despite its large majority in parliament, the government often had to struggle to pass legislation as the formerly unified NSF fell apart. Nevertheless, most of the fighting was now taking place verbally, within parliament and among government officials, and peacefully—without violence and not in the streets.

National Elections

Throughout the spring of 1992, as Prime Minister Stolojan struggled to keep the economic reforms on schedule in the face of inflation, growing unemployment, and trade union opposition, all political activity focused on the electoral law being debated in parliament.[67] Everything about the elections was controversial, even the timing. Having abandoned the NSF in March and having created the DNSF, Iliescu's supporters wanted to hold simultaneous elections for president and parliament so that they could take advantage of Iliescu's prestige and ensure a large turnout of DNSF voters. Some also wanted to postpone the elections until fall in order to buy time to set up new organizations throughout the country (taking over NSF facilities wherever possible). Other groups, including Roman's NSF, wanted quick parliamentary elections separate from the presidential ones to prevent a DNSF victory. Stolojan's government was pushing for early elections in July, before scheduled economic reforms could bring further hardship and popular alienation. Foreign governments and investors were also advocating early elections to consolidate both democratization and privatization. Nevertheless, enough members of parliament were persuaded of the advantages of delay (it did, after all, keep them in office and on salary longer) that the date was set for September 27.

There were also disagreements in parliament over the type of electoral system to adopt, but eventually the proportional representation system was retained, with party lists in each of the forty-two counties and seats distributed among the counties according to population (70,000 for a lower chamber seat, 160,000 for the upper chamber). In order to reduce the number of parties in parliament, a national threshold was established of 3 percent for a single party or up to 8 percent for a multiparty coalition such as the DCR; any group receiving a lower share of the total votes would not enter parliament, with an exception made for national minorities, who were guaranteed at least one representative in the house no matter how small their share of the vote.

As the elections turned out, neither the opposition nor Iliescu and his DNSF did as well as each had hoped.[68] The DCR ran a disastrous campaign and won just 20 percent of the popular vote, well down from its 33 percent in the local elections. Rivalries and bickering among the leaders of its various parties—and the backing of the National Peasant Party leader, Corneliu Coposu—produced a relatively unknown presidential candidate, a geologist, Emil Constantinescu; a better choice might have been someone already known to the public (such as Nicolae Manolescu, the charismatic but controversial head of the Civic Alliance Party and highly respected as a literary critic and intellectual) or possibly another prominent politician from a coalition party. Moreover, those coordinating the DCR campaign chose to attack Iliescu and the government on issues of corruption and neocommunism rather than stressing economic problems or mobilizing support for their own policies. Finally, DCR candidates often were older, not young and pragmatic, and they still had not learned how to organize and coordinate a political campaign. Roman's more experienced supporters were just as disappointed in the election outcome, however, as the NSF took just 10 percent of the vote. Iliescu's DNSF emerged with a winning plurality of 28 percent, but this was far below the party's 62 percent in the 1990 elections.

Iliescu did win the presidency again, but the PRNU candidate, Funar, took the nationalist vote in the September 27 first round (almost 11 percent), forcing the incumbent president into a humiliating second-round runoff two weeks later with the novice Constantinescu from the DCR. Iliescu won the presidential runoff easily, but the loss of his DNSF majority in parliament would produce serious legislative problems for him, because no party or coalition would have a majority of seats. Now the importance of rules and choices became apparent. Had the electoral law required a 5 percent threshold instead of 3 percent, then only five parties (or coalitions) would have made it into the legislature: Iliescu's DNSF, the opposition DCR, Roman's NSF, Funar's PRNU, and the Hungarian HDUR (which had run election candidates separately from the DCR). In those circumstances, the DCR, Roman's NSF, and the HDUR (along with the other ethnic minorities in the lower chamber) could have formed a viable majority coalition in parliament. The 3 percent threshold, however, brought the remaining extremist parties into parliament, reduced the seats won by others, and allowed Iliescu to form a minority government in which the DNSF relied informally on the former communists, the PRNU, and the Greater Romania Party—the radical red-brown groups. In 1994 the cooperation would be formalized into a coalition, and these groups would gain cabinet posts.

After his 1992 election, however, Iliescu struggled until November 4 to put
together a new government. He indeed tried several alternatives such as persuad-
ing the DCR and NSF to join in a "national unity" government, but they refused,
mistrusting any overtures from him and hoping that he would be forced to call
new elections. Instead, he repeated his experiment with Stolojan and appointed as
prime minister a nonparty economist and technocrat, Nicolae Văcăroiu.
Although Văcăroiu would not prove to be as popular as Stolojan, he would hold
the government together through many no-confidence votes over the next three
years with the help of the extremist parties.

The 1992 elections had satisfied no one, but all parties respected the outcome.
In addition, the party system in Romania was beginning to show a number of patterns similar to those in other postcommunist systems: weak historical parties,
splits in the postcommunist umbrella parties and in the anticommunist opposition groupings, alliance readjustment in the face of electoral defeat, the presence
of antisystem parties (red and brown), and the primacy of personality over policy
in generating and maintaining political support. Indeed, Romania closely resembled the other post-Leninist systems in Eastern Europe where, "instead of reflecting or articulating the interests of social groups, the emerging party systems
appear[ed] to be reflecting the faultlines, fissures and fads among political
elites."[69]

Minority Government: Weakness, Compromise, and More Learning

In 1993, Romanian politics entered a period of prolonged frustration, negotiation, and compromise. Political learning would continue, economic reforms
would proceed very slowly, and most controversies would remain inside the halls
of government rather than in the streets. One of the quick learners in the new
Romanian political system was Iliescu, who—after the violence of 1990—managed to adapt his own instincts and methods to the new political environment and
work behind the scenes to accomplish his goals. Another surprise was Prime
Minister Văcăroiu. When the new government was announced in November
1992, few observers thought that the unprepossessing Văcăroiu would last more
than a few months. Indeed, one of the most consistent features of Romanian politics over the next several years was the frequent speculation about how much
longer Văcăroiu could last. In 1995, however, he was still in office, helped by the
disunity of the opposition and the absence of viable alternatives.

Yet another important personality emerged from the 1992 elections. Adrian
Nastase, foreign minister since the very first post-Ceaușescu government, was
elected to the Chamber of Deputies in 1992 at the head of the DNSF party list and
then was chosen to be president of that body, where he soon became crucial to

both Iliescu and Văcăroiu in passing their legislative proposals. An imposing figure in his forties, with legal training and experience in the West, Nastase brought to his new position exceptional skills in negotiating, bargaining, and compromise. As foreign minister, Nastase had worked closely with both Roman and Iliescu, reporting to Roman as head of government, but also responsible directly to Iliescu because of the president's special powers in foreign policy. When the president and prime minister became political enemies, Nastase remained loyal to Iliescu and was rewarded with the DNSF party leadership. However, his close association with Iliescu, his moderate views on foreign policy in nationalistic surroundings, his potential to succeed the president, and frequent charges of corruption made him almost as controversial a figure as Iliescu himself.

The weakness of the new government turned 1993 into a year of political immobility, economic frustration, and a continued learning experience for Romanian politicians. It would later become clear that 1993 represented the turning point in Romania's economic decline: Farm output rose 12.4 percent and industrial output and gross domestic product about 1 percent each. At the time, however, Romanians experienced a 10–15 percent rate of unemployment, 300 percent inflation, and a 12 percent budget deficit. On May 1, an end to consumer subsidies (due in part to the insistence of the IMF) brought higher prices, as did an 18 percent value-added tax introduced on July 1.[70] The streets of Bucharest on several occasions were filled with thousands of demonstrators protesting the declining living standards, but no major violence occurred.

In March, the opposition in parliament, unhappy with Văcăroiu's economic program, tried to pass a vote of no confidence, which was narrowly defeated due to red-brown support for the government. Widespread threats of strikes in May led Iliescu to intervene personally to allow wage increases that contributed to the inflation. Members of parliament expressed their frustration at the economic difficulties by blocking legislation that would have permitted foreigners to own land and by investigating a series of government corruption scandals that nearly produced a second no-confidence vote in July just before the summer adjournment. Again, as in the March no-confidence vote, Nastase's political skills helped to save the government. During the summer recess, at a conference with Nastase presiding, Iliescu's Democratic National Salvation Front changed its name to the Party of Social Democracy in Romania (PSDR), symbolically distancing itself from the NSF and the early days of postrevolutionary violence.

Meanwhile, the IMF and the World Bank held up promised loan packages because of the budget deficit, and by late 1993 Iliescu, with an eye on Western approval, was urging a quicker pace for economic reforms. Nevertheless, Văcăroiu, responding to the protests and no-confidence votes in parliament, ordered price controls and import restrictions in October, both being further retreats from market reform. He and Iliescu were still attempting to attract members of the DCR into a coalition, but their overtures were always rejected. Not until August 1994, after an attempt by the DCR to impeach Iliescu and repeated threats by the red-brown parties to bring down his government unless they were granted portfolios, would Văcăroiu formally add several members of Funar's PRNU to the cabinet.

Despite the economic problems, Romania's progress toward political democracy—demonstrated by the 1992 elections—was earning rewards abroad. The European Community accepted Romania as an associate in February 1993, and in October the Council of Europe granted Romania full membership. The U.S. Congress extended most-favored-nation trade status the same month, and thereafter military interaction with the United States, Germany, and the North Atlantic Treaty Organization (NATO) began and quickly intensified, with Romania the first postcommunist state to join NATO's Partnership for Peace in early 1994.[71] Romania's support for international trade sanctions against a traditional ally, Yugoslavia, hurt its economy but improved the country's relations with Europe and the United States.

In 1994, progress on economic reforms began again. An austerity budget was adopted in late May at the insistence of the IMF, which then approved a new loan of $500 million to bring Romania's total foreign debt to about $4 billion. By mid-year, inflation had slowed to a manageable 1.6 percent per month, and in 1994 Romania had an overall inflation rate of 70 percent, GDP grew 3.4 percent, and exports rose almost 20 percent. Industrial restructuring and privatization of large enterprises had barely begun, but 1995 would see a renewal of that process and the establishment of a stock exchange. By then the private sector accounted for 35–40 percent of GDP, and Western banks were signaling their approval with major loans.

Romania's Neighbors

Despite these positive economic developments, menacing events were taking place near Romania's borders. Aside from the war in former Yugoslavia, which threatened to draw in Romania and had already deprived it of a traditional trade partner, disputes involving Hungary and Russia remained unresolved, and in both cases the issue was Romania's national boundaries. A bilateral friendship treaty with Hungary was blocked by Hungarian reluctance to accept the existing borders without Romanian promises to respect international guidelines on the treatment of its Hungarian minority. West European organizations such as NATO and the European Union exerted pressure on both sides to settle their differences as a requirement for future membership, and the Council of Europe was especially active in promoting human rights for ethnic minorities in the formerly communist East European states, criticizing the Romanians and forcing them to defend policies toward ethnic Hungarians.

The Russian situation was even more complicated. Iliescu had expressed support for Russian President Boris Yeltsin in that leader's 1993 struggle with his parliament, and Văcăroiu had even visited Moscow and signed agreements on trade, culture, science, and tourism. Yet one major controversy remained between the two states: Romanians overwhelmingly supported unification with Moldova, which had been seized by the USSR in World War II but was still inhabited mainly by Romanians and had been independent since 1991. Most Moldovans, in contrast, wished to remain an independent state, but their sovereignty was being violated by the Russian 14th Army, which occupied a small section of Moldova east of the Dnestr River containing a large number of Russian and Ukrainian inhabitants (although a plurality of the population even here was Romanian). Russian and Ukrainian groups on the east bank, supported by the Russian army, were trying to secede from Moldova, and Romania offered support to the Moldovans. This question fanned nationalist flames in Bucharest and provided a goal on which the extreme nationalists and most parties in the DCR could agree: immediate unification with Moldova. In this case, the Romanian government and the PSDR followed a less aggressive policy of support for Moldova without insisting on unification.

Conclusions

During the first five years after the 1989 revolution, Romanians suffered a traumatic period of violence and economic hardships—this after the horrors of the dictator Ceaușescu's last decade in power. When events are viewed in this context, we might conclude that by 1995 the country had traveled a considerable distance in establishing a democracy. Two sets of elections had been held, a new constitution had been written and implemented, and the new institutions of government were resolving most disputes peacefully albeit with considerable rancor. Romanians had moved first to establish the framework for democratic processes and then had begun to implement the needed economic reforms. In 1995, economic conditions were still very difficult, but there were signs that improvement was on the way.

Serious difficulties remained, however. Iliescu still polarized the country, and his continuing position in power was a crucial issue. Many Romanians viewed him as the devil incarnate, running the country for the benefit of his friends among the old *nomenklatura*. Others viewed him as a competent politician, not infallible but doing his best under difficult circumstances. In any case, he would be eligible for reelection one more time in 1996, and Romania had come far enough in establishing its democracy that the issue presumably would be decided according to democratic procedures at the ballot box. Nevertheless, the country remained deeply divided between those who supported and those who rejected not only the president but the legitimacy of the entire system that he headed.

Many Romanians claimed that their revolution had been "hijacked" by former communists—regime reformers—who had covered up crimes of the past and now controlled the privatization process to serve their own interests. Certainly there had been little action taken against former supporters of Ceaușescu and his regime; some of his family and closest associates had been arrested, tried, and imprisoned, but few had served much time in jail. The issue of retribution—or lustration—had been resolved by the May 1990 elections, when Romanians voted overwhelmingly for the NSF and its implied promises to forget the previous regime and its crimes.

The *Securitate* was ostensibly cleansed and reborn as the Romanian Intelligence Service (RIS), a powerful organization close to Iliescu, its members keeping out of public view. The RIS head was appointed by parliament on the nomination of the president, and questions about the RIS have been raised frequently in parliament and constantly in the press. Transitions such as Romania's—where regime reformers play major roles—leave institutional traces that can threaten the new democracy;[72] in Latin America this usually means an autonomous military, but in Romania the police were just as, if not more, important. Citizens who mistrust Iliescu point to the RIS as evidence of his perfidy, whereas his supporters argue that its character has indeed changed significantly and the organization now serves to protect the Romanian nation and its officials.

Romanian society remained polarized in its attitudes toward Iliescu and the new regime in 1995, but a viable opposition capable of replacing Iliescu and his colleagues through electoral processes had yet to emerge. Divided by rival personalities, ideology, and issues of policy, the opposition parties presented a constant threat to the government with their no-confidence motions; however, they did not provide a credible alternative. Even worse, from their point of view, by 1994 they had driven the government into a formal coalition with the extremist red-brown parties, and government policies—especially on issues of concern to the Hungarian minority such as education—began to reflect this alliance.

It was difficult for individual members of parliament to challenge the president, the government, or their own leadership effectively. They remained weak political actors, because whatever privileges and support services existed were channeled through the parties in this proportional representation system, as were committee assignments. There were no budgets, staffs, or offices for individual members, and it was difficult to establish connections to constituents.

Another threat to the survival of the new system was corruption, endemic throughout the country, both in politics and in the economy. Many of those benefiting (even legally) since 1989 had also profited under Ceaușescu: The formerly privileged were now acquiring new resources in postcommunist Romania, and this contributed to the resentment of those who felt excluded. Society was polarized between the haves and the have-nots (in terms of economic as well as political power), and the gap was growing wider as more and more families sank below the poverty level. To many Romanians, the parliamentary debates they watched on television seemed frivolous and far removed from the pressing issues facing them in their daily lives. A deep mistrust of government continued to characterize the Romanian polity, contradicted by another legacy of communism: the habit of relying on the government to provide such daily items as food, employment, health care, and education.

In many ways, however, the system was working. There were signs that political officials felt accountable to those who had chosen them: Văcăroiu, for example, accountable to parliament for his daily survival; Iliescu, with his eye on the presidential elections in 1996; Nastase, concerned with holding his party together in parliament and providing majorities for the government in many legislative struggles. Each of the three men behaved in accordance with the powers and responsibilities of office, each with an eye on the next legislative or electoral battle. Members of parliament also were worried about the problems of the electorate in general and how such issues might affect their own reelection.

In addition, a free press was flourishing, despite complaints about government favoritism and intimidation and lack of resources for the opposition press. The state-owned television network continued to support the government, however, and there were battles in parliament and the press over its direction, as over the role of the RIS. Although television began to be slightly more objective in its coverage of politics, both it and the RIS remained tools of the president and could be formidable weapons if so used. Respect for human rights was therefore less firmly established than accountability—the practical political necessity to win periodic elections.

In sum, new political procedures had been established and were beginning to work, but the new methods had yet to resolve the problems of most people. Nineteen ninety-five Romania had, in some ways, turned the clock back to 1925— and yet the lessons learned and the structures established in those seventy years had changed the country in fundamental ways. The communists had entirely restructured the economy to emphasize obsolete and costly industries rather than inefficient agriculture, and the country's rich natural resources had been degraded. Another new constitution had been introduced, but the communist period had led Romanians to mistrust government and avoid its reach whenever possible. Yet Romanians also had come to expect a great deal from government, and the 1989 revolution only raised their expectations. They would not be easily satisfied, and they looked to elected officials to deliver. A democratic government would have to deal with these problems and at least give signs of progress if it wished to be reelected.

Despite these difficulties, the constitutional government was still in place. No dictatorship—civilian or military—had been imposed, an event that seemed quite possible on several occasions in 1990 and 1991. Instead, by 1995 the framework for political democracy had been established. Many of the rules and processes were still being worked out as the government responded to intense pressures at home and abroad, and the population had yet to see material rewards from the new system. There had been no turnover in power from one party to another, from one president to a successor, and hence there was as yet an incomplete "devolution of power from a group of people to a set of rules."[73] Romania in 1995 was not yet a consolidated democracy, but the country had accomplished far more since 1989 than most observers could have expected.

CHRONOLOGY

1866	First constitution
1866–1914	Carol I
1914–1927	Ferdinand
1923	Second constitution
1930–1940	Carol II
1940	Carol II abdicates; son Michael becomes titular monarch
1940–1944	World War II and rule by Marshal Ion Antonescu
1944–1958	Soviet occupation
1944–1947	Coalition governments
1947	King Michael into exile, communist rule begins
1958	Soviet troops leave
1944–1965	Gheorghe Gheorghiu-Dej
1965–1989	Nicolae Ceaușescu
December 1989	Ceaușescu overthrown and executed; National Salvation Front establishes provisional government under Ion Iliescu
May 1990	First national elections; Iliescu and NSF win
June 1990	Miners come to Bucharest
June 1990–September 1991	Roman government
September 1991	Miners again come to Bucharest
September 1991–November 1992	Stolojan government
November–December 1991	New constitution approved
February 1992	Local elections
September–October 1992	Second national elections; Iliescu wins
November 1992	Văcăroiu forms a minority government
1994	Economic recovery begins
1996	Elections expected for president, parliament, and local officials

NOTES

1. See note 3 in the Introduction to this book and the accompanying text.

2. See the introduction to Guillermo O'Donnell and Philippe C. Schmitter, *Transitions from Authoritarian Rule: Tentative Conclusions About Uncertain Democracies* (Baltimore:

Johns Hopkins University Press, 1986). Schmitter concludes elsewhere that the mode of transition least favorable to the consolidation of democracy is a revolution with mobilized masses and force; Philippe C. Schmitter, "Dangers and Dilemmas of Democracy," *Journal of Democracy* 5 (April 1994): 65. See also pp. 5-9 of the Introduction to this book and the accompanying notes.

3. Keith Hitchins, *Rumania, 1866–1947* (New York: Oxford University Press, 1994), pp. 17, 19.

4. Andrew C. Janos, "Modernization and Decay in Historical Perspective: The Case of Romania," in Kenneth Jowitt, ed., *Social Change in Romania, 1860–1940: A Debate on Development in a European Nation* (Berkeley: University of California, Institute of International Studies, 1978), pp. 87–88.

5. Some of the descriptions of Romanian social and economic development rely heavily on my "Politics, Nationalism, and Development in Romania," in Gerasimos Augustinos, ed., *Diverse Paths to Modernity in Southeastern Europe* (New York: Greenwood Press, 1991), pp. 135–168.

6. The picture is much more complicated than these data suggest; see Per Rőnnas, *Urbanization in Romania* (Stockholm: Stockholm School of Economics, Economic Research Institute, 1984), pp. 172, 232.

7. Joseph Rothschild, *East Central Europe Between the Two World Wars* (Seattle: University of Washington Press, 1974), p. 290; Henry L. Roberts, *Rumania: Political Problems of an Agrarian State* (Hamden, Conn.: Archon Books, 1969), p. 7 and table 8, p. 362; Daniel Chirot, *Social Change in a Peripheral Society* (New York: Academic Press, 1976), p. 134; Roberts, *Rumania*, p. 15.

8. Chirot, *Peripheral Society*, pp. 148–149. Lampe's analysis would seem to support this hypothesis; see John R. Lampe and Marvin R. Jackson, *Balkan Economic History, 1550–1950: From Imperial Borderlands to Developing Nations* (Bloomington: Indiana University Press, 1982), pp. 186–190.

9. Janos, "Modernization and Decay," p. 103; Lampe and Jackson, *Balkan Economic History*, p. 352; Barbara Jelavich, *History of the Balkans*, vol. 2 (New York: Cambridge University Press, 1983), 161–163.

10. Hitchins, *Rumania*, pp. 379–380.

11. Rothschild, *East Central Europe*, p. 296.

12. William Crowther, *The Political Economy of Romanian Socialism* (New York: Praeger, 1988), p. 37; Chirot, *Peripheral Society*, p. 146; Lampe and Jackson, *Balkan Economic History*, p. 428.

13. Janos, "Modernization and Decay," p. 96. In comparing Romania to the other Balkan states, Lampe makes a more positive assessment, but, as he points out, often the enterprise owners and skilled workers were not ethnic Romanians; see Lampe and Jackson, *Balkan Economic History*, pp. 238–277, esp. 241–242, 274–276.

14. Crowther, *The Political Economy of Romanian Socialism*, pp. 31, 37–38.

15. Michael Kaser, *Health Care in the Soviet Union and Eastern Europe* (Boulder: Westview Press, 1976), p. 235.

16. See Janos, "Modernization and Decay," p. 99, and the sources cited.

17. Lampe and Jackson, *Balkan Economic History*, pp. 502–504. On the relationship between education and stability, see Janos, "Modernization and Decay," pp. 95–101.

18. Daniel Chirot, "Social Change in Communist Romania," *Social Forces* 57 (December 1978): 461–462.

19. John Michael Montias, *Economic Development in Communist Rumania* (Cambridge: MIT Press, 1967), pp. 89, 92. See also Ghita Ionescu, *Communism in Rumania, 1944–1962* (New York: Oxford University Press, 1964).

20. See Crowther, *The Political Economy of Romanian Socialism*, p. 56, citing Montias, *Economic Development in Communist Rumania*, pp. 25–27.

21. Crowther, *The Political Economy of Romanian Socialism*, p. 58.

22. Chirot, "Social Change in Communist Romania," p. 472.

23. See the survey of sources in Ronald Linden, *Bear and Foxes: The International Relations of the East European States, 1965–1969* (Boulder: East European Monographs, 1979), pp. 260–263, note 21. See also David Floyd, *Rumania: Russia's Dissident Ally* (New York: Praeger, 1965); Montias, *Economic Development*; Stephen Fischer-Galati, *The New Rumania* (Cambridge, MA: MIT Press, 1967); Kenneth Jowitt, *Revolutionary Breakthroughs and National Development: The Case of Romania, 1944–1965* (Berkeley: University of California Press, 1971); and Michael Shafir, *Romania: Politics, Economics, and Society* (Boulder: Lynne Rienner, 1985).

24. See my *Nicolae Ceauşescu: A Study in Political Leadership* (Boulder: Lynne Rienner, 1989).

25. Crowther, *The Political Economy of Romanian Socialism*, p. 154.

26. *New York Times*, April 15, 1989.

27. On the distinction between totalitarianism and authoritarianism, see the Introduction to this book. I argue that Romania was totalitarian for much of the Gheorghiu-Dej period, authoritarian during the 1960s and early 1970s, and totalitarian again by the 1980s. See my "Stalinism in Romania," in Sanford R. Lieberman et. al., *The Soviet Empire Reconsidered* (Boulder: Westview Press, 1994), pp. 27–47. For early Romanian descriptions of systematization, see *Scînteia*, August 4, 1974, or Ion St. Ion, "Perfecţionarea repartizării pe teritoriu a forţelor de producţie," in *Perfecţionarea organiăzrii şi conducerii vieţii economice de stat şi sociale* (Bucharest: Ed. Academiei, 1972). On its results, see Dinu C. Giurescu, *The Razing of Romania's Past* (New York: World Monuments Fund, 1989).

28. The many abandoned children found in orphanages after the fall of Ceauşescu resulted from these policies; see Gail Kligman, "The Politics of Reproduction in Ceauşescu's Romania," *East European Politics and Societies* 6 (Fall 1992): 364–418, and my "Women in Romanian Politics: Elena Ceauşescu, Pronatalism, and the Promotion of Women," in Sharon L. Wolchik and Alfred G. Meyer, eds., *Women, State, and Party in Eastern Europe* (Durham, NC: Duke University Press, 1985), pp. 121–137, 388–393.

29. The letter was translated in *New York Review*, April 27, 1989, p. 9. See also the analysis by Michael Shafir and related materials in Radio Free Europe Research, *Romanian Situation Report* 3 (March 29, 1989), pp. 1–14. The six signers were Gheorghe Apostol, Alexandru Bîrlădeanu, Corneliu Mănescu, Constantin Pîrvulescu, Grigore Ion Răceanu, and Silviu Brucan.

30. Schmitter, "Dangers and Dilemmas of Democracy," p. 65.

31. Some observers contend that this was a conspiracy prepared in advance; see, for example, Anneli Ute Gabanyi, *Die unvollendete Revolution* (Munich: Piper, 1990). Others view the events of December 1989 as a spontaneous popular revolt during which politically experienced individuals managed to gain control, a more likely scenario; see the reports by Michael Shafir in Radio Free Europe, *Report on Eastern Europe* 1 (1990): passim; David Kideckel, *The Solitude of Collectivism: Romanian Villagers to the Revolution and Beyond* (Ithaca: Cornell University Press, 1993), ch. 8; Nestor Ratesh, *Romania: The Entangled Revolution* (Washington, DC and New York: Center for Strategic and International Studies

and Praeger, 1991); Katherine Verdery and Gail Kligman, "Romania After Ceauşescu: Post-Communist Communism?" in Ivo Banac, ed., *Eastern Europe in Revolution* (Ithaca: Cornell University Press, 1992), pp. 117–147.

32. *Scînteia poporului*, December 23, 1989, p. 1. See also my "The New Leaders and the Opposition," in Daniel N. Nelson, ed., *Romania After Tyranny* (Boulder: Westview, 1992), pp. 45–65.

33. *Scînteia poporului*, December 24, 1989, p. 1.

34. *Adevărul*, February 1, 1990.

35. That is, no minimum percentage of the total vote was required for a party to enter parliament. See Michael Shafir, "The Electoral Law," Radio Free Europe, *Report on Eastern Europe* 1 (May 4, 1990): 28–31.

36. *Adevărul*, May 26, 1990.

37. This was translated and printed in Radio Free Europe, *Report on Eastern Europe* 1 (April 6, 1990): 41–45.

38. See *Struggling for Ethnic Identity: Ethnic Hungarians in Post-Ceauşescu Romania* (New York: Human Rights Watch, 1993), and my "The New Leaders and the Opposition," pp. 56–57, and the sources cited.

39. See Dan Ionescu, "Violence and Calumny in the Election Campaign," Radio Free Europe, *Report on Eastern Europe* 1 (May 25, 1990): 37–42; Crisula Stefanescu, "Romanian Radio and Television Coverage of the Election Campaign," Radio Free Europe, *Report on Eastern Europe* 1 (June 8, 1990): 42–45; Vladimir Socor, "National Salvation Front Produces Electoral Landslide," Radio Free Europe, *Report on Eastern Europe* 1 (July 6, 1990): 24–32; Kideckel, *The Solitude of Collectivism*; Ratesh, *Romania: The Entangled Revolution*; and Verdery and Kligman, "Romania After Ceauşescu."

40. U.S. Commission on Security and Cooperation in Europe, *Report on the Parliamentary and Presidential Elections in Romania* (Washington, DC: May 30, 1990), p. 1.

41. Such people certainly survived at lower levels but not at the very top. There were, however, exceptions: Some former supporters of Ceauşescu had been rewarded with high positions for betraying him (General Victor Stanculescu, for example).

42. On pacts and divisions among elites, see the Introduction to this book. For a recent discussion of the disastrous legacy of Leninism, see Kenneth Jowitt, *New World Disorder: The Leninist Extinction* (Berkeley: University of California Press, 1992).

43. Romanian television showed the demonstrators but not the miners; I was in Romania at the time. The reasons behind these events remain controversial. The best eye-witness accounts include Vladimir Tismaneanu, "Homage to Golania," *New Republic*, July 30 and August 8, 1990, pp. 16–18; Kathleen Hunt, "Letter from Bucharest," *New Yorker*, July 23, 1990, pp. 74–82; and Sam Beck, "The Struggle for Space and the Development of Civil Society in Romania," in Hermine G. DeSoto and David G. Anderson, *The Curtain Rises: Rethinking Culture, Ideology, and the State in Eastern Europe* (Atlantic Highlands, NJ: Humanities Press International, 1993), pp. 232–265. See also Michael Shafir, "The Parliamentary Inquiry into the June 1990 Events," Radio Free Europe, *Report on Eastern Europe* 1 (February 22, 1991): 20–28, and the sources cited.

44. On the implications of this, see my "The New Leaders and the Opposition," p. 46.

45. On these points, see David M. Olson, "Political Parties and Party Systems in Regime Transformation: Inner Transition in the New Democracies of Central Europe," *The American Review of Politics* 14 (Winter 1993): 619–658.

46. "Lustration"—bringing past crimes to light, as in the denazification attempts in post–World War II Germany—was advocated only by radical opponents of the regime; a few of Ceaușescu's close associates were prosecuted, but their sentences were light and they often were paroled, ostensibly due to health. For discussions of lustration elsewhere in Eastern Europe, see the 1992 spring and summer issues in *East European Constitutional Review* (both vol. 1, pp. 24–26 [spring]; 15–22 [summer]).

47. Guillermo O'Donnell and Philippe C. Schmitter, *Transitions from Authoritarian Rule: Tentative Conclusions*, p. 13.

48. Dan Ionescu, "Social Tension Threatens Frail Romanian Economy," *RFE/RL Research Report* 1 (March 6, 1992): 32.

49. Dan Ionescu, "National Salvation Front Holds Convention," Radio Free Europe, *Report on Eastern Europe* 2 (March 29, 1991): 6–11; Michael Shafir, "Sharp Drop in Leadership's Popularity," Radio Free Europe, *Report on Eastern Europe* 2 (April 12, 1991): 23–24.

50. All of these laws are described in some detail in the 1991 issues of Radio Free Europe's *Report on Eastern Europe*. See also *East European Reporter* 1 (October 28, 1991): 23, and 1 (November 25, 1991): 142–144.

51. For discussions of these events in English, see Dan Ionescu, "Riots Topple Petre Roman's Cabinet," Radio Free Europe, *Report on Eastern Europe* 2 (October 18, 1991): 18–22, and Ionescu, "The New Government," Radio Free Europe, *Report on Eastern Europe* 2 (November 8, 1991): 29–34.

52. Stephen Holmes, "Back to the Drawing Board," *East European Constitutional Review* 2 (Winter 1993): 25.

53. Herman Schwartz, "In Defense of Aiming High," *East European Constitutional Review* 1 (Fall 1992): 25. For a Romanian interpretation of the new document, see Vasile Gionea, "La nouvelle Constitution de la Roumanie," *Revue Roumaine d'Études Internationales* 27 (1993): 79–89.

54. The historical province of Transylvania today makes up roughly the northwestern third of Romania. The counties where Hungarians form a majority (Covasna and Harghita) are in the southeast of Transylvania, the former border region, and therefore in the geographical center of Romania.

55. See Michael Shafir, "Romania," in "The Politics of Intolerance," *RFE/RL Research Report* 3 (April 22, 1994): 87–94, and the sources cited.

56. The constitution was published in English by the Foreign Broadcast Information Service as a supplement to the *Daily Report: East Europe*, FBIS–EEU–91–246–S (December 23, 1991).

57. See articles 32–33, 38, 41–43, 45–46, 135.

58. Minorities do have the right to an interpreter in court (article 127); see also articles 27.2.6, 31.3, 30.7, and 49.1.

59. On the parliament and bicameralism, see Elena Stefoi-Sava, "Romania," in *East European Constitutional Review* 4 (Spring 1995): 78–83.

60. A motion of no confidence is introduced in joint session by at least one-fourth of the total number of deputies and senators. Discussed three days later, it must be passed by a majority of the total number of legislators. For a comparative discussion, see James McGregor, "The Presidency in East Central Europe," *RFE/RL Research Report* 3 (January 14, 1994): 23–31.

61. Michael Shafir, "Romania's New Institutions: The Constitutional Court," *RFE/RL Research Report* 1 (October 23, 1992): 47–50; Adrian Campbell, "Local Government in

Romania," in Andrew Coulson, ed., *Local Government in Eastern Europe* (Brookfield, VT: Edward Elgar, 1995), pp. 76–101.

62. An excellent discussion of the process and outcome is provided by Michael Shafir in "Romania: Constitution Approved in Referendum," *RFE/RL Research Report* 1 (January 10, 1992): 50–55. On the original version, see his "Romania's New Institutions: The Draft Constitution," Radio Free Europe, *Report on Eastern Europe* 2 (September 20, 1991): 22–33. On Hungarian issues, see Aurelian Craiutu, "A Dilemma of Dual Identity," *East European Constitutional Review* 4 (Spring 1995): 43–49.

63. See Michael Shafir, "Romania Prepares for Local Elections," *RFE/RL Research Report* 1 (January 31, 1992): 18–23.

64. Campbell, "Local Government in Romania," pp. 79–80.

65. Michael Shafir, "Romanian Local Elections Herald New Political Map," *RFE/RL Research Report* 1 (March 13, 1992): 29.

66. Michael Shafir, "Agony and Death of an Opposition Alliance," *Transition* 1 (May 26, 1995): 23–28. See also the many articles on individual parties by Shafir and Dan Ionescu in *RFE/RL Research Report* and its successor, *Transition*.

67. See the following articles by Michael Shafir in *RFE/RL Research Report*, "Romania's New Electoral Laws," 1 (September 11, 1992): 24–28; "Romania's Election Campaign: The Main Issues," 1 (September 11, 1992): 29–31; and "Romania: Main Candidates in the Presidential Elections," 1 (September 4, 1992): 11–18. See also James McGregor, "How Election Laws Shape East Europe's Parliaments," in *RFE/RL Research Report* 2 (January 22, 1993): 11–18, and Elena Stefoi, "Electoral Law in Eastern Europe: Romania," in *East European Constitutional Review* 3: 2 (Spring 1994): 55–58. The electoral laws were #68 and #69 (1992); *Monitorul oficial* #164 (July 16, 1992).

68. For analyses of the results in English, see *East European Reporter* 6 (November–December 1992): 3–9, and the many articles in *RFE/RL Research Report* 2 (1992).

69. Arista Maria Cirtautas, "In Pursuit of the Democratic Interest: The Institutionalization of Parties and Interests in Eastern Europe," in Christopher G.A. Bryant and Edmund Mokrzycki, eds., *The New Great Transformation* (New York: Routledge, 1994), p. 36. On East European patterns, see the conclusion in Gordon Wightman, ed., *Party Formation in East-Central Europe* (Brookfield, VT: Edward Elgar, 1995), pp. 228–251; the editor's introduction and conclusion in Thomas F. Remington, ed., *Parliaments in Transition* (Boulder: Westview, 1994), esp. pp. 5–10, 217–224, and the sources cited; Paul G. Lewis, "Democratization and Party Development in Eastern Europe," *Democratization* 1 (Autumn 1994): 391–405; and Maurizio Cotta, "Building Party Systems After the Dictatorship," in Geoffrey Pridham and Tatu Vanhanen, eds., *Democratization in Eastern Europe* (New York: Routledge, 1994), pp. 99–127.

70. For an overview of economic developments in 1993–1995, see the coverage in *RFE/RL Research Report* and *Transition*. The data cited here and below come from Colin Jones, "Romania: The Tide Turns," *Banker* 144 (December 1994): 29–31, *Romania Economic Newsletter* 5 (April–June 1995): 1; and *Financial Times*, August 15, 1995.

71. On changes generated in part by the PFP process, see Dumitru Cioflina, "Restructuring and Modernizing the Romanian Armed Forces," *NATO Review* (August 1994): 32–35. On these years in general, the best sources in English remain *RFE/RL Research Report* and *Transition*.

72. Adam Przeworski, *Democracy and the Market* (New York: Cambridge University Press, 1991), pp. xi, 94. On the RIS, see Dan Ionescu, "Big Brother Is Still Watching," *Transition* 1 (May 26, 1995): 20–22.

73. See p. 3 of this book and Preworski, *Democracy and the Market,* p. 14.

SUGGESTIONS FOR FURTHER READING

For the broad sweep of Romanian history, see Vlad Georgescu, *The Romanians: A History* (Columbus: Ohio State University Press, 1991). Keith Hitchins, *Rumania, 1866–1947* (New York: Oxford University Press, 1994), gives the most comprehensive and readable interpretation of social and political developments in the modern period. On issues of ethnicity and nationalism, see Katherine Verdery, *Transylvanian Villagers* (Berkeley: University of California Press, 1983), and Irina Livezeanu, *Cultural Politics in Greater Romania* (Ithaca: Cornell University Press, 1995). The best political treatments of the interwar era remain those by Roberts and Rothschild (see note 7), and the many books and articles by Stephen Fischer-Galati should also be consulted, e.g., *Twentieth Century Rumania*, 2d ed. (New York: Columbia University Press, 1991).

On the communist period, see William Crowther, *The Political Economy of Romanian Socialism* (New York: Praeger, 1988); Mary Ellen Fischer, *Nicolae Ceauşescu: A Study in Political Leadership* (Boulder: Lynne Rienner, 1989); Michael Shafir, *Romania: Politics, Economics, and Society* (Boulder: Lynne Rienner, 1985); Katherine Verdery, *National Ideology Under Socialism* (Berkeley: University of California Press, 1991); and the sources listed in note 23. Edward Behr has written a popular study of Ceauşescu: *Kiss the Hand You Cannot Bite: The Rise and Fall of the Ceauşescus* (New York: Villard Books, 1991). Daniel N. Nelson, ed., *Romania in the 1980s* (Boulder: Westview, 1981), contains chapters by many scholars writing on Romania at the time.

Nelson's *Romania After Tyranny* (Boulder: Westview, 1992) includes works by major scholars working on the postcommunist period, including Vladimir Tismaneanu. Sources on the revolution of 1989 and the miners' violence of June 1990 are found in notes 31 and 43 respectively. The most detailed analyses of postcommunist Romania, usually by Michael Shafir or Dan Ionescu, appear in the journals of Radio Free Europe—*Report on Eastern Europe* 1–2 (1990–1991), and *RFE/RL Research Report* 1–3 (1992–1994)—and in their sequel, *Transition*, published by the Open Media Research Institute (OMRI) since 1995. The OMRI daily reports are now available free on internet (omripub@omri.cz). Other important journals with regular coverage of Romania include *East European Constitutional Review, East European Politics and Societies, Problems of Post-Communism*, and *Slavic Review*. For translations of the Romanian press, see Foreign Broadcast Information Service, *Daily Report: East Europe.*

7

POLAND:
A TROUBLED TRANSITION

SARAH MEIKLEJOHN TERRY

In the forty-odd years that Moscow held sway over Central and Eastern Europe, Poland was the USSR's least stable satellite, repeatedly wracked by political and economic crises. It was also the first to have a noncommunist government in place in that dramatic autumn of 1989. That this event occurred before anyone in the West or East, including in Poland itself, foresaw the collapse of Soviet power in the region profoundly affected the early course of democratization and has continued to influence later stages of the transition and consolidation. Thus, the first set of issues to be explored here involves the consequences of Poland's role as pacesetter in Eastern Europe—a role that presents us with a number of interesting angles on postcommunist transitions.

Another set of issues concerns the extent to which Poland possessed or lacked the prerequisites traditionally viewed as necessary to sustain a democratic order.[1] On the negative side, as with most of its Central and East European neighbors, Poland had only fleeting experiences with democracy: first, immediately after World War I with the resurrection of an independent Polish state following more than 100 years of partition and repression; and, second, the bogus coalition phase under Soviet military occupation from 1945 to 1947. Neither period lasted long enough, however, to create stable democratic institutions, much less to instill habits of democratic behavior; the first was cut short by Marshal Józef Piłsudski's 1926 military coup, the second by the brutal Stalinization of the country beginning in 1948. On the economic front, the dislocations of the interwar years—caused largely by the need to patch together the disparate Russian, Prussian, and Austrian partitions—were compounded by wartime losses that, on a per capita basis, surpassed those of any other country, including the USSR. The following four decades of communist mismanagement left the economy in a severe state of macroeconomic disequilibrium, with hyperinflation that by the close of 1989 was approaching an annual rate of 1,000 percent, a hard-currency and ruble debt of $50 billion, and a population sorely tried by more than a decade of economic deprivation and failed reforms.

On a more positive note, and in contrast to most communist states, Poland in 1989 retained a large private agricultural sector—although for the most part it was fragmented and backward, with a rapidly aging labor force. The much smaller nonfarm private sector (in services and small-scale industry) provided only the embryonic beginnings of an entrepreneurial middle class. In the political realm, Poland also had a jump start over most of its neighbors in establishing the foundations—and, I emphasize, only the foundations—of civil society as a result of the decade-long experience of the Solidarity movement as well as the role of the Catholic Church in sheltering opposition activity. Clearly we need to ask how this overall lack of the attributes of democracy has affected the transition as well as the extent to which individual leaders have been able to compensate for this void to promote democratization and market reforms in largely unfavorable conditions.

A third set of questions relates to the dual-track nature of the transition in Poland and other postcommunist states—that is, the simultaneous attempt to construct both pluralistic democracy and a market economy. As I have argued elsewhere, this is a task that is both historically unprecedented and fraught with contradictions. Although market and democracy are generally seen as mutually reinforcing in the long term, in their formative stages they tend to be mutually obstructive. In particular, we need to explore the extent to which the pain inflicted by the economic transition has generated political instability, which in turn impedes the creation of the legal and institutional infrastructure for economic restructuring and privatization, in the end contributing both to a prolongation of the postcommunist recession and to further political polarization.[2]

Finally, a fourth set of questions concerns the impact of external actors on Poland's transition. Without question, the primary external factor through the end of 1989 was the Soviet Union, without which Poland would never have fallen under communist domination—or, at the very least, would have embarked on its postcommunist transition decades earlier—but which in the end played a crucial role in permitting the final breakthrough to noncommunist rule. Since 1989, an array of Western and international organizations—from the World Bank and International Monetary Fund (IMF) to the European Union (EU) and European Bank for Reconstruction and Development (EBRD)—have played an indispensable, if sometimes controversial, role in keeping Poland's transition on track when domestic events seemed to threaten it.

The remainder of this chapter is divided into four sections. The first looks at Poland's extended prelude to transition. The second examines the events surrounding the final breakdown of the *ancien regime* in 1988–1989 and the actual transfer of power, including the external context in which it evolved. The third section, which is the heart of the chapter, analyzes the political and economic dimensions of the first six years of postcommunist rule. The concluding section assesses the prospects for the consolidation of democracy in Poland.

Prelude to Transition: The Unruly Satellite, 1956–1988

Timothy Garton Ash once described the communist collapse in Eastern Europe in terms of "ten years, ten months, ten weeks, ten days"—a reference to the snow-balling pace of that collapse in Poland, Hungary, the German Democratic Republic, and Czechoslovakia, respectively.[3] Although the metaphor is catchy, it is not entirely accurate. In particular, the antecedents of the transition in Hungary can be traced back at least to the introduction of the New Economic Mechanism in 1968. In the case of Poland, they go back even further, to the crisis of 1956 which, unlike its Hungarian counterpart (or the Prague Spring of 1968), did not lead to Soviet military repression. Instead, it began a cyclical pattern of partial liberalization followed by partial retrenchment, leading sooner or later to renewed crisis, liberalization, and retrenchment—a pattern that repeated itself over the next three decades.

The 1956 crisis—a broad-based movement in support of far-reaching destalinization that involved virtually all social groups as well as reform elements within the ruling Polish United Workers' Party (PUWP)—led eventually to reinstatement of postwar "national communist" leader Władysław Gomułka and to modifications in a number of policy areas. After 1956, there were to be five more crises: 1968, 1970, 1976, 1980–1981, and 1988–1989.[4] In 1968, students and intellectuals protesting censorship and cultural repression were not supported by the workers; instead, the short-lived protests were exploited by Gomułka's hardline rivals to justify a largely anti-Semitic purge of intellectual and reform party circles. Gomułka survived this challenge—but only because Soviet leader Leonid Brezhnev was reluctant to risk a leadership shake-up in Poland while he still had his hands full with the Prague Spring reformers in Czechoslovakia.

In the 1970 Baltic port riots, the situation was reversed when worker protests against steep food price increases, announced just before the Christmas holidays, were not supported by the intellectuals. The strikes were brutally suppressed; but this time Gomułka did not survive in office. The new leadership team of Edward Gierek and Piotr Jaroszewicz was soon forced not only to withdraw the price increases, but also to make concessions to other groups—especially the peasants, the cultural intelligentsia, and the Church. Taking advantage of emerging East-West détente and the sudden availability of Western credits, the new team also embarked on an ambitious (in the event, reckless) program of economic expansion and modernization. By 1976, the Gierek strategy was in deep trouble. Western credits, often misappropriated or inefficiently used, had failed to produce the increases in export goods needed for repayment; instead, they were fast being transformed into an unsustainable external debt burden. By now most of the concessions of the early 1970s had also been reversed. Renewed cultural restrictions had soured the intellectuals' initially tolerant view of Gierek; Church-state relations had been irreparably damaged by the imposition of constitutional amendments that appeared to compromise the status of the Church and the civil rights of believers and to institutionalize the "Brezhnev Doctrine," which limited the sovereignty of Poland and other Warsaw Pact states. But the fatal blow to Gierek's strategy was the resumption of discriminatory policies against the private farm sector, a move that predictably led to a new round of domestic food shortages and another attempt, in June 1976, to raise food prices.

In the wake of the June riots, the dynamics of opposition politics in Poland changed in several important respects. In contrast to 1970, a disaffected intelligentsia now rushed to support workers arrested or dismissed from their jobs with the formation of KOR (Committee for Defense of the Workers). Equally important was the rapprochement between left-wing intellectuals and the Catholic Church, both disillusioned with the regime's failed promises. The result was the emergence of a broad-based opposition movement—involving not only the Church and intelligentsia (left-wing and Catholic alike) but also a growing segment of the working class and the independent peasantry—that led to the birth of the independent Solidarity trade union four years later.

The August 1980 strikes marked a major turning point, not only in Polish domestic politics but in Polish-Soviet relations and Soviet-East European relations generally. The rise of Solidarity led to a sixteen-month standoff between a communist party in crisis and a totally unprecedented trade union movement, and this time the workers were supported by the intellectuals and, for the most part, by the Church as well. In December 1981, under intense pressure from Moscow—including the threat of military intervention—martial law was declared. Solidarity was suspended but not destroyed; instead, it spawned an underground movement that continued to sap the legitimacy of the regime long after martial law was lifted in 1983.

By 1988, a combination of continuing political stalemate and economic stagnation sparked two rounds of worker strikes—the first in April–May, the second in August–September—and an anguished reappraisal on the part of the PUWP. By mid-1989, "roundtable" negotiations with Solidarity had led to partially free parliamentary elections and, to the surprise of all sides, the formation of a Solidarity-led government. Space does not allow for detailed consideration of each crisis; instead, I will focus here briefly on the major players in this process—including not only (or even primarily) individuals, but also the institutions and social forces that laid the groundwork for the unexpectedly rapid transformation of 1989.

First and foremost among the institutional players was the PUWP itself. Its prewar predecessor, the Polish Communist Party, was disbanded in 1938 on orders of the Comintern, with most of its leaders falling victim to Stalin's Great Purge. The successor Polish Workers' Party, established in the wartime underground in 1942 and into which the left wing of the Polish Socialist Party was forcibly merged in 1948, forming the PUWP, retained an anti-Soviet bias that smoldered beneath the surface during the next four decades. Unlike most communist parties in Eastern Europe, the PUWP was spared a full-scale purge in the early 1950s; in part as a result of this fact, one of the elements of continuity in the PUWP was the presence of a reform faction, which, although never strong in the leadership, did have influential voices among professional groups and in the media. The 1970s and early 1980s witnessed subtle changes in the PUWP's fortunes that would prove critical to its downfall a decade later. First, Gierek's program of accelerated development, coupled with concessions to the Church and cultural intelligentsia, attracted new recruits to the party in the early 1970s, especially among young professionals. Then, as Gierek defaulted on his promises in the second half of the decade, and with the rise of Solidarity in 1980–1981, deep disillusionment set in. An estimated one-third of PUWP members had also joined Solidarity; with the imposition of martial law, which delegitimized the party in the eyes of its own members, many turned in their party cards. Even with the lifting of martial law in 1983, the PUWP experienced a progressive weakening as recruitment plummeted.

A second official institutional player—at times, the effective arbiter of Polish politics—was the military. The Polish People's Army began its life during and after World War II as a military establishment totally subordinated to Moscow, with its senior officer corps (including the defense minister) composed of Red Army officers assigned to the Polish army. Following 1956 and the repatriation of most of the Soviet officers, the Polish military gradually acquired a degree of professional autonomy. Ironically, this was advanced by the participation of Polish units in the 1968 Warsaw Pact invasion of Czechoslovakia and suppression of the 1970 Baltic port strikes, both of which led to severe demoralization within the officer corps and the subsequent statement by then Defense Minister General Wojciech Jaruzelski that "Polish soldiers will not be used to shoot at Polish workers." With the 1976 crisis, during which Jaruzelski reiterated his warning, the army emerged as the arbiter of Polish politics, effectively determining when military force would (or would not) be used to quell civil unrest and when the regime would have to seek a political solution. This position was reinforced not only in August 1980 (when Jaruzelski rejected Gierek's demand for a state of emergency) and December 1981 (when he succumbed to pressure to impose martial law and suppress Solidarity) but also later as the PUWP's influence flagged in the mid- to late 1980s.[5]

Among the unofficial actors, the Church (and the Catholic intelligentsia) played an extraordinary role—as the defender of Polish national and cultural identity and, after 1956, as the lone and increasingly independent institution capable of sustaining a quasi-independent press. Especially after the mid-1970s, it also provided a protective umbrella for a growing number of opposition groups spawned in the aftermath of the June 1976 crisis. Finally, the 1978 election of Karol Cardinal Wojtyła, the charismatic archbishop of Cracow, as Pope John Paul II, followed by his tumultuous return visit to his homeland in June 1979, gave the opposition the psychological shot in the arm that proved to be a catalyst in the rise of Solidarity. During and after martial law, and despite its long-standing concern to avoid any situation that might lead to Soviet military intervention, the Church continued to tilt toward the Solidarity-led opposition and to reject the regime's efforts to play off the Church against the opposition.

Toward the other end of the spectrum was the "left" opposition, which emerged in the 1960s from an increasingly fractured PUWP and contributed in two crucial ways to the rise of Solidarity. The first was the strategy for breaking the regime's monopoly of social organization and communication first articulated by the disillusioned Marxist philosopher, Leszek Kołakowski, in 1970. Accepting that Soviet proximity guaranteed the survival of the communist regime for the foreseeable future—and also that the latter was incapable of reforming itself—Kołakowski argued that "the rigidity of the system depends partly on the degree to which the people living under it are convinced of its rigidity" and that monopolistic bureaucratic rule could be resisted by exploiting contradictions in the system. A second cause for the rise of Solidarity was the initiative taken by a leader of the 1968 student movement to seek a rapprochement between the left opposition and the Church. Writing in 1976 and later, and implicitly drawing on Kołakowski's earlier work, Adam Michnik (a founding member of KOR) called for a reappraisal of the left's attitude toward the Church—to begin to see it not as an adversary but as a partner in the struggle against totalitarian power.[6]

Although initially less cohesive and articulate than either the Catholic or left oppositions, the working class and peasantry were no less central to Poland's chronic instability. The workers, in particular, were at the forefront of every postwar crisis except the student-led protests in 1968, the cumulative lessons of which were that economic concessions granted to restore stability were invariably temporary and inadequate and that only an independent trade union organization could ensure that the workers' interests would be represented in the longer term. Thus, in a very real sense, the rise of Solidarity marked the first truly Marxist revolution in history, in which the Polish proletariat found its revolutionary class consciousness and rose up against an oppressive ruling class, appropriately dubbed the "red bourgeoisie."

Although the peasantry played a less visible role, it was nonetheless an important factor in the progressive escalation of social tensions and political paralysis. Poland was the only East European country in which collectivization of agriculture was not pushed to completion; indeed, it never came close. After 1956, when existing collectives were allowed to disband, the private sector (mostly small inefficient farms) accounted for approximately three-fourths of agricultural land and output. At the same time, successive leaderships never abandoned the long-term goal of socializing the farm sector; rather than do it quickly and forcibly, however, it would be accomplished by attrition and persistent economic pressure. Although formally independent, the private farm sector was subject to a wide range of discriminatory policies in its access to essential inputs and investments, as well as to obligatory deliveries at artificially low state prices. These policies resulted in chronic food shortages, especially of meat products, which directly contributed to social unrest in the 1970s and 1980–1981.

The final ingredient in this volatile mix was what might best be called the Soviet factor. Moscow not only saw Poland as the geopolitical linchpin of its influence in Eastern Europe; it also viewed the Poles as unreliable allies. (As Stalin was rumored to have said, converting Poland to socialism was like trying to put a saddle on a cow.) As a result, Soviet policy over the years was an unlikely mix of intermittent leniency on some issues combined with unrelenting pressure on others. In periods of acute instability, Moscow would tolerate temporary concessions— whether to the workers and peasants, the cultural intelligentsia, or the Church. Once the situation was under control, however, Warsaw would feel renewed pressure for political, cultural, and economic conformity. The most important hold that the Soviets had over the PUWP was in the area of economic policy. As a key component in Moscow's military-industrial complex, Poland was under relentless pressure not to cut back on key sectors of defense-related production (no matter how unprofitable)—indeed, to expand production in these areas. These pressures played a major role in the excesses of Gierek's "development strategy" in the 1970s and, thus, in Poland's mounting debt burden and economic collapse by the end of the decade. (Following Mikhail Gorbachev's rise to power in the Soviet Union in 1985, Poland would gradually be given more room for maneuver at home; but that is a subject for the next section of this chapter.)

Two additional points are worth emphasizing. The first concerns the continuity of key actors from several of the institutional players. Among the most important were the following: Defense Minister (later prime minister and PUWP first secretary) General Wojciech Jaruzelski; Tadeusz Mazowiecki, Poland's first noncommunist prime minister, who began his career as a student leader of the Catholic intelligentsia in the mid-1950s and later served as an adviser to Solidarity; Bronisław Geremek, a prominent dissident historian and another Solidarity adviser, who played a leading role in the 1989 roundtable talks and subsequently in the postcommunist parliaments; Adam Michnik and Jacek Kuron, both leaders of the 1968 student protests, founding members of KOR, and Solidarity advisers—the former to become editor-in-chief of Poland's leading daily newspaper after 1989, the latter a government minister and a prospective presidential candidate; and Lech Wałęsa himself, an electrician in the Gdansk shipyards who first emerged during the 1970 Baltic port strikes, reemerged as the leader of Solidarity in 1980 and, after years of internment and police surveillance during and after martial law, led Solidarity into the roundtable talks.

It is sometimes said that familiarity breeds contempt. In the Polish case, however, the interaction of these (and many other) leaders from both sides of the political divide, not only in the immediate context of the final crisis of communist rule but over the preceding decade (or decades), tended to breed grudging respect and a degree of certainty about how the other side would respond. This level of familiarity, occasionally tinged with a hint of trust, was a crucial factor in facilitating first the successful conclusion of the roundtable negotiations and then the sudden and unexpected transfer of power that followed in summer 1989.

The second point that merits attention here was the progressive exhaustion by 1988–1989 of alternatives to a genuine opening of the political system to some form of power sharing. After the lifting of martial law in 1983, Jaruzelski (with the grudging acquiescence of a badly weakened PUWP) made several unsuccessful attempts at co-opting some elements of the opposition. These "pseudocorporatist" initiatives invariably failed because they were seen as "too much, too soon" by party hardliners but "too little, too late" by the population and opposition, leaving the political landscape littered with regime-appointed "representative" bodies that were viewed with indifference or contempt. As one Solidarity activist reportedly quipped, "Jaruzelski is like a man with a choice between being on time for his train or being ten minutes late; so he decides to compromise and is five minutes late."

Toward the Roundtable
and the First Noncommunist Government

Six years after the imposition of martial law, Poland again teetered on the brink of crisis. The partial economic recovery of the mid-1980s had run out of steam; the debt had ballooned to nearly $40 billion, some 60 percent above the 1981 level, due to Warsaw's inability to meet interest and principal payments; and the failure of the Jaruzelski regime to adopt comprehensive reforms was proving a major obstacle to new Western credits, especially an IMF-backed stabilization package. A November 1987 referendum, intended to elicit popular support for essential austerity measures, was mishandled and inconclusive. Thus, as the last full year of communist rule began in 1988, the dynamics of the standoff between PUWP and opposition changed yet again. For its part, the party remained deeply divided over how to bridge the credibility gap; although a majority of the leadership continued to resist any form of power sharing, a growing reform faction was convinced that the cooperation of the moderate opposition could be gained only by offering tangible concessions. Unwilling to accept anything less and increasingly alarmed by the potential for widespread social unrest in a deteriorating socioeconomic environment, Solidarity itself was appealing for an anticrisis pact with the regime.[7]

Before the stalemate could be resolved, however, Poland would be wracked by two more waves of industrial strikes, two shake-ups in the party leadership, the resignation en masse of the Council of Ministers, and a bitter five-month struggle within the PUWP over whether and under what conditions to negotiate with

Solidarity. The fireworks began when, despite lack of a clear mandate from the November referendum, the regime went ahead with steep price increases in early 1988, with predictable results. Following the first round of strikes in late April and early May, the opposition stepped up its pressure for an anticrisis pact, implying a willingness to meet the regime halfway. Reviewing the dire economic situation and the numerous obstacles to reform, a major article by two Solidarity advisers in the independent Catholic weekly *Tygodnik Powszechny* warned that society must resist the "understandable but dangerous" temptation to view regime failures with "masochistic satisfaction": "Despite the risks associated with supporting the regime's program, there is no [realistic] alternative more beneficial for the interests of the country. . . . [A] failure of the present reform attempts must lead to a prolonged impasse with negative consequences that are difficult to foresee." At the same time, the authors chastised the regime for lack of cooperation with independent circles, noting that there was "not even a forum for contacts" and proposing a ten-point program as a starting point for negotiations.[8]

Despite tantalizing hints that some within the leadership wanted to pick up on this initiative—and apart from the first shake-up in the Politburo and Secretariat that brought more reformers into the leadership—Jaruzelski's poststrike moves indicated that he would pursue his economic reforms more aggressively, but not that he was prepared at this point to alter his posture vis-à-vis the opposition. That decision (or indecision) bore bitter fruit in a second and more virulent wave of strikes in late August and early September 1988, marking the eighth anniversary of Solidarity's birth and altering the face of Polish politics in irreversible ways. The most salient reality of the new situation was that Solidarity and its leader, Lech Wałęsa, reemerged on center stage. In contrast to the spring strikes, when the failure of the majority of workers to rally to the union's banner left its future in limbo, Solidarity's reinstatement quickly became the nonnegotiable demand of strikers from the coal pits of Silesia to the Baltic shipyards. That the strikes ended without the union's formal relegalization was possible only because of Wałęsa's personal intervention, in which he urged moderation and patience— and only after the regime, in a concession it had dismissed out of hand for nearly seven years, agreed to negotiations (the so-called roundtable talks) in which the status of the union would be on the agenda.[9]

Before the talks could begin, however, the PUWP had to sort out its internal divisions in a bruising tug-of-war not only between reformers and hardliners, but also within the reform faction between pragmatists who favored compromise and those (ironically including some of the most stalwart reform advocates) who were unwilling to share what they expected to be their moment of glory with Solidarity. With the resignation of the previous government (as scapegoats for the August strikes), the prime minister's post fell to one of the latter, Mieczysław Rakowski. A former editor of the liberal party weekly *Polityka* and long-time advocate of economic reforms, Rakowski was nonetheless the person who, next to Jaruzelski, bore the greatest onus for crushing Solidarity in 1981 and who had remained one of the most vociferous opponents of talks with Wałęsa.[10] It soon became clear that Rakowski's agenda included the introduction of his own "economic consolidation" plan—but without the participation of grassroots movements such as Solidarity.[11]

In the end, Rakowski's tactics backfired. Having first tried to buy off the Church by offering cabinet posts to several Catholic intellectuals without recognition of the banned union, he then attempted to derail the roundtable talks by labeling key Wałęsa advisers as "extremists" whose participation could not be tolerated. Solidarity's response was to close ranks; by November reinstatement of the union had become not merely the subject of future negotiations but a sine qua non, as a symbol of the party's sincerity in offering society an authentic voice in the reform process. By mid-December, more than 100 prominent intellectuals and Solidarity activists had organized themselves into a Citizens' Committee (with a standing secretariat and fifteen commissions covering all major policy areas) to serve as a pool of expertise for Wałęsa.[12]

Faced with a united opposition and escalating tensions, Jaruzelski had little choice but to go to the mat with his internal opposition in a two-stage Central Committee plenum in December and January. The initial stage yielded little more than the second shake-up in party leadership within six months and a revealing display of the PUWP's disorientation. When it reconvened in January, the plenum approved the opening of talks with the opposition—but only after two days of rancorous debate and an unprecedented confidence vote in the leadership prompted by Jaruzelski's threat to resign if the party rejected his position.[13]

A final factor pushing the party toward compromise was an apparent change of heart in Moscow. Already in the wake of the August strikes, the Soviet press had begun to take a favorable view of an anticrisis pact, criticizing the foot-dragging of "conservative and bureaucratic forces" who "have become adept" at resisting change and implying that the strikers had finally forced the leadership to address "unresolved economic and social problems." Most remarkable was a *Le Monde* interview with Nikolai Shishlin, head of the international section of the CPSU's Propaganda Department. In the interview, entitled "Union Pluralism Is No Heresy," Shishlin implied that Moscow was tilting in favor of stability regardless of ideological compromises: "If we do not have a solution ready-made for ourselves, we have even less of one for Poland where pluralism is so developed. . . . We are not afraid of a reemergence of Solidarity. . . . The men who participated in Solidarity are today in a position to play a more important role." In February 1989, with the roundtable talks in progress, the Soviets sent an even stronger signal by publishing a highly positive profile of Wałęsa, depicting him as "a man who rose from the people," a "man of principle."[14]

Thus, although it was hardly a foregone conclusion that the roundtable would yield positive results,[15] by early 1989 conflicts within both regime and opposition had been resolved in the way most auspicious for a breakthrough—in favor of reformers in the PUWP and moderates in Solidarity, with hardliners and radicals respectively pushed to the sidelines.[16] In just two months, from February 6 to April 5, the two sides were able to reach an agreement—more procedural than substantive, to be sure—that had eluded them for nearly a decade. At the same time, each side (perhaps fortuitously) miscalculated the relative strength of the other in ways that would dramatically alter Poland's political landscape in the space of a few months.

For our purposes here, the political provisions of the roundtable agreement were most important.[17] First, new parliamentary elections would be called for June 1989, in which 65 percent of the seats in the Sejm (now to be the lower and more powerful house of parliament) would be reserved for the communist-led coalition—38 percent for the PUWP itself and 27 percent for its junior coalition partners, the United Peasant Party (ZSL) and Democratic Party (SD). The remaining 35 percent of the seats were to be openly contested. Second, Poland's Senate (abolished in 1947) would be reconstituted as the upper house of parliament with more limited advisory and veto powers; all 100 seats there would be openly contested. In return, Solidarity agreed to the establishment of a new executive presidency, expressly designed for Jaruzelski, with extensive powers in foreign and defense policy and carefully circumscribed emergency powers that were intended simultaneously to reassure Moscow of Warsaw's continued loyalty but to impede the arbitrary exercise of presidential power at home. Other elements of the package included relegalization of Solidarity, opposition access to the media, and agreement in principle to reorganize local government along democratic lines.

The short two-month time frame to organize for the elections put Solidarity at a distinct disadvantage—no doubt a calculated move on the part of the PUWP. Nonetheless, the Citizens' Committee proved effective in minimizing competition among opposition candidates, at times eliciting charges of undemocratic behavior from Solidarity radicals opposed to the roundtable compromise. The result was that the PUWP suffered a one-two punch at the hands of the electorate, with Solidarity sweeping all 161 Sejm seats it was allowed to contest (35 percent of the 460-seat total), plus 99 of the 100 seats in the reconstituted Senate. The communist-led coalition eventually secured its allotted 299 Sejm seats, but only after all but five of its candidates fell short of the required 50 percent voter approval in the preliminary round. Particularly humiliating was the defeat of 33 of 35 unopposed coalition candidates on the so-called national list, including eight members of the PUWP's Politburo, whose names were crossed off the ballot by more than half of the voters. (Jaruzelski escaped defeat by not standing for election.) Adding insult to injury was the fact that nearly half the seats guaranteed to the PUWP (80 of 173) were won by candidates who ran against nominees selected by the central party apparatus.[18]

Electoral aftershocks nearly derailed the transition process, which was ultimately salvaged by a combination of bold initiative, calculated compromise, and judicious Soviet intervention. Following the June debacle, Jaruzelski threatened to withdraw from the presidency, a post that even Solidarity leaders felt must remain in PUWP hands to ensure Moscow's neutrality. In the end, he was elected by a single vote of a joint session of parliament, thanks only to the abstention of a number of Solidarity electors. This was followed by a tense standoff over the replacement of Rakowski, the new PUWP first secretary, as prime minister. Jaruzelski's choice, Interior Minister Czesław Kiszczak, was unacceptable to Solidarity, less out of personal animosity (it was, after all, Kiszczak's negotiations with Wałęsa in September 1988 that opened the door to the roundtable talks) than because the general's role in the imposition of martial law eight years earlier disqualified him in the eyes of most of the union's constituency.

Although Kiszczak was confirmed, brewing dissension in the ranks of the PUWP's hitherto coalition partners (the ZSL and SD) gave Wałęsa the opening he had initially hoped to avoid—the opportunity to form a Solidarity-led government. On August 7, less than one week after Kiszczak's confirmation, Wałęsa, sensing the danger of political paralysis, appealed to the ZSL and SD to join Solidarity in a coalition. By the end of the month, Kiszczak had withdrawn, the ZSL and SD parliamentary groups had endorsed Wałęsa's proposal, and Jaruzelski had nominated Catholic journalist and Solidarity adviser Tadeusz Mazowiecki as the new prime minister. The transfer of power was further complicated by the foot-dragging tactics of new PUWP chief Rakowski, who was understandably anxious not to see the position to which he had so long aspired rendered irrelevant. Following an emergency Central Committee plenum in mid-August, the party demanded "parity" in the new government (six ministries for the PUWP, six for Solidarity, and three each for the ZSL and SD). Rakowski himself attacked the PUWP's erstwhile allies for their alleged "opportunism" and warned that, unless the party were given a role consistent with its "state potential," it would be unable to "take co-responsibility for the course of developments."[19]

The beginning of the end of the standoff came on August 22 with a forty-minute phone conversation between Rakowski and Gorbachev, in which the latter reportedly told the former to "stop blocking the inevitable" and to cooperate with a Mazowiecki government. Moscow's message was reinforced a few days later when Vladimir Kryuchkov, chairman of the Soviet State Security Committee (KGB), visited Warsaw and called Mazowiecki a "man of principles" whom he wished "every success." In the end, the new twenty-three-member government installed in early September included eleven Solidarity ministers, four each from the ZSL and PUWP (the latter including the defense and interior posts as provided by the roundtable agreement) and three from the SD, plus an independent international legal expert as foreign minister.[20] This was followed in October by the beginning of the end of the PUWP itself: a declaration of independence by the party's parliamentary delegation—in effect telling the central party apparatus that, as elected representatives of the people, they would have an autonomous and decisive voice in shaping the party's program. Implying, moreover, that significant elements within the party still hoped for its resurrection "on the ruins of the policies of the new government," they warned that obstructionist tactics would be disastrous for the whole country and pledged to cooperate with Mazowiecki's government and all other people "of democratic orientation."[21] The "exit phase" of the transition was over.

What conclusions can we draw from the death throes of Polish communism? Apart from the utter bankruptcy of the system, and in the context of this book, three come immediately to mind. The first is that Poland was neither a case of "transformation" (*reforma*) nor "replacement" (*ruptura*). Rather, it was a hybrid form (what Huntington has called "transplacement"),[22] a "pacted opening" intended by all sides—the PUWP, its coalition partners, Solidarity, and Moscow—to be a limited power-sharing agreement that, as a result of miscalculations (again on all sides), turned into a full-scale replacement of executive and legislative power.

A second conclusion is that individuals did, indeed, make a difference. Although the crisis of 1988–1989 was an outgrowth of long-standing political and socioeconomic conflicts, individual leaders among the institutional players were crucial in facilitating the peaceful, if dramatic, transfer of power. On the opposition side, most visible was Wałęsa, whose uncanny political instincts helped him grasp the moment, first, for the revival of Solidarity and then for the formation of a Solidarity-led coalition; others included Geremek, who guided the Solidarity team through the all-important political working group of the roundtable as well as new Prime Minister Mazowiecki. On the PUWP side, credit must be given to Jaruzelski for finally deciding to "catch his train" and seek genuine reconciliation; others in the party leadership were instrumental in his change of heart (or in giving him the courage of his convictions), most notably General Kiszczak, whereas some recalcitrants (e.g., Rakowski) continued to pursue obstructionist tactics to the end. Also noteworthy were leaders of the ZSL and SD, who seized the opportunity of Wałęsa's offer to form an opposition-led coalition, even at substantial risk to their own political futures. Finally, one must mention Soviet leader Gorbachev (along with some of his closest advisers), whose willingness to bend to the winds of history facilitated the emergence of the first noncommunist government in Eastern Europe in more than forty years.

The third conclusion is the most ironic—namely, that without multiple miscalculations among the various players the roundtable compromise and the breakthrough to a Solidarity-led government might never have occurred, at least not in the way that it did. Both Solidarity and the PUWP underestimated the impact of partially free elections. On the Solidarity side, it was widely assumed that the union, in a minority position in parliament and excluded from the government, would be spared the onus of responsibility for the first stage of clearing away the debris of communism; that it would have four years to prepare for taking power after the first truly free elections. The PUWP also miscalculated: that their 65 percent coalition majority would hold, that Solidarity would be incapable of mounting a cohesive and orderly campaign in less than two months, and that

Moscow would refuse to accept a change of regime in Poland. But perhaps the greatest miscalculation was on Moscow's part: that a change of leaders in Eastern Europe would not mean a change of regime, that socialism in some form (in Gorbachev's image?) would survive.[23] In brief, had the PUWP, and Moscow in particular, realized in advance what was about to happen, they might never have agreed to the roundtable compromise.

THE FIRST SIX YEARS

In less than a year, what had seemed a stunning breakthrough was overtaken by even more dramatic events elsewhere as communist regimes collapsed across Eastern Europe. While others celebrated with mostly free elections, the Poles, last year's pacesetters, were stuck with an anachronistic compromise—the "contractual Sejm," widely perceived as lacking in democratic legitimacy, and a communist general in a presidency designed to guarantee the country's loyalty to a soon to be defunct Warsaw Pact. Over the next six years, Poland would hold an unscheduled presidential election plus two more rounds of parliamentary elections, each under a different electoral regime, with no parliament serving more than half of its four-year term. In the same period, the country had no less than six governments of varying political colorations, none surviving much more than a year (and one not quite six months). Throughout, president and parliament were at loggerheads over their respective powers, and the Poles had yet to adopt a democratic constitution. Nonetheless, Poland was the first postcommunist country to implement an economic austerity program ("shock therapy") and the first to emerge from its postcommunist recession, with 1995 promising to be the third straight year of 4–5 percent growth in gross domestic product (GDP).

The apparent discrepancy between endemic political volatility and steady economic recovery is perhaps best explained by the "Balcerowicz paradigm." Leszek Balcerowicz, Poland's first postcommunist finance minister, has identified what he calls a "period of extraordinary politics" as crucial to a rapid and successful transition—a window of opportunity in which a new leadership can take advantage of broad social and political consensus in favor of radical change to undertake bold reforms, before the petty bickering and infighting of "ordinary politics" return.[24] In Poland, the period of "extraordinary politics" corresponded to the Mazowiecki government (September 1989 through most of 1990), which, despite Solidarity's minority position in the Sejm, enjoyed unprecedented popular legitimacy; it also corresponded to the implementation of Balcerowicz's austerity program, which subsequent governments (campaign promises notwithstanding) found themselves unable to reverse. At the same time, hardships imposed by the austerity program helped put an abrupt halt to "extraordinary politics."

During Poland's first postcommunist year, the role played by individual leaders was overwhelmingly positive; indeed, the availability of leaders with vision and understanding of what was needed, in both institutional and policy terms, was critical to the decisive nature of the reforms adopted. This is not to say that mistakes were not made; but in light of the daunting problems that the new government faced, the pluses clearly outweighed the minuses. With the return of "ordinary politics," however, the impact of individual behavior on the political scene turned more negative as personal conflicts and ambitions began to crowd out common perceptions of, and an overriding commitment to, national interest. Among the early offenders was none other than Solidarity leader Lech Wałęsa.

The December 1990 Presidential Election

The first event to roil Poland's political waters was Wałęsa's call in the summer of 1990 for a new presidential election, this time by popular vote rather than by parliament. Although he justified his move and his decision to be a candidate himself by citing the need to rid the country of a symbol of the communist past (Jaruzelski), his real motivation appears to have been personal ambition, especially his frustration over being sidelined by a government dominated by Solidarity intellectuals. In addition, he consciously set out to split Solidarity by calling for a "war at the top," declaring that the union-based government posed a new authoritarian threat and basing his own campaign on blatantly populist and contradictory promises both to accelerate reforms and to soften the austerity program of the Mazowiecki government; he also criticized Mazowiecki for his reluctance to settle accounts with the communists. With his policy under attack, the farsighted but uncharismatic prime minister had little choice but to run for president himself against Wałęsa, in the end unsuccessfully.[25]

In all probability, the Poles would eventually have held early elections to replace Jaruzelski with a democratically elected president; nonetheless, Wałęsa's initiative was premature and detrimental in several respects. First, Jaruzelski had shown no inclination to use his executive powers to thwart reform. Second, it put the cart before the horse in the sense that what Poland most needed at this point was a new constitution, in which the respective powers of president and parliament would be properly delineated, followed by fully free parliamentary elections. Third, as the catalyst for the fragmentation of Solidarity, the presidential election destroyed the political consensus that had held the country together not only through the anxious moments of 1989 but also through the first months of the economic program introduced in January 1990. Without the disruption of a presidential election, it was quite possible that the Mazowiecki government could have served out its four-year term, ensuring consistency in economic policy and lending credibility to Poland's democratic consolidation. As it happened, the campaign served to reopen contentious issues that have continued to dominate political debate.

Finally, coming as it did just as the economy was plunging into postcommunist depression, the election graphically demonstrated the vulnerability of Polish voters to demagogues peddling snake oil—in this case, in the person of Polish-

Canadian "businessman" Stanisław Tymiński, who came from nowhere to declare his candidacy and take 25 percent of the vote in the first round, placing second to Wałęsa and knocking Mazowiecki out of the runoff round. Tymiński's initial appeal was based on his flamboyant style and image as a "Polish boy who made good in the West" and who, by implication, could lead his countrymen to painless prosperity—all of dubious credibility. Not only did he support policies at odds with market reforms, presenting himself as a defender of state-owned enterprises (SOEs) and an opponent of foreign investment (which he warned would leave Poland hostage to the West), but subsequent revelations also suggested a check-ered past and links to the communist-era secret police.[26]

Elected easily in the second round, Wałęsa quickly discovered that he could change economic course only at the unacceptable risk of losing the support of the IMF and Poland's external creditors. Thus, the second postcommunist govern-ment, appointed in January 1991 under new Prime Minister Jan Krzysztof Bielecki, a radical market reformer, continued to pursue the policies of its prede-cessor. But the campaign had wreaked havoc on the public mood. In particular, the revival of anticommunist rhetoric had further undermined the legitimacy of the "contractual Sejm," leading to growing pressure for early parliamentary elec-tions; equally important, Wałęsa's (and Tymiński's) attacks on the Mazowiecki government had put debate over economic policy and the state budget back on center stage. It was the second issue, the economy, that brought Bielecki's govern-ment down in September 1991, barely nine months after its installation; but it was the first issue, the revival of anticommunist rhetoric, that set the stage for the next turning point in Poland's transition, the first fully free parliamentary elections.

Parliamentary Politics: October 1991

The dissolution of the roundtable parliament was preceded by a six-month strug-gle over the law that would govern election of the next one. With two-thirds of the "contractual Sejm" from parties with roots in the old PUWP-led coalition, it was a foregone conclusion that they would try to maximize chances for their political survival by holding out for adoption of a proportional representation system with no threshold, an effort in which they were joined by several small post-Solidarity groups with a similar incentive. The result was a proliferation of "couch parties"—in Polish parlance, *partie kanapowe*, so called because all members could fit on a single sofa—many with little or no social base and idiosyncratic, often inconsis-tent platforms.[27]

In an insightful essay entitled "A Political System Under Construction," one analyst has added a historical dimension to our understanding of Poland's politi-cal confusion at this stage. Comparing the context of the political transition in 1918 with that after 1989, Mirosława Grabowska noted that despite 125 years of partition, Poland emerged from World War I with a well-defined and more or less complete spectrum of political parties. The key parties, from right to left, could all trace their beginnings back to the 1890s; each had a leadership experienced in political and social activism, a distinctive program, and its own press. Grabowska also noted that the South European countries that underwent transitions from authoritarian to democratic rule in the 1970s and early 1980s similarly benefited from well-developed party structures and that "the degree of organization of political forces was an important factor in the very process of creating a democratic order—and, especially, the durability of that order." By contrast, the 1989 transition began "in a situation in which political options [had] not yet been articulated, and political groupings [did] not exist or [were] poorly organized and uninstitutionalized." In such a situation, it is the "process itself that becomes the formative factor," in which "political parties react to events and changes rather than shape them"; the transition then "resembles an airplane with no one at the controls."[28]

More than 100 parties and other political organizations contested the 1991 elections, which drew out only 43 percent of the electorate and in which no party received more than 12 percent of the valid votes (see Table 7.1).

In all, twenty-nine parties and groups won at least one seat in the Sejm (eleven only one each). The top five vote-getters, accounting for just over half the votes (21 percent of eligible voters) and 57 percent of the seats, were spread so widely across the political spectrum as to make a majority coalition virtually impossible to create, much less sustain. Complicating matters further, the two largest parties, the centrist Democratic Union (UD) and the Democratic Left Alliance (SLD), were effectively relegated to the opposition: the latter because no one was willing to include the former communists in a coalition; the former because most right-of-center parties were unwilling to join a government led by the UD, the party most closely identified with the previous two governments, due to deep differences over both the pace of economic reform and the role of the Church in political life.

The standoff left two alternatives, neither very promising. The first was for a cluster of smaller, self-defined, right-wing parties to form a coalition. To control even a bare majority of deputies, however, such a coalition would have to include parties with widely disparate agendas, whereas a more coherent rightist coalition could routinely command only 40 percent of votes in the Sejm. The second alternative was to concede that no orientation had won the election, that the Sejm was too fragmented to form a viable coalition, and that the best solution was to transfer primary responsibility for appointing a government to the president and to enhance the powers of the government vis-à-vis parliament. This was clearly the course preferred by Wałęsa, who, during the immediate postelection turmoil, proposed a set of constitutional amendments (a "little constitution") that would have had precisely this effect. But most in the Sejm saw Wałęsa's proposals as a transparent power grab rather than as a sincere attempt to give Poland a stable government capable of keeping the reform program on track as the president himself claimed.[29]

TABLE 7.1   Results of Poland's Parliamentary Elections, October 27, 1991

Party	Percent of Vote	Number of Sejm Seats
Democratic Union (UD) [S]	12.31	62
Democratic Left Alliance (SLD) [C]	11.98	60
Catholic Electoral Alliance (WAK) [S]	8.73	49
Center Citizens' Alliance (POC) [S]	8.71	44
Polish Peasant Party (PSL) [C]	8.67	48
Confederation for an Independent Poland (KPN)	7.50	46
Liberal Democratic Congress (KLD) [S]	7.48	37
Peasant Alliance (PL) [S]	5.46	28
Solidarity Trade Union [S]	5.05	27
Polish Beer Lovers' Party (PPPP)	3.27	16
Christian Democracy (ChD) [C]	2.36	5
Union of Real Politics (UPR)	2.25	3
Solidarity of Labor (SP) [S]	2.05	4
German Minority	1.70	7
Party of Christian Democrats (PChD)	1.11	4
Party "X"	0.47	3
Silesian Autonomy Movement (RAS)	0.35	2
Polish Western Union (PZZ)	0.23	4
Other[a]	10.32	11
Totals	100.00	460

[S] post-Solidarity parties; [C] former communist and communist allies.

[a] Eleven groups were elected to one seat each, including the postcommunist Democratic Party (SD).

SOURCE: David McQuaid, "The Parliamentary Elections: A Postmortem," *Report on Eastern Europe* 2 (November 18, 1991): 16.

The election yielded two (really two and one-half) governments before parliament was again dissolved in May 1993. After nearly two months of wrangling at the end of 1991, the Sejm imposed a minority, three-party, right-wing coalition on a reluctant Wałęsa. Under Center Alliance leader Jan Olszewski, a former Solidarity lawyer and critic of Poland's free-market reforms, the new government was quickly embroiled in a protracted crisis not only over the state budget (where Olszewski was intent on increasing state subsidies in defiance of the terms of a multibillion dollar IMF stabilization loan) but also over Church-state relations (especially the abortion issue), the division of power between president and parliament, and the volatile question of "decommunization." Less than six months after the installation of the new government, Olszewski was ousted primarily as a result of the budget stalemate, although the immediate occasion was the furor caused by a scurrilous attempt to discredit critics of his government as alleged informers for the old regime.[30]

Following a two-month interlude during which Peasant Party (PSL) leader Waldemar Pawlak (then Wałęsa's personal choice for prime minister) was unable to form a government,[31] a new, seven-party, center-right coalition took office in July 1992 under UD deputy Hanna Suchocka. Despite its short tenure (ten months this time) and the tenuous nature of its parliamentary majority, the Suchocka government brought changes in both the style and substance of policy-making. Although not Wałęsa's choice for the job, she signaled at the outset a willingness to cooperate with the president—a stance that facilitated adoption of the badly needed "little constitution." On the economic front, her tough stance on the budget deficit and determination to put reforms back on track, combined with the first signs of economic recovery during the second half of the year, helped restore Poland's international credibility. At the same time, Suchocka's tenure was not without controversy. Her plan to begin the painful task of downsizing and restructuring the bloated coal and steel sectors sparked a wave of labor unrest; and her support for the divisive and highly restrictive abortion law—ironically, a position that made her acceptable to most of her right-wing coalition partners—contributed to the erosion of popular support. In the end her government, like its predecessors, fell victim to the budget, losing a no-confidence motion by a single vote.[32]

Parliamentary Politics: September 1993

The lessons of the short, troubled life of the 1991 parliament were not lost on its incumbents. Before being disbanded, it approved a new electoral law which, while still based on proportional representation, imposed a 5 percent threshold for single parties and 8 percent for coalitions. As Table 7.2 shows, the revised law had the intended effect of limiting the number of parties represented in the Sejm (the thresholds applied only to the lower house, as the Senate continued to be elected under a plurality system).

Nonetheless, the election produced its own surprises. This time, with a 53 percent turnout, the two postcommunist parties (the SLD and PSL) won 303 of 460 seats in the Sejm—almost exactly the 65 percent allotted to the PUWP-led coalition under the 1989 roundtable agreement—as well as 73 of 100 seats in the Senate. A third left-wing party, the Union of Labor (UP), with roots in Solidarity, won another 9 percent of the seats. On the right, only the quirky populist-nationalist Confederation for an Independent Poland (KPN) inched over the threshold to take 5 percent of the seats; proreform centrist parties (the UD and BBWR) won barely 20 percent.

That the first East European country to give its communist rulers the bum's rush should be one of the first to return their postcommunist successors to office

TABLE 7.2   Results of Poland's Parliamentary Elections, September 19, 1993

Party	Percent of Vote	Sejm Seats	Senate Seats
Democratic Left Alliance (SLD)	20.41	171	37
Polish Peasant Party (PSL)	15.40	132	36
Democratic Union (UD)	10.59	74	4
Union of Labor (UP)	7.28	41	2
Confederation for an Independent Poland (KPN)	5.77	22	–
Non-Party Bloc to Support Reform (BBWR)	5.41	16	2
"Fatherland" Catholic Election Coalition	6.37	–	1
Solidarity Trade Union	4.90	–	9
Center Alliance	4.42	–	1
Liberal Democratic Congress (KLD)	3.99	–	1
Union of Real Politics (UPR)	3.18	–	–
Self-Defense	2.78	–	–
Party "X"	2.74	–	–
Coalition for the Republic	2.70	–	–
Peasant Alliance (PL)	2.37	–	1
German Minority (4 committees)	0.71	4	1
Other	0.98	–	5
Totals	100.00	460	100

Electoral system: For the Sejm, proportional representation with a 5 percent threshold for single parties, 8 percent for electoral coalitions (ethnic minorites were not subject to the thresholds); for the Senate, a plurality of votes cast.

SOURCE: Louisa Vinton, "Poland Goes Left," *RFE/RL Research Report* 2 (October 8, 1993): 22–23.

through the ballot raises some intriguing questions: most importantly, why Poles voted as they did and what it means for Poland's transition over the longer term. Despite the temptation to find simple explanations, the answer to the first question goes well beyond the oft-cited "nostalgia for the past," although socio-economic factors were an important part of the equation. Without question, the center and center-right parties that dominated earlier governments were being punished for the pain of the transition, a graphic reminder of society's short collective memory concerning the real causes of that pain. In addition, one should keep in mind that communism collapsed not because society rejected socialist-era values but because the *ancien regime* had failed abysmally to honor them. Thus, with substantial segments of society still attached to key features of the "nanny state," the absence or relative weakness of parties on that part of the political spectrum without ties to the communist past tended to favor the postcommunists.

But other explanations are equally compelling. For instance, the left retained much of its organizational infrastructure as well as its core constituencies. For the SLD, this meant the old *nomenklatura*, significant segments of the blue-collar workforce and other state-budget employees, and pensioners—the first out of old loyalties, the others out of understandable fear for their future in a market economy. Much the same was true for the PSL in rural areas, where it was the beneficiary not only of the collapse of the state farm system but also of the association of Solidarity-based peasant parties with the first post-1989 governments. In addition, both the SLD and PSL were better able to get out their supporters and, in a low-turnout election, secure a disproportionate share of votes cast. (Preelection polls showed the SLD with support of 10 to 12 percent of voters. With a 53 percent turnout, that share was leveraged to 20 percent.) A final factor in the SLD's showing was a growing recognition that the reformed Social Democrats (the nucleus of the Alliance) were a far cry from the old PUWP—that a vote for them was not a vote for a return to the past and that they were again legitimate players in the new Poland.[33]

By contrast, most center and right-wing parties continued to suffer from the political immaturity and fluidity characteristic of the 1991 elections. Often organized from the top down, around a self-styled leader surrounded by a small entourage of supporters, these parties lacked the voter identification of parties built from the bottom up and based on clearly defined social interests.[34] In other cases, even well-established parties suffered from self-inflicted shots to the foot— especially overconfidence and an unwillingness to make the compromises (both personal and programmatic) necessary for mutually beneficial electoral alliances. Most damaging in this respect was the failure of the UD to join forces with the smaller, ardently pro-reform Liberal-Democratic Congress (KLD), which, running on its own, fell short of the required 5 percent threshold.[35] Had the two parties run as an electoral coalition, they would have come close to matching the PSL's representation. Moreover, had Wałęsa not siphoned off votes with his "nonparty" initiative (the BBWR), a combined centrist bloc would have rivaled the SLD contingent.

A final factor affecting the fortunes of the center-right was a growing uneasiness (even aversion) among voters over the Church's intrusion into politics. The aggressive campaign by the episcopate to legislate its social agenda—especially to outlaw abortion and require Catholic education in the public schools—cost it support among women and other social groups that formerly saw the Church as a bastion in defense of nation and culture in the struggle against communist dictatorship. Not only did this hurt right-wing parties with close ties to the Church, but the UD, which was split on Church-state issues between the Suchocka wing and its more secular center-left, also lost votes. Again, the obvious beneficiaries here were the avowedly secular SLD and the Catholic but anticlerical PSL.

Yet, despite the left's substantial majority in parliament, its victory was not without problems, the most obvious of which was a flawed popular mandate. Of those who voted in the 1993 elections, only 36 percent voted for the SLD and PSL; another 35 percent voted for parties that were not represented in the Sejm. If one includes nonvoters, almost 70 percent of the electorate was not represented, while only 19 percent had voted for the SLD or PSL. And, despite common roots in the past, a SLD-PSL coalition was not the only feasible outcome. Eager to shed their communist lineage, the Social Democrats (the main component of the SLD) initially sought negotiations with several post-Solidarity parties. The most likely candidate, the UD (the only one with enough votes for even a narrow parliamentary majority) was still reluctant to be the first to join forces with the former communists. Even then, the SLD hoped to bring the smaller UP into a three-way coalition, but the latter eventually pulled out as well. Left with no choice but the PSL as its sole partner and despite serious differences between the two (especially over economic policy), the SLD opted to cede the prime minister's post to PSL leader Pawlak as a quid pro quo for SLD control over the main economic ministries and the post of Sejm speaker. No doubt the Social Democrats also assumed that, as the senior coalition partner, they would prevail on most policy matters.[36]

Almost from the outset, however, Pawlak proved the superior manipulator, and the government was plagued by internal divisions as well as rising tensions between it and the president. In contrast to a year earlier, Wałęsa wasted no time in expressing his displeasure with the choice of Pawlak. Even before the coalition took office, the president, predicting that the "postcommunists would be no more successful than the anti-communists," seemed to savor the prospect that he might have to step in and govern over the heads of the parties. Within the coalition, differences centered on economic policy. Although the SLD had campaigned on promises to restore some budget subsidies (and raise the deficit), party leaders were quick to back down after the election in order not to jeopardize IMF support and crucial debt-reduction negotiations. The PSL was far more committed to restoring subsidies, especially to the badly strained agricultural sector; in addition, it was deeply skeptical of market reforms in general and privatization and foreign investment in particular. As a result, Pawlak repeatedly frustrated SLD attempts to push ahead with a mass-privatization plan for large SOEs.[37]

Another area of tension concerned Poland's foreign policy orientation, with Pawlak and the PSL leaning toward restoration of ties in the East even as the Social Democrats were reiterating their commitment to European integration. In addition, the president's *droit de regard* over the posts of foreign, defense, and interior minister (the three "power ministries")—a right somewhat short of a full veto power as provided for in the roundtable agreement—was a continuing source of conflict in his relations with the government. On the latter point, the forced resignations of the foreign and defense ministers at the end of 1994 set the stage for a three-month standoff between Pawlak and Wałęsa, in which the prime minister rejected the president's choices for replacement ministers and the president (to the dismay even of opposition parties) threatened to dissolve parliament yet again. In a reckless move to boost his sagging political fortunes in advance of his reelection campaign, Wałęsa also attempted to use the crisis to breathe new life into the touchy issue of the political role of the military.[38] With concern over the impact on Poland's economic recovery growing, the standoff was resolved in March 1995, when the SLD took charge of the government in its own right with the appointment of Józef Oleksy as the country's sixth prime minister since 1989. The new government quickly approved Wałęsa's choices for the disputed ministries, announced (to the PSL's chagrin) that it would retain the proreform finance and privatization ministers, and reaffirmed its commitment to a predominantly Western orientation, including pursuit of early membership in the EU and the North Atlantic Treaty Organization (NATO).

What, then, has the return of the left meant for Poland's transition to democracy? On the negative side, it brought another bout of political hiccups, disrupting the reform process and, at least briefly, raising anxiety levels in the international financial and investment communities. It may also have added to the dyspepsia of the Polish electorate, although only time will tell on that score. But in the longer term it may augur well for the country's stability in that we may eventually look back on the 1993 elections as the beginning of the normalization of Polish politics in several respects. First, unless the electoral law is changed back to proportional representation with no threshold (highly improbable at this point), political groupings now have incentives to coalesce, which may mean that "couch parties" will soon be a thing of the past. Already the more established UD and KLD have overcome their differences to form the Freedom Union (UW), which recently elected former Finance Minister Balcerowicz as party leader. Second, and equally important, having taken responsibility for government, the postcommunist parties will henceforth have to share the blame for the pain of the transition. Over time this should help lower the temperature of political debate and, by fostering a culture in which all parties that abide by the rules of the democratic process are viewed as legitimate players, lessen the vulnerability of Polish voters to demagogic appeals of the Tymiński variety.

The Constitutional Conundrum

In retrospect—and in contrast to the swift action taken on the economic front—failure to adopt a new constitution early in the postcommunist period appears to have been a classic example of an inability or unwillingness to take advantage of Balcerowicz's period of "extraordinary politics" in this equally important area. With the inevitable return of "ordinary politics," the process of crafting and refining the institutional structures of Polish democracy became hopelessly embroiled in the ongoing struggle over specific policy issues. For many, the argument against early adoption of a new constitution centered on the "illegitimacy" of the "contractual Sejm." Others, including Geremek, the first chairman of the commission tasked with hammering out a new constitution, argued that the flawed legitimacy of the Sejm could have been overcome by submitting a draft to popular referendum and that it was a mistake not to take advantage of the "wave of enthusiasm that accompanied the fall of communism" to adopt a fully democratic and consistent constitution.[39]

Once Wałęsa's "war at the top" destroyed the Solidarity consensus, the task of constitution writing became infinitely more complicated, repeatedly delayed by the turnover of governments and parliaments. Among the most contentious issues were those related to the respective powers of president and parliament—in particular, powers concerning the formation and dissolution of the government and control over the "power ministries." The "little constitution" adopted in the fall of 1992 left presidential authority in the latter area intact (although still not uncontested in the political arena), but only partially sorted out the first set of problems. This interim arrangement set up a kind of ping-pong game in the formation of a government, with the initiative passing back and forth between president and parliament in cases of conflict. If neither side could gain majority support for its choice, the president could either dissolve parliament or appoint a government for six months; should that government fail to win majority support, parliament would automatically be dissolved and new elections called. Otherwise, the president could dissolve parliament only if it failed to adopt a budget within a set time frame.[40]

Three years later, in mid-1995, the Constitutional Commission still had seven drafts under consideration, most of which would curtail the president's powers in favor of parliament. Indeed, although he seemed to emerge victorious from his standoff with Pawlak early in the year, Wałęsa's threat to dissolve parliament during the crisis brought quick retaliation from the Sejm in the form of an amendment to the "little constitution," leaving parliament in place even after formal dissolution until new elections were held. That amendment, which easily survived Wałęsa's veto attempt, was almost certain to be written into the new constitution, as were further restrictions on the president's control over the "power ministries" and, especially, the military.[41]

Apart from the balance among basic political institutions, the most difficult constitutional issues focused on Church-state relations, with the Church predictably pressing hard for incorporation of its social and political agenda. Perhaps most surprising was that, even with left-wing parties in control of the Constitutional Commission, the Church was able to extract major concessions (although some provisions may still be subject to further negotiations). The episcopate, aptly described by the editor of the leading Catholic weekly as "allergic" to the separation of Church and state, succeeded in having the word "separation" replaced by "neutral autonomy," leaving ill-defined latitude for the Church to influence public policy. The drafters also accepted compromise language on right-to-life and freedom-of-conscience issues (the latter implying limitations on parental rights with respect to non-Catholic sects), as well as a clause to the effect that Church-state relations would be governed by the concordat signed between

Poland and the Vatican by the Suchocka government in 1993 (although the SLD has opposed it and ratification has repeatedly been postponed).[42]

Perhaps the best explanation for these and other compromises is that a key figure in the drafting process, Social Democratic Chairman Aleksandr Kwaśniewski was also the leading candidate for president in the election set for November 1995 and, as such, was not eager to antagonize the Church. Still, the greatest uncertainty concerning the constitution remained the timing of its adoption. Once the Constitutional Commission has an agreed draft, it is sent to a joint session of parliament, which may amend it or send it back for further revisions but ultimately must approve the text by a two-thirds majority. It then goes to the president, who has sixty days to propose his amendments, which must also be approved by a two-thirds majority in parliament. Only at this point can a national referendum to ratify the constitution be called. With Wałęsa threatening to veto any draft that weakens his powers, Kwaśniewski hoping to replace him after the November election, and the Church pledging to campaign from the pulpit against any provisions contrary to its interests, prospects that this complicated and much-delayed process could be completed any time soon—and especially before the presidential election—were fading fast in mid-1995.[43]

The Economic Dimension

When the Mazowiecki government took office in September 1989, Poland's budget deficit stood at 10 percent of GDP, and inflation for the entire year was nearly 250 percent (approaching an annual rate of 1,000 percent by year's end).[44] Over the next two years, GDP fell by nearly 20 percent and industrial production by more than one-third. Yet, in 1992, Poland became the first postcommunist country to pull out of recession with increases of 1.5 percent in GDP and 2.6 percent in industrial production. Over the next two years, GDP grew 4–5 percent annually (7.5 percent in 1994 by one estimate) and industrial production grew 6 and 9 percent in 1993 and 1994 respectively, with a 23 percent rise in private industrial output in the latter year. In the first quarter of 1995, industrial output rose an additional 10 percent; unemployment fell from a peak of 16.9 percent in mid-1994 to 15.4 percent in March 1995. Perhaps most impressive, the budget deficit declined to 2.8 percent of GDP in 1994, a level that should make most West European governments envious.

On the basis of such statistics, Poland is often trotted out as "Exhibit A" of successful shock therapy. Although this perception is partially true, it is also somewhat misleading; indeed, the juxtaposition of rapid versus gradual reform is itself misleading. As a growing number of economists have argued,[45] in economic transformations from central planning to the market there are two types of tasks: those that can and must be done quickly, and those that cannot or do not necessarily have to be. Prominent in the first group are changes associated with macro-

economic stabilization, that is, price and trade liberalization to wring inflation out
of the economy and sharp curbs on state subsidies to bring down the budget
deficit. In contrast, tasks such as privatization and the creation of the legal and
institutional infrastructure for a market economy can only be implemented over
a longer time frame.

Perhaps the most important lesson to be drawn from the Polish experience goes
back to the Balcerowicz paradigm, the period of "extraordinary politics" that
allows for bold reforms—in this case the macroeconomic stabilization program
put in place by Mazowiecki and Balcerowicz in January 1990 and from which subsequent governments were unable to deviate significantly. This was hardly the
result of a policy consensus or self-discipline; on three occasions elections have
been won on promises of weakening the austerity program: Wałęsa's presidential
election in 1990 and the parliamentary elections in 1991 and 1993. Instead,
Poland's relative policy consistency has been the result primarily of fiscal insol-
vency and external imperatives. Once the Balcerowicz plan was in place, it became
nearly impossible to reverse its main features without incurring punitive sanctions or, more accurately, foregoing welcome benefits in the form of IMF/World
Bank loans and debt relief. Poland's reward has been a 50 percent reduction (finally solidified in late 1994) of its debts to Western governments and banks, which
was followed by the granting of an investment-grade credit rating in June 1995, a
change that should allow the country to raise capital at favorable rates on international markets.

Nonetheless, the Polish economy was not yet out of the woods. Success in trim-
ming the budget deficit had its downside in the form of severe pressure on the
earnings of public-sector employees—workers in the numerous SOEs, state
bureaucrats, health care workers, and teachers—as well as the country's 9 million-
strong contingent of pensioners. Inflation also persisted at a worrisome 30 percent
annual rate, and the government's target of 17 percent for 1995 seemed unrealistic. In addition, the farm sector was especially hard hit, with overall agricultural
production in 1994 fully 10 percent below 1989 levels and 15 percent below 1991.
At least three factors were at work here. First, the small-scale and undercapitalized
nature of the bulk of Polish agriculture hindered its adaptation to the market.
Second, the ideological bias of the early postcommunist governments against both
the small, inefficient private plots and the highly subsidized state farms led to policies that were destructive to both; indeed, in what was probably the most serious
flaw in Balcerowicz's policy, his austerity program neglected the special needs of
agriculture by imposing prohibitively high interest rates that stifled essential
investments. Third, the dynamics of agricultural trade changed dramatically,
especially with the collapse of the Soviet Union; not only did Polish farmers lose
most of their markets in the East, they also have seen a reversal of their trade sur-
plus with the EU and, most painful of all, must now compete with subsidized EU
goods on the domestic market.[46]

Nor can there be much doubt that continuing political volatility and the turnover of governments has had a negative impact on other aspects of the economic transition, especially on the scope and pace of privatization. Even as privatization of small and medium enterprises—as well as some large joint-venture deals—has pushed the Polish economy ahead to the point where more than 60 percent of GDP now comes from the private sector, transformation of large SOEs has repeatedly been set back by the differing approaches of successive governments. A mass-privatization plan, designed to give all Polish adults an equity stake in the economy through an innovative mutual-fund scheme, was drafted already in 1990 but has been sent back for reconsideration by every subsequent government. Pawlak, in particular, almost single-handedly succeeded in delaying the program during his eighteen-month tenure. Soon after the Social Democrats took charge of the government in March 1995, the mass-privatization program was revived, with the first phase set to be launched in late 1995 with support from the World Bank and the EBRD. Yet the roller-coaster struggle over control of state assets may be far from over. In July 1995, parliament passed a new privatization law limiting the powers of the privatization ministry and even of the government as a whole. Under the new law—the president's veto of which was narrowly overridden by parliament—sales of individual SOEs must be approved by the entire cabinet rather than by the privatization minister himself; the government must also win parliament's approval to sell off SOEs in strategic sectors of the economy (such as defense industry, banking, mining, and telecommunications). Wałęsa and other opponents of the law—including the Solidarity trade union, which has threatened to mount a general strike over the issue—argue that it will slow privatization and leave the process hostage to antireform forces.[47]

Thus, despite impressive strides in overall economic recovery, the unevenness of the transition has contributed to the persistence of a negative popular mood. Unemployment, although declining, is still high and concentrated in areas highly dependent on old-line, state-owned, heavy industries. As a result of the growing income gap between the private and state economies, there is a widespread perception of unfairness in the transition process—that the benefits of recovery have bypassed much of the population and that elements of the old system, especially the *nomenklatura*, have been able to translate political clout under communism into economic power in the new system by misappropriating state property. Popular apprehension over rising levels of crime and corruption is growing, as is suspicion of the market in general and foreign investors and international institutions in particular. Just how this level of disaffection will feed into the political process will become clear only in the next round of elections for president in November 1995 and for parliament no later than fall 1997. In both cases, one of the key questions will be whether the current coalition partners can escape the punishment for the continuing unevenness of the transition that the voters visited on centrist and right-wing parties in 1993. In anticipation of the presidential election, industrial workers were voicing their demands for a larger slice of the recovery pie—in particular, for a greater share of privatized assets and for wage increases comparable to the increases in productivity that had fueled Poland's export-led growth.[48]

LESSONS AND PROSPECTS

If nothing else, the first six years of Poland's transition demonstrate the difficulty of "crafting"—that is, the deliberate shaping of political outcomes by adopting specific institutional forms. If we were to apply the rule of thumb often used to assess a country's progress toward democracy, Poland has clearly passed the "two-turnover" test. Yet this is less an indicator of democratic consolidation than of continuing political volatility, which can be seen in part as a hangover from the roundtable compromise, but which is primarily a reflection of the weakness of political institutions and civil society as well as the ongoing struggle over economic policy.

A second and related lesson concerns the limits on the contributions that individuals can make to the transition process. Although there can be no doubt that mature and pragmatic leadership on both sides greatly facilitates a smooth transfer of power from an authoritarian regime to the opposition, the Polish experience also suggests that strong leadership is a necessary but insufficient condition for later stages of democratic consolidation. That is, although leaders of vision and ability are still essential for the tasks of institution building and market reforms, they cannot make up for the political immaturity and volatility of an unschooled electorate or the competing ambitions of new actors in the political arena. Moreover, where participation in the liberalization and exit phases is limited to relatively few actors, their number and lack of political experience tend to rise dramatically thereafter, adding to the potential for instability.

Third, the Polish case provides a useful reminder of the peculiar complexity of postcommunist transitions. Not only are the political and economic dimensions inextricably linked, each complicating the other in various ways, but the extent of the economic and social distortions inherited from decades of communist mismanagement is also greater than in earlier transitions. Most of these earlier transitions took place in countries at a lower level of socioeconomic development—when both privatization and a change of development strategy are far easier to implement. The Polish and most other postcommunist economies, however, are highly industrialized. Moreover, their industrial structures are profoundly dysfunctional—distorted by past Soviet-imposed priorities, plagued by low productivity and technological obsolescence, and mired in environmental nightmares that pose still uncharted threats to public health and future productivity. Nonetheless—and this is the fourth and perhaps most important lesson—the Polish case shows that even in the face of overwhelming odds bold action in that period of "extraordinary politics" can be surprisingly effective in accelerating the economic transformation.

What, then, are the prospects for Polish democracy? Despite the many obstacles facing Poland in the near term—and despite fears voiced in some quarters that the country could lapse into an "Italian model," characterized by frequent elections and government changes—I am cautiously optimistic, preferring to see the glass as half-full rather than half-empty. Yes, mistakes that might have been avoided have been made; yes, personal ambitions and voter dyspepsia have thwarted consistent policymaking; and, yes, the severity of the post-1989 economic downturn has left the country with diminished capacity to meet pressing social needs (pension benefits, education, public health, and environmental protection, to mention only the most important) that will be crucial to future growth and stability. Yet, given its starting point in 1989, Poland has made remarkable progress on both the political and economic fronts, more than many observers could have imagined six years ago.

The primary key to Poland's future lies in continuing economic recovery, which should lead to a moderation of social and political tensions. That recovery has both domestic and international dimensions. On the domestic side, we still cannot say with any certainty at what point the development of the country's markets will become self-sustaining even in the face of ongoing political turmoil. Clearly that point had not yet been reached in mid-1995 despite the job creation and industrial growth generated by a burgeoning private sector. To reach that self-sustaining "takeoff" stage, the political system must prove capable of resolving remaining aspects of the transition, most importantly, completion of the privatization and restructuring of large sectors of heavy industry still in state hands as well as the consolidation of the country's legal and institutional infrastructure.

At the same time, the success of Poland's continuing recovery may now depend as much on the international environment as on domestic developments. Like other Central and East Europeans, the Poles see their future prosperity and security as inextricably linked to their integration into the EU and NATO, which, realistically speaking, will not come before the first decade of the twenty-first century. This illustrates yet another difference between the East European transitions and those in Southern Europe in the 1970s and early 1980s. At that time, the cold war division of Europe gave the West a powerful incentive to forestall either a possible "Eurocommunist" victory or prolonged instability by quickly integrating these countries into Western economic, political, and security structures. Today that sense of urgency is gone; moreover, the EU must sort out its numerous internal differences before it will be ready for another round of expansion, and NATO is struggling to redefine its mission. Much of Poland's economic growth to date has been export-led; for that to continue will require increasing access to world markets, especially those of the EU, which will also stimulate foreign investment. The other critical external factor will be the situation in the former Soviet Union. Should Russia or Ukraine, in particular, be seriously destabilized, Poland would be at risk of spillover effects—mass migrations, or the infiltration of criminal elements—that could compromise both its domestic stability and its international credibility.

POSTSCRIPT

Since this chapter was completed in mid-1995, the Polish scene has been altered yet again, first, by the defeat of Solidarity founding father Lech Wałęsa at the hands of social democratic leader Aleksandr Kwaśniewski in the November 1995 presidential election, and second, by the forced resignation in January 1996 of Prime Minister Józef Oleksy over charges that he spied for Moscow.[49] The latter crisis was quickly resolved with the appointment of an "independent" former communist as prime minister and a partial reshuffling of other government posts. Nonetheless, this latest round of political turmoil may yet disrupt Poland's ongoing economic transformation and complicate its hopes of early integration into the EU and NATO.

Before I address these longer-term problems, a few reflections on the presidential election are in order. The most obvious question is whether Wałęsa self-destructed or whether Kwaśniewski won on the basis of popular appeal and a voter backlash over the pain of the transition. The easy answer would be that the outcome was a combination of both; but, in light of the narrow margin of victory (51.7 for Kwaśniewski to Wałęsa's 48.3 percent), it was probably due more to the latter's self-inflicted wounds, not only during this latest campaign but over the five-year course of his presidency. Many Poles who would never think of voting for the former communists could nonetheless not forgive Wałęsa for his deliberate breakup of the post-1989 Solidarity coalition in his ambition-driven campaign for the presidency in 1990; nor could they forget his erratic performance in that post.

The real surprise in the first round of the election was that Wałęsa was able to recover from single-digit poll ratings to take one-third of the vote, close to his rival's 35 percent. The explanation for this is not that he regained genuine popularity, but that he was able to translate a well-tested recipe for anticommunist rhetoric into a widespread perception that he was the only nonleft candidate who had any chance of defeating Kwaśniewski. In the second round, however, Wałęsa squandered his apparent advantage with an unseemly and rude performance in a nationwide televised debate, reinforcing his less than presidential image in the minds of the electorate. In addition, his belated endorsement from the Church, which suffered a major setback in the election, may well have cost him more votes than he gained.

Kwaśniewski's campaign was not without its damaging revelations: failure to report his wife's questionable financial dealings and misrepresentation of his own academic credentials. Nonetheless, he was able to capitalize on quite disparate voter expectations: on the one hand, his image as an energetic and articulate exponent of economic modernization and integration with the West—an image that played particularly well among younger voters for whom even Solidarity, not to mention communism, belonged to a dimly remembered past; on the other hand, expectations among the losers in the transition—the jobless, pensioners, along with state-budget workers and many farmers—that Kwaśniewski as president could restore the social safety nets that once kept them afloat.

Thus, the sources of Kwaśniewski's victory soon became his dilemma: Which of his constituencies should he reward, and which should he disappoint? If he would pursue a proreform and pro-West agenda, he would have to disappoint the hard core of his party's support; in order to retain his credibility, he would also have to distance himself from the old communist *nomenklatura*. No doubt Kwaśniewski was well aware of this dilemma even before his electoral victory in November, but he undoubtedly did not foresee how quickly his intentions would be tested.

The governmental crisis began in late December 1995, with what initially appeared to be a postelection bout of sour grapes on Wałęsa's part to discredit his successor. In brief, allegations were leaked to the press that Prime Minister Oleksy had turned over state secrets to Russian agents, not only in the decade before the collapse of communist rule, but even after he assumed the posts of speaker of parliament in late 1993 and prime minister in March 1995. By early 1996, the crisis has taken on broader dimensions: the admission that Oleksy had a long-standing "friendship" with a resident KGB agent in the Soviet embassy in Warsaw and, thereafter, with his successor; the implication that there were other high-level moles among the postcommunists; Oleksy's politicization of the legal system with the dismissal of reformist prosecutors who had targeted wrongdoing by high-level former communists; and the appointment as deputy interior minister of an Oleksy crony who specialized in surveillance of anticommunist dissidents prior to 1989.

Although final judgment as to the veracity of the charges had to wait for a full airing of the evidence (in the hands of military prosecutors), it soon became clear that this was much more than an act of vengeance from a defeated president. A more plausible explanation of the timing of the allegations was that the outgoing interior minister, Andrzej Milczanowski—himself a highly respected and twice-jailed Solidarity activist from the 1980s—decided to lift the veil on an investigation that had been in progress for at least two years in the hope of preventing his successor (appointed by none other than Oleksy himself) from closing the case (and possibly destroying the evidence).

Oleksy's resignation set off a flurry of efforts to reconfigure or overturn the governing coalition. The PSL initially saw the crisis as an opportunity to retake the prime minister's post and reassert its protectionist antireform agenda, threatening otherwise to jump ship and form a new coalition with the Freedom Union and other opposition parties. For its part, the UW called for the formation of a non-party government of experts to restore credibility, hinting at a no-confidence motion with the implied threat of forcing another round of preterm elections; more extreme opposition voices called for a ban on the SLD altogether. It quickly became clear, however, that the PSL had no viable candidate for prime minister, that the UW and the PSL were too much at odds over basic policy issues to join in a coalition, that the opposition as a whole was too fragmented to challenge the existing coalition—and that, in any event, a prolonged period of political uncertainty (and especially a new round of elections) could only damage Poland's economic recovery and international credibility.

With the initiative back in its hands, the SLD nominated maverick former communist Włodzimierz Cimoszewicz as its compromise choice for prime minister. A 45-year-old lawyer with an independent streak, Cimoszewicz had declined to join the postcommunist social democratic party formed after the collapse of PUWP in late 1989 but had remained in the leadership of the left alliance in the Sejm. By February 1996, his government was shaping up to be even more solidly proreform than the outgoing one. Retention (despite strong PSL opposition) of Privatization Minister Wiesław Kaczmarek ensured that the ambitious SOE sell-off plan (some $720 million in 1996) would go forward. Among other proreform officials retained was Grzegorz Kolodko, the independent finance minister and deputy prime minister, who feared that new elections would derail badly needed pension and social-welfare reforms to keep deficit reduction on track. In addition, Kwaśniewski replaced Oleksy's newly appointed interior minister with one of his own close aides, apparently to restore credibility to the investigation of spy charges against the ousted prime minister.

Although still in opposition, the UW had cause to be reasonably satisfied with the near-term outcome; some observers even suggested that Cimoszewicz could "cautiously move towards the Polish-style 'historic compromise'"[50] that proved elusive in 1993. What this could mean for the stability of the current SLD-PSL coalition was still in question. The PSL, basically a one-issue party, accepted the Cimoszewicz nomination in hopes of extracting concessions on economic policy, especially a slowdown in the privatization program. Having failed in that effort, the Peasants had to decide whether they would prefer junior status in the existing coalition, with minimal clout on key issues of economic policy, to new elections and a likely opposition role. Should the PSL choose to withdraw, it would be problematic whether the SLD and UW could patch together an alternative government.

The other issue hanging over the new president was the impact that the spying charges against Oleksy could have on prospects for early integration into the EU and NATO, in particular whether Poland would be seen in the West as a reliable partner or as a potential security risk. Under the best of circumstances, Kwaśniewski probably expected a large helping of problems on his presidential plate; what he ended up with looked more like a can of worms.

Chronology

1918–1921	Poland emerges from 125 years of partition among Russia, Prussia, and Austria
May 1926	Marshal Józef Piłsudski's coup d'état ends Poland's brief experiment with parliamentary democracy
September 1939	German attack on Poland launches World War II, with the fourth partition of Poland under terms of the Nazi-Soviet Non-Aggression Pact
1944–1945	"Liberation" from Nazi occupation by the Soviet Army; establishment of a communist-dominated government
1947–1948	Noncommunist opposition defeated in flawed elections; "national communist" leader Władysław Gomułka purged; Stalinization begins
1956	First major challenge to communist leadership following Khrushchev's "secret speech"; Gomułka returned to power
1968	Student/intellectual demonstrations protesting Gomułka's ideological rigidity
1970	Worker riots protesting austerity measures lead to ouster of Gomułka and installation of new leadership under Edward Gierek and Piotr Jaroszewicz
1976	New round of worker riots over food price increases leads to emergence of a broad-based quasi-underground opposition movement
1980	Another attempt to raise consumer prices leads to a nationwide wave of strikes and the formation of the independent Solidarity trade union
1981	After a sixteen-month political stalemate, and under intense pressure from Moscow, martial law is imposed by General Wojciech Jaruzelski
1983–1988	Martial law is lifted, but Poland remains in lingering political and socioeconomic stagnation and crisis
1989	Roundtable talks between the regime and Solidarity (February–April) lead to the latter's victory in partially contested elections and to the formation of the first noncommunist government in Eastern Europe (September) under Tadeusz Mazowiecki
1990	"Shock therapy" austerity reforms introduced in January; Solidarity leader Lech Wałęsa defeats Mazowiecki in December presidential election to replace General Jaruzelski
January–September 1991	Second noncommunist government, under Jan Krzysztof Bielecki, continues reforms begun by Mazowiecki

October 1991   First fully free elections produce fragmented parliament and
                  fragile right-wing government that lasts less than six
                  months
July 1992   Minority centrist coalition under Hanna Suchocka takes
                  office; passes "little constitution"
May 1993   Suchocka government loses surprise no-confidence motion by
                  one vote
October 1993   New parliamentary elections result in victory of postcommu-
                  nist Alliance of the Democratic Left (SLD) and the Polish
                  Peasant Party (PSL) with a 35 percent plurality; government
                  formed under Peasant Party leader Waldemar Pawlak
March 1995   Pawlak government falls over conflicts with Wałęsa on eco-
                  nomic and political issues; SLD-led government under Józef
                  Oleksy, Poland's sixth since 1989, takes office pledging to
                  renew push for economic reforms and privatization
November 1995   SLD candidate Aleksandr Kwaśniewski defeats Wałęsa in
                  Poland's second presidential election, placing parliament,
                  government, and the presidency all in the hands of former
                  communists
January 1996   Prime Minister Oleksy is forced to resign following charges
                  that he passed state secrets to Soviet and then Russian
                  agents; in an effort to retain control of the government, the
                  SLD nominates "independent" former communist
                  Włodzimierz Cimoszewicz, deputy speaker of the Sejm, as
                  the new prime minister; but the SLD-PSL coalition remains
                  shaky, and preterm elections for a new parliament are still
                  possible

NOTES

1. See Mary Ellen Fischer's Introduction to this book, esp. note 3 and accompanying
text.

2. See Sarah Meiklejohn Terry, "Thinking About Post-Communist Transitions: How
Different Are They? A Comment," *Slavic Review* 52 (Summer 1993): 333–337. See also
Valerie Bunce, "Sequencing of Political and Economic Reforms," in John P. Hardt and
Richard F. Kaufman, eds., *East-Central European Economies in Transition: Study Papers
Submitted to the Joint Economic Committee, Congress of the United States* (Washington, DC:
U.S. Government Printing Office, November 1994), pp. 49–63. In a very insightful article
that generally supports my view of the exceptional nature of postcommunist transitions,
Leszek Balcerowicz wrote that "it is misleading to speak of 'simultaneous transitions' in
postcommunist Europe," arguing that: "It takes more time to privatize the bulk of the state-
dominated economy than to organize free elections and at least some rudiments of political parties. . . . [T]his asymmetry in speed *produces a historically new sequence:* mass
democracy . . . first, and market capitalism later." Leszek Balcerowicz, "Understanding

Postcommunist Transitions," *Journal of Democracy* 5 (October 1994): 76, emphasis in the original. Although I shall not dispute the specific point, I do argue that both the political and economic transitions are long-term, complex processes that interact in sometimes unpredictable ways. One election, however free, does not complete the political transition any more than the introduction of a macroeconomic stabilization plan, which also can be implemented rapidly, ensures a successful economic transition.

3. Timothy Garton Ash, *The Magic Lantern: The Revolution of '89 Witnessed in Warsaw, Budapest, Berlin, and Prague* (New York: Random House, 1990), p. 78. As Ash himself recounts it, the quip (made in Prague one week into the changes in Czechoslovakia) went as follows: "In Poland it took ten years, in Hungary ten months, in East Germany ten weeks; perhaps in Czechoslovakia it will take ten days."

4. This account of Poland's crises between 1956 and 1988–1989 draws primarily on the following sources: Sarah M. Terry, "The Future of Poland: Perestroika or Perpetual Crisis?" in Wm. E. Griffith, ed., *Central and Eastern Europe: The Opening Curtain?* (Boulder: Westview Press, 1989), pp. 178–217; and Sarah M. Terry, "June 1976: Anatomy of an Avoidable Crisis," in Jane Leftwich Curry and Luba Fajfa, eds., *Poland's Permanent Revolution: People vs. Elites, 1956 to the Present* (Washington, DC: American University Press, 1996), pp. 109–166.

5. See esp. Andrzej Korbonski, "Poland: Changed Relationship Between the Polish United Workers' Party and the Polish People's Army," in Jeffrey Simon and Trond Gilberg, eds., *Security Implications of Nationalism in Eastern Europe* (Boulder: Westview Press, 1986), pp. 257–275.

6. Leszek Kołakowski, "Hope and Hopelessness," *Survey* 17 (Summer 1971): 37–52; and Adam Michnik, "What We Want and What We Can," *Europa* (June 1981): 34. See also Michnik's book *Kościół, lewica, dialog* (Paris: Instytut Literacki, 1977).

7. For coverage of the events leading up to the roundtable negotiations, see Terry, "The Future of Poland," pp. 202–213; also Janusz Ziółkowski, "The Roots, Branches, and Blossoms of Solidarność," in Gwyn Prins, ed., *Spring in Winter: The 1989 Revolutions* (New York: Manchester University Press, 1990), pp. 40–62.

8. Ryszard Bugaj and Andrzej Wielowieski, "Wobec malejących szans," *Tygodnik Powszechny*, June 19, 1988; for additional details, see Terry, "The Future of Poland," pp. 209–210 and notes 25 and 26, below.

9. The promise was made to Wałęsa in early September by then Interior Minister General Czesław Kiszczak, who, despite his role as Jaruzelski's deputy at the time of martial law, played a critical role in facilitating the compromise, marking yet another instance in which the military made the choice between the use of force and political compromise to resolve a crisis situation.

10. In 1981–1982, Rakowski served as deputy prime minister with special responsibility for labor relations. In late 1987, Rakowski circulated a confidential memorandum in which he rejected the concept of pluralism, suggesting that the word *przeciwnicy* ("enemies" or "foes") was preferable to *opozycja* ("opposition"), because the latter might be seen as legitimizing regime critics; for additional details, see Terry, "The Future of Poland," pp. 211–212 and note 35, in this chapter. In an interview in *Le Monde* on February 11, 1989, during the roundtable talks, Rakowski still opposed legalization of Solidarity.

11. See, e.g., Anne Applebaum, "Premier Plans to Circumvent Solidarity," *Boston Globe*, November 27, 1988; and *Radio Free Europe Research* (hereafter *RFER*), Polish Situation Report 19 (December 16, 1988). No doubt Rakowski believed he had the support of most of the PUWP; following Kiszczak's promise of roundtable talks, party organizations in

thirty-eight of Poland's forty-nine provinces protested to Warsaw and, by the end of September, the leadership was privately reassuring them that it had no intention of going ahead with the relegalization of Solidarity in the near term.

12. *RFER*, Polish Situation Report 1 (January 11, 1989), item 1a.

13. In a revealing interview on the eve of the plenum, Central Committee Secretary for Ideology Marian Orzechowski described the PUWP as suffering from a "loss of direction, an ideological breakdown" caused by the fact that what was hitherto seen as "irrefutable has proved to be ineffective or mistaken, and new ideas and concepts have not yet crystallized." *Nowe Drogi*, no. 10 (October 1988), pp. 4–10. For reports of the plenum, see Jan B. de Weydenthal, "Striving for Change in Poland," *RFER*, RAD Background Report 245 (December 27, 1988); and *RFER*, Polish Situation Reports 1 (January 11, 1989) and 2 (January 20, 1989).

14. Bernard Guetta, "Le pluralisme syndical n'est pas une heresie," *Le Monde*, September 7, 1988. See also Terry, "The Future of Poland," p. 213, and notes 41 and 42 in this chapter; and *New York Times*, March 3, 1989.

15. The Central Committee (CC), and especially Rakowski, made a last-ditch attempt to limit the scope of the talks by attaching conditions that were clearly unacceptable to Solidarity, most importantly: acceptance of Poland's "constitutional order" (a code word for the "leading role" of the PUWP); and agreement to abide by the restrictive 1982 law on trade unions (under which Solidarity was originally banned) and to enforce a two-year moratorium on strikes (an impossible demand since it was not Solidarity that initiated either strike wave in 1988). In addition, the CC resolution stated that the primary task of the talks would be to draw up a common electoral platform in exchange for offering the "constructive opposition" an unspecified number of seats in "non-confrontational" elections. See the Associated Press dispatch, January 18, 1989; and *New York Times*, January 19 and 20, 1989. To the opposition, this smacked of co-optation. As Solidarity adviser Andrzej Stelmachowski told *Polityka* as the roundtable was getting under way: "It is necessary to distinguish opposition to the state from opposition to the government. We would like to renounce opposition to the state . . . [but] we do not wish to give up the possibility of criticizing the government." "Po Magdalence przed okrągłym stołem: z profesorem Andrzejem Stelmachowskim rozmawia Marian Turski," *Polityka*, no. 5, February 4, 1989.

16. Adam Przeworski, *Democracy and the Market: Political and Economic Reforms in Eastern Europe and Latin America* (New York: Cambridge University Press, 1991), p. 68.

17. Following the opening session on February 6, the negotiating teams broke up into three main working groups (on political reform, trade union pluralism, and economic issues), plus at least eight smaller groups (on agricultural reform, the courts and legal reform, health care, education, ecology, mass media, mining, and local self-government).

18. Concerning the election results, see *RFER*, Polish Situation Reports 10 (June 16, 1989) and 11 (July 6, 1989).

19. On the circumstances surrounding the formation of the Mazowiecki government, see *RFER*, Polish Situation Reports 13 (August 22, 1989) and 14 (September 12, 1989).

20. For Moscow's reaction, see Michael Shafir, "Soviet Reaction to Polish Developments: Widened Limits to Tolerated Change," *RFER*, RAD Background Report 179 (September 20, 1989), pp. 1–13; also *New York Times*, August 24, 1989.

21. Concerning the progressive disintegration of the PUWP, see Louisa Vinton, "Disintegration of Polish Communist Party Continues Unabated," *RFER*, RAD Background Report 207 (November 28, 1989), pp. 1–11; and J. B. de Weydenthal,

"Communists Dissolve Party, Set Up New Social Democratic Group," Radio Free Europe, *Report on Eastern Europe* 1 (February 16, 1990): 23–27.

22. For a comparative typology of transitions, see Samuel P. Huntington, *The Third Wave: Democratization in the Late Twentieth Century* (Norman: University of Oklahoma Press, 1991), pp. 113–114. Transformation occurs when "elites in power" bring about democracy, replacement when opposition groups take the lead, and transplacement when "joint action by government and opposition groups" produces democratization.

23. In the spring of 1990, I had the opportunity to ask a former adviser to Gorbachev at what point in the fall of 1989 the Soviet leader had realized the depth of the transformation taking place in Eastern Europe. He replied that, for himself, that recognition came in mid-November (after the opening of the Berlin Wall and with changes in Prague under way). But, he added, Gorbachev continued to believe at least to the end of 1989, and even into the first months of 1990, that "reform socialism" in some form would survive.

24. Balcerowicz, "Understanding Postcommunist Transitions."

25. Concerning the presidential election, see Louisa Vinton, "The Debate over the 'Political Calendar'," Radio Free Europe, *Report on Eastern Europe* 1 (November 2, 1990): 13–19; and Louisa Vinton, "Poland: The Presidential Elections," Radio Free Europe, *Report on Eastern Europe* 1 (December 21, 1990): 10–21. Upon taking office Mazowiecki had explicitly opted for reconciliation over retribution, drawing what he called a "thick line" between the communist past and the democratic future; for a discussion of the reconciliation-versus-retribution dilemma in postauthoritarian transitions, see Huntington, *The Third Wave*, pp. 211–231.

26. Concerning Tymiński's disruptive role, see Vinton, "Poland: The Presidential Elections." Following his defeat in the runoff against Wałęsa, and as more information about his past emerged, the fortunes of Tymiński's Party "X" quickly waned.

27. For accounts of the battle over the electoral law and the October 1991 elections, see, e.g., David McQuaid, "The 'War' Over the Election Law," Radio Free Europe, *Report on Eastern Europe* 2 (August 2, 1991): 11–28; and Krzysztof Jasiewicz, "From Solidarity to a Fragmented Parliament," *Journal of Democracy* 3 (Spring 1992): 55–69.

28. Mirosława Grabowska, "System partyjny—w budowie," *Krytyka* (Warsaw), no. 37 (1991), pp. 24–33.

29. For details on party orientations and the aftermath of the elections, see Sarah M. Terry, "What's Right, What's Left, and What's Wrong in Polish Politics," in Joseph Held, ed., *Democracy and Right-Wing Politics in Eastern Europe in the 1990s* (Boulder: East European Monographs, 1993), pp. 33–60; also Louisa Vinton, "After the Elections: A 'Presidential Government'?" and "Five-Party Coalition Gains Strength," Radio Free Europe, *Report on Eastern Europe* 2 (November 8, 1991): 22–28; and 2 (December 6, 1991): 5–12.

30. For an overview of the Olszewski government, see Louisa Vinton, "Olszewski's Ouster Leaves Poland Polarized," *RFE/RL Research Report* 1 (June 19, 1992): 1–10. The list of "agents" tallied suspiciously with Olszewski's political opponents in parliament and government (including even Wałęsa).

31. Pawlak's failure to form a government at this time was due in part to the reluctance of other parties to join a coalition led by the postcommunist PSL, but in part to the perception that the choice of Pawlak was Wałęsa's bid to control the government and enhance his own powers.

32. For overviews of the Suchocka government and the circumstances of her ouster, see Louisa Vinton, "Wałęsa Applies Political Shock Therapy," *RFE/RL Research Report* 2 (June 11, 1993): 1–11; Louisa Vinton, "Poland: Governing without Parliament," *RFE/RL Research*

Report 2 (June 25, 1993): 6–12; and David S. Mason, "Poland," in Stephen White, Judy Batt, and Paul G. Lewis, eds., *Developments in East European Politics* (London: Macmillan, 1993), pp. 36–50.

33. Concerning the September 1993 elections, see, e.g., Louisa Vinton, "Poland's Political Spectrum on the Eve of the Elections," *RFE/RL Research Report* 2 (September 10, 1993): 1–16; Louisa Vinton, "Poland Goes Left," *RFE/RL Research Report* 2 (October 8, 1993): 21–23; and Anna Sabbat-Swidlicka, "The Polish Elections: The Church, the Right, and the Left," *RFE/RL Research Report* 2 (October 8, 1993): 24–30.

34. On the 1991 elections, see note 28, above; concerning the continuing disorientation in the party system, see Andrzej Siciński, "Społeczeństwo obywatelskie," *Życie Gospodarcze, no. 15 (April 9, 1995), p. 7 (supplement).*

35. The Liberal-Democratic Congress differed significantly from other rightist parties in its unswerving commitment to free-market reforms and to a secular state. Thus, it had little in common with other right-wing parties; it was also at odds with the UD's left (Kuron) wing on socioeconomic issues but in agreement on Church-state relations; its relationship with the UD's pro-Church (Suchocka) wing was just the reverse.

36. For an account of the month-long coalition negotiations, see Anna Sabbat-Swidlicka, "Pawlak to Head Poland's 'Postcommunist' Government," *RFE/RL Research Report* 2 (October 29, 1993): 24–32. One irony was that the UP was more rigidly "leftist" in its stance on socioeconomic issues than the SLD leadership.

37. For Wałęsa's remarks, see Sabbat-Swidlicka, "Pawlak," p. 32; concerning the growing tensions between government and president, and between the SLD and PSL, see Louisa Vinton, "Poland: Velvet Restoration," *Transition* 1 (January 1995): 42–48.

38. The crisis, quickly dubbed the "Drawsko affair," began in October 1994 with Wałęsa demanding the defense minister's resignation, claiming that senior officers had lost confidence in him and implying that the military might again be preparing to interfere in politics—a contention that a subsequent Sejm investigation showed to be grossly exaggerated; see Paul Latawski, "In Defense of Presidential Prerogative," *Transition* 1 (May 26, 1995): 40–43.

39. See Wiktor Osiatyński, "Bronisław Geremek on Constitution-making in Poland," *East European Constitutional Review [EECR]* 4 (Winter 1995): 42–45.

40. For a detailed account, see Louisa Vinton, "Poland's 'Little Constitution' Clarifies Wałęsa's Powers," *RFE/RL Research Report* 1 (September 4, 1992): 19–26.

41. See Latawski, "In Defense of Presidential Prerogative"; and *EECR* 4 (Winter 1995): 18–20, and 4 (Spring 1995): 18–21.

42. See the "Constitution Watch" section in *EECR* 4 (Winter 1995): 18–19, and 4 (Spring 1995): 20–21; concerning the concordat, see also Andrzej Korbonski, "A Concordat—But No Concord," *Transition* 1 (June 9, 1995): 13–17.

43. Despite the compromises provisionally struck with the Church, conservative elements of the Conference of Bishops remained deeply dissatisfied with some articles, denouncing the draft as "nihilistic"; see Jane Perlez, "Shrinking Gap Between Church and Polish State," *New York Times*, July 17, 1995.

44. Unless otherwise indicated, this section is based on the following two sources: Ben Slay, "The Polish Economic Transition," in Hardt and Kaufmann, *East-Central European Economies*, pp. 463–479; and "Polish Economic Monitor," *PlanEcon Report* 11 (May 19, 1995): 1–28.

45. See, e.g., Balcerowicz, "Understanding Postcommunist Transitions"; and Ben Slay, "The Postcommunist Economic Transition: Barriers and Progress," *RFE/RL Research Report* 2 (October 1, 1993): 35–44.

46. Between 1990, when Poland lowered or eliminated most of its trade barriers, and 1994, food imports from the EU rose 250 percent, whereas exports to the EU declined some 10 percent, leaving Poland with negative trade balances in both 1993 and 1994; see Caroline Southy and Anthony Robinson, "Agriculture: Living Museum on the Land," *Financial Times* (supplement on Poland), March 28, 1995.

47. The *Financial Times* of London provides the most complete ongoing coverage of the twists and turns in Poland's privatization policy. See especially the following: "Pace of Poland's Privatization Too Slow, Says PM," June 24, 1995; "Poland to Launch Mass Sell-Off Programme," July 14, 1995; and "Strike Threat as Wałęsa Defeated on Sell-Off Veto," July 22, 1995.

48. See, e.g., Christopher Bobinski and Anthony Robinson, "Poland's Unions Eye Bigger Slice of Prosperity," *Financial Times*, May 26, 1995.

49. Sources for this Postscript include coverage of presidential election and the subsequent fall of the Oleksy government in the *New York Times*, the *Financial Times*, and the Warsaw weekly *Polityka* (especially the interview with former Interior Minister Andrzej Milczanowski, in no. 2 [January 13, 1996], pp. 15–16); concerning the extended charges against Oleksy, see also Adrian Karatnycky, "Red Cloud Over Poland," *Wall Street Journal*, January 22, 1996; concerning the subsequent shake-up, see *Economist*, February 3, 1996, pp. 42–43, and the *Financial Times*, February 5 and 8, 1996.

50. *Financial Times*, February 1, 1996.

Suggestions for Further Reading

For the broad sweep of Polish history, from the origins of the Polish state in the tenth century through the partitions in the late eighteenth century to Poland's rebirth in the twentieth century, see Norman Davies, *God's Playground: A History of Poland*, 2 vols. (New York: Oxford University Press, 1981); a single-volume version was published as *Heart of Europe: A Short History of Poland* (New York: Oxford University Press, 1984). The most comprehensive account of Poland's political developments in the interwar years can be found in Antony Polonsky, *Politics in Independent Poland 1921–1939: The Crisis of Constitutional Government* (London: Oxford University Press, 1972). Students of regional political economy may also want to look at David E. Kaiser's *Economic Diplomacy and the Origins of the Second World War: Germany, Britain, France, and Eastern Euruope, 1930–1939* (Princeton, N.J.: Princeton University Press, 1981). Those interested in the "Polish question" during World War II may wish to look at Sarah Meiklejohn Terry, *Poland's Place in Europe: General Sikorski and the Origin of the Oder-Neisse Line, 1939–1943* (Princeton, N.J.: Princeton University Press, 1983).

The early communist period is ably covered by M. K. Dziewanowski's *The Communist Party of Poland: An Outline of History* (Cambridge: Harvard University Press, 1959) and Adam Bromke's, *Poland's Politics: Idealism Versus Realism* (Cambridge: Harvard University

Press, 1967). For detailed accounts of Poland's recurring crises between 1956 and 1988–1989, see Jane Leftwich Curry and Luba Fajfa, eds., *Poland's Permanent Revolution: People Versus Elites, 1956 to the Present* (Washington, DC: American University Press, 1996); also the author's chapter "The Future of Poland: Perestroika or Perpetual Crisis?" in William E. Griffith, ed., *Central and Eastern Europe: The Opening Curtain?* (Boulder: Westview Press, 1989), pp. 178–217. For a book-length study on the sociopolitical origins of the Solidarity trade union movement and civil society in the making, see Michael Bernhard, *The Origins of Democratization in Poland* (New York: Columbia University Press, 1993.)

As the first Soviet bloc country to shed its communist past, Poland has generated more than its share of the postcommunist transition literature. Of book-length studies, one of the first to examine the broad spectrum of political, economic, and international issues is Richard F. Staar, *Transition to Democracy in Poland* (New York: St. Martin's Press, 1993). More recent and focused studies of the domestic dimension of Poland's transitions include: Ben Slay, *The Polish Economy: Crisis, Reform, and Transformation* (Princeton, NJ: Princeton University Press, 1994); and Raymond Taras, *Consolidating Democracy in Poland* (Boulder: Westview Press, 1995). Ongoing coverage of developments in Poland may be found in the successor to the *RFE/RL Research Report* (1992–1994): *Transition*, published by the Open Media Research Institute in Prague.

8

RUSSIA: PROBLEMS AND PROSPECTS FOR DEMOCRATIZATION

CAROL R. SAIVETZ

Ever since former Soviet president Mikhail S. Gorbachev introduced the terms *glasnost* and *perestroika* into the political lexicon during the 1980s, interested observers have offered theories about the processes unfolding in the former Soviet Union and the ultimate direction of political evolution there and now in Russia and the other successor states. Would the former Soviet Union follow the paths of the democratizing states of Latin America, or would the development of post-communist states be significantly different? Can Russia navigate the seas of political transition while also making the transition to a market economy? What might democracy look like in Russia? Although there are no definitive answers to these and many other questions about the political-economic processes occurring in Russia today, we can make some preliminary observations about Russian democratization.

Classic democratic theory has typically focused on the prerequisites for democracy and the institutional arrangements that guarantee it. Over the years, theorists concentrated, for example, on such factors as requisite levels of economic development, especially the emergence of a middle class;[1] others argued that it is far easier to accommodate competing interests in relatively homogenous societies.[2] Scholars who studied similar questions in the Third World context asked whether particular developmental crises had to be resolved in a delineated chronological order.[3] Yet another group explored the impact of arrangements of governmental structures on the development of democracy.[4]

In contrast, studies of what Samuel Huntington calls the "third wave"[5] of democratizations focus much more on the choices of individual leaders at crucial junctures in the "transition" process. And although it has been argued that "heroics may in fact be key,"[6] individual decisions in this context "respond to and are conditioned by the types of socioeconomic structures and political institutions already present."[7] This decision-oriented approach to understanding the processes at work helps us to assess the kinds of political decisions made by Gorbachev during his time in office and by Russian President Boris Yeltsin (who remains in office as of this writing) precisely because it takes into account aspects of Russia's democratization that are uniquely post-Soviet and Russian.

In assessing Russia's prospects for democratization, it is also useful to distinguish between the concepts "transition" and "consolidation" as they have been used in the literature. "Transition" generally refers to questions about who initiated the process and under what circumstances, whereas "consolidation" refers to the actual governmental structures and procedures that are put in place and the institutionalization of the system. Of course, it is not always clear where the one process ends and the other begins.

This chapter considers the transition and consolidation processes, examining the Gorbachev era and the years since the collapse of the Soviet Union. The first section analyzes the Gorbachev period as one of transition; the second section looks at the period since the collapse of the Soviet Union in an effort to assess the beginnings of the consolidation process. The chapter then explores current political developments in Russia that seem specifically post-Soviet and Russian. These include the apparent weakness of civil society in Russia; the impact of the new geopolitical context in which Russia finds itself;[8] the multiethnic composition of the Russian Federation; and the way in which all of these issues affect questions of citizenship and borders. Finally, I speculate on the prospects for future Russian development given the differences between Russia and other societies undergoing transitions to democracy as well as the extensive economic problems Russia faces.

MIKHAIL GORBACHEV: THE DIFFICULT TRANSITION

In examining regime transitions, an interesting question is why a particular transition has occurred in the first place, especially in instances where reformers within the ruling authoritarian regime have initiated the process. Possible spurs to liberalization (as the beginning of such a transition) include defeat in war, economic collapse, and loss of regime legitimacy. In the Soviet case, there was little to indicate that Gorbachev, when he was named general secretary of the Communist Party of the Soviet Union (CPSU) in March 1985, would turn out to be a reformer, much less a revolutionary. True, he was younger and more vigorous than his predecessors and, perhaps, more impatient with the inefficiencies and corruption of the Soviet regime and more anxious to solve foreign policy problems. Yet, upon his accession to power, Gorbachev faced precisely the same problems that had triggered democratization processes in other "third wave" countries.

In the foreign policy sphere, the USSR suffered no single defeat but a series of major foreign policy setbacks. In 1985, the Kremlin was saddled with several "basket cases" in the Third World, was backing states such as Angola and Afghanistan that were fighting counterinsurgency struggles, and was cut out of the Middle East peace process. In Europe, the late General Secretary Yuri Andropov had backed the USSR into a corner by first threatening to withdraw and then actually withdrawing from talks between the North Atlantic Treaty Organization (NATO) and the Soviet Union on limiting intermediate-range nuclear forces. And finally, the declining performance of the Soviet economy prevented Moscow from competing successfully with the United States in the arms race. In the economic realm, the Soviet Union was, in the words of one observer, living on borrowed time.[9] Central planning had led to a marked decline in the growth of the Soviet gross national product (GNP), punctuated by crises in agriculture and the exhaustion of accessible coal and natural gas reserves. Moreover, military expenditures were taking an ever-increasing share of the state budget. This economic downturn had implications not only for foreign policy but, perhaps more importantly, for the legitimacy of the communist system itself. One might question whether or not the Soviet regime ever enjoyed affective legitimacy; nonetheless, the worsening economic position of the average citizen certainly diminished the prospects for continuing instrumental legitimation.

Gorbachev's first responses to what are now seen as the failures of the Soviet system were strictly in line with earlier attempts at reform: exhortations to party leaders to be more responsive to the needs of the Soviet people and slogans, such as *uskorenie* (literally, a speeding up), to get the system moving more efficiently. At the Twenty-Seventh Party Congress in February 1986, Gorbachev indicated that the Soviet Union's economic problems were his top priority. Within a year, Gorbachev moved beyond *uskorenie* to introduce state-mandated quality-control criteria (*gospriemka*); then, through the 1987 Law on Enterprises, he reduced ministerial interference in the day-to-day operation of individual enterprises. Virtually simultaneously he promoted so-called cooperatives, which were designed to produce much-needed consumer goods and to provide services, from better restaurants to medical care, that were lacking in the Soviet system.

In the political sphere, Gorbachev at first tried to accomplish his reforms by working within the existing political system. In the pre-Gorbachev period, the CPSU was the government: All power resided in the Politburo, headed by the general secretary of the CPSU and supported by the Central Committee and the Secretariat. The old Supreme Soviet met twice yearly for only four days each session, a fact that severely limited its ability to function as a true legislative body. Thus, initially and in strictly political terms, *perestroika* translated into Gorbachev's attempts to democratize the CPSU. At a Central Committee plenum in January 1987, Gorbachev proposed contested elections for party officials; at the Nineteenth Party Conference convened in June 1988, he called for the democratization of party life by correcting what he called "deformations" and by streamlining the party apparatus. The act of convening the conference itself was a statement of the opening up of the party's political processes. Both Boris Yeltsin, leader of the prodemocratic forces, and Yegor Ligachev, head of the conservatives, were permitted to address the dignitaries who had gathered. Most dramatically, in February 1990, the party rescinded article 6 of the Soviet Constitution, which guaranteed to the party the leading role in Soviet society.

Gorbachev's closely related policy of *glasnost* dovetailed with his political renovations. Gorbachev used the term as early as the spring of 1985; however, as time went on, the parameters of acceptable public debate were clearly broadened. By June 1986, *glasnost* had been seen not only in the aftermath of the Chernobyl nuclear disaster, but also in the discrediting of bureaucrats who blocked the reforms outlined above.[10] Within the year, *glasnost* was also visible in the marked changes in the Soviet media as newspapers, magazines, and journals all published open discussions of the Soviet past, including hitherto taboo subjects such as Stalinism. *Glasnost* and *perestroika*, originally two separate policies, became inextricably intertwined. Although unprecedented in the Soviet context, the liberalization these two policies represented seems to be a definite feature of the transitions in other countries. In the words of Guillermo O'Donnell and Phillipe Schmitter: "Authoritarian rulers may tolerate or even promote liberalization in the belief that by opening up certain spaces for individual and group action, they can relieve various pressures and obtain needed information and support."[11] From Gorbachev's perspective, *glasnost* served multiple purposes. Through it he hoped to find experts and bold thinkers who could help him accomplish the modernization of Soviet society. Simultaneously, by providing a forum in which to air grievances about the Soviet economic and political systems, *glasnost* helped to discredit recalcitrant bureaucrats who were blocking reform. Finally, Gorbachev hoped that *glasnost* would enable him to enlist the support of the public against the bureaucracy and for *perestroika*.

However hopeful Gorbachev and his supporters among the liberal intelligentsia were that *glasnost* would help the reform process, they quickly found out that it also created problems. First, the disclosures about the past that were supposed to move the USSR forward exacerbated the legitimacy problems that Gorbachev had been trying to address. Questions about Stalin only raised doubts about his successors and the legitimacy of those components of the Stalinist system that remained in place. Second, the "standpatters,"[12] or hardliners, used *glasnost* to further their political agenda. Conservatives delivered speeches and wrote long dispositions criticizing Gorbachev and describing how much better things used to be. The most striking—and, at the time, most frightening—example of this phenomenon was the letter written by Leningrad schoolteacher Nina Andreevna and printed in *Sovetskaia Rossiia* on March 13, 1988. The letter, a long, impassioned defense of Stalinist principles, did indeed come from Nina Andreevna but was embellished by none other than Yegor Ligachev and then published while

Gorbachev was on an official visit to Yugoslavia. The letter frightened those who presumed that *glasnost* would be used only in the name of further reform; moreover, it took Gorbachev several weeks to respond to the attack.

Finally, *glasnost* seems to have unleashed pent-up interethnic tensions within the Soviet Union and facilitated non-Russian resistance to the central Soviet authorities. This is not the place to detail pre-1985 Soviet nationality policy. We must mention, however, Stalin's role in drawing up ethnic boundaries that left many ethnic groups divided; we must also note that language and cadre policies were frequently the touchstones of serious unrest. For Gorbachev, the earliest manifestation of this was the December 1986 rioting in Alma Ata, Kazakhstan, when the ethnic Kazakh first secretary of the Kazakh Communist Party was replaced with a Russian. Open public discontent was also evident when Crimean Tatars demonstrated on Red Square. Among the other flare-ups that apparently resulted from the opening up of Soviet society by 1988–1989 were the outbreak of fighting in Nagorno Karabakh (an ethnic Armenian enclave within Azerbaijan) as well as in Georgia, where nationalists demonstrated for more autonomy from the central Moscow authorities and where Ossetians pushed for reunification with their ethnic brethren in the Northern Caucasus. It was in the Baltic republics, however, that Gorbachev encountered his most difficult situation. Beginning in August 1987, on the anniversary of the signing of the 1939 Nazi-Soviet pact, citizens of the Baltic republics—Estonia, Latvia, and Lithuania—protested their annexation by the USSR; a year later, the text of the pact was published in Estonia. With hindsight, it is clear that Gorbachev did not realize that *glasnost* would release the nationality genie from the Soviet bottle. Ultimately, these expressions of cultural and ethnic distinctiveness would culminate in 1991 in demands by many of the non-Russian republics for sovereignty and independence from Moscow and would elicit calls from the standpatters to crack down on nationalist expression.

These attempts at reform—whether ill-conceived or not—were part of a cyclical process of reforms and reactions producing greater reforms and deeper reactions, eventually leading Gorbachev to introduce fundamental changes in the Soviet political system. The unsuccessful attempt to introduce competitive elections to the CPSU in 1987 was followed by structural changes in the party apparatus initiated at the June 1988 Nineteenth Party Conference. By December 1988, a new law on state elections had been adopted that outlined new electoral procedures for two totally new legislative bodies, the Congress of Peoples' Deputies (CPD) and the new Supreme Soviet—new state bodies through which Gorbachev hoped to govern and to bypass what had become the major obstacle to reform, the CPSU. The CPD was to be composed of 2,250 deputies (750 elected from districts determined by population; 750 from districts based on ethnic composition; and 750 representing social organizations including 100 from the CPSU). According to the new law, meetings of 500 or more voters could nominate local candidates for the CPD, as could social organizations and the CPSU. In each district more than 50 percent voter turnout was required, and the winner needed to garner more than 50 percent of the vote or a run-off would be held. The elections of March 26, 1989, produced a legislature less representative than the old Supreme Soviet[13]—especially because of the 100 seats reserved for the CPSU. Yet, the elections also produced some stunning defeats, for example, in Leningrad, where the party boss was defeated because he received less than 50 percent of the vote despite running unopposed.

The first meeting of the CPD, the new Soviet parliament, mesmerized Soviet citizens: Work stopped as people watched the proceedings on television. Much of the wrangling occurred over procedural issues, including the election from the CPD of the smaller, more permanent legislature—the new Supreme Soviet. In those elections, Boris Yeltsin failed to secure a place until another deputy offered his seat to the future Russian president. The Soviet public then watched as Yeltsin criticized the party's monopoly on power; as Yuri Vlasov, an Olympic weight lifter, criticized the KGB; and as Andrei Sakharov, physicist and human rights leader, criticized the Afghan War and then was himself castigated for his remarks. The CPD created a commission to investigate the 1939 Nazi-Soviet pact and the shooting of demonstrators in Tbilisi, Georgia, in April 1989. Perhaps most important of all, liberal deputies created the interregional group—a caucus within the parliament—which went on to set up a new political movement, Democratic Russia.

Following the CPD elections, a second round of elections was held for new parliaments in the republics in which nascent political parties, including Democratic Russia, competed. Although none of these political organizations can properly be labeled a "party" in the Western sense of the word, they aggregated and articulated interests, and, thus, their very existence represented a degree of pluralism unparalleled in the communist era. There can be no question that Gorbachev saw the elections to the new Congress and the CPD itself as a means of legitimizing the new-style Soviet regime, and, in a sense, they did. Elections were at least partially contested, and the CPD did openly discuss pressing political issues. However, there were limits to that new legitimacy (and, by extension, democratization). Seats were held for the CPSU, and the nomination process was encumbered in such a way as to guarantee seats for other traditional Soviet organizations. Ultimately, if Gorbachev was indeed seeking legitimacy, the fact that he himself never stood for election (whereas Boris Yeltsin did, in June 1991) meant that his presidency was never "ratified" by the population at large.

In the end, of course, it was the August 1991 attempted coup against Gorbachev that hastened the demise of the Soviet Union. A discussion of the events leading up to the coup and the details of the coup itself are beyond the scope of this chapter, but several brief points need to be made. First, as the cycle of reform and reaction continued, Gorbachev repeatedly attempted to position himself in the "middle" in order to attract support from both the democrats, on the one hand, and the hardliners on the other. He could use hardliners such as Nina Andreevna and Yegor Ligachev to promote himself as the democrats' best hope; at the same time, he could use Boris Yeltsin—who remained a member of the party until the

Twenty-Eighth Party Congress—to show the hardliners how moderate he was. Yet, as the reforms transformed the political landscape, this strategy became increasingly difficult to maintain.

Second, as Samuel Huntington and others argue, for transformations initiated by an incumbent regime to take hold (what Huntington calls "transplacements"),[14] reformers within the regime need to be able to control the standpatters—just as moderate democratic opponents hope to control radicals. Gorbachev tried unsuccessfully to co-opt the conservatives: In October 1990, he backed away from the Shatalin 500-Day Program, which was designed to transform dramatically the Soviet economy; and in January 1991, the military violently broke up a pro-independence demonstration in Vilnius, Lithuania, either with Gorbachev's approval or, as he himself claimed, without his prior knowledge. Either way, the events in Vilnius demonstrated how little control Gorbachev actually exercised over the standpatters within the party.

Third, in the spring of 1991, Gorbachev began negotiations with the leaders of the other republics to draw up a new union treaty, that is, a new, more equal arrangement among the republics of the USSR. The negotiations intensified following a referendum in which the Soviet electorate supported a vaguely worded proposition in favor of continued union.[15] The April 23, 1991, treaty governing relations among the new Union of Soviet Sovereign States gave republics the right to appoint one house of the legislature that would possess veto powers. Republics would also have a voice in the cabinet and could block amendments to the treaty; they would own their land and natural resources; and they would collect taxes and remit a set percentage to the Union government in Moscow. The treaty was scheduled to be signed on August 20, 1991, and it was to prevent its signing that the coup conspirators acted. With the new union treaty in place, relations among the states would have significantly diminished the power of the center and of the vestiges of the CPSU.

Fourth, the coup failed for several reasons. The conspirators apparently miscalculated in relying on both the passivity of the masses and the loyalty of the armed forces. Enough demonstrators appeared outside the Moscow White House to make the coup leaders think twice about massive use of force. For his part, Boris Yeltsin, as leader of the democratic forces, displayed great leadership and skill in facing down the conspirators and their tanks. His policy of cultivating support among the armed forces paid off in that many units refused to march on Moscow. In the final analysis, the price of total repression, not to mention of reinstituting the old system, was just too great. The conspirators also proved themselves inept, and some have been described as drunk throughout those tense three days.

Finally, the coup was in reality the end of the USSR. When Gorbachev returned to Moscow after being placed under house arrest in the Crimea, he appeared a broken man. Instead of going immediately to the White House to thank those who had supported liberalization, he waited until the next day and then delivered a rambling speech to the Supreme Soviet that called for a socialist renewal. Although he tried to create—again—new governmental structures and to renegotiate the union treaty, he lost power precipitously. Russia, in effect, moved to supplant the USSR, and then, beginning with the Baltic republics (which were recognized as independent shortly after the coup), republic after republic declared independence from Moscow and took over the state property within its territory. On December 1, 1991, Ukraine voted overwhelmingly for independence and within a week, Russia, Ukraine, and Belarus had agreed to create the Commonwealth of Independent States (CIS). By December 25, 1991, Gorbachev had resigned, and eleven of fifteen republics were members of the new commonwealth.

Because the old Soviet government ceased to exist, it would seem fair to argue that this was the end point of the transition process. In fact, O'Donnell and Schmitter define the transition as the interval between the old authoritarian regime and the beginnings of a new order.[16] One final word on the Gorbachev transition: During the transition Gorbachev clearly lost control of the liberalization process that he initiated, becoming in Coit Blacker's phrase "hostage to revolution."[17] As noted, he could not control the hardliners or bring them along through the process; indeed they calculated that they could reverse it. Moreover, his erstwhile partner within the opposition, Boris Yeltsin, represented not the moderates but the radicals—thus making a "pact" unlikely. Gorbachev, by the end of the USSR, had dismantled the economic system but had not replaced it with a new distributive mechanism; equally problematic, he had only partially dismantled the old political system. At the highest levels of power the rules of the game were uncertain at best, and the old government institutions had been discredited; however, at the middle and local levels within the still remaining structures, the old apparatchiks remained in power. This brief analysis of the Gorbachev transition period is vital as we shift our focus to the consolidation of a new regime in Russia because, in the words of Douglass North, "history matters."[18] The remnants of the old order and the choices made by Gorbachev were informed by Russian and Soviet history and in turn shaped (and continue to shape) the options available to Boris Yeltsin as he began the consolidation process.

BORIS YELTSIN: CONSOLIDATION AND CRISIS

Following the abortive coup, Boris Yeltsin outlawed the CPSU within the Russian Republic and, in the months leading up to the Soviet collapse, in effect appropriated the property and powers of the unraveling Soviet state. Little, however, was done to prepare for the realities of governing the Russian Federation. Many had assumed that with the collapse of the Soviet Union and the disgrace of the CPSU democracy would triumph. Instead, the next few years would demonstrate that consolidation is sometimes more difficult to manage than transition.

According to most theorists, "democratic consolidation" means the institutionalization of the procedural minimums of democracy.[19] This definition implicitly refers to consolidation as the end point of the democratization process, but it may be more useful to look at consolidation as a long series of events, as Larry Diamond does in arguing that it is the process by which "democracy becomes so broadly and profoundly legitimate among its citizens that it is very unlikely to break down."[20] Thus, the ideal end of the process would be a "consolidated democracy," one in which the procedural minimums have been institutionalized.[21] The task of consolidation, as complex as it is, becomes more so by the need to govern efficiently until a consolidated democracy is achieved. On the most general level, laws promulgated by the political center must be implemented in the peripheries, and the revenues needed by the center must be collected. Huntington summarizes the complexities of the consolidation process when he describes three sets of problems facing democratizing governments: transitional problems, such as establishing new governmental institutions and laws; contextual problems, by which he means societal and economic problems; and systemic problems that face all governments, especially the linkage between performance and legitimacy.[22] Michael McFaul adds that "[For] Russia to consolidate a market economy and a political democracy requires the demolition of the Soviet *ancien regime* and the creation of a completely new political and socioeconomic system."[23]

Initially, Yeltsin attacked the contextual problems, specifically the economy, without paying attention to the creation of wholly new political institutions. In January 1992, he strove to continue the market transformation begun in the late Soviet period by liberalizing prices and sought to govern through the institutions left over from the Soviet era—that is, the Russian CPD that had been elected in 1990, when the CPSU was still the most potent force in Soviet society. Additionally, by maintaining old structures, Yeltsin kept in force the Soviet-era constitution, which ostensibly gave all power to the legislature. The reality of the Soviet era, however, was that true power had resided with the party bosses in the Politburo.

Although tensions between Yeltsin and the Russian CPD were evident in late 1991, they became more acute with independence. Ironically, the Russian CPD had initially supported Yeltsin in his fight with Gorbachev, because it hoped to replace the old Soviet Congress of Peoples' Deputies as the supreme legislative body when the Soviet Union collapsed.[24] After the demise of the USSR and its CPD, however, the Russian CPD between January 1992 and October 1993 became increasingly antireform and anti-Yeltsin, setting up a dynamic that dominated Russian politics during that period: the stalemate between Yeltsin and the parliament that culminated in the October 1993 shelling of the Russian White House.

President Versus Parliament

The most contentious issue between Yeltsin and the parliament was the economy. Yeltsin and his young advisers, led by Yegor Gaidar, favored tight monetary policy, liberalization of prices, and other policies associated with "shock therapy."

Many of the deputies, however, were former members of the old *nomenklatura* who favored, if not a restoration of the old system, then at least a continuation of government credits to the enterprises they ran and a much slower pace of economic reform. In fact, Civic Union, perhaps the most potent opposition force from the middle of 1992 until the spring of 1993, opposed the pace of Gaidar's macroeconomic stabilization and supported a strong Russian state.[25] Another issue galvanizing the opposition was foreign policy. A faction of ardent nationalists emerged in the parliament who resented Russia's loss of empire and its loss of superpower status. They vocally criticized then Foreign Minister Andrei Kozyrev and Russia's policies toward the so-called near abroad (the other Soviet successor states), the West, and the Bosnian crisis. Finally, personality was clearly an important factor in the ensuing struggle. Ruslan Khasbulatov, a Chechen and speaker of the parliament, by all accounts resented Yeltsin's young entourage and was angered that they were not under the direct control of the speaker. The convergence of these issues can be seen in the crisis-ridden nature of each session of the CPD.

In the April 1992 CPD session, opposition forces demanded that Yeltsin relinquish the extraordinary powers that he had been granted by parliament the previous November. Simultaneously, the forces that were to become the Civic Union demanded that the pace of economic reform be slowed considerably, and the nationalists began their open criticism of Kozyrev and the direction of Russian foreign policy. In a behind-the-scenes compromise, Yeltsin retained his powers but let go some of the young reformers and replaced them with representatives of the industrialists. He also began pushing for a new constitution that would create a presidential system modeled after the French Fifth Republic. Even though Yeltsin staved off defeat and retained his extraordinary powers, Khasbulatov and the other opposition forces used the spring, summer, and early fall of 1992 to regroup. It seemed at the time that the ascendancy of the Civic Union posed the greatest threat to "shock therapy," but other forces in fact turned out to be greater threats: Khasbulatov consolidated his hold on the apparatus of the CPD's presidium, and in October communists created the National Salvation Front.

Thus, the December 1992 meeting of the CPD became a true test of the relative strength of Yeltsin and the Congress. Yeltsin chastised the parliament for blocking reform while Khasbulatov demanded that the government resign. During the session, Yeltsin offered a number of concessions, including giving the Supreme Soviet the right to confirm the appointments of the ministers of defense, foreign affairs, interior, and security. Then, a frustrated Yeltsin announced that he would hold a referendum of "trust"; but the proposal was supported only by approximately 200 delegates. Ultimately it was agreed that a referendum would be held, but on the outlines of a new constitution, not on the popularity of the parliament and Yeltsin. Additionally, Yeltsin agreed to choose a new prime minister from a short list of three candidates approved by the parliament. In the balloting, Gaidar ran a poor third, so rather than risk another bruising battle with the parliament, Yeltsin appointed Viktor Chernomyrdin the new prime minister.

The December 1992 compromise was, however, short-lived. In January and again in February 1993, Khasbulatov abrogated what had amounted to a political cease-fire by reneging on the agreement to hold a referendum. (In this, he had the support of the chairman of the Constitutional Court, who claimed that a referendum would split Russian society.) The speaker also openly challenged Yeltsin's powers by going out into the provinces, where he pushed for the local soviets to resist presidential power. In March 1993, the CPD session rejected the earlier power-sharing proposals, curtailed Yeltsin's powers even more, and canceled the planned referendum. Yeltsin retaliated by introducing "special rule" and reinstating a referendum that was tantamount to a vote of confidence in the president. This in turn prompted the parliament to attempt to impeach him, but it fell short by seventy-two votes.[26]

Just two weeks later, the next CPD session reached a compromise on the referendum question. A referendum would be held on April 25 and would consist of four questions: Do you support the president? Do you support economic reform? Are you in favor of early elections for president? Are you in favor of early elections for a new parliament? Anti-Yeltsin forces within the parliament, however, tacked on a provision that 50 percent of the population must vote for the referendum to be valid. It was thought to be next to impossible to organize the referendum in less than one month, making a 50 percent turnout highly unlikely; moreover, some regions—most noticeably Chechnya—refused to conduct the referendum. Surprisingly, in a last-minute move, the Constitutional Court ruled that only the last two questions required the 50 percent turnout to be binding. The final results were at least a partial victory for Yeltsin: On question 1, 58.7 percent of those voting supported Yeltsin; on question 2, a surprising 53 percent favored a continuation of the reform process; on question 3, 49.5 percent favored an election for president; and on question 4, 67 percent supported new parliamentary elections. Unfortunately for Yeltsin, 50 percent of the electorate did not vote, and thus the call for early elections was nonbinding.[27]

Following the referendum, Yeltsin concentrated on the content of a new constitution and procedures for its adoption. A draft promulgated just five days after the referendum gave tremendous powers to the presidency and created a bicameral legislature with severely circumscribed powers. In June 1993, Yeltsin convened a constituent assembly to discuss and amend the constitution. Simultaneously, because the referendum did not validate new parliamentary elections, the CPD continued to meet, not only to draft its own version of the constitution, but also to continue its war against Yeltsin and reform. The parliament refused to pass the state budget, blocked legislation to promote privatization, and became increasingly assertive in foreign policy (for example, declaring the Crimean city of Sevastopol to be Russian rather than Ukrainian). Thus, by September 1993, nothing had been resolved: The battles between Yeltsin and the CPD continued, and no new constitution seemed possible.

On September 21, 1993, Yeltsin formally dissolved the Congress of People's Deputies and announced new elections for December 11. Apparently, he had been planning this move for some time. Over the previous year, reports had circulated that Yeltsin had contemplated introducing direct rule as early as mid-1992.[28] Yeltsin himself said in September, "I wrote this edict with my own hand, with my own pen. I told nobody anything about it and kept the edict in my safe for a whole month."[29] Immediately afterward, Aleksandr Rutskoi, the Russian vice president and an ally of Khasbulatov, proclaimed himself president; meanwhile the speaker appealed to the armed forces not to obey any order from Yeltsin. Within days, the rhetorical standoff turned more serious when defenders of the parliament armed themselves against attack and refused to leave the building, even after all services to it had been cut. On October 3, the situation deteriorated when mobs, responding to appeals from Rutskoi and Khasbulatov, attacked the Moscow mayor's office and the Ostankino television station. Yeltsin declared a state of emergency, and troops loyal to the president ejected the mob from the television station and shelled the parliament building. Rutskoi and Khasbulatov were arrested when the renegade parliamentarians ultimately surrendered.

Yeltsin's victory cleared the way for a constitutional referendum and for new parliamentary elections. In many ways, the post–October 1993 period may be seen as a second attempt at consolidation—this time addressing the need to create new governmental and societal institutions. The draft constitution provided for a new bicameral legislature and a very strong presidential republic. Representatives to the lower house, or Duma, were to be elected under a dual system: 225 deputies were to be elected by party lists in a proportional representation system with a 5 percent threshold; an additional 225 were to be elected in single-member districts under a first-past-the-post system. For some reason, a passage providing for a run-off in the single-member districts was deleted in the final electoral law. The upper house, or Council of the Federation, was to be composed of two elected representatives from each of the Russian Federation's regions and republics (some of which are ethnically defined). After some wavering, Yeltsin opted not to stand for election at the same time but to continue in office until the 1996 end of his term.

The situation surrounding the December 1993 elections was less than ideal and less than democratic. In the aftermath of the shelling episode, Yeltsin banned extreme nationalist and communist groups; many were not permitted to field candidates during the election campaign. The Yeltsin government also suspended the publications of the banned groups (for example, *Pravda*, *Den*, and *Sovetskaia Rossiia*); in addition, several other papers were censored, including some that had traditionally sided with Yeltsin. Papers appeared with blackened areas to indicate where censored articles or passages would have appeared. Finally, all political parties were at a serious disadvantage in regard to time. They had to coalesce, garner the requisite 100,000 signatures necessary to run candidates, and campaign—all within nine weeks. Even the constitutional referendum was prejudiced by the fact that the constitution itself was not promulgated until November 10.

This review of the period between January 1992 and December 1993 raises two fundamental and interrelated questions as to Russian consolidation. First, why did the serious disagreements over solutions to the contextual problems devolve into an ongoing constitutional crisis? Second, what forces seem to make Russian consolidation distinct?

At the most basic level, Yeltsin's choice to attack the economic problems without first creating new post-Soviet institutions in effect gave the opponents of reform a power base in the old Soviet-era legislature, the Russian CPD, which they were then compelled to defend. Many had secured election in 1990 by virtue of having been part of the old Soviet *nomenklatura*, enjoyed the perquisites of being deputies, and were certainly not about to vote themselves out of office. Russell Bova has suggested that for representatives of the *ancien regime* to retire "gracefully" there must be some avenue to wealth and security other than through political power.[30] Yet, it was precisely the question of private property and who would profit from privatization that galvanized such tremendous opposition both to Yeltsin and to his reforms. Moreover, as Yeltsin adviser Andranik Migranyan has written, in the absence of partisan politics the deputies were mobilized to protect their corporate prerogatives.[31] Khasbulatov's actions throughout late 1992 and into 1993 reinforced this tendency. Within the parliament, Khasbulatov's control of committee appointments not only enhanced his personal power, but also meant that he controlled the political power wielded by other deputies.[32] Outside parliament, Khasbulatov provided deputies who were loyal to him with housing, cars, and the use of official dachas, just to name a few of the additional perquisites.

By the same token, the proreform deputies found their strength eroding and their fortunes hurt—ironically—by many of Yeltsin's policies. First, Yeltsin's desire to remain above party politics hurt the democrats because the president was isolated and the deputies resented his aloofness. With hindsight, we can argue that Yeltsin needed a strong and disciplined parliamentary faction that would work with him.[33] Never completely united, the democrats disintegrated into several factions that disagreed over nuances in policy and tactics. Second, Yeltsin's move to the presidency and his staffing of the executive branch with democrats weakened their numbers in parliament.[34] Finally, the president's attempts in 1992 and early 1993 to patch together a coalition to fight the emerging red-brown (communist-fascist) grouping in the CPD by making concessions to Civic Union threatened the pace of economic reform and enhanced the managers' and industrialists' stake in the parliament.

Structural factors must be added to this explanation. When Yeltsin was himself speaker of the parliament, that office was imbued with tremendous power. However, when Yeltsin was elected president, there was never a formal diminution of the speaker's power.[35] For his part, Khasbulatov added to his powers as parliamentary speaker by appropriating much of the old Central Committee staff,[36] attempting to control the newspaper *Izvestiia*, and creating a private parliamentary guard of 5,000 men that actually engaged in a shoot-out with regular police.

Equally important, because the 1978 Soviet-era constitution guaranteed to the parliament the sole right to call a referendum and, even more importantly, empowered it to rewrite the constitution itself, the only way out of the ongoing stalemate was through extraconstitutional means. Democrats found themselves in the ironic situation of supporting the continuation of Yeltsin's extraordinary powers and upholding his right to abrogate the constitution. Indeed, in his call for direct rule, Yeltsin admitted that he was acting unconstitutionally but justified his action as necessary to promote reform.

Legacies: Defining Borders and Creating Civil Society

As the Russian constitutional crisis unfolded, it was exacerbated by several legacies from the Soviet past. An enduring problem, that of defining Russian borders, was actually dual in nature: It entailed questions surrounding the rights of ethnic Russians left stranded in the other successor states and Russia's obligations to them, and also the relationship between Moscow and the republics and regions within the Russian Federation. Russia, as a state, has never existed within its current borders. This is highly significant because, in the words of Philippe Schmitter: "If there is one overriding political requisite for democracy, it is the prior existence of a legitimate political unit."[37]

At the most basic level, many Russian officials today as well as average citizens feel that Russia should encompass the whole of the former Soviet Union.[38] More specifically, the unraveling of the Soviet Union placed 25 million ethnic Russians outside the boundaries of the federation. In some successor states they have been considered full-fledged citizens (as in Ukraine), but in others they have been subjected to stringent new definitions of citizenship based on language or ethnicity (as in Latvia). Yet even in Ukraine—which had defined a citizen as one living on the territory of Ukraine—Russian separatist movements have sprung up. For example, in Crimea, Russian nationalists have repeatedly declared their intent to rejoin Russia—a move supported by nationalists in the CPD. This would obviously enlarge the electorate and, perhaps, skew it in an ultraconservative direction. Many in the Russian diaspora apparently voiced support for Vladimir Zhirinovsky in the December 1993 elections. Moreover, concern over the fate of ethnic Russians in the "near abroad" has become a catalyst not only to nationalists but also to democrats, such as Sergei Stankevich, for increasingly hardline policies toward the other successor states. As noted above, this issue became increasingly salient in the old parliament and helped to shift the Russian political center to the point that officials, from Boris Yeltsin down, began to exert extreme pressure on these other successor states to guarantee the ethnic Russians either dual citizenship or CIS citizenship.

Concern for the 25 million ethnic Russians outside Russian borders provides useful rhetoric for politicians; more immediately pressing, however, is the need to define the rights of the constituent regions and republics of the Russian Federation itself. During the Soviet era, Russia's ethnically based republics were considered autonomous, whereas the regions and districts were not. Many regions, therefore, took advantage of the breakup of the USSR and the weakness of the central government in Moscow to declare their own sovereignty. Sakha, for example, seized the right to keep more than one-half of its hard currency earnings from diamonds; Chechnya attempted to secede outright. Outbreaks of ethnic fighting, as in the Northern Caucasus, further challenged Moscow's authority and continue to do so today.[39]

When Yeltsin convened the constituent assembly to rewrite the constitution in June 1993, the key issue turned out to be the powers of the ethnically defined republics and the territorially based regions and districts of the Russian Federation—not the balance of power between president and parliament. Yeltsin tried to use the negotiations over federal relations in his fight with the parliament. In August 1993, in what amounted to a last effort to woo the provinces, Yeltsin established the Federation Council, which was to be composed of two representatives from each of the eighty-nine regions and republics. This devolution of power to the provinces proved to be a risky maneuver because, in the end, the first meeting of the new Federation Council that summer failed to approve either the draft constitution or any other founding documents and, as the October crisis showed, despite Yeltsin's concessions to the republics and regions many supported parliament. The new Russian constitution, finally adopted in December 1993, guarantees equal rights to republics and regions; however, republics are permitted to have constitutions, whereas regions may have only charters. Moreover, the continuation of concessions (made earlier as Yeltsin was trying to win provincial support) is left decidedly vague, although the constitution does provide for the Federation Council to be composed of two representatives from each of the republics and regions.

Moscow's tenuous control over the turbulent regions and republics goes to the heart of two interrelated questions that affect the consolidation process: It highlights Huntington's systemic problem of linkage between performance and legitimacy; it also highlights the inherent difficulty of building democracy in a multiethnic society. The potential splintering of the Russian state militates against Moscow's ability to govern. Left in place after December 1993 are contradictions between the federal constitution and several subnational constitutions and a great deal of local legislation. Laws passed in the regions and republics directly contradict those promulgated in Moscow; old-style politicians remain in control in many areas and challenge the reforms initiated by the Yeltsin government; finally, the withholding of revenues by these regions and republics worsens the Russian deficit and increases inflationary pressures. This, obviously, spills over and complicates solutions to the contextual problems, namely, that of economic reform.

If consolidation is to go forward, however, the demands of local jurisdictions must be accommodated by federal authorities. Experience seems to indicate that the best way to manage these issues—especially if the demands are ethnically based—is through a federal system. In Russia, the constituent elements (Chechnya, for example) would have to agree to be part of the federation, and authorities in Moscow would have to cede a certain degree of autonomy to those areas. In February 1994, Moscow signed a treaty governing relations with Tatarstan, a reluctant member of the Russian Federation. The treaty fell short of Tatarstan's demand for full sovereignty, but it did recognize Kazan's right to conduct foreign policy and foreign trade; moreover, the treaty guaranteed the right of Tatarstan to decide questions of republican citizenship and exempted young men from the republic from serving in the Russian armed forces. The language of the treaty was purposefully vague—calling Tatarstan a "state united with Russia"—in order to allow each side to claim it had won the battle for political power. At the time of its ratification, this treaty was seen as a model that could be followed by other recalcitrant republics and regions. Ultimately, successful democratic consolidation would seem to require either (1) devising another equitable founding document and then being able to put it into practice, or (2) using the Tatarstan model. During the last six months of 1994, several other republics and regions followed Tatarstan's example; however, Chechen president Dzhokhar Dudayev's refusal to accept anything less than full independence precipitated a war that devastated Chechnya and weakened president Yeltsin's authority.

Another legacy of the Soviet past that will have a major impact on successful Russian consolidation is the relative weakness of civil society. Larry Diamond has defined civil society as the "realm of organized social life that is . . . autonomous from the state, and bound by a legal order or set of shared rules."[40] If this is conceived of as an intermediary realm—one that lies between the state and society—then modern Russians face a stark reality: This realm was outlawed under Soviet rule, and all organizations were controlled by the party. Only in the period of *glasnost* and *perestroika* did interest groups spring up that were independent of the state and at least partially tolerated. Geoffrey Hosking, in his book *The Awakening of the Soviet Union,* argues that the emergent green movement as well as such groups as Memorial represented the rudiments of civil society in the late Soviet period.[41] Other analysts have concluded that the current Russian scene evidences nascent pluralism, but a pluralism that is weak and not yet institutionalized.[42] To further complicate the picture, it may well be that in an era of simultaneous political and economic transition, nascent groups such as trade unions have difficulty deciding which interests they represent.[43]

Civil society requires an institutionalized legal order that will protect that intermediate domain. The parliament has passed laws on freedom of the press, assembly, and religion, to name a few, but we have also seen repeated attempts to rein in the media and to limit civil liberties and civil rights. Theorists writing about civil society argue that as a corollary the organized interests in society should seek to influence policy, not to capture the decisionmaking apparatus. It is argued further that "the state itself must have sufficient autonomy, legitimacy, capacity, and support to mediate among the various interest groups and balance their claims."[44] Thus, a formidable obstacle to a healthy civil society is the decay, corruption, and disorganization of the Russian state.[45] O'Donnell and Schmitter write about the resurrection of civil society; however, in Russia the more appropriate term may be the creation of civil society.

This discussion implies that civil society requires a degree of toleration and moderation within political culture, and the absence of such toleration may be seen in the vituperative nature of political debate in Russia today. During 1992 and 1993, both Yeltsin and the opposition were guilty of name-calling and stereotyping. For example, Yeltsin repeatedly called all opponents fascists or communists; the opposition—from both the left and the right—accused Yeltsin of wanting to establish a dictatorship. There also seemed to be little understanding of the nature of political compromise, which is so essential to civil society. Every time Yeltsin moved to compromise with the old parliament, Khasbulatov viewed it as a sign of weakness and sought to change the rules of the game. The rules must become institutionalized, however, as the process of democratic consolidation proceeds; in a democracy, outcomes are unclear but the rules are certain. During 1992 and 1993, personal and institutional rivalries—and legacies from the past—slowed the process drastically but did not bring it to a standstill.

1994 AND AFTER: TOWARD CONSOLIDATION?

The period from 1992 through late 1993 highlights Huntington's observation regarding the linkage between performance and legitimacy. Given the stalemate between the parliament and the president during that time, it seemed as if nothing was being accomplished in Moscow. The ability of each side to issue edicts that annulled those of the other gave the appearance that neither side cared much about the problems of the population at large. It also added to the sense that the fight was over perquisites and power and not over the fundamental economic and political problems facing Russia. This was perhaps epitomized by reports that Muscovites were strolling the Arbat during the shelling of the White House. In the words of O'Donnell, if consolidation is to occur, then the state, to be acceptable to the people, must "not [be] perceived by most of the population as just an arena for the pursuit of particularistic interests."[46]

With the elections in December 1993, Russia moved to a different phase in the consolidation process, one that is simultaneously new and not so new. The Russian electorate did indeed indicate its frustration with politics-as-usual; the party that garnered the largest single block was Vladimir Zhirinovsky's Liberal Democratic Party (22.8 percent), followed by Russia's Choice (15.4 percent) and the Russian Communist Party (12.4 percent).[47] Although many explanations have been offered for Zhirinovsky's success, we can note only a few. He apparently appealed to voters who were tired of "shock therapy" but who did not want to return communists to power. Moreover, the democrats apparently underestimated the strength of "nostalgia" for empire and for Russia's superpower status—an issue that Zhirinovsky used rather effectively. Finally, the democrats seemed complacent: Public opinion polls, almost until election day, gave them a decisive edge. However, although the first-past-the-post system should have given them an incentive to form coalitions, they did not. No agreement was ever reached on backing a single candidate where it seemed that the democrats might be splitting the vote. Even after the disastrous election results, the democratic factions continued to blame each other for their electoral failures.

As for the constitutional referendum, a majority of the mandated 50 percent turnout had to approve the constitution in order for it to pass. Official results after the referendum stated that enough people had voted and that the constitution was valid. Later, however, sources within democratic circles claimed that the results had been tampered with, that fewer than 50 percent of the population had actually voted. Ironically, only Rutskoi formally challenged the constitution and the new Duma. In many respects, this makes perfect sense. Although Yeltsin may well want the new, equally conservative parliament to disappear, if he declared the referendum results invalid, he would lose the new political powers he acquired in the constitution. And the deputies, although they might want to rewrite the constitution to give themselves more formal powers, could lose their seats in parliament if there were to be new founding elections. They suddenly discovered that they have a large stake in the system that Yeltsin devised. Thus, the postelection period offers new opportunities and new problems for economic and political reform—as well as a second chance at consolidation in Russia.

The new Russian system is strongly presidential. Under the 1993 constitution, the president has the right to initiate policy and to make governmental appointments. The latter, however, must be approved by the legislature. If the Duma refuses to confirm a nominee for prime minister three times, the president can dissolve it and call new elections. Judicial appointments are to be confirmed by the Council of the Federation. Parliament can pass a no-confidence vote, which the president may ignore the first time; if a second no-confidence vote is passed within three months, the president must respond either by dissolving the parliament or dismissing the government. The new constitution also puts in place an exceptionally cumbersome impeachment procedure, making the likelihood of impeachment minimal.

Ironically, despite Yeltsin's presidential republic, the stalemate between the new Duma and the presidency began where the old confrontationist policies left off. Immediately following the elections, Gaidar and Minister of Finance Boris Fedorov resigned, leaving the field to Chernomyrdin and the centrists. Yet, economic reform in Russia continued, although everyone predicted the demise of marketization as a result. Simultaneously, the Duma demonstrated its independence and conservatism by voting an amnesty for the August 1991 coup conspirators and for the leaders of the October 1993 uprising. In many respects, the only difference between the old stalemate and the new one is that thus far it is not a constitutional crisis of the same magnitude.

This is not the place to discuss the theoretical literature on the comparative strengths and weaknesses of a presidential system versus a parliamentary system. Certainly examples of both abound. In the context of democratizing societies, it has been argued that parliamentarianism offers voice to more segments of society and that all members of a coalition have an incentive to cooperate if they do not want the government to fall.[48] Presidentialism, however, seems to preclude precisely that kind of representation and coalition building.[49] In the words of two Russian observers: The constitution "virtually precludes the possibility of forming a coalition government, a practice that many traditionally democratic countries use to attain civic harmony."[50] Whether or not Russia can avoid the pitfalls of presidentialism remains to be seen.

A strong presidential system was chosen because it seemed the way out of the contextual and institutional problems that newly independent Russia faced. It also may reflect the Russian penchant for a strong state to solve economic and political problems. A poll taken in late 1992 indicated that there was more support for a government that "strove toward security" than one that "protected individual liberties";[51] 1994 data indicated that approximately 25 percent of the respondents felt that Russia did not need democracy.[52] As Phillipe Schmitter writes: "The trick is to make binding and collective choices ... between alternative institutional arrangements that are compatible with existing socioeconomic structures and cultural identities."[53]

The problem is that presidentialism may degenerate into what Guillermo O'Donnell calls "delegative democracy."[54] Key features of this system are a president who sees him- or herself above politics and views the constraints imposed by parliament or a court as nuisances. In delegative democracies, the parliament, the press, and other institutions are free to voice their opinions, but the president is equally free to ignore these views. There is much in this description that rings true of Russia under Yeltsin. Two crises in late 1994 illustrate this point fully. The first was the precipitous drop in the dollar value of the ruble in mid-October 1994; the second was the Russian invasion of Chechnya.

The October ruble crisis highlighted the fragility of the government's attempts at financial stabilization and again raised the specter of a loss of governmental legitimacy through nonperformance. Although official figures through the summer of 1994 had indicated that Russia was making tremendous strides to curb inflation, the drop of the ruble probably occurred because of inflationary pressures created by continuing agricultural subsidies and interenterprise debt. The drop may also have been accelerated by the inaction of Viktor Gerashchenko, the director of the State Bank and an ally of antireform forces, who refused to intervene to prop up the ruble. Additionally, the weakness of the ruble may have been fed by speculators—both legal and illegal—who sought to protect and enrich themselves at the expense of the average Russian citizen. Independent investigations carried out by Yeltsin's Security Council and the Duma blamed different parties for the crisis. In the efforts to find a simple explanation for the crisis and a scapegoat, Yeltsin replaced Gerashchenko and shuffled his economic advisers. As in the April 1992 confrontation, he limited the number of reformers in his inner circle and in effect surrounded himself with advisers who recommend inherently contradictory policies. In the aftermath of the ruble crisis, Yeltsin survived a no-confidence vote in the Duma; but the slim margin by which he won indicated the growing opposition to the president.

The second crisis, the war in Chechnya, has been far more serious. First, Chechen opposition is yet another legacy of Russia's past. Incorporated into the tsarist empire after fifty-plus years of fighting, the Chechens were victimized by Stalin in the 1940s. They seized upon the weakness of the USSR in the fall of 1991 to secede outright from Russia. Second, as Moscow sought to create a new constitutional order, it promulgated a new federal treaty to govern relations between Moscow and the republics and regions but never recognized Chechnya's independence. If it was hoped that the Tatarstan model could work for Chechnya, such hopes were dashed when neither side proved willing to engage in serious negotiations until it was too late and there was virtually no room for compromise. Instead, Moscow took advantage of clan divisions within the republic by rallying opponents of Chechen President Dudayev. When a Russian-instigated coup attempt failed, Moscow apparently felt that it had no choice but to invade. In addition, many in Yeltsin's entourage apparently felt that Chechnya would be an easy victory that would boost the president's flagging popularity.

Third, the invasion of Chechnya has proven to be an embarrassment for the military, as the total victory promised within a few days eluded the Russian army. The initial operation was criticized by several high-ranking military officials, including General Aleksandr Lebed, who gained prominence as commander of the army in Moldova, and General Boris Gromov, the deputy defense minister. Gromov and two other deputy defense ministers were relieved of their responsibilities in a move to silence critics of the war and to demonstrate that Yeltsin remained in charge. These obvious divisions within the military heightened its politicization and, at that time, were seen to increase the possibility of some kind of military intervention into the consolidation process.

Fourth, the war skewed the democratization process in Russia. Insofar as the third wave of democratization depends on choices made by leaders, Yeltsin's decision to invade (if indeed he made it) threatens the very processes he claims to support. The war in Chechnya has been almost universally condemned by politicians—both from the right and the left. Yegor Gaidar called for Yeltsin to dismiss those in the president's inner circle who advised the intervention, and Grigory Yavlinsky, the leader of the Yabloko faction and a major reformer, openly demanded Yeltsin's resignation. The opposition claims (and there seems to be much truth in this) not only that Yeltsin is relying on the advice of nonelected individuals such as his bodyguard, Aleksandr V. Korzhakov, but also that he has exceeded his constitutional authority in so doing. In the words of Aleksei Manannikov, then deputy chairman of the Federation Council's International Affairs Committee: "Russia is now governed by a military-civilian junta disguised as the National Security Council. . . . The Security Council has no right running this country. If it continues Russia will be ripe for an authoritarian dictatorship."[55]

Conclusion

Mikhail Gorbachev may have initiated the transition process, yet it has fallen to Boris Yeltsin to oversee the consolidation of Russian democracy. Yeltsin, as I have argued, made a false start in 1992–1993 when he failed to create wholly new post-Soviet governmental institutions and had to try again beginning in December 1993. Yet, as the crisis in Chechnya indicates, Russia continues to face serious political problems. Yeltsin's authoritarian tendencies and his isolation from the Duma were readily apparent during the siege by Chechen rebels of the southern Russian town of Budennovsk in June 1995. As the crisis there unfolded, Yeltsin, in a move that elicited criticism from all factions in the Duma, flew to Halifax, Nova Scotia, for a meeting of the Group of Seven. In his absence, Prime Minister Chernomyrdin negotiated with the rebels, secured the release of the hostages, and facilitated longer-term negotiations to bring an end to the conflict. Chernomyrdin's handling of the crisis increased his standing with the population and seemed to create a potentially serious challenge to Yeltsin's leadership. At the same time, the Duma scheduled a vote of no confidence in the government, which passed 241–70, with 20 abstentions. Under the December 1993 constitution, Yeltsin could ignore this first vote of no confidence, but if the Duma were to vote no confidence again the president would be obligated to dismiss either the government or the Duma. In reality, the Russian president averted losing a second no-confidence vote by agreeing to fire Sergei Stepashin, the director of the Federal Security Service, Viktor Yerin, the minister of internal affairs, and Nikolai Yegorov, the deputy prime minister, all of whom shouldered much of the responsibility for hostilities in Chechnya and for the failed hostage rescue attempt in Budennovsk. The move, however, was simply a sop to the Duma, because the new ministers were hardliners like those whom they replaced. Indeed, the cease-fire and negotiations begun by Chernomyrdin have broken down; in early 1996, the war threatened to spread into neighboring regions.

Whether Russia will move forward in the consolidation process will depend as well on the ability of the current—or some future—government to move decisively on the economic problems confronting the new state. These include inflation, the problem of interenterprise debt, the creation of a market, and the completion of the privatization process. Simultaneously, Russia must contend with the rapid growth of criminality and the seeming omnipresence of organized crime. Moreover, the solutions to these problems must be supported by the appropriate legal and financial infrastructures. If this cannot be done, then Russia risks heading into what O'Donnell calls a "national level prisoner's dilemma" in which it is in the interest of all actors to protect themselves by acting alone and by establishing special relations with the state agencies that provide the sought-after benefits.[56] This is reminiscent of comments made about the activities of deputies to the old CPD and clearly would not provide a healthy environment in which to consolidate democracy.

The catch-22 is that the government must function efficiently, and to do this it must create a consensus. Yet in order to create a consensus, it must be perceived as efficient and legitimate. By the end of 1995, neither seemed to be occurring. In parliamentary elections held in December, the Russian Communist Party successfully played on the population's dissatisfaction with the economy, crime, and the war in Chechnya to emerge as the largest faction of the Duma. And, with presidential elections scheduled for June 1996, Communist Party chief Gennady Zyuganov is currently far ahead of Yeltsin and Grigory Yavlinsky in the polls. Zyuganov has criticized the government's handling of market reform and privatization and has called for the renationalization of the extractive industries. In response, Yeltsin has also called for a slowing of the marketization process and promised to pay back wages owed to millions of workers. Whether these promises will placate disgruntled, impoverished workers remains to be seen. Of course, Yeltsin, as the erstwhile champion of Russian democratization, has survived many previous crises. Yet, in early 1996, the prospects for economic stabilization and transition have dimmed, with serious implications for the democratic consolidation process.

CHRONOLOGY

March 1985	Gorbachev elected general secretary of the Communist Party of the Soviet Union by the party Politburo
February 1986	Twenty-Seventh Party Congress; Gorbachev indicates that domestic reform is his top priority
January 1987	At a party plenum, Gorbachev proposes contested elections for party officials
March 1988	Nina Andreevna's hardline letter is printed in *Sovetskaia Rossiia*
June 1988	Nineteenth Party Conference
March 1989	Contested elections for the Soviet Congress of People's Deputies
May 1989	First meeting of Soviet Congress of People's Deputies

February 1990	Party rescinds article 6 of Soviet Constitution, which guaranteed the CPSU leading role in society
Spring 1990	Elections for republic Congresses of People's Deputies including the Russian CPD (March)
June 1991	Boris Yeltsin is elected president of the Russian Federation
August 1991	Attempted coup against Gorbachev by hardliners within party
December 8, 1991	Presidents of Ukraine, Russia, and Belarus met in Minsk to create the Commonwealth of Independent States
December 25, 1991	Gorbachev resigns as president of the Soviet Union; the USSR ceases to exist
December 1992	Parliamentary session in which antireformers openly challenge Yeltsin; Chernomyrdin becomes prime minister
March 1993	Two meetings of parliament: The first cancels Yeltsin's planned referendum, but also fails to impeach Yeltsin; the second reinstates the referendum
April 1993	Referendum held on Yeltsin and on reform process
September 1993	Yeltsin dissolves parliament
October 3–4, 1993	Supporters of Khasbulatov and Rutskoi take to the streets; Yeltsin calls on the army to storm the Russian White House
December 1993	Elections for new Duma and vote in constitutional referendum
October 1994	Ruble crisis
December 1994	Russian troops invade Chechnya
June 1995	Chechen rebels seize hostages in southern town of Budennovsk; Chernomyrdin negotiates in Yeltsin's absence and secures release of hostages and a cease-fire in Chechen War
December 1995	Parliamentary (Duma) elections in which Russian Communist Party secures major victory

Notes

1. See, for example, the arguments presented in Charles E. Lindblom, *Politics and Markets* (New York: Basic Books, 1977).

2. Dankwart A. Rustow, "Transitions to Democracy: Toward a Dynamic Model," *Comparative Politics* 2 (April 1970): 337–363.

3. See the series done in the late 1960s by the Social Science Research Council, especially Leonard Binder, *Crises and Sequences in Political Development* (Princeton: Princeton University Press, 1971).

4. See, for example, Maurice Duverger, *Political Parties* (New York: Wiley, 1954), or Alfred Stepan and Cindy Skach, "Constitutional Frameworks and Democratic Consolidation," *World Politics* 46 (October 1993): 1–22.

5. Samuel P. Huntington, *The Third Wave* (Norman: University of Oklahoma Press, 1991).

6. Nancy Bermeo, "Rethinking Regime Change," *Comparative Politics* 22 (April 1990): 5.

7. Terry Lynn Karl, "Dilemmas of Democratization in Latin America," in Dankwart A. Rustow and Kenneth Paul Erickson, eds., *Comparative Political Dynamics: Global Research Perspectives* (New York: HarperCollins, 1991), p. 170.

8. See Bruce D. Porter and Carol R. Saivetz, "The Once and Future Empire: Russia and the 'Near Abroad,'" *Washington Quarterly* 17 (Summer 1994): 75–90.

9. Peter Rutland, "Economic Crisis and Reform," in Stephen White, Alex Pravda, and Zvi Gitelman, eds., *Developments in Soviet and Post-Soviet Politics* (Durham, NC: Duke University Press, 1992), p. 202.

10. David Wedgewood Benn, "'*Glasnost*' and the Media," in White, Pravda, and Gitelman, *Developments*, p. 183.

11. Guillermo O'Donnell and Philippe C. Schmitter, *Transitions from Authoritarian Rule: Tentative Conclusions About Uncertain Democracies* (Baltimore: Johns Hopkins University Press, 1986), p. 9.

12. The term "standpatters" is Huntington's in describing those opposed to the liberalization and transformation of the society in question. In the Russian context, they would be the hardliners. Huntington, *The Third Wave*, esp. ch. 3.

13. In the old Supreme Soviet, representation by gender, profession, and age, among other categories, was guaranteed. The more open elections of 1989 did not result in the same kind of distribution.

14. Huntington, *The Third Wave*, esp. ch. 3. See also the Introduction to this book.

15. The wording of the referendum question was as follows: "Do you consider necessary the preservation of the Union of Soviet Socialist Republics as a renewed federation of equal sovereign republics, in which the rights and freedoms of an individual of any nationality will be fully guaranteed?"

16. O'Donnell and Schmitter, *Transitions*, p. 6.

17. Coit Blacker, *Hostage to Revolution* (New York: Council on Foreign Relations, 1993).

18. Douglass C. North, *Institutions, Institutional Change and Economic Performance* (Cambridge: Cambridge University Press, 1990), p. vii.

19. See, for example, Huntington, *The Third Wave*, pp. 6–7, for definitions of democracy.

20. Larry Diamond, "Toward Democratic Consolidation," *Journal of Democracy* 5 (July 1994): 15.

21. See the discussion in Don Chull Shin, "On the Third Wave of Democratization: A Synthesis and Evaluation of Recent Theory and Research," *World Politics* 47 (October 1994). Shin uses the term "consolidation" to mean something beyond institutionalization, thus continuing the confusion.

22. Huntington, *The Third Wave*, pp. 208–210.

23. Michael McFaul, "Why Russia's Politics Matter," *Foreign Affairs* 74 (January/February 1995): 89.

24. See Alexander Rahr, "Winners and Losers of the Russian Congress," *RFE/RL Research Report* 1 (May 1, 1992): 2.

25. Formally created on June 21, 1992, the new organization was a merger of Nikolai Travkin's Democratic Party of Russia, Aleksandr Rutskoi's People's Party of Russia, and Volsky's All-Russian Renewal Union (representing the military-industrial complex).

26. A total of 617 deputies voted for impeachment; however, for the motion to carry, the anti-Yeltsin forces needed to muster 689 votes.

27. Wendy Slater, "No Victors in the Russian Referendum," *RFE/RL Research Report* 2 (May 21, 1993): 12.

28. As early as late fall 1992, Serge Schmemann estimated that 20 percent of the deputies regularly voted with Yeltsin, 35 percent voted against him, and the rest were an unstable swing vote. See Schmemann, "Power of Russian Parliament's Leader Becoming a Vexing Issue for Yeltsin," *New York Times*, October 25, 1992, p. 18.

29. *RFE/RL Daily Report*, no. 219, November 15, 1993.

30. Russell Bova, "Political Dynamics of the Post-Communist Transition, a Comparative Perspective," *World Politics* 44 (October 1991): 129.

31. Andranik Migranyan, "Prezidentsii porek—garant stabil'nost'," *Nezavisimaia gazeta*, June 5, 1993, as cited in Thomas F. Remington, "Menage à Trois: The End of Soviet Parliamentarianism," paper presented at the American Association for the Advancement of Slavic Studies, Honolulu, Hawaii, November 1993.

32. See the discussion of how Khasbulatov operated in Remington, "Menage à Trois," p. 12.

33. Rahr, "Winners and Losers," p. 1.

34. Remington, "Menage à Trois," p. 5.

35. Remington, "Menage à Trois," p. 5.

36. Schmemann, "Power of Russian Parliament's Leader," p. 18.

37. Philippe C. Schmitter, "Dangers and Dilemmas of Democracy," *Journal of Democracy* 5 (April 1994): 65.

38. Jessica Eve Stern, "Moscow Meltdown," *International Security* 18 (Spring 1994): 43.

39. For more details on negotiations between the center and the regions and republics, see Vera Tolz, "Thorny Road Toward Federalism in Russia," *RFE/RL Research Report* 2 (December 3, 1993): 1–8.

40. Larry Diamond, "Toward Democratic Consolidation," *Journal of Democracy* 5 (July 1994): 5.

41. Geoffrey Hosking, *The Awakening of the Soviet Union* (Cambridge: Harvard University Press, 1990).

42. See the essays in Carol R. Saivetz and Anthony Jones, *In Search of Pluralism: Soviet and Post-Soviet Politics* (Boulder: Westview Press, 1994).

43. McFaul, "Why Russia's Politics Matter," p. 89.

44. Diamond, "Toward Democratic Consolidation," p. 14.

45. M. Steven Fish, "Russia's Fourth Transition," *Journal of Democracy* 5 (July 1994): 32.

46. Guillermo O'Donnell, "On the State, Democratization, and Some Conceptual Problems: A Latin American View with Glances at Some Postcommunist Countries," *World Development* 21 (1993): 1358.

47. Figures included in Timothy J. Colton, "The Russian Voter in 1993," paper presented at conference, "The Russian Elections of December 1993," Harvard University, April 1994.

48. Stepan and Skach, "Constitutional Frameworks," p. 20.

49. Stepan and Skach, "Constitutional Frameworks," p. 6.

50. Dmitry Volkov and Aleksei Zubro, "Constitution: Boris Yeltsin's Basic Law," *Segodnia*, November 11, 1993, p. 1, as cited in Erik P. Hoffmann, "Challenges to Viable Constitutionalism in Post-Soviet Russia," *Harriman Review*, 7 (November 1994): 41.

51. Mark Rhodes, "Political Attitudes in Russia," *RFE/RL Research Report* 2 (January 15, 1993): 43.

52. *RFE/RL Daily Report*, No. 155 (August 17, 1994).

53. Schmitter, "Dangers and Dilemmas of Democracy," p. 64.

54. Guillermo O'Donnell, "Delegative Democracy," *Journal of Democracy* 5 (January 1994): 55–69.

55. Michael Specter, "Yeltsin Declares Chechen War Over and Ousts 4 Critics in Military," *New York Times*, January 20, 1995, p. A10.

56. Guillermo O'Donnell, "On the State," pp. 1363–1365.

SUGGESTIONS FOR FURTHER READING

In the last days of the Soviet Union and in the five years since the collapse of the USSR, a number of good books have appeared which detail both Gorbachev's attempts at reform and the unraveling of communist power. David Lane's *Soviet Society Under Perestroika* (Boston: Unwin Hyman, 1990) describes the impact of Gorbachev's policies on various aspects of Soviet life; Marshall I. Goldman's *What Went Wrong With Perestroika* (New York: Norton, 1991) analyzes the economic mistakes the Soviet President made. Two edited collections—Stephen White, Alex Pravda, and Zvi Gitelman, *Developments in Soviet and Post-Soviet Society* (Durham: Duke University Press, 1992) and Carol R. Saivetz and Anthony Jones, *In Search of Pluralism* (Boulder: Westview Press, 1994)—offer examinations of the impact of Gorbachev's reforms and carry the analysis forward to the early days of the post-Soviet period. One other very good book on the Gorbachev era is Dusko Doder and Louise Branson, *Gorbachev: Heretic in the Kremlin* (NY: Penguin Books, 1991).

Given the fluidity of events since the collapse of the Soviet Union, there are few books out dealing with the Yeltsin period. The best sources are chapters in books and articles that have appeared in scholarly journals. There are several chapters on Russian politics in Thomas F. Remington, ed., *Parliaments in Transition: The New Legislative Politics in the Former USSR and Eastern Europe* (Boulder: Westview Press, 1994). The same is true of Timothy J. Colton and Robert Tucker, eds., *Patterns in Post Soviet Leadership* (Boulder: Westview Press, 1995). The best biography of Yeltsin during the Soviet period is John Morrison's *Boris Yeltsin: From Bolshevik to Democrat* (New York: Dutton, 1991); and of course there is Yeltsin's autobiography, *Against the Grain* (New York: Summit Books, 1990).

Among the articles that stand out are: Michael McFaul, "Why Russia's Politics Matter," *Foreign Affairs* 74 (January/February 1995); Russell Bova, "Political Dynamics of the Post-Communist Transition, a Comparative Perspective," *World Politics* 44 (October 1991); and Jessica Eve Stern, "Moscow Meltdown," *International Security* 18 (Spring, 1994).

Translations of Soviet and Russian press commentaries are available in the *Current Digest of the Soviet Press,* now called the *Current Digest of the Post-Soviet Press.* Many of the same articles (in translation) can be found in the U.S. government's Foreign Broadcast

Information Service (FBIS). The FBIS is very useful because it also includes transcripts of television shows and radio broadcasts.

Finally, an invaluable source of information and analysis about Soviet and Russian events are the publications of Radio Free Europe/Radio Liberty and now the Open Media Research Institute. The former published the weekly *Research Report*, and it has been succeeded by OMRI's *Transition*. Both also provide(d) information daily over the internet.

CONCLUSION

MARY ELLEN FISCHER

What have our eight chapters told us about the process of establishing democracies? Are there common features among the chapters that justify our choosing such disparate examples, and do the earlier cases especially contain useful lessons for emergent democratic systems today? At a minimum, we can identify the following similarities, each of which appears in every case: (1) a crisis in the old regime; (2) societal constraints shaping institutions; (3) crucial individuals making choices; (4) group conflicts affecting the transition; and (5) pervasive uncertainty. Yet these similarities themselves are diverse: sources of instability in old regimes vary widely; constraints differ from one society to another; individuals are by definition unique; groups often diverge in leadership and relative strengths and therefore differ in their abilities to affect new systems; the very absence of predictable patterns of behavior creates uncertainty.

Our conclusions here can merely outline some tentative patterns that need further exploration. The following features emerge as the cases play out: (1) the old regime contributes to its own demise by failing to solve or even by exacerbating structural problems, usually economic or military, or by embracing ideas incompatible with its survival; (2) in successful new democracies, the new institutions are crafted to fit societal constraints; (3) capable individuals who make shrewd choices are crucial in establishing democracies, but good leaders alone may not be sufficient, because other factors may intervene to doom the attempt; (4) the balance among different groups will shape the transition, and a peaceful transition may leave powerful groups intact and allow them important roles in the new democracy; (5) uncertainty diminishes as new rules and patterns of behavior evolve.

In addition, in regard to our earlier cases, several lessons emerge at once, each with significant implications for contemporary attempts: (1) time is required to establish what we define in the Introduction as "democracy"—a set of rules, periodic accountability on the part of political leaders, and respect for individual and group rights; (2) democratic processes can indeed precede democrats; (3) models and foreign support can substitute for at least some of the traditional prerequisites; and (4) therefore, procedural democracy is a good way to begin, although it may not satisfy the expectations of many citizens. All of these lessons provide hope for contemporary efforts to create new democratic systems, and we shall return to them later in this Conclusion.

ORIGINS AND MODELS

The origins of our eight cases—that is, the nature of the *ancien regime* and the sources of regime change—are quite diverse. Most obvious is the distance in time between the seventeenth century and the late twentieth century. Not only does this imply huge differences in the levels of socioeconomic development and technology among our case studies, but it also means that England and colonial America had no existing models to follow, no clear concept of democracy, nor any contemporary democratic system to emulate. The colonies certainly made use of English and classical concepts and precedents, but in 1784 there were no living democracies nor practicing democrats. The remaining six cases not only had clear models but also enjoyed foreign support in establishing new systems: in the cases of Germany and Japan, there was an occupying army as well as economic aid; in Argentina, political support from other states in the Western Hemisphere and economic support from organizations such as the IMF; and in formerly communist Eastern Europe, considerable political pressure and (some) economic aid from the United States, its European allies, and international financial bodies.

England and the American colonies had other advantages, however, advantages that allowed them to nurture and finally develop sustainable democratic systems. Both time and geography were important: time enough to develop procedures and behavioral norms within constitutional structures, and geographic locations that insulated them from outside, nondemocratic threats. Germany and Japan had a measure of time, but their transitions were accelerated by the devastation of the war and the totality of the occupations. Argentina does have some geographical advantages—raw materials to export and a square mileage sufficiently large for economic viability but not so large as to be unable to cope with its many problems (like Russia)—but time has been a problem: The population expected fast results, and successive democratic regimes have not delivered economic improvement quickly enough; hence, the result is melancholy. The three postcommunist cases are quite disadvantaged in both ways: they have no time to speak of, as people's high expectations have already been dashed, and geography has led to disaster in the ethnic mosaic of the former Soviet bloc, where all borders are subject to historical controversy.

Although England and the United States did have significant advantages, without models, what stimulated them to start the process of establishing democratic systems? Here we come to one of our common patterns: In all cases, the old regime goes through some type of crisis that produces change. Sometimes it is defeat in war; at other times a structural imbalance—often economic or military—within the society itself seems to spark change. Ideas also play a role in regime change, however, and here is an important question to ask when evaluating the origins of new democracies: Are ideas or societal factors more important in stimulating democratization? Furthermore, can the idea of democracy—an understanding of the process and a determination to establish such a system—overcome societal disadvantages? To put it yet another way, can foreign or historical models substitute for missing socioeconomic features that would facilitate a democratic transition? Certainly our contemporary cases lack many of the facilitating factors specified in pre-1974 studies of democratization as prerequisites to democracy: society-wide economic, social, and cultural conditions like economic prosperity, a diversified social structure, a national culture that tolerates dissent and seeks compromise. Indeed, in the postcommunist cases, not only are such positive elements missing, but specific features of the authoritarian background make success appear unlikely. After World War II, however, Germany and Japan were also disadvantaged by their authoritarian traditions and past democratic failures.

If we look at the origins of regime transition in our eight cases, we find that structural economic difficulties in each society contributed significantly to instability. In England, for example, rising inflation and military costs in conjunction with falling tax receipts and bad harvests created serious budget deficits for Charles I, forcing him to quarrel with his parliaments over increasing his revenues. This eventually contributed to revolution. A century later, efforts by the English king and parliament to increase taxes on the American colonies precipitated their revolution. In Argentina, the failure of the export-import model and then of the import-substitution model led the military government in the late 1970s to attempt neoliberal economic policies; discredited by falling living standards (and defeat in war), the military government entered into an informal "pact" with reformers, and a democratic election took place in 1983.

In Romania, Ceauşescu's devastating economic policies provoked intense resentment, finally motivating Romanians to overthrow and execute him in December 1989—although the immediate impetus for revolt came from their rising hopes and expectations as other East European communist systems collapsed. In a similar vein, economic issues—price hikes or labor demands—were at the center of Poland's dramatic series of protest movements throughout the communist period, even though it was withdrawal of Soviet support from the PUWP in August 1989 that eventually ended communist rule. Moreover, in the USSR, Gorbachev after 1985 initiated his *glasnost* and *perestroika* and even *demokratizatsia* to improve the disastrous condition of the economy; however, the Soviet economy proved much harder to reform than he had anticipated, and as economic conditions deteriorated, his support and the Soviet regime collapsed. Even in the remaining two cases, Germany and Japan, where military defeat in World War II, not the economy, destroyed the pre-1945 regimes, economic issues played a key role in bringing the Nazis and the Japanese militarists to power and in justifying their rule, and economic shortages later contributed to their defeat.

War—or the military budget—was another catalyst that precipitated crisis in each of our old regimes. For Charles I, war with the Scots (and the hostility of the French) forced him into confrontation with parliament. A century later, the military burdens and rivalries of the British Empire contributed to friction between London and the American colonies, and Britain soon found the costs of military occupation too great to emerge victorious; the Americans won the war for independence and established a new political system. Military defeat in World War II and occupation by the victors destroyed the old regimes in both Germany and Japan and began their democratic transitions. Defeat in the Falklands/Malvinas War precipitated the replacement of Argentina's military rulers by their democratic opponents. And although the communist states did not suffer defeats on the battlefield, the high cost of military competition with the United States was a major cause of the Soviet Union's difficulties—and, therefore, contributed to the collapse of communist rule in Poland and Romania as well.

Although economic and military pressures precipitated regime crisis in all of our cases, just as important were the ideas existing within each *ancien regime* that contributed to its loss of legitimacy.[1] In England, for example, religious quarrels divided Charles I from many of his supporters and from parliament, which was itself divided, and compromise on issues of religious principle was difficult for both Charles and his subjects. In addition, Charles I's concepts of kingship and the role of parliament differed sharply from those of his English subjects. Indeed, his violations of the Ancient Constitution justified parliament in resisting him, its goal being to restore the correct balance in the system. Even Cromwell would try to reestablish the old balance on the basis of traditional concepts of parliament's proper role. The Stuart monarchy would indeed be reestablished, but it would again be overthrown (peacefully) to bring to the throne monarchs who would accept English ideas of political process.

In the American colonies, many ideas and institutional structures from England crossed the ocean and then took root in a new form, causing disagreement within colonial legislatures and between legislators and royal governors appointed by the king. Indeed, the English encouraged both legislatures and local autonomy in the colonies, thus transplanting the concept of representation that would eventually lead Americans to reject the English parliament's authority to tax them. Later, the very concept of a constitution, which in England involved unwritten rules based on history and tradition, was transformed in America and given a new basis: reason, equality, and natural rights. This doctrine of natural law, set forth in the Declaration of Independence, provided a decisive break with the past and would eventually justify much greater popular participation in politics than even the American founders envisioned. Even so, the doctrine had roots in the old society, in English theorists such as John Locke and in the Scottish Enlightenment.

Much later, in twentieth-century Argentina, seeds of discontent grew in various authoritarian systems—both populist and military—which failed to live up to their own promises of economic equality and prosperity or national greatness, respectively. The communist states also could not fulfill their ideological goals of economic development and world revolution. Thus, across the ages, the ideas of the old regimes eventually weakened or destroyed their legitimacy and contributed to their demise, even in Nazi Germany and pre–World War II Japan, where expansionist ideological goals eventually outreached regime capacity and set those countries on a path to military defeat.

All our cases, therefore, emerged from periods of regime crisis, but the first two had no contemporary models to emulate. Instead, the English in the seventeenth century were trying to re-create their own imagined past and failed to do so. Later, the American founders in the eighteenth century found important precedents in such English accomplishments as representative government, parliamentary power, religious toleration, and the rule of law. Those precedents, as well as the Americans' idealized views of classical democracy and the ideas that sprang from the Enlightenment, were sufficient to justify the American Revolution and provide a framework for a new system based not on tradition but on rational/legal legitimacy.

Our more recent cases followed several existent models. After 1945, for example, the Germans and Japanese had not only contemporary constitutions to study but also democratic (or protodemocratic) institutions from their own past; Argentina returned to its own presidential system, originally modeled on the U.S. scheme; and the postcommunist states since 1989 have looked mainly to the constitutions of France and Germany. Perhaps the answer to our question about the relative importance of ideas and societal factors lies in this question of models: In effect, the availability of models—the institutions and concepts of democracy and the ideas of democrats—reduces the importance of the traditional socioeconomic prerequisites. If, therefore, foreign examples and foreign support (as in the cases of Germany and Japan) may substitute for these internal characteristics, then a more accurate phrase for these socioeconomic "prerequisites" would be "facilitating factors."

SOCIETAL CONSTRAINTS

The selection of models and shaping of institutions in all of our cases have depended in part on societal constraints, and our successful cases have adjusted the democratic framework to fit the society and its traditions. The English, for example, eventually resolved their fierce struggle between king and parliament in 1688 by opting for parliamentary supremacy, relying on political and legal precedent rather than separation of powers to balance the government. Their concept of representation—choosing informed individuals to make decisions—eventually led them to the single-member-district, "first-past-the-post" election process with close ties between representative and constituents.

Although the Americans copied the English electoral system, the traditions of diversity and localism in the colonies together with fears of a tyrannical ruler produced a federal structure in which the components—the states—would exercise considerable power, although much less power than under the Articles of Confederation. Indeed, the framers of the U.S. Constitution of 1787 sought to strengthen the central government while placing strict limits on that government. Federalism, for example, is a concept whereby power is divided between the central government and the states and, in the U.S. Congress, between two chambers with different constituencies: the Senate, with equal representation for each state, and the House, where representation is based on population. Within the federal government the three branches would check and balance each other, as would the House and Senate in Congress, thus preventing any body or individual or geographic region from becoming too powerful, but also slowing change and often producing gridlock.

The U.S. Constitution also imposed limits on the whims of voters through indirect election of the president and Senate, the appointment process in selecting the federal judiciary, and separated powers and overlapping jurisdictions in the federal system so that a "majority" of American voters would never decide anything directly. As in England, the party system would develop later as a response to the electoral system, and interest groups as a response to representative government. Thus, the institutions of these two old democracies bear the imprint of two very different societies: in England a strong, all-powerful parliament was needed to offset the power of the king; in America the Constitution, erected on the foundations of English colonial rule, was crafted to reflect the diverse interests of the states and to protect against both a tyrannical government and a tyrannical popular majority.

In Germany as well, political institutions were built on earlier foundations and shaped to avoid the mistakes of Imperial Germany and the Weimar Republic. The new government was federal in structure, in order to conform to German traditions and distribute power widely throughout the system, but Prussia was broken up. The power of the central German government now rests in the legislature, where the chancellor is the key figure rather than the president. Responsible to the *Bundestag*, the chancellor is nevertheless difficult to replace without going to the voters in a new election—unless the legislators can come up with an alternative by way of a positive no-confidence vote. Thus, the chancellor of the Federal Republic is stronger than his Weimar predecessor, but not too strong. The electoral law balances proportional representation with single-member districts and has a 5 percent threshold in order to exclude tiny parties and to achieve a compromise between viable government and representation of the many societal interests— the dilemma of governability versus participation. In addition, the many rights guaranteed to citizens are balanced by rights reserved to the government to defend itself against parties or groups aiming to destroy it—an attempt to prevent another Hitler. Carefully crafted, with considerable interference and support from the occupying powers, the German Basic Law created a procedural democracy before many Germans had recovered sufficiently from the trauma of war and defeat to become real democrats. That would come later, when political participation and support for the new system emerged in the 1960s.

Like the German Basic Law, the new Japanese Constitution after World War II was a combination of Japanese traditions and reactions against past mistakes. Before the war the Japanese Constitution had provided a democratic framework, but the political system had evolved instead into a militaristic oligarchy. Determined to prevent a replay, MacArthur had the constitution written quickly, according to his priorities, and the Japanese acquiesced—in part to retain Emperor Hirohito. Despite U.S. influence, many features of the new democracy were congruent with traditional Japanese culture: the emperor, the centralized (rather than federal) structure, the continuing power of the bureaucracy, and the electoral system, which encouraged factions and local ties in candidate selection and reelection. There were important new features, however: The document renounced war as an instrument of national policy and enumerated political and social rights in considerable detail. In contrast to Germany, where fears of the past led constitutional framers to create a state strong enough to defend itself against hostile internal groups, in Japan fears of past militarism and authoritarian rule placed strict limits on the state and its powers.

In Argentina, the end of military rule was accomplished peacefully, through an informal agreement to hold elections in 1983 and to put the constitution back into force. This meant a return to civilian rule and the strong presidential system of the past, in which the president dominated both the legislative and judicial branches of government. It also meant that the power of the military remained a potential threat to the presidency and to democracy itself. In addition, the hardships of neoliberal economic policies alienated large segments of the population, including most labor unions. Although Raúl Alfonsín managed to preserve the democratic system, his Radical Party lost the 1989 election to Carlos Menem's Peronists. Menem then managed to reduce the influence of traditional societal forces such as the military and labor unions while retaining the tradition of a strong and personalistic presidency, but traces of Argentina's past were clearly visible in the new democratic system.

Romania's 1991 constitution clearly bears traces of the past, resulting as it does from a process dominated by old-regime reformers but with considerable input from their opponents. Deriving its republican form and guarantees of socioeconomic as well as political rights from the communist period, the document also reflects the country's historical admiration for France, adopting some features of the Fifth Republic's semipresidential system. The centralized administrative structure controlled from the capital combines both French and communist traditions, and this rejection of federalism and local autonomy—along with other constitutional provisions regarding language and nationhood—reflects the nationalism that has been a feature of Romanian politics throughout the twentieth century. The new parliament returns to the bicameralism of the 1920s, but the electoral law based on proportional representation—in which voters choose parties rather than candidates—is very much a reaction against the communist one-party system and single-member districts: despite a threshold of 3 percent, enough tiny parties gained representation in the 1992 elections so as to make a majority coalition very difficult to maintain. The last European state to throw off its communist regime (excepting Albania), Romania nevertheless managed to create and implement a new constitutional framework for democratic politics within two years—a framework shaped by the Romanian political past.

Poland, in contrast, the first East European state to install a noncommunist government, still did not have a new constitution by 1996. A number of adjustments to the old communist framework allowed democratic politics to proceed—most notably the roundtable agreements of 1989, which created a strong presidency, and the "Little Constitution" of 1992, which adjusted relations between president and parliament—but the legal basis for Polish politics reflects the communist past. The postcommunist electoral laws, in contrast, have reacted against that past. To ensure the fullest possible inclusion of interests in the new government, the 1991 law set up an extreme form of proportional representation with no threshold. This produced a legislature with so many tiny parties as to make governing very difficult. The 1993 law improved the situation somewhat with a 5 percent threshold, but by then political apathy produced such a low voter turnout that the viable legislative coalition that finally emerged represented only a small plurality of voters. By 1996, the hard constitutional choices still remained to be made—those involving the role of the church, for example, or the powers of the president. For the new system to be successful, compromises would have to be worked out as to which aspects of Poland's past should be accepted and rejected.

Russia also remained in political disarray in 1996. A prolonged struggle over a new constitution had led Boris Yeltsin to dissolve parliament by force in 1993 and impose a new constitution (ratified by popular referendum but shaped by presidential fiat). Such a constitution, of course, gave tremendous powers to the president, in line with the Russian tradition of a strong ruler. The German electoral system somehow was incorporated into the Russian electoral law—one-half single-member districts, one-half proportional representation by party list—and despite the disappointing results in 1993 for Yeltsin's supporters, the same system was approved for 1996. The legislature did reflect Soviet traditions and Russian realities by retaining its bicameral structure in a federal system, with the upper house representing territorial units and the lower house elected according to population. After 1993, many procedures and responsibilities remained to be clarified, disputes over internal and external boundaries led to disobedience and violence, and traces of the Soviet past, including recalcitrant bureaucrats, a nervous military establishment, and remnants of police organizations, remained behind to threaten the new system—but at least Russia had a democratic framework within which to operate.

In all of our cases, the new institutions have been or are being crafted to fit societal constraints: using federalism, for example, to accommodate geographic or ethnic diversity; choosing proportional representation or single-member districts to reflect varying concepts of representation; including provisions to strengthen or weaken the central government, depending on historical experience or immediate needs. In transitional situations, therefore, it does not seem difficult to create institutions that reflect the society and its past. Instead, because all our contemporary cases have involved compromise with members of the old regime, the basic need in these recent attempts might be to create institutions that retain enough indigenous elements to take root yet also escape the confines of the past sufficiently to become fully democratic. In addition to establishing democratic procedures, in other words, the new states must find ways to fulfill the substantive democratic requirements of government accountability and respect for individual and group rights.

INDIVIDUALS AND CHOICES

Another feature common to all of these new democracies is strong leaders. That should not be surprising, for in a period when traditional legitimacy has been destroyed and rational/legal legitimacy is trying to emerge, charismatic legitimacy may be necessary to fill the gap. As a result, individuals and their choices should prove crucial to the success of the new systems as they did in earlier cases. In seventeenth-century England, neither Charles I nor Cromwell was able to fulfill his goals. Charles, for example, hastened his own demise by his poor judgment and inflexibility, choosing force when he should have compromised (or vice versa), listening to the wrong advisers, and proving himself untrustworthy. Cromwell, relying on his faith in himself as one of the Elect, tried to restore a traditional balance between government and parliament that could not exist without a king; in the absence of new models (except for the army), he was unable to create a stable system that could outlive him. Both men contributed to the destruction of the old regime, but neither could provide a replacement.

Individuals were crucial in the founding of the United States: Thomas Jefferson, author of the Declaration of Independence; John Dickinson, author of the Articles of Confederation; the authors and interpreters of the Constitution, such as James Madison, Alexander Hamilton, and John Jay; the first president, George Washington, who set the precedent for the peaceful transfer of power after two terms in office; and John Marshall, who as chief justice of the U.S. Supreme Court established a monumental precedent befitting the American system of checks and balances: judicial review. The choices they made gave the republic a new foundation—natural law based in human reason—and thus paved the way for democracy. When the Articles of Confederation proved unworkable, these framers of the Constitution devised a new system of representation, a bicameral legislature representing the states and also the people *within the states*, to form "a more perfect union."

In Germany, Konrad Adenauer was skilled in handling the occupation authorities, shaping the Basic Law, and then governing Germany as chancellor until 1963. His strategy was clear: When necessary, do what the Americans, British, and French want so that they will leave more quickly. In these concessions he was opposed by Kurt Schumacher, whose very resistance helped Adenauer in his negotiations with the Allies. Indeed, these leaders of the CDU/CSU and the SPD disagreed on many issues of internal and foreign policy, thus providing Germans with clear political alternatives that helped democratic politics to rebuild a positive reputation after the failures of Weimar. In Japan, also, individuals and their choices established democracy: MacArthur's decision to create an entirely new system immediately by fiat; Emperor Hirohito's decision to support the new constitution; and Shigeru Yoshida's ability first to persuade the Japanese Diet to accept MacArthur's constitution and then to implement it in ways that would make it compatible with Japanese traditions. Yoshida, like Adenauer, argued for cooperating with the occupiers to encourage their going home, and both men gained the right to amend the constitutions thereafter.

During Argentina's consolidation of democracy in the 1980s, the dominant actors were the elected presidents. The first new president, Raúl Alfonsín, was caught between the still-powerful military and its radical opponents demanding retribution. This conflict, based on remnants of the authoritarian past, was complicated by intensifying economic hardships as neoliberal economic policies continued to produce a decline in living standards for many voters. Alfonsín's party therefore lost the elections of 1989 to Carlos Menem, who used populist promises to win the presidency and then abandoned his themes of social justice and intensified the neoliberal policies. This brought more years of economic hardship, but Menem was able to weaken any opposition—including the military, labor unions, and political rivals—through shrewd maneuvering and compromise. He then made sufficient political concessions to obtain congressional approval in 1994 for several constitutional amendments, most designed to check presidential power, but one that allowed him to run again for a four-year term in 1995. He did so and won, his victory allowing him to continue his strong and personalistic rule, in the tradition of Argentine politics. In Menem's case, however, he maintained himself in office not by force but by shrewd political maneuvering within the democratic system.

In Romania, the major figure has remained President Ion Iliescu. Others have also played important roles, but for limited periods of time. Iliescu led the new government from the very beginning, won the overwhelming election victory in

May 1990, and then made the disastrous choice to invite the miners into Bucharest. He learned from that experience, however, and thereafter worked behind the scenes to accomplish his objectives. Reelected in 1992, he could run for a final term in 1996. Iliescu stimulates dislike rather than fear in his enemies, as the president of a democracy should, and has managed to govern in conjunction with parliament and three successive prime ministers of his choice despite his party's loss of a majority in the 1992 elections. He continues to preside over and polarize Romania.

Lech Wałęsa will be viewed as the crucial individual in Poland's transition. Important choices were made by others, such as Wojciech Jaruzelski and Adam Michnik, before and during the roundtable talks of 1989, but Wałęsa led Solidarity then as before and was instrumental in its astonishing electoral victory. Largely excluded from government in the first months of noncommunist rule, he chose to run for president in 1990, a fateful decision not only because he won but also because the presidential election forced the postponement of any attempts to seize the moment and write a new constitution. Afterward it was too late. Deep political divisions emerged within parliament and between parliament and the president, and by 1995 Poland was still working with the much-amended constitution carried over from the communist years.

In Russia, the dominant roles have been played by Mikhail Gorbachev and Boris Yeltsin, who overshadow those around them. It was Gorbachev who initiated the changes in the Soviet Union and then lost control of events; it was Yeltsin who picked up the reins of power in Russia and completed the disintegration of the former system; and it has been Yeltsin who has led independent Russia since 1991. Gorbachev's choices were crucial to the destruction of the old regime, but Yeltsin's choices have created tremendous problems for the new system. His failure to move quickly in early 1992 meant that he—like Wałęsa—lost the democratic moment and gave opponents time to regroup. In 1993, he made the fateful choice to dissolve parliament by force and impose a new constitution. And, in 1994 and 1995, he was weakened by health and indecisiveness; the new democracy has weakened along with him.

These issues involving individuals and choices are essentially those of leadership. Charles I failed miserably as a king, and although Cromwell could lead an army, he could not establish a republic in seventeenth-century England. In Cromwell's case, therefore, other factors intervened to prevent success; good leadership may be important for success but is not sufficient in itself. In the United States, Germany, and Japan, individual leaders made wise choices, and democratic systems emerged. In Argentina, both Alfonsín and Menem were crucial to the consolidation of the new system. The postcommunist leaders—steeped as they were in methods of communist rule or opposition—have had more difficulty;[2] Iliescu and even Wałęsa seem to be learning how to make use of democratic procedures to accomplish their goals, but Yeltsin remains problematic. Nevertheless, in postcommunist systems, as in earlier cases, shrewd choices by capable leaders are crucial in establishing democratic rule.

GROUPS

In addition to individuals, groups are important in all of our cases. If we divide the players into regime hardliners, regime reformers, opposition moderates, and opposition radicals,[3] for example, we might interpret events in seventeenth-century England as follows: Regime hardliners (supporters of Charles's concept of kingship) were eliminated early, but Charles himself made it difficult for his reformist supporters to carry the day. As a result, opposition moderates such as Cromwell eventually came to dominate the process, although finally even the moderates were sufficiently radicalized to execute the monarch. Radical opponents of the old regime (such as the Levellers) did not win out, however, and Cromwell continued to dominate the situation until his death. Then regime reformers managed to restore the monarchy, but it and England would never be the same.

In the United States, Germany, and Japan, war destroyed the old regime, leaving only vestiges of groups that opposed the new system, and these were not allowed to play political roles. Thus, in the United States, the founding process was soon dominated by disputes among victorious opponents of the old regime—disputes about the powers held by the central government or the shape of new institutions. In Germany and Japan, the occupation authorities ensured that old-regime supporters were eliminated from the founding process so that discussions took place largely between the occupation authorities and indigenous democrats (or at least indigenous opponents of the old regime). What finally consolidated support for the new system, however, was its success in each case, especially the economic recovery that followed on the heels of democratization.

In Argentina, an informal pact between old-regime reformers and opposition moderates produced the 1983 elections. Thereafter, Alfonsín had to balance the (military) hardliners against the radical opposition while reassuring the business groups (old-regime reformers) who supported his neoliberal economic policies. The first strategy frustrated both the hardliners and the radicals, whereas the economic reforms alienated labor and others suffering from economic dislocation, often moderate and radical opponents of the old regime. Alfonsín managed to preserve democracy, but his support among old-regime reformers was not sufficient for his party to win the 1989 elections. Menem was more successful: As a Peronist, he appealed to labor and other disaffected groups and won election, but he also intensified the neoliberal policies. He had time enough for the economic reforms to take hold, however, and he was able to control the military and weaken other groups opposing his policies. By the time of the 1995 elections, the military regime was far in the past, and our four transition groups had broken down, penetrated effectively by Menem, who gained enough support throughout the system to win reelection.

In Romania, supporters of Ceauşescu (regime hardliners) were largely eliminated from politics, and the new government was formed by regime reformers such as Iliescu, with some participation from the moderate and radical opposition. The violence of 1990 then radicalized the moderates and polarized society between reformist former communists controlling the government and radical opponents, who accused Iliescu and his colleagues of neocommunism. Divisions over economic issues soon appeared within the governing coalition, and in 1992 Iliescu lost his majority in parliament. Thereafter, he was forced to govern in informal and then formal coalition with the red-brown extremist parties, some of whose leaders had been supporters of Ceauşescu. Iliescu enjoyed considerable support within the bureaucracy, among industrial workers, and in rural areas, but society remained polarized, and his opponents—urban residents and intellectuals—tended to be both articulate and vocal in their disapproval of him and his policies.

In Poland, a complex coalition of regime reformers and opposition moderates—pushed by industrial strikes and mass protests—eventually managed to subdue hardliners and radicals sufficiently to initiate and carry through the roundtable talks in 1989, thereby creating a "pacted" transition. The results of the first election in 1989 thrust power unexpectedly into the hands of the opposition moderates, and for the next several years they governed in unstable coalitions. Then, after the third set of elections in 1993, the old-regime reformers and their allies formed a governing coalition. These groups had changed fundamentally in the intervening period, however, as their policies demonstrated, and they were beginning to act like democrats.

Russia under Gorbachev followed a different sequence of events. A division emerged within the Soviet Politburo between hardliners and reformers; eventually the reformers themselves disagreed: Liberalizers like Gorbachev wished to reform but preserve the old system, and democratizers like Yeltsin wished to bring more radical change. Eventually, Yeltsin was forced out of the party leadership and became a regime opponent. He used the Russian republic as his power base, where he was elected to the legislature and then president. A struggle ensued as regime reformers, including Gorbachev, tried to hold the center between hardliners and regime opponents. The hardliners attempted a coup and failed, leaving regime opponents such as Yeltsin in the dominant position. Thus, the Soviet regime collapsed in 1991, and Yeltsin emerged as the major figure in the new state of Russia.

This examination of groups helps us to define certain patterns that may emerge during regime transition, but does it really tell us something of value about the cases or about attempts to establish democracy? Some lessons emerge. First, if war (or revolution) is involved, as it was in England, the United States, Germany, and Japan, the new system is shaped by opponents of the old regime; therefore, in these cases, it is they who form the important groups we should consider in establishing democracy. In England, for example, regime opponents won the war and executed the king, but they were unable to establish a viable new system; only because of this eventual failure did moderate supporters of the monarchy emerge once again as important players in the political process. In the other three cases, the major actors in the new system had been opponents of the old regime.

Second, even when old-regime hardliners are excluded from political power, they remain a force in society and the new democratic officials must work out a conscious method for dealing with them—the Nazis in Germany, the militarists in Japan, the military and their civilian allies in Argentina, the police in Romania, the Communist Party in Russia, and the *nomenklatura* in any postcommunist system—and they will be particularly strong if the transition is peaceful. There will be pressure on the government for retribution, but the urge to seek out and punish individuals will sooner or later give way to the pragmatic need for cooperation in building a new system.[4]

Third, in postcommunist transitions, regime reformers often play a dominant role, as they have in Russia, Romania, and—except from 1991 to 1993—in Poland. Their success, however, seems to depend upon the extent to which they are able to operate in a new environment and learn different ways of dealing with their opponents. In this sense, Iliescu is doing better than Yeltsin.

Fourth, the speed with which new political institutions are established seems to depend more upon individual choices than group structures. In Poland, for example, even though regime opponents initially won control of the new government and economic reform proceeded quickly (putting Poland ahead of most postcommunist states in terms of economic recovery), in political terms—establishing new institutions and a new constitution—Wałęsa's decision to run for president postponed progress. In Romania, in contrast, even though regime reformers controlled the new government, a new constitution was written and implemented within two years, but the economic transition proceeded more slowly.

A fifth and final point: Although this four-part division is useful in analyzing the transition, it loses its relevance as a new regime emerges and creates its own political groupings based on socioeconomic and ideological cleavages that develop in the new system.

THE PERMANENCE OF THE NEW INSTITUTIONS

What can we say about the permanence of these new democratic institutions? Is there any chance that they will succeed? In evaluating future prospects for our cases, we must remember that democracy is not a solution in itself but a process for finding solutions. If, therefore, the democratic process is successful in solving the problems confronting these societies, the new institutions have a good chance for survival. No democracy is permanent, however; even the four oldest cases face

threats to their stability from time to time and adjust or amend specific procedures to enhance their chances for remaining viable.

One major set of problems threatening our recently installed democracies
involves their economies. In all four countries an economic crisis contributed to
the previous regime's demise, leaving the crisis for the new regime to resolve. In
Argentina, recovery took so long that Alfonsín's party lost its bid for reelection
after six years in office. Six years later the economy had recovered sufficiently for
Menem to win a second term, but large segments of the population had not
shared in the recovery, and he needed shrewd political strategies to gain his victory.

The postcommunist states today face much graver economic difficulties than
did Argentina. Not only must they achieve macroeconomic stability by controlling budget deficits and inflation, but they also need to reform banking and
finance, privatize the huge share of the economy that is state-owned, establish
industrial policies for guiding trade and investment, reorient trade, and simultaneously fulfill the population's basic needs during the interim. There are signs that
both Poland and Romania have started to recover: Gross domestic product does
show some growth, and inflation seems to have leveled off. Nevertheless, privatization—especially of the large industrial enterprises—has barely begun, and large
numbers of people in both countries are suffering under extreme poverty. Most
ominously, the huge Russian economy in 1995 continued to decline.

One advantage these postcommunist states do have is the desire of their populations to create democratic systems, but they equate democracy with higher living standards, and their faith in such a political system will not survive economic
deprivation forever.[5] Of course, politicians do manage to buy time. Like Menem
in Argentina and Iliescu in Romania, they can gain election in times of economic
hardship with promises to relieve hardship, and then implement quite different
policies later. Eventually, however, in a democratic system they or their parties
should be accountable for their promises.

In order for a democratic system to survive in such difficult times, the important groups and actors must foresee a chance to win under the rules or else understand that the dangers of nondemocratic action are too great to risk. At least two
factors are important here. First, inside the system, power must be distributed
among a variety of competing groups in such a way that no one group can dominate the system. As Tatu Vanhanen and Richard Kimber observe, "democracy
emerges when no group is any longer able to establish or maintain hegemonic
power."[6] At that time, no single group will take the risk of breaking the rules.
Second, the external environment must impose sanctions for breaking the rules
and rewards for observing them: holding up or granting loans, raising or lower-
ing trade barriers, slowing or speeding affiliation with international organizations
such as the European Union, to mention only a few examples.[7] The external pressure cannot be clumsily applied, however, or internal nondemocrats could take

advantage of the opportunity to play on the nationalistic, even xenophobic, tendencies of the citizens.

This raises another major issue—in addition to the economy—facing many postcommunist regimes: defining territorial borders. As Dankwart Rustow pointed out many years ago, a democracy needs a well-defined territory and stable boundaries,[8] and many of the postcommunist states lack both. Poland is somewhat luckier than Romania and Russia in the security of its borders and the homogeneity of its population, but the latter two states have territorial disputes and military conflicts on their borders, and Russia faces dozens of internal boundary quarrels and civil war in several areas, most notably in Chechnya in 1995 and 1996.

Nevertheless, one pattern that does emerge from our cases—even in Russia to some extent—is that uncertainty does decline over time. It can never disappear completely, for democracy is a process, not a permanent and stable condition. Even as they enter the twenty-first century, Britain, the United States, Germany, and Japan all face some uncertainty about the stability of their political systems, although these older democracies are clearly more secure than the less mature systems. Even in the four most recent cases, however, there was less uncertainty in 1995 than just five years earlier. The new democracies are by no means secure, but they do have some chance for survival.

LESSONS

Our eight cases tell us a great deal about how to establish democracies, including the types of regime crises that precipitate a democratic founding, the ways in which societal constraints shape the new institutions, and the roles of crucial individuals and groups in the demise and creation of regimes. We also find that uncertainty tends to decline over time, although it never evaporates completely.

Moreover, the earlier cases contain some valuable lessons for the more recent attempts to establish democracies. Transition theorists assert that the traditional prerequisites of democracy are really outcomes. England and the United States did have most of the socioeconomic requirements—what we might term facilitating factors—such as economic prosperity or potential for growth and a diversified social structure with a propertied middle class. Indeed, they should have had those features, since the early democratization theories were based mainly on their experiences. The English did not, however, have the norms of behavior usually associated with democracy, including a tolerance for disagreement and diversity and a preference for compromise. Instead they showed considerable intolerance—of both religious and political differences—during their revolution despite popular views about concepts of representation, participation, and constitutional balance. Even the Americans, who based their system on the fundamental equality of human beings, did not translate their ideals into political practice until much later.

Neither the English in the seventeenth century (except for the Levellers) nor the Americans in the eighteenth century were trying to establish a modern democracy, of course, because they had no working models. What they did have was time to experiment with constitutional frameworks and allow democratic processes to evolve and democratic norms of behavior to emerge. Thus, we can conclude that establishing democracy takes time and that England and the United States had many decades to develop democratic processes and actors (judicial review, parties, interest groups) despite the absence of models and to develop democratic norms of behavior despite the absence of democrats. These processes and norms of behavior were therefore outcomes, not prerequisites, of democracy. Once the framework was in place, the rest could appear later. Representative democracy— elected legislators engaged in debate and policy formulation—can precede democrats and help to produce supportive processes and norms of behavior.

In Germany and Japan as well, many democratic norms of behavior were initially absent, and there were few democrats. Nevertheless, these countries had models to follow and foreign encouragement to do so, and so their democratization proceeded quickly—in years, not decades or centuries—and in each case military occupation provided a period of transition, giving the new democratic system time to test new institutions. Models and foreign support can therefore substitute for time, as long as other prerequisites are in place: institutions are shaped to fit societal constraints, crucial individuals make the right choices, and hostile groups are successfully neutralized. Finally, the earlier cases tell us that procedural democracy is a good way to begin. In both England and the United States the framework of procedures emerged first; only later did parties and interest groups appear, democratic norms of behavior develop, and participation extend to most citizens along with the protection of their rights. The framework also preceded democratic practices in Germany and Japan as well, and democrats were created by their participation in the processes.

All of these lessons give us some hope for the contemporary cases. Despite the melancholy of Argentina, the polarization of Romania, the frustration of gridlocked Poland, and the chaos of Russia, there is at least some hope that these countries can develop into sustainable, substantive democracies. Each of the new political systems has a procedural framework (although a new Polish Constitution has yet to be written, a democratic structure is nevertheless operating), and these frameworks can produce democrats, even in the absence of some of the traditional prerequisites for democracy. The postcommunist states also have highly literate populations and, although the communist system trained them to *avoid* work, they do have skills. These countries (like Germany and Japan in 1945) do not have traditions of participation and tolerance, but perhaps (like Germany and Japan after 1945) they can substitute models and foreign support and establish democratic systems. This does not mean they will do so. The postcommunist transitions, although accompanied by some violence, have been less destructive than the military defeat and occupation of Germany and Japan, leaving intact remnants of the former regimes. Other political and economic legacies of communist party rule create special problems for establishing democratic systems. Some of these transitions may stall along the way so that the regimes remain semi-democratic,[9] with periodic accountability to voters but limited respect for individual rights. Some may even succumb to a dictatorship, populist or military. Nevertheless, the chances for these new regimes to establish democracy seem greater in 1995 than they did in 1990. Uncertainty diminishes with time.

NOTES

1. On legitimacy, see note 5 in the Introduction to this book and the accompanying text.

2. See Timothy J. Colton and Robert C. Tucker, eds., *Patterns in Post-Soviet Leadership* (Boulder: Westview, 1995).

3. Terms closely associated with the transition theorists mentioned in the Introduction to this book; see especially Samuel P. Huntington, *The Third Wave* (Norman: University of Oklahoma Press, 1991), and Adam Przeworski, *Democracy and the Market* (New York: Cambridge University Press, 1991).

4. Such attempts have been made in the Czech Republic and the former German Democratic Republic; see note 46 in Chapter 6 of this book. For a general discussion of the lustration issue (that is, bringing past crimes to light, as in the denazification attempts in post–World War II Germany), see Huntington, *The Third Wave*, pp. 211–231.

5. One question beyond the scope of this study is whether democracy requires neoliberal reforms or is compatible with an economic system that ensures a more egalitarian distribution of goods and services. On these issues, see Przeworski, *Democracy and the Market*; and Luiz Carlos Bresser Pereira et al., eds., *Economic Reforms in New Democracies* (New York: Cambridge University Press, 1993), especially the chapter by Przeworski, "Economic Reforms, Public Opinion, and Political Institutions"; and Larry Diamond and Marc F. Plattner, eds., *Capitalism, Socialism, and Democracy Revisited* (Baltimore: Johns Hopkins University Press, 1993).

6. Tatu Vanhanen and Richard Kimber, "Predicting and Explaining Democratization in Eastern Europe," in Geoffrey Pridham and Tatu Vanhanen, eds., *Democratization in Eastern Europe* (New York: Routledge, 1994), p. 64.

7. For more, see Adrian G. V. Hyde-Price, "Democratization in Eastern Europe: The External Dimension," in Pridham and Vanhanen, *Democratization in Eastern Europe*, pp. 220–252.

8. Dankwart A. Rustow, "Transitions to Democracy," *Comparative Politics* 2 (April 1970): 337–364.

9. Such as O'Donnell's "delegative democracy"; see Guillermo O'Donnell, "Delegative Democracy," *Journal of Democracy* 5 (January 1994): 55–69.

ABOUT THE BOOK

Balancing historical and contemporary cases, this comparative text examines the crucial question of what promotes or prevents the successful founding of democratic systems. Underscoring lessons learned from successful regime change and assessing current efforts to establish democracies whose ultimate fate is yet uncertain, this book will enable students to evaluate the chances of success for societies making the transition from an authoritarian or communist regime. The case studies are placed in context by a substantial introduction surveying theories of democracy and democratic transition and a conclusion comparing the cases and suggesting common patterns in the establishment of successful democracies.

Created for upper-level students, this book can be used as a primary text to be supplemented by theoretical readings or as a source of additional case studies. Extensive notes provide a wealth of suggestions for further reading and research.

ABOUT THE EDITOR
AND CONTRIBUTORS

Mary Ellen Fischer is the Joseph C. Palamountain Professor of Government at Skidmore College and a Fellow at the Russian Research Center, Harvard University. Her many publications on Romanian, Russian, and East European politics include *Nicolae Ceaușescu: A Study in Political Leadership*.

Roy H. Ginsberg is associate professor of government and director of the International Affairs Program at Skidmore College. A specialist on the European Union, he is the author of *Foreign Policy Actions of the European Community: The Politics of Scale*, and coauthor of *The United States and the European Union in the 1990s: Partners in Transition*, now in its second edition.

Steven A. Hoffmann is professor of government and chair of the Department of Government at Skidmore College. He has published widely on the politics of East and South Asia and the Middle East, including a book titled *India and the China Crisis*.

Tadahisa Kuroda is professor of history and associate dean of the faculty at Skidmore College. His most recent publication in the field of American history is *The Origins of the Twelfth Amendment: The Electoral College in the Early Republic, 1787–1804*.

Patricia-Ann Lee is professor of history at Skidmore College. A specialist in Tudor-Stuart England, her publications on a variety of topics include "Aylmer, Knox, and the Debate on Queenship," in *The Historian*, and "Reflections of Power: Margaret of Anjou and the Dark Side of Queenship," in *The Renaissance Quarterly*.

Erwin L. Levine is professor emeritus of government at Skidmore College. Among his many publications are a two-volume political biography of Theodore Francis Green of Rhode Island and an introduction to American government (five editions). Most recently, he coauthored *PL 94-142: The Education for All Handicapped Children Act of 1975*.

Carol R. Saivetz is a Fellow at the Harvard Russian Research Center and lecturer in social studies, also at Harvard. The most recent of her numerous articles and books dealing with Soviet and now Russian affairs include *In Search of Pluralism: Soviet and Post-Soviet Politics* and "Russian Foreign Policy: Political Debates, the 'Near Abroad,' and the West," forthcoming. She is currently working on a book tentatively entitled *Russian Foreign Policy from Perestroika to Post-Communism*, focusing on the interconnections between Russian domestic politics and the evolution of post-Soviet Russian foreign policy.

Sarah Meiklejohn Terry is associate professor of political science at Tufts University and a Fellow at the Russian Research Center, Harvard University. She is the author of numerous publications on East European politics including *Poland's Place in Europe: General Sikorski and the Origins of the Oder-Neisse Line, 1939–1943*, and *Soviet Policy in Eastern Europe*.

Aldo C. Vacs is associate professor of government at Skidmore College. He has published extensively on Latin America, political economy, development, democratization, and international relations, including *Discreet Partners: Argentina and the USSR Since 1917*, and "Authoritarian Breakdown and Redemocratization in Argentina," in James M. Malloy and Mitchell A. Seligson, eds., *Authoritarians and Democrats: Regime Transition in Latin America*.

INDEX

Acheson, Dean, 123
Adams, Abigail, 65
Adams, John, 61, 63, 70, 74, 76, 77
Adenauer, Konrad, 9, 87, 100–102, 109, 111, 289
Afghanistan, 255, 258
Agitators, 37, 39, 40, 42
Agriculture, 179–181, 214, 218–219, 234, 238
Aid, 11, 111, 164, 280, 281, 284, 296
Albania, 287
Alfonsín, Raúl, 9, 15, 149, 157–162, 167–171, 173, 286, 289–291, 294
Algiers, 69
All-Russian Renewal Union, 277(n25)
American Revolution, 56, 66, 68, 283
Ancien Regime. See old regime
Andreevna, Nina, 256, 258, 274
Andropov, Yuri, 255
Angeloz, Eduardo, 161
Anglican church, 23, 28, 30, 33, 36
Angola, 255
Anti-Comintern Pact, 120
Anti-Semitism, 110, 215
Antonescu, Ion, 181, 194, 206
Argentina, 151, 153, 164, 167
    under Alfonsín, 149, 157–162, 168–171, 173, 291
    authoritarianism in, 6, 15, 151–155, 172, 284, 289
    Constitution of, 159, 167–168, 170, 172, 173, 286, 289
    democracy in, 149–151, 156, 157, 159, 162, 168, 169, 286, 289, 296
    democratization in, 1, 2, 5, 11, 12, 15, 150, 151, 157–158, 172, 281–284, 286, 289, 291–294, 296
    economic reforms in, 20(n40), 150–166, 169–172, 282, 286, 289, 291
    economy in, 15, 151–153, 158, 159, 161–164, 170, 173, 297

human rights in, 159, 160, 166, 170
judicial system in, 167, 170
labor unions in, 158–160, 164–165, 170, 286
leadership in, 9, 156, 168–171, 289, 290
under Menem, 149, 162–171, 173
military in, 149, 159–161, 166, 170, 283, 286, 289, 291–292, 293
under military rule, 151, 153–154, 172
political participation in, 149, 156, 157, 162, 168–170, 172
political parties in, 149, 166, 168–169, 171
political system in, 151, 152, 170, 171, 284, 286, 289
populism in, 6, 152, 154–155, 162, 170–172, 289
Aristotle, 64
Arminianism, 28, 30, 36, 52(nn 13, 14)
Articles of Confederation, 14, 66–73, 81, 285, 288–289
Austria, 93
Austria-Hungary, 180
Authoritarianism, 5, 6, 8, 12, 19(n22), 23, 88–90, 92, 150, 208(n27), 256, 260, 273
    in Argentina, 6, 15, 151, 153–155, 172, 284, 289
Awakening of the Soviet Union, The (Hosking), 268
Aylmer, G. E., 38
Azerbaijan, 257

Bacon, Lord, 61
Balcerowicz, Leszek, 226, 235, 238, 246(n2)
Baltic Republics, 257, 260
Banat, 180
Baptists, 44
BBWR. *See* Non-Party Bloc to Support Reform
Belarus, 260, 275
Bessarabia, 180
Bielecki, Jan Krzysztof, 228, 245